Adobe® Photoshop® Lightroom® 2 FOR Digital Photographers ONLY

Rob Sheppard

Wiley Publishing, Inc.

Adobe® Photoshop® Lightroom® 2 for Digital Photographers Only

Published by
Wiley Publishing, Inc.
10475 Crosspoint Blvd.
Indianapolis, IN 46256
www.wiley.com

Published by Wiley Publishing, Inc., Indianapolis, Indiana

Published simultaneously in Canada

ISBN: 978-0-470-27804-8

Manufactured in the United States of America

10 9 8 7 6 5 4 3 2 1

Library of Congress Control Number: 2008933793

about the author

Rob Sheppard has had a longtime and nationally recognized commitment to helping photographers connect with digital imaging technology. He was one of the small group of people who started *PCPhoto* magazine nearly ten years ago to bring the digital world to photographers on their terms. He was the editor of *Outdoor Photographer* magazine (second only to *Popular Photography* in circulation) for 12 years and now is editor at large. He is the author/photographer of more than 25 photo books, including *Adobe Camera Raw for Digital Photographers Only* and *Digital Photography Simplified.*

He also writes a column in *Outdoor Photographer* called "Digital Horizons" and teaches around the country, including workshops for the Palm Beach Photographic Centre, Santa Fe Photography and Digital Workshops, BetterPhoto.com, xTrain.com, and the Great American Photography Workshop group. His Web site for workshops, books, and photo tips is at www.robsheppardphoto.com; his photo blog is at www.photodigitary.com.

As a photographer, Rob worked for many years in Minnesota (before moving to Los Angeles), including doing work for the Minnesota Department of Transportation, Norwest Banks (now Wells Fargo), Pillsbury, 3M, General Mills, Lutheran Brotherhood, Ciba-Geigy, Anderson Windows, and others. His photography has been published in many magazines, ranging from *National Geographic* to *The Farmer* to, of course, *Outdoor Photographer.*

credits

Acquisitions Editor
Laura Sinise

Project Editor
Jama Carter

Technical Editor
Michael Guncheon

Copy Editor
Lauren Kennedy

Editorial Manager
Robyn Siesky

Vice President & Group Executive Publisher
Richard Swadley

Vice President & Publisher
Barry Pruett

Business Manager
Amy Knies

Project Coordinator
Erin Smith

Graphics and Production Specialists
Carrie A. Cesavice
Nikki Gately
Andrea Hornberger

Quality Control Technician
Melanie Hoffman

Proofreading
Laura L. Bowman

Indexing
Slivoskey Indexing Services

Cover Design
Mike Trent

Book Designer
LeAndra Hosier

foreword

Writing a book is somewhat like giving a presentation — which Rob, by the way, does many times a year and does very well.

In a presentation, the presenter must grab the audience's attention in the first few seconds. Body language and enthusiasm help during those critical moments. That attention must then be held with informative facts, but just as important, with entertaining wit and with eye-catching slides. And of course, the presenter's knowledge of the subject and energy is key.

Like a guitar solo, the presentation must have a beginning, middle, and end. It has to be well organized, or else the audience may get lost in a sea of facts. At the end of the presentation, the audience should say, if the presenter has done his or her job well, "That was one of the best presentations I've ever been to." That's different from, "I learned a lot," or "those were great photographs," and so on.

In reading the draft of Rob's book, I felt as though I was at one of his fun-filled and info-packed presentations, which I've attended many times, usually with standing-room only. Rob grabs the reader right up front, offering the features *and benefits* of Lightroom. I stress "and benefits" because, as I learned in my ten-year stint at a New York ad agency, stating only the features alone does little good unless you state the benefits as well.

I like Rob's title for this book, *Adobe Photoshop Lightroom 2 for Digital Photographers Only*. If I were the copywriter, I'd add my own subtitle: *Everything You Possibly Want to Know About Working and Playing in Lightroom*. The book is that complete, and is the most complete book I've seen on Lightroom.

Getting back to giving an organized presentation, Rob's technique for organizing your work (workflow) in Lightroom takes the guesswork out of common Lightroom questions: Where do I start, what do I do along the way, and where do I finish?

If you don't know the answer to these questions, you'd be somewhat like Christopher Columbus: When he left Spain, he did not know where he was going. When he got to the New World, he did not know where he was. When he got back to Spain, he did not know where he had been.

It's an old joke, but true. You must be organized — you must know where you want to go, do what you want to do. Otherwise, you waste a lot of time sailing around on the wrong course, so to speak.

Rob is a very sharing person, which you'll realize in the first few pages of this book. And speaking of sharing (and getting back to my presentation analogy just one more time), Lightroom is great for sharing your photographs — with prints and especially on the Web and with slideshows. Here, again, Rob's presentation of the work makes learning fun.

Rob loves Lightroom, and I am sure you will fall in love with some of the application's features, too. But as Rob suggests, don't dump perhaps your first love, Photoshop. The two applications can work hand in hand to give you ultimate creative control over your images — with lighting-fast speed.

Take my word; you're in for a good read and good presentation in the following pages.

Rick Sammon

www.ricksammon.com

preface

With Adobe Photoshop Lightroom 2, I have to say, "Wow!" After working with it from the start of its development by Adobe, I really feel at home with this software, not because it is a great piece of software, but because it is truly going to revolutionize the way photographers work with photos. It brings me back to working in the traditional darkroom, something I had longed to do with color, but really only felt successful with black-and-white. I now have the control over a color image that photographers have longed for.

The great *LIFE* magazine photographer Andreas Feininger once said that the uncontrolled photograph was a lie (and this was more than 40 years ago, before Photoshop) because it misrepresented the way we saw reality. He felt that truth could only come when the photographer controlled the image so that it truthfully represented how we saw the world. Of course, a photographer can control an image and lie, too, but this has always been true. Feininger would find that Lightroom allows the photographer the control needed to bring photos back to the truths of black-and-white photography.

Lightroom's ability to give photographers a totally integrated program, from editing and organizing to image processing to photo sharing, is unmatched by any other Adobe program. Plus it offers some amazing processing capabilities, as you will soon learn, that no one else is doing. I love the way the program handles images and makes working with them intuitive and a joy.

The official name of the program is Adobe Photoshop Lightroom — a bit unwieldy, don't you think? So you will often see it referred to simply as Lightroom in this book. Most people commonly call it Lightroom anyway. Adobe wanted to include Lightroom as part of the Photoshop brand, which is how it got its official name.

I admit to a bias in doing this book that is the same one I have for most of my books. I am uninterested in programs like Lightroom or Photoshop as software programs with a big list of features. I really only care about what they can do for the photographer. I get excited, not from working in Lightroom, but from seeing my photos come to life in the program. Lightroom has very obviously been designed more specifically for the photographer than Photoshop ever has been.

My goal in writing this book has been to explain Lightroom features to you, the reader and photographer, and give you some perspective on how you can use them. As in my other books, I wanted to produce a book that addresses photographers' needs and concerns, one that makes photography as important as the technology. It's easy to be wowed by cool features in Photoshop or Lightroom, but it's a different thing altogether to make that cool feature really fit in your workflow.

acknowledgments

Acknowledgments are both hard and easy. It is easy to say a lot of people helped with a book given no book can be done by one person. Once again, I thank everyone who has ever given me information or challenged me to do better in communicating to readers about digital photography, including the great editors at Wiley. Project editor Jama Carter and tech editor Michael Guncheon always worked to be sure I was showing the reader the correct and best way to understand Lightroom.

I will always thank all the great folks who have been at my workshops and seminars and have taught me what photographers really need to know about digital photography and Lightroom. Without them, I would never have known the nuances of what photographers with a great range of knowledge and skills really understand and don't understand about digital photography.

I have to especially thank my family, particularly my wife, Vicky, a terrific partner who tolerates me photographing all over the place and, when home, saying I will just be a minute (but rarely am) and then spending much time in my office working at the computer.

contents at a glance

contents

chapter 4 Organizing Images in the Library Module 83

chapter 5 Basic Workflow in the Develop Module 101

chapter 8 Making a Better Show in Slideshow 203

chapter 9 Making Sense of the Print Module 225

chapter **10 From Good to Great Printing with Print 251**

chapter **11 The Web Module 271**

Part I

WHAT IS LIGHTROOM ALL ABOUT?

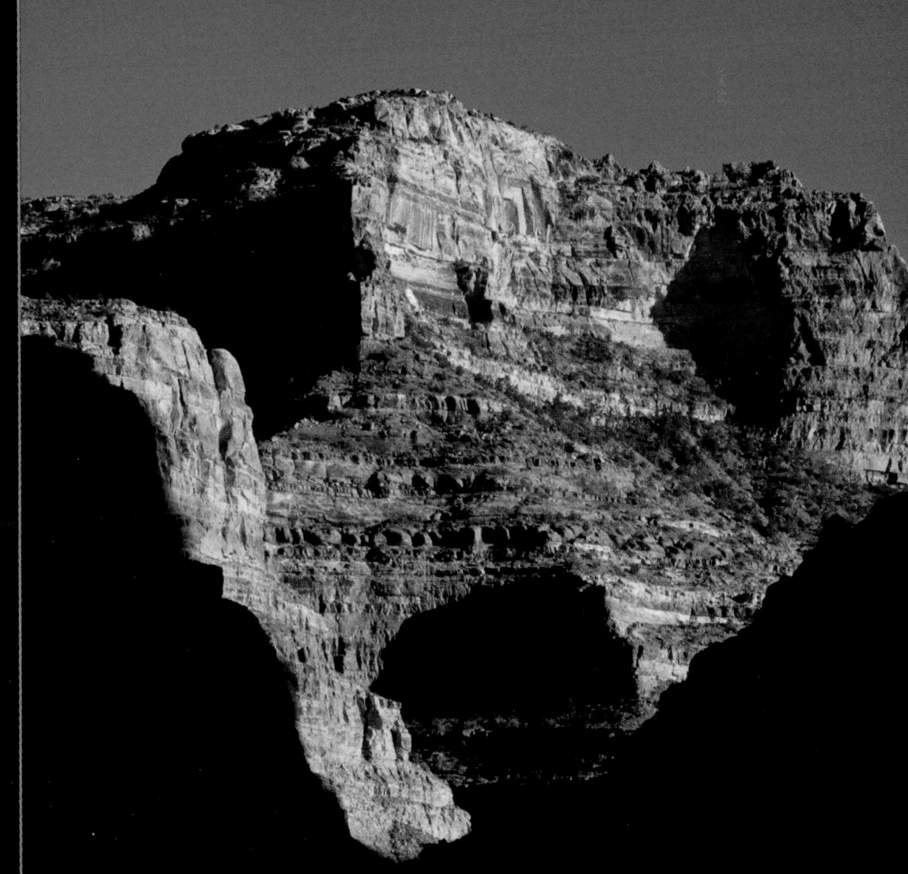

Chapter 1

INTRODUCTION TO THE PHOTOSHOP LIGHTROOM CONCEPT

Adobe Photoshop Lightroom is a program that was designed specifically for photographers. As part of the Photoshop family of Adobe software, Lightroom, as most photographers refer to it and how you will see it in this book, has become the preferred method of working with photographs for many photographers because it enables them to edit, catalog, process or develop, print their images, and more, all in one powerful program.

Adobe Photoshop, by comparison, is a great program, but it was designed for people who use photographs, not necessarily for photographers. And Photoshop itself is still a very powerful program for working with photography; but Lightroom, as shown in figure 1-1, offers new approaches that are more intuitive and often more efficient for photographers.

Lightroom really resonates with photographers because it parallels how a photographer thinks, which means the Lightroom learning curve is not as difficult as with Photoshop.

In this chapter, you discover what makes Lightroom different and how that difference is important to you as a photographer.

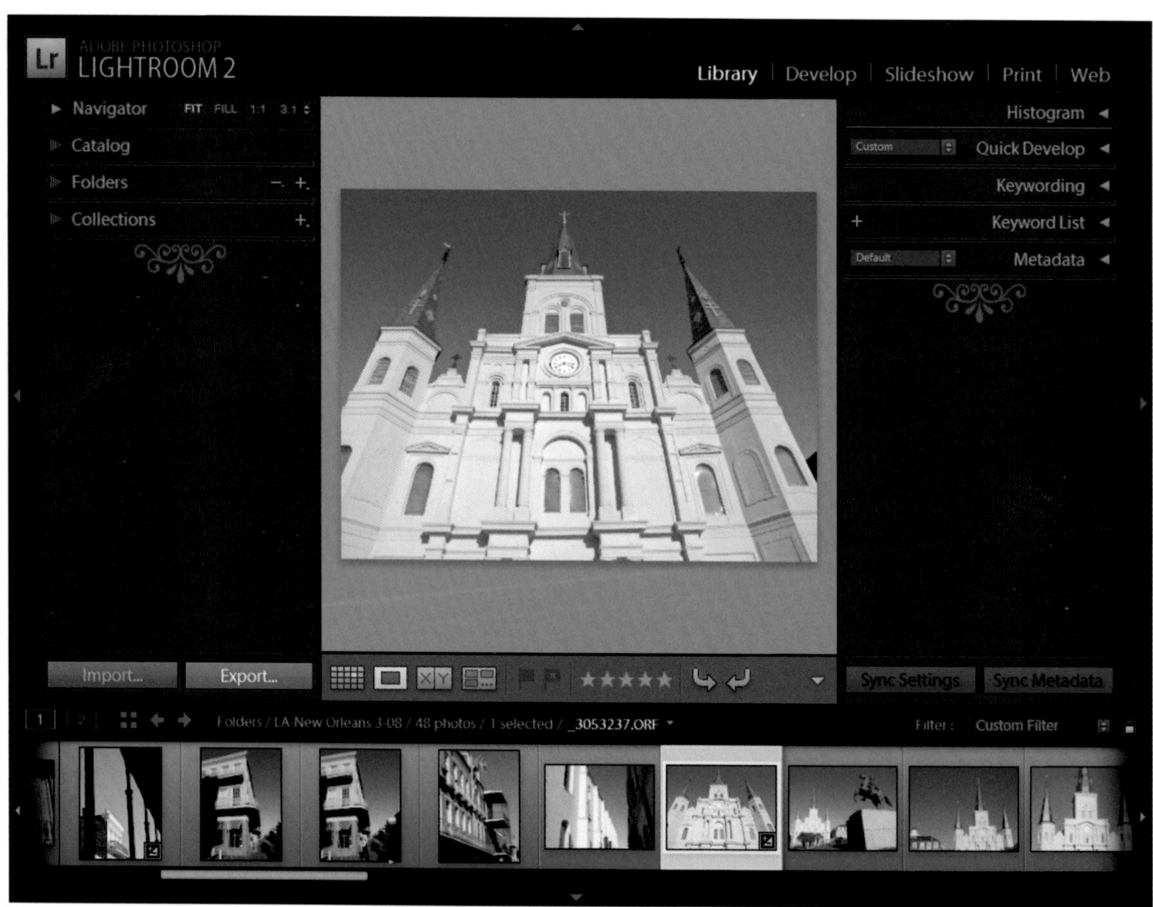

1-1

What Is Lightroom About?

In many ways, Photoshop is still the premier image-processing software available today. But, as I mentioned, it was never designed specifically for photographers. There are many things about Photoshop that make photographers crazy!

Lightroom was not developed to replace Photoshop. It was designed to help the advanced amateur or pro gain more control over his or her images while maintaining an efficient and effective workflow. Adobe's first effort to make the Photoshop processing "engine" (all the algorithms and high-level computer engineering that happen under the hood) more accessible to the average photographer was Photoshop Elements. Photoshop Elements introduced many photographer-friendly ideas that influenced later software. Just compare the interface of Photoshop Elements, shown in figure 1-2, with that of Lightroom.

Photoshop Elements was a great effort, to be sure. However, Lightroom goes far beyond that. It is a program built from the ground up for photographers, and more specifically, professional and advanced photographers. It was developed to enhance the photographer's experience of working with RAW and other image files so that the photographs are as important as the program.

Lightroom is not about designing fancy graphics, creating wild composites, or prepping images for the printing press — all things that Photoshop does very well. It is about organizing digital images to make them more accessible, processing them quickly, and then getting them to an audience through slide shows, prints, or Web galleries (and, of course, image files).

1-2

Designed for Speed and Efficient Processing

Lightroom really takes a different approach to handling digital image files compared to an image-processing program like Photoshop. Lightroom allows you to work with your images right from the start, when you import them into the computer from your memory card. You can edit the good and the bad, group them into categories, and process or develop as many of the photos as you want. This makes a true digital photograph workflow possible using one software program.

Simply having the ability to do those things in one program makes your work faster and more efficient. You don't have to open multiple programs, which is a big benefit, but Lightroom goes further. The tools that you need for a specific type of work are all in one place, right by the image you are working on, as shown in figure 1-3. You don't have to search through multiple menus or palettes. If you've spent any time doing those things in other programs, you know how much time that can take, even if you know the program very well.

Lightroom even enables you to work with multiple images. You can look carefully at a group of images and compare details in them so you can more easily pick a particular image. You also can apply multiple adjustments to a photograph, and then copy and apply those same adjustments to a whole group of similar photographs.

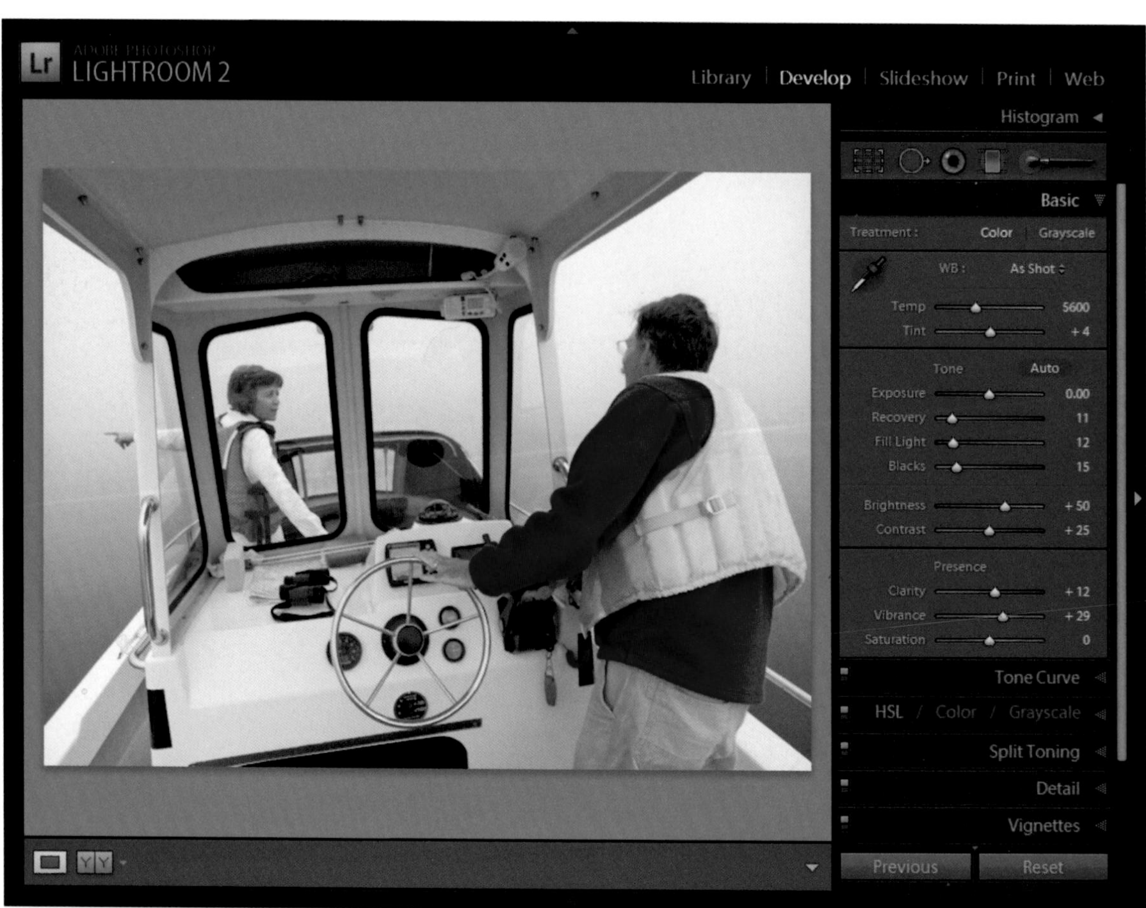

1-3

The following example proves how powerful this is. I was scheduled to give an evening lecture for the public at a CSU Summer Arts program. I got into the lecture hall a little before 5 p.m. My lecture was scheduled for 8 p.m. When I saw my images projected through their digital projector, I discovered that the projector over-enhanced the reds in my photographs. These were nature images that included a lot of reds in them, and so this was a problem.

Yet with Lightroom, I was able to make corrections to every single image, still keep a dinner appointment, and get to the lecture hall in plenty of time for my presentation. Speed and efficient processing were absolutely critical for me. I doubt I could have done it without Lightroom.

Another example of Lightroom's speed and efficiency is how it works with specific formats. RAW files have always demanded more in their processing, required special software, created larger files than many photographers' computers were able to handle well, and so on. In short, they were often a pain to use.

Lightroom was designed to make RAW processing an easy, integrated part of image work on the computer.

Adobe Camera Raw (the RAW processing program that comes with Photoshop) first changed how RAW files could be integrated into a Photoshop-oriented workflow, as shown in figure 1-4, and continues that approach today. Other RAW conversion software programs offer excellent results and their own workflow, plus they process colors slightly differently, and so they do have advantages for some photographers. However, the fact that Camera Raw fit the Photoshop workflow really made quite a difference for most photographers.

1-4

Adobe software engineers had long wanted to make RAW file processing easier, more efficient, and better integrated with how a photographer works. Lightroom does exactly that. If you compare the features of Camera Raw to Lightroom, you'll notice that a good part of Lightroom's Develop module is very similar to Camera Raw. In fact, when Camera Raw 4 came out, you could see Lightroom influencing Camera Raw! The Adobe engineers are using what they learn from photographers' experiences with one product to refine the others.

If Lightroom processed just RAW files quickly and efficiently, the program would be a success. Lightroom also works quite well with other formats. It will do its magic with well-crafted JPEG files, which makes organizing, processing, and using them more efficient and more effective than ever. In addition, the actual JPEG files are not altered by Lightroom — all adjustments are saved as instructions and not actually applied to the files until the image is exported from Lightroom.

Non-Destructive Processing

Non-destructive processing is a really big deal. This is something unique to Lightroom in that it deals with *all* files non-destructively.

Non-destructive processing means that you can adjust a file without damaging its original data. The look of the image changes, but no pixels are harmed. What happens is that the program creates a set of instructions on how to process an image and saves those instructions, but it does not permanently apply those instructions until a new file is created when the image is exported or printed.

RAW file processing is non-destructive simply because of the nature of a RAW file. A RAW file is basic data minimally processed from the sensor — you can convert it to another format, but the original data cannot be altered in any way through processing. However, JPEG files have been traditionally processed in a way that changes pixels. That's how Photoshop works, though Camera Raw 4 also processes JPEG files non-destructively.

Changing pixels is not how Lightroom works. Instead, it affects JPEG, TIFF, and RAW files with instructions for adjustments. You can adjust and readjust any file as much as you want without affecting its quality. It is only when you export the file that it finally changes, with the adjustments actually applied to the pixels.

There is another advantage to non-destructive processing in Lightroom that is often missed: it reduces the number of image files you have to keep. For example, you don't need multiple files at different resolutions for printing — you simply print directly from the Lightroom file. You don't need a whole new set of image files for a slide show — you just work on the slide show in Lightroom. And you don't need to make up a whole series of file sizes for clients — you can always get exactly what you need from the Lightroom file.

PRO TIP

RAM is still important for any image-processing software. With too little RAM, your computer slows down as it uses the virtual RAM or memory it creates with your hard drive. Have at least 1GB of RAM for Lightroom (2GB is better if you are also running Photoshop at the same time).

Lightroom Compared to Photoshop

Here's something I need to clear up right away. There is little in Lightroom that you can't do in Photoshop (including Bridge). Lightroom is not some amazing new approach to processing images in the computer that can't be duplicated anywhere else. In fact, a lot of Camera Raw shows up in Lightroom, as well as ideas from Adobe Bridge and Photoshop Elements (and Lightroom ideas are now showing up in Camera Raw, Bridge, and Photoshop, too).

Lightroom is not a new program that bumps Photoshop out of the top position in image processing. It is, as I've explained, one that responds specifically to photographers' needs for working on images in the computer. It is about making a process easier, more convenient, and more intuitive for photographers, and because of that, it will become the primary way many photographers will work with digital photos.

To be more explicit:

> **Lightroom is a program designed to include features optimized for photographers.** Photoshop is a multi-featured program designed to meet a great deal of users' needs, from graphic artists to art directors to video artists to photographers and more.

> **Lightroom offers a flat hierarchy of controls you can access quickly.** By this, I mean that Lightroom's controls are all readily accessible within any given work area, such as Develop (image adjustment). You don't have to search for the controls under multiple menus or palettes. Photoshop offers hierarchies of controls with different levels of access to meet the diverse needs of its users, but that does mean a complexity in how the interface is laid out.

> **Lightroom has a small RAM footprint and boots up very quickly.** Photoshop has a large RAM footprint and loads slowly.

> **Lightroom is designed for fast work by a photographer.** Photoshop is designed for complex work by many types of users, and speed is not the primary goal (although recent versions of Photoshop do have speed refinements built into them).

> **Lightroom offers a targeted set of controls to deal with images.** Photoshop gives you an infinite amount of control over how you deal with images.

> **Lightroom only offers tools that affect the photographer.** Photoshop offers text, special effects, high-level commercial printing controls, and other specialized tools.

> **Lightroom has no compositing or manipulation tools.** Photoshop includes advanced compositing and image-manipulation tools.

> **Lightroom integrates the workflow process into a linear and photocentric process that can be used nonlinearly as needed.** Photoshop separates parts of a photographer's workflow process into nonlinear patterns that are often illogical for photographers.

I could compare the two for a long time. My point is not that either program is better, but that they are different and offer different processes for the user.

Photoshop has a lot of tools that you can use in a number of ways. And all of its tools can get a little overwhelming, as shown in figure 1-5. Lightroom takes a very different approach. Its tools are aligned in a way that matches photographers' workflow needs.

Bottom line: Lightroom is a highly capable program that helps photographers organize and process images faster and more efficiently. It offers a better and more photocentric workflow than Photoshop. For many photographers, Lightroom offers a complete and effective way of working with digital images, and they will need nothing else, especially with the new tools that have been added to version 2.

1-5

Can Photographers Forget about Photoshop?

Some photographers will be able to give up Photoshop. If Lightroom does everything you need, why bother with Photoshop? I'm afraid that I can't answer that question for you. You'll have to see how well Lightroom meets your needs.

Full disclosure: I love Lightroom. I now use Lightroom as my primary way of working with digital images. Lightroom is far better than Bridge for organizing and storing images. It is also faster (though the latest version of Bridge is reasonably fast compared to past versions, which were very slow). Lightroom makes working with RAW files a real pleasure, and the printing module simplifies that process.

However, because Lightroom cannot do everything that Photoshop can do, I am not about to give up using Photoshop. Image processing includes making overall adjustments to an image, but very often you need to make local or small area changes. Photoshop, with its selection tools, layers, layer masks, and history brush, offers a wealth of power for adjusting an image in precise and defined areas. Lightroom is not made for that, but luckily, Photoshop and Lightroom work together really well.

For folks who like special effects, from image-warping filters to composited images, Photoshop is the place to go. And if your work involves going beyond preparing an image for slide shows or printing, you may need the added color-handling and graphics-oriented tools you'll find in Photoshop.

Who Benefits from Lightroom?

Lightroom is for digital photographers, obviously. It is aimed at pros, but Lightroom is a great choice for anyone who shoots a lot of photographs, needs to organize and access them readily, and needs a way of processing them quickly and easily to a saved file, slide show, print, and/or Web gallery. You can see one photo's progression through the modules in Lightroom in figures 1-6 through 1-10.

Lightroom is for serious photographers who don't need the full-featured options of Photoshop or its price. And it is for photographers who want to work quickly and efficiently with most images, while retaining the ability to use Photoshop in a more targeted way for specific images that need its power (and its more detailed workflow). I know Photoshop well and have worked with it for many years. However, Lightroom has allowed me to work with large numbers of my photographs quickly and efficiently, thereby ensuring that my time in front of the computer is well spent. I love digital photography and working on my images to get the most out of them, but I don't enjoy working on images in the computer just to spend time at the computer.

Lightroom is definitely for the photographer who doesn't want to deal with the learning curve of Photoshop or is intimidated by all the tools Photoshop offers the user. Yet it is also for the sophisticated Photoshop user who wants a simpler approach to working with large numbers of photos more quickly, especially RAW files.

1-6

Survey :
CA-JoshuaTree-816.JPG

1-7

Lr
LIGHTROOM 2
Library
Develop
Slideshow
Print
Web
Histogram
Basic
Treatment :
Color
Grayscale
WB :
As Shot
Temp
5150
Tint
- 3
Tone
Auto
Exposure
+ 0.57
Recovery
0
Fill Light
0
Blacks
13
Brightness
+ 50
Contrast
+ 25
Presence
Clarity
+ 29
Vibrance
+ 33
Saturation
0
Tone Curve
HSL / Color / Grayscale
Split Toning
Detail
Vignettes
Previous
Reset

1-8

LIGHTROOM 2
Library
Develop
Slideshow
Print
Web
Preview
Options
Layout
Overlays
Backdrop
Titles
Playback
Template Browser
Collections
Export JPEG...
Export PDF...
All Filmstrip Photos
ABC
Preview
Play
12 photos
Custom Filter

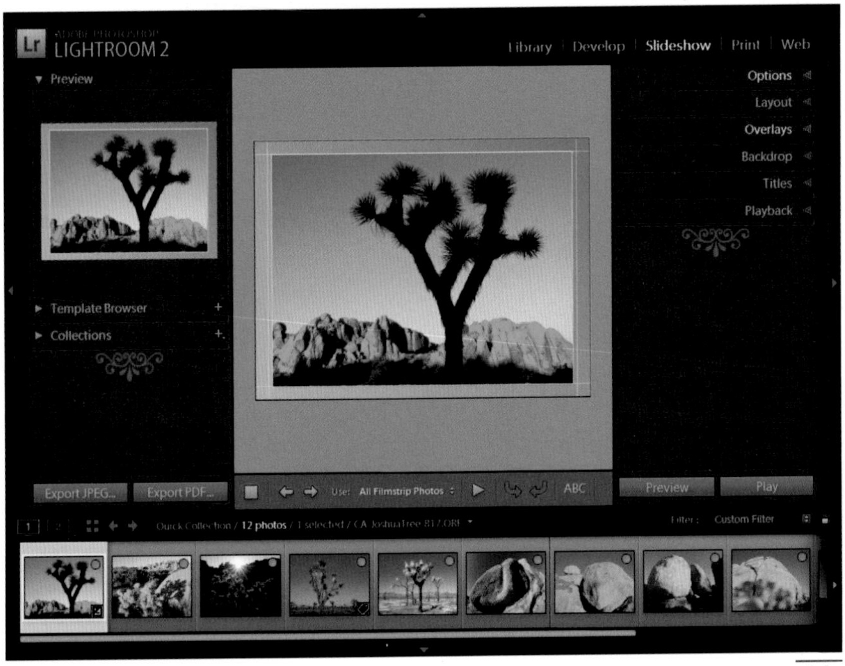

1-9

LIGHTROOM 2
Library
Develop
Slideshow
Print
Web
Preview
Joshua Tree National Park
A portfolio of landscapes
Rob Sheppard
Template Browser
Lightroom Templates
Blue Sky
Charcoal
Classic
Dusk
Earl Grey
Exif metadata
Flash gallery (default)
HTML gallery (default)
Preview in Browser...
1 / 3
12 photos
Custom Filter

1-10

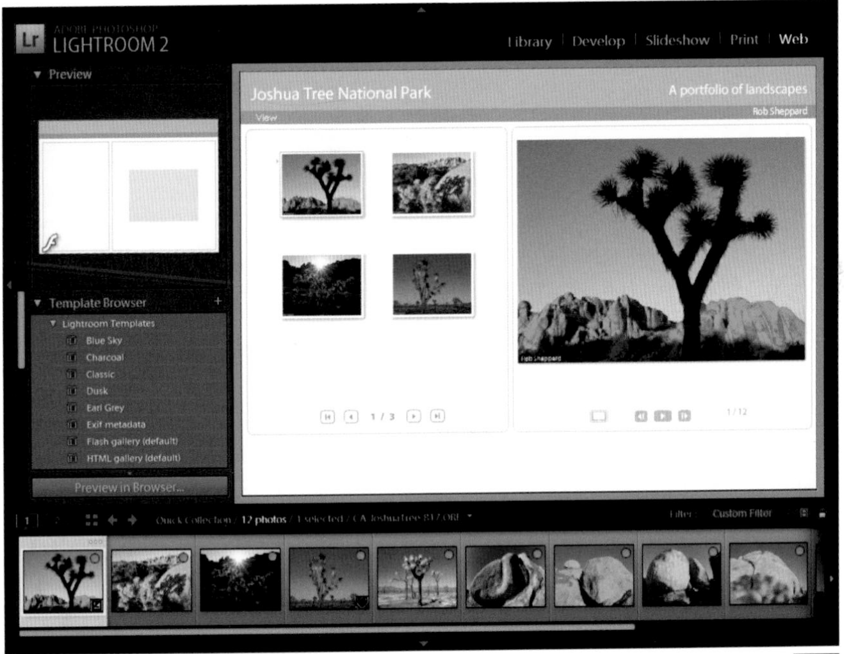

Chapter 2

THE BASICS OF LIGHTROOM

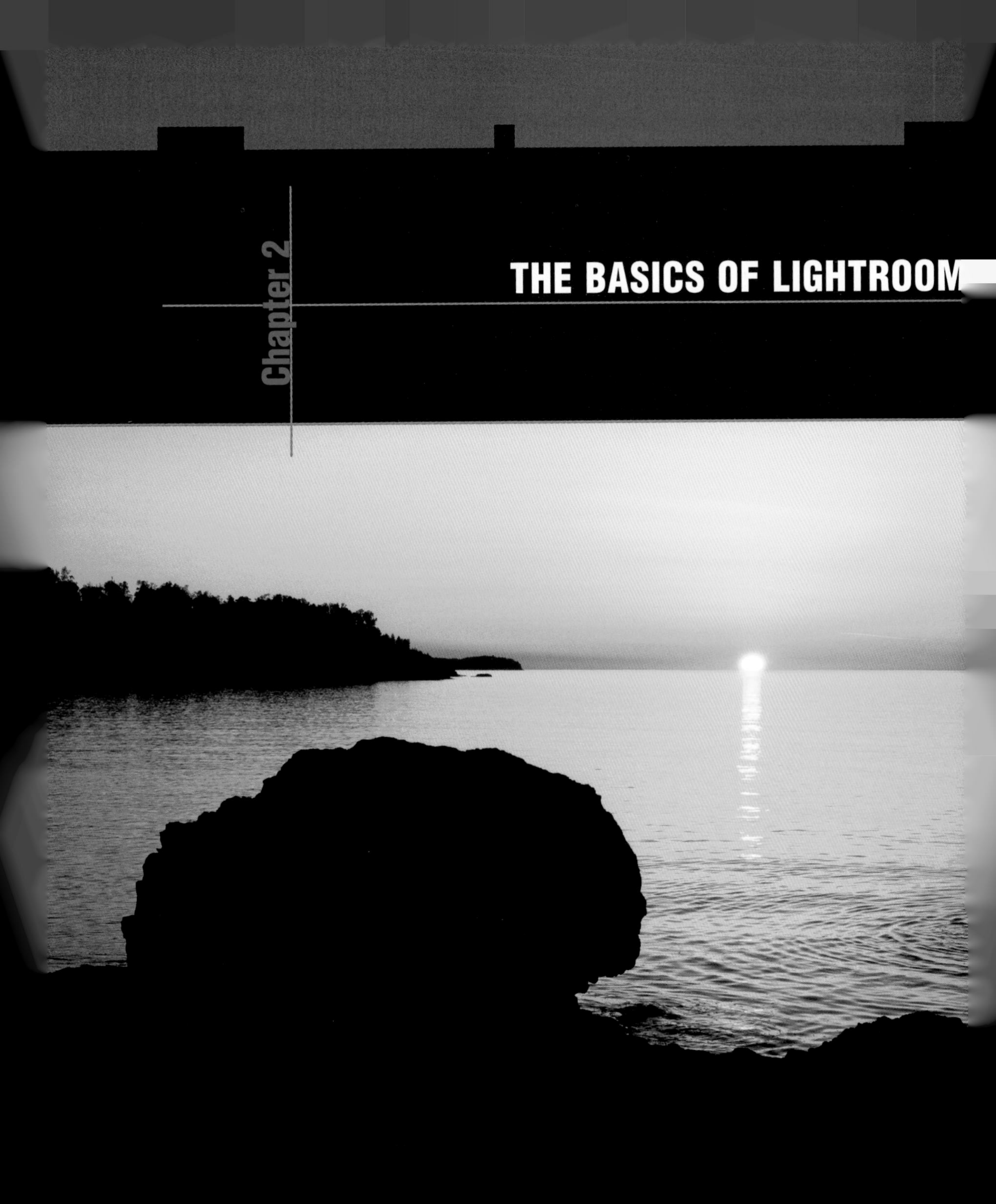

When Lightroom first came out, a lot of people wondered if the world really needed another digital photography program. Lightroom has definitely proven itself to be a valuable tool for the working photographer.

As you see when you open the program, Lightroom is based on modules, so once you import images into its control, you can jump around within the program as much as you want. Some people think very linearly, others think nonlinearly. Lightroom works for both mind-sets. This program is laid out in such a way that once you understand the basics, you can quickly make it an important element of your digital photography.

How Lightroom Is Organized

Lightroom takes a very different approach, compared to most image-processing programs, in how a photographer accesses its features. The program is organized linearly around a set of five work modules, while the interface itself is arranged spatially into four distinct regions or panels, as shown in figure 2-1. This approach really works. It keeps controls grouped according to their function and places them at the ready when you need them for doing specific work on digital images. It also means that you don't have to constantly go to menus at the top of the screen. Lightroom has top menus, but most of the time you don't need to use them.

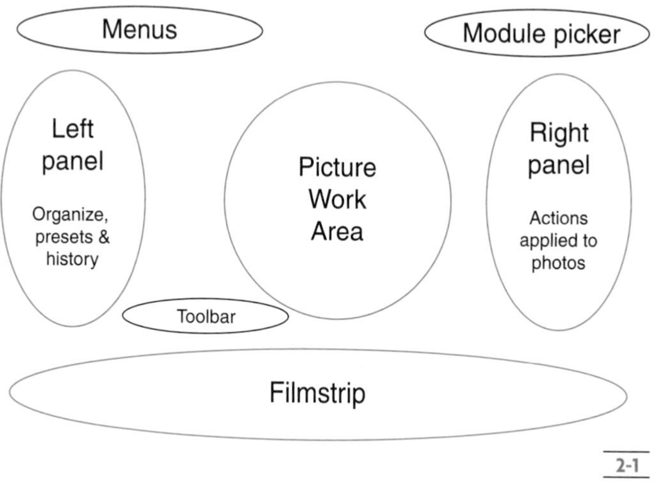

2-1

Modules

Lightroom's modular organization is very efficient in that it allows you to access specific parts of the program as you need them. Consider these modules workrooms that let you make changes to an image, and the controls in each workroom all relate to a specific function. According to Adobe, modules can be added or subtracted from the program, so the company may add more in the future (or you may be able to add special modules created by independent software developers).

The modules are

- > Library
- > Develop
- > Slideshow
- > Print
- > Web

In addition, these modules are actually based on three functions, as shown in figure 2-2: Library, Develop, and Output (Slideshow, Print, and Web). The most important functions for photographers are Library and Develop. You will spend most of your time there.

The modules themselves appear at the top right of the Lightroom interface in figure 2-3. I am going to keep the same photo in the interface for each module so you can better see how the modules change the interface. The image is a sunrise from a shoot along the shore of Lake Superior in Northern Minnesota.

To select any one module, just click on it. You can use them in order, starting at Library and finishing with Print, or you can select any one of them at any time. The Filmstrip at the bottom of the screen provides constant access to photos. You learn more about using each module in later chapters.

Library

Library is where you "keep" your photos for Lightroom to work on, though you are actually using virtual files. The files stay on your hard drive in the folders where you are storing them. Library has outstanding organizing capabilities that keep a reference as to where images are on the hard drive or other media. This is the place to systematize and sort photos. This module (also shown in figure 2-3) gives you image import and export options, folder editing and organizing capabilities, labeling and other information options, and even a chance to quickly process images.

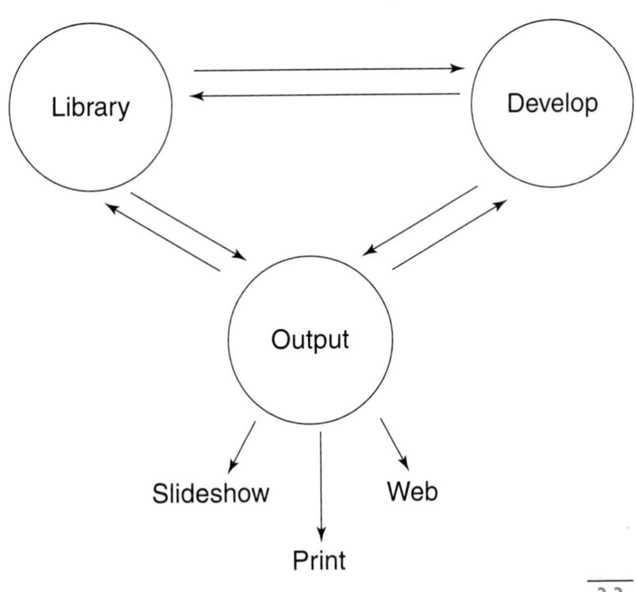

2-2

2-3

Develop

Develop is where photos are processed, as shown in figure 2-4. This is where you adjust and optimize images, using some controls that are just like those in Camera Raw and others that are more advanced. Develop has controls from basic exposure to color tuning, cropping, and even lens aberration correction. You can see the control groupings in figure 2-4.

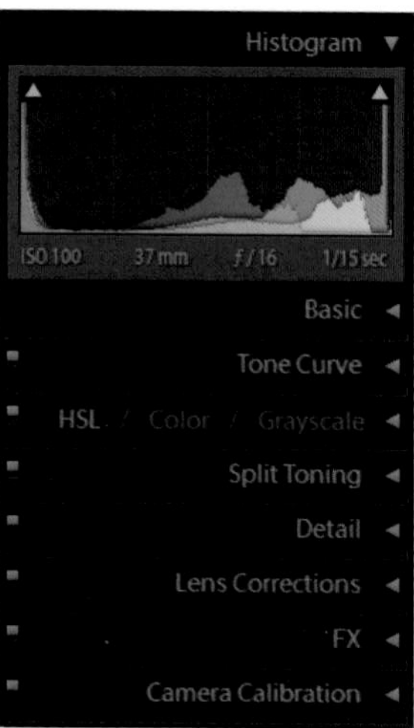

2-4

This module also introduces an interesting and often useful way to work quickly with images: the Presets panel, shown in figure 2-5. You can use presets that come with the program as well as create your own. All the other modules include something similar, offering pre-made adjustments for images.

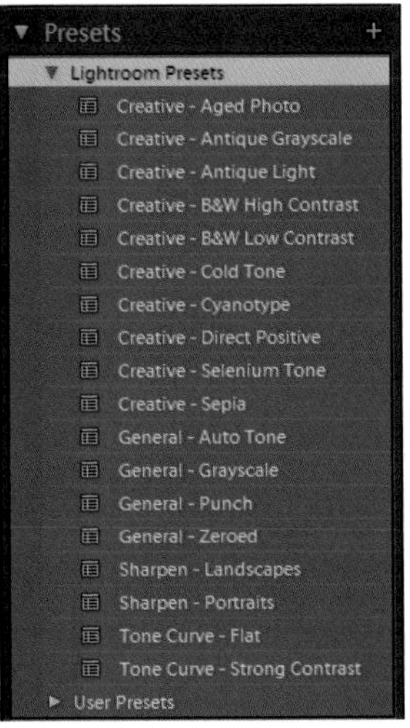

2-5

Slideshow

Slideshow (shown in figure 2-6) gives you some basic capabilities for showing off groups of images, just like the old slide shows from the days when most people shot film. If you have a digital projector, you can even project these images like in the old days. Slideshow gives you control over how the images are displayed, including the ability to add some very cool image enhancements such as borders and drop shadows. It does not allow exporting of music with the slide show, however.

X-REF

For more information on color tuning, see Chapter 6.

2-6

Print

The next module is Print (as shown in figure 2-7). Adobe engineers knew that photographers like to make prints, so they created a module to gather together printing options. This is the first time in any Adobe product that all printing-related functions are put into one place. You actually have a lot of control here for the print; and because Lightroom groups the adjustments and settings in a manner that is logical for printing, you can truly focus on what matters in printing and not be distracted by a lot of unrelated stuff.

Web

The last module is Web (as shown in figure 2-8). This offers you an easy way of making Web galleries for a Web site. This is a fairly simple module with two basic forms of galleries — one HTML, the other Flash. You control the text you need and how the galleries display the work.

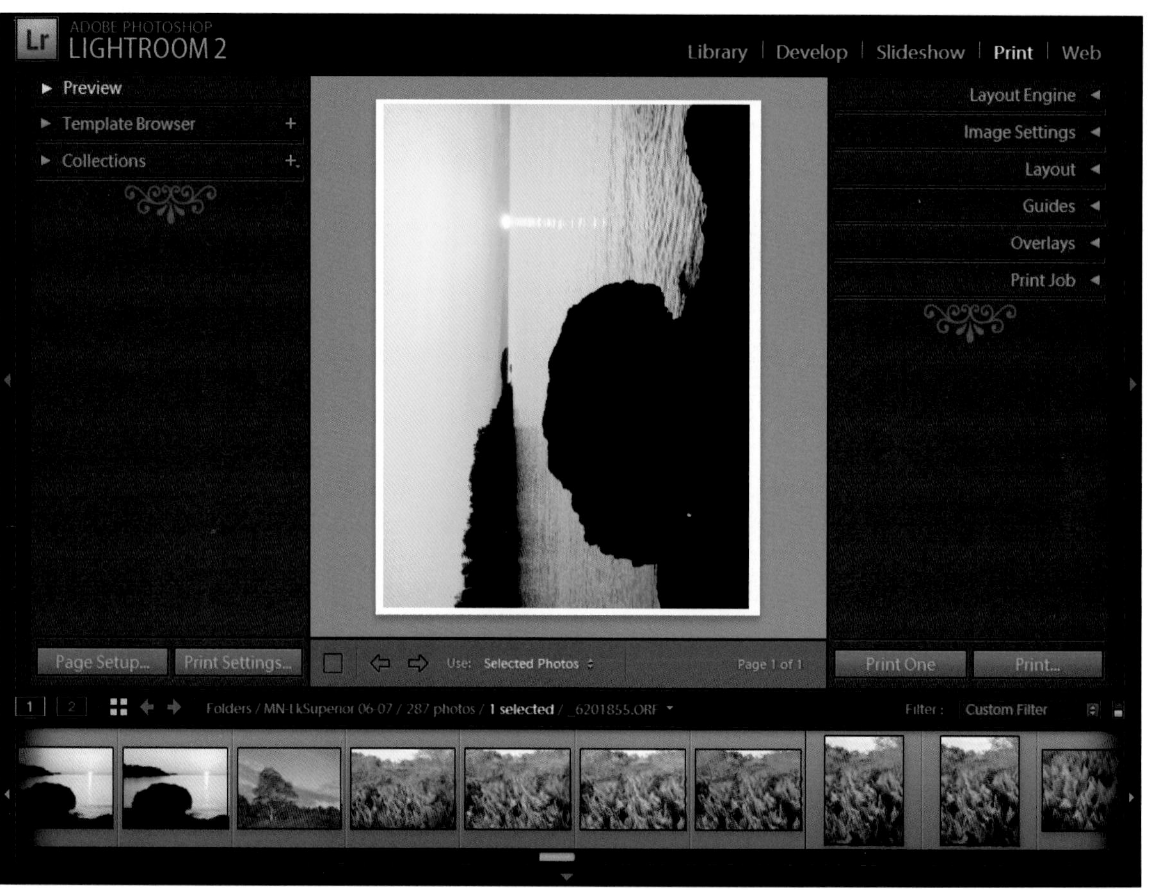

2-7

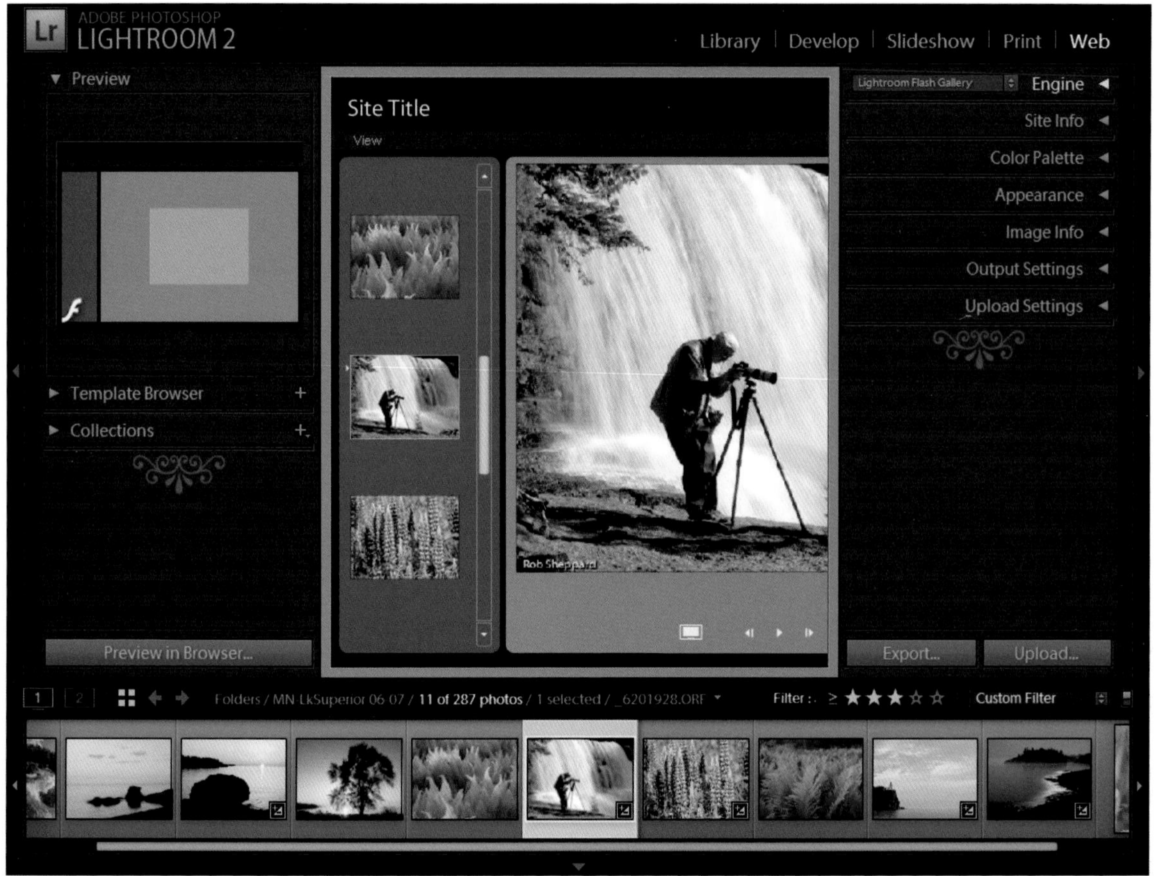

2-8

Skip Between Modules

A really great thing about Lightroom is that you can skip back and forth among these modules as needed. If you test a slide show (shown in figure 2-9), for example, and find one image is off in exposure compared to others, you can immediately go to Develop (shown in figure 2-10), fix that exposure, and then go back to the slide show. That is a really cool feature. I can tell you that working with images for slide shows or printing has been annoying at times when I had to go back and readjust an image, and then start over with it for the slide show or print. This totally changes how you work with images in that way.

One way of looking at these modules, too, is to group the last three modules as output modules, as shown earlier in figure 2-2. Slideshow, Print, and Web all give you options to output your images. These modules don't really have quite the depth of Library and Develop when seen alone, but put them together, and you gain some very useful tools for output.

ADOBE PHOTOSHOP
LIGHTROOM 2
Library
Develop
Slideshow
Print
Web
Options
Layout
Overlays
Backdrop
Color Wash
Opacity
100
Angle
45
Background Image
Opacity
Background Color
Titles
Playback
Use: All Filmstrip Photos
ABC
Slide 3 of 11
Preview
Play
Folders / MN-LkSuperior 06-07 / 11 of 287 photos / 1 selected / _6201855.ORF
Filter :
Custom Filter

2-9

ADOBE PHOTOSHOP
LIGHTROOM 2
Library
Develop
Slideshow
Print
Web
Navigator
FIT
FILL
1:1
3:1
Presets
Snapshots
History
Histogram
Basic
Tone Curve
Region
Highlights
0
Lights
0
Darks
0
Shadows
0
Point Curve :
Medium Contrast
Copy...
Paste
Previous
Reset
Folders / MN-LkSuperior 06-07 / 11 of 287 photos / 1 selected / _6201855.ORF
Filter :
Custom Filter

2-10

Panels

Each module has the same basic setup for panels within the interface. There are four regions defined by panels that identify and contain ways of dealing with an image, as shown in figure 2-11 and figure 2-12. Each panel changes depending on the module (compare figure 2-11 with figure 2-12); however, appropriate work panels appear at the right and left that offer you adjustments and controls over your images. The center work area is photo based and highlights the image (or images) you are working on. It can include one or multiple images. The final panel is the Filmstrip at the bottom that lets you go quickly through a selected group of photos.

2-11

2-12

You can turn panels on and off to better see the photo (or group of photos) at the center in two ways. First, you can just press Tab and the two side panels disappear, as shown in figure 2-13. They return when you press Tab again.

Second, you can hide them one at a time by clicking the small arrows at the far sides of the panels (in reality, the arrows are just reminders — you can click anywhere near them on the bars where they reside). The arrows are dark gray until you mouse over them. Figure 2-14 shows Lightroom with the left panel hidden (and the top menu is hidden, too). The panels come back temporarily if you move your mouse to the far edge of the interface where the panel is, and are hidden again if you move the mouse over the middle of the photo. They remain visible if you click again on the arrow.

LIGHTROOM 2
Library
Develop
Slideshow
Print
Web
Library Filter:
Text
Attribute
Metadata
None
Custom Filter
Sort: User Order
Thumbnails
Filter:
Custom Filter

2-13

Library Filter:
Text
Attribute
Metadata
None
Custom Filter
Histogram
Quick Develop
Keywording
Keyword List
Metadata
Sort: User Order
Thumbnails
Sync Settings
Sync Metadata
Filter:
Custom Filter

2-14

You can hide the Filmstrip panel, too. Click the little arrow at the bottom of the interface, below the Filmstrip, and the strip of photos hides, as shown in figure 2-15. It comes back temporarily if you mouse over the bottom of the screen or stays on if you click the arrow again.

When the Filmstrip is hidden, you can press Tab and the side panels become hidden, then if you press T, the toolbar also hides, leaving you with just the image on which you are working, as shown in figure 2-16. Pressing Tab does not bring back the Filmstrip, just the side panels. Press Shift+Tab and you can make the side panels, the top module picker, plus the Filmstrip appear and disappear. Press T again to get the toolbar back.

PRO TIP

The larger the monitor you can work with, the easier it is to work with all of the panels at once. Using smaller monitors, especially those on laptops, often means you have to hide certain parts of the interface so the part you are working with is large enough.

2-15

2-16

If you don't like the way the panels are sized on your computer, you can adjust how big each one is by moving your cursor over the dividing bar between the panels. This changes your cursor to a bar with arrows and allows you to make a panel larger or smaller by clicking and dragging.

PRO TIP

There are a number of ways of working with the panels to make them turn on and off. You might want to remember these function keys: F6 hides the Filmstrip, F7 hides the left panel, and F8 hides the right panel. Also, F5 hides the top bar where the module names are.

Adobe's Five Rules for Lightroom

When you look in the Help menu in Lightroom, you'll find something called The Five Rules, as shown in figure 2-17. This is a set of five rules for using Lightroom, which were actually used as guidelines in the development of the original version of the program. They are not rules as in absolutes or laws you must follow, but are really guidelines that direct how you can work with Lightroom. They are also still used by the program developers to guide their work. Adobe's five rules for Lightroom are

> **Module Picker.** Use the Module Picker to choose your path through Lightroom.

> **Panels.** Control the modules using the panels.

> **Filmstrip.** Navigate your photos using the Filmstrip.

> **Key Commands.** Expedite your work by learning import and keyboard shortcuts.

> **Finally . . .** Enjoy.

A note before looking at these in more detail: As you click on each of the five rules, the appropriate part of the interface will highlight in yellow.

Use the Module Picker to Choose Your Path Through Lightroom

As you've seen, Lightroom is structured into modules. It is not done that way simply to keep different functions separate; it also makes it easier for photographers to work through images in an intuitive way.

This is a framework to constantly keep in mind as you are learning Lightroom. If you have trouble remembering where a certain control is, think about the modules and where that control might logically be. Any time you click to activate a module, a new set of controls and choices appears in the panels at the left and right sides of the screen.

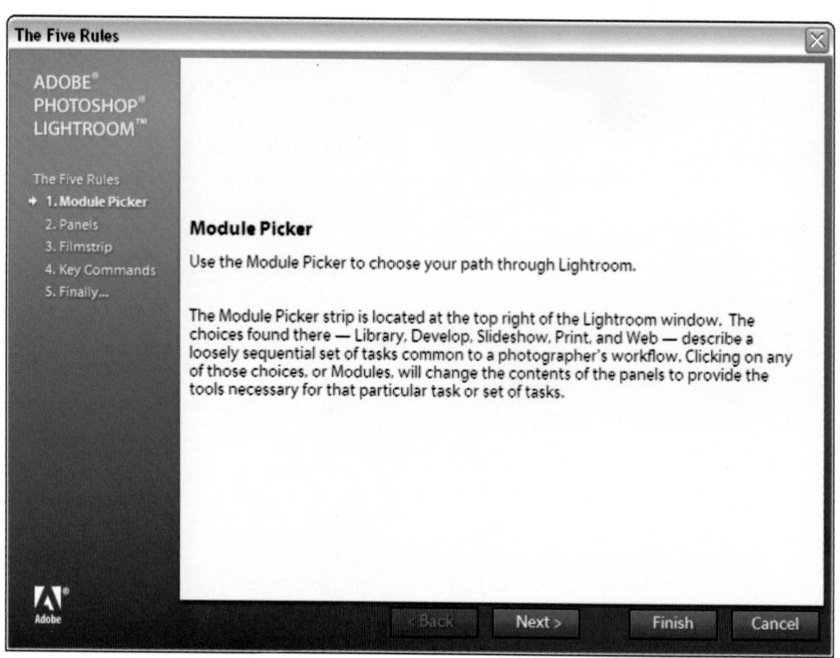

2-17

These modules are also a great framework for a workflow:

1. **Start with the Library module; do library (organizing) sort of work there.**
2. **Process the image or images in Develop.**
3. **Go to the output modules to use your image in presentations, either as a slide show, a print, or a Web gallery.**

Control the Modules Using the Panels

Nearly everything you need to do with an image you can find in the panels at the sides of the central work area (a few controls are found in the toolbar at the bottom of the central work area). All controls and adjustments are grouped into sets of similar functions. This makes them much easier to use than the menu structure of Photoshop. While you can use the menus at the top of Lightroom, you won't be using them much.

You can find nearly every standard photo adjustment you need here. Each panel has controls and adjustments appropriate to the task the module defines. Panels at the left hold preset browsers, while panels at the right hold the actual tools. The panels also include section headers to group controls by category. Open a category by clicking on the section header (for example, see Basic in the Develop module in figure 2-18) or close the choices to make the interface simpler by clicking again on the category.

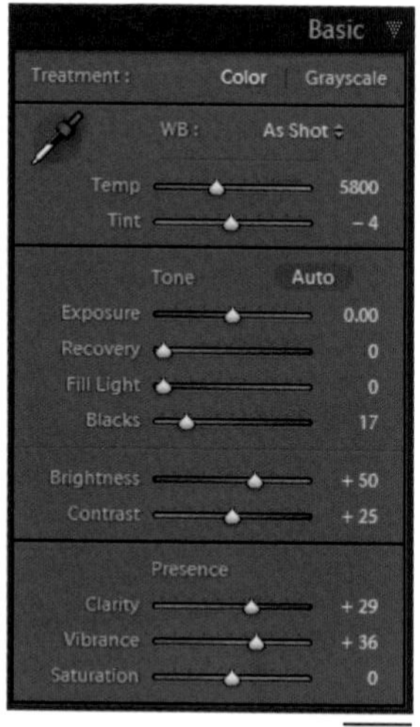

2-18

Navigate Your Photos Using the Filmstrip

Lightroom is designed so that images are always accessible to you. You don't have to constantly open an "open" dialog box and search for images on your hard drive. All photos from a particular group (folder, keyword search, or collection) are in the Filmstrip. This is a linear view of the current images in the Catalog group that you have selected.

You can change what is in the Filmstrip whenever you need to by going back to the Library and choosing a different group of images. The Filmstrip, as shown in figure 2-19, provides a place to see your images from a particular group of shots (a folder, collection, or sorted group) in any module, that is, the Filmstrip stays consistent across modules.

Expedite Your Work by Learning Important Keyboard Shortcuts

You can work with Lightroom more quickly and efficiently if you learn a few key commands that you access directly from the keyboard. More than a few keystrokes make the process of working an image go more smoothly, but start with these important key commands:

- **Tab.** Hides side panels. This is a quick way to simplify the interface. The side panels of controls are hidden, shifting the focus to just your photo, and the Filmstrip remains available. See either panel instantly by moving your cursor to the sides; hide them again by moving the cursor away. Press Tab again and the panels return.
- **Shift+Tab.** Hides/unhides both side panels, the top bar, and the Filmstrip panel, as shown in figure 2-20.
- **F.** Cycle full-screen mode. This removes extraneous and potentially distracting elements such as the top menus that are rarely used.
- **L.** Dim the lights mode. This is really a cool key command to remember. Press L once and the whole interface dims except for your photos in the center work area, as shown in figure 2-21. Press L again and the screen turns black except for your photo. This is a very quick and useful keystroke that lets you better examine your photo without any distractions around it.
- **~.** Flag the selected photo(s).This will put a little white flag with your image in Library and mark it as a "Pick."
- **Ctrl+/ or ⌘+/.** Module-specific shortcuts. There are a ton of keyboard shortcuts in Lightroom; for example, those that appear with the Library Module are shown in Tables 2-1 through 2-6. You can find some that you might want to try in a specific module by using this keyboard command. Note that Mac users should use ⌘ for Ctrl and Option for Alt in the keyboard shortcuts.

2-19

2-20

Table 2-1: Library Module View Shortcuts

Keystroke(s)	***Function***
Esc	Return to previous view
Enter	Enter Loupe or 1:1 view
E	Enter Loupe view
C	Enter Compare mode
G	Enter Grid mode
Ctrl+Enter	Enter Impromptu Slideshow mode
F	Cycle to next Screen mode
Ctrl+Alt+F	Return to Normal Screen mode
L	Cycle through Lights Out modes
Ctrl+J	Grid View Options
J	Cycle Grid Views
\	Hide/Show the Filter Bar

Table 2-2: Library Module Ratings Shortcuts

Keystroke(s)	***Function***
1-5	Set ratings
Shift+1-5	Set ratings and move to next photo
6-9	Set color labels
Shift+6-9	Set color labels and move to next photo
0	Reset ratings to none
[	Decrease the rating
]	Increase the rating

2-21

Table 2-3: Library Module Flagging Shortcuts

Keystroke(s)	Function
'	Toggle Flagged Status
Ctrl+↑	Increase Flag Status
Ctrl+↓	Decrease Flag Status

Table 2-4: Library Module Target Collection Shortcuts

Keystroke(s)	Function
B	Add to Target Collection
Ctrl+B	Show the Target Collection
Ctrl+Shift+B	Clear Quick Collection

Table 2-5: Library Module Photo Shortcuts

Keystroke(s)	Function
Ctrl+Shift+I	Import photos
Ctrl+Shift+E	Export photos
Ctrl+[	Rotate left
Ctrl+]	Rotate right
Ctrl+E	Edit in Photoshop
Ctrl+-	Zoom out
Ctrl+=	Zoom in
Z	Zoom to 100%
Ctrl+G	Stack photos
Ctrl+Shift+G	Unstack photos

Continued

Table 2-5 *(Continued)*

Keystroke(s)	***Function***
Ctrl+R	Show in Explorer
Backspace	Remove from Library
F2	Rename File
Ctrl+Shift+C	Copy Develop Settings
Ctrl+Shift+V	Paste Develop Settings
Ctrl+←	Previous selected photo
Ctrl+→	Next selected photo
Ctrl+L	Enable/Disable Library Filters

Table 2-6: Library Module Panel Shortcuts

Keystroke(s)	***Function***
Tab	Hide/Show the side panels
Shift+Tab	Hide/Show all the panels
T	Hide/Show the toolbar
Ctrl+F	Activate the search field
Ctrl+Alt+↑	Return to the previous module

Finally . . . Enjoy

I really like this little rule. I'm glad the Lightroom developers included it. Some folks treat Photoshop so very, very s-e-r-i-o-u-s-l-y. I think that having a fun, playful attitude toward Photoshop helps you in that program, too, but it is especially important in Lightroom. Lightroom is made to encourage experimentation and trying out features. You can quickly go from one thing to another, make comparisons, try new tools, and so forth. Treat Lightroom as a fun way to deal with your images and look for the fun in the process. You are likely to discover many new ideas that way.

PRO TIP

Lightroom is set up to give you some very specific, context-sensitive options when you right-click on something in the Lightroom interface. No matter whether you are a Mac or PC user, you should be using a right-click mouse. By right-clicking on a photograph, for example, you will get a context-sensitive menu of the things that you can do with that photograph, ranging from setting a rating to exporting the image. By right-clicking on a folder in Library, for another example, you'll get a menu of folder-specific options that allow you to do such things as rename the folder or save metadata in it.

The Craft of Lightroom and Photography

One thing that I like to stress in all my workshops and books is the craft of photography and the digital darkroom. Craft is the learned skill of doing something well; it suggests the idea that someone is making or constructing something in a way that requires care and ingenuity. Photography is definitely a craft — an art and a science developed with practice by using and learning the many tools involved so that through trial and error, one masters the skills needed through a period of apprenticeship. Sometimes I'll tell my group that we need to keep photography in digital photography.

While it is true that most photographers don't have a true, traditional apprenticeship (though some do, becoming assistants to top photographers while they hone their craft), one cannot pick up a camera and immediately become an excellent photographer.
You need to learn how to control the equipment, from f-stops to shutter speeds, and how to deal with the medium. You need to learn how to make a photograph with care and ingenuity. Most pros and advanced amateurs understand that. They know that it takes some time to master exposure and composition, for example, as demonstrated in the scene shown in figure 2-22 and figure 2-23. Figure 2-22 is an overexposed,

2-22

2-23

amateurish composition of a waterfall taken at Inks Lake State Park in Texas. Figure 2-23 shows more control and mastery over both the exposure and composition.

Just as it took you some time to master f-stops and shutter speeds, it will take some experience with Lightroom for you to really master its capabilities. Yes, it is set up for photographers; yes, it is designed to be intuitive for the pro and advanced photographer. However, this does not mean that once you know the basics of this program, you have mastered its craft. You must spend some time with the program, playing with its controls and working on a lot of images to really know how to benefit from its power.

I also stress the idea of craft because Lightroom is especially made to make RAW file processing easier and more efficient. There is still a serious misunderstanding about RAW that is very dangerous for any photographer: If you shoot RAW, you can always fix image problems in the software. The idea that RAW makes it so easy to correct poor shooting technique that you don't have to worry about being as careful when shooting is, to put it bluntly, wrong. It is not the best way to use Lightroom or any other image-processing software. Crafting a fine image starts when you first pick up the camera.

Customizing Lightroom's Identity Plate

Lightroom has a neat little feature that will appeal to many pros who use the program with clients — for example, on a laptop while in the field. This is the ability to change the Identity Plate, as Adobe calls it, which is the program identity part of the interface at the top left where it says Adobe Photoshop Lightroom. You can actually put in your own name (or studio name). The Identity Plate can also be added to slides in the Slideshow module, to prints in the Print module, and to Web pages in the Web module.

To do this, follow these steps:

1. **Choose Edit ➪ Identity Plate Setup in Windows (shown in figure 2-24) and Lightroom ➪ Identity Plate Setup on a Mac.** The Identity Plate Editor dialog box appears.
2. **Select Enable Identity Plate and type your name in the name space at the left (with the Use a styled text identity plate option selected).** There is a drop-down menu that has a default of Custom at first — this menu lets you save or remove specific Identity Plates. Your name appears in the Identity Plate area at the top left, as shown in figure 2-25. The default is an interesting font, but it is not particularly consistent with the rest of the interface.

However, you can change the font for both your name and the module picker buttons. You pick a font with the Font drop-down menu after selecting the appropriate letters, and then choose a module word font by using the drop-down menus below that area in this dialog box, as shown in figure 2-26. The font choices are obvious, from left: the typeface, font style, and size. Color is not as obvious — you click the square box to the right of font size to get a Color Picker, as shown in figure 2-27.

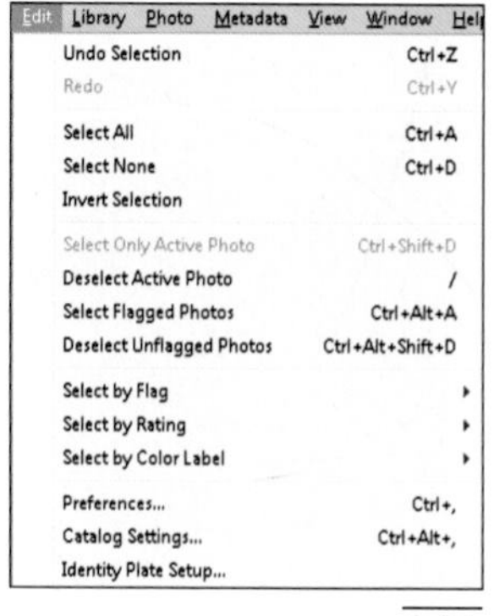

2-24

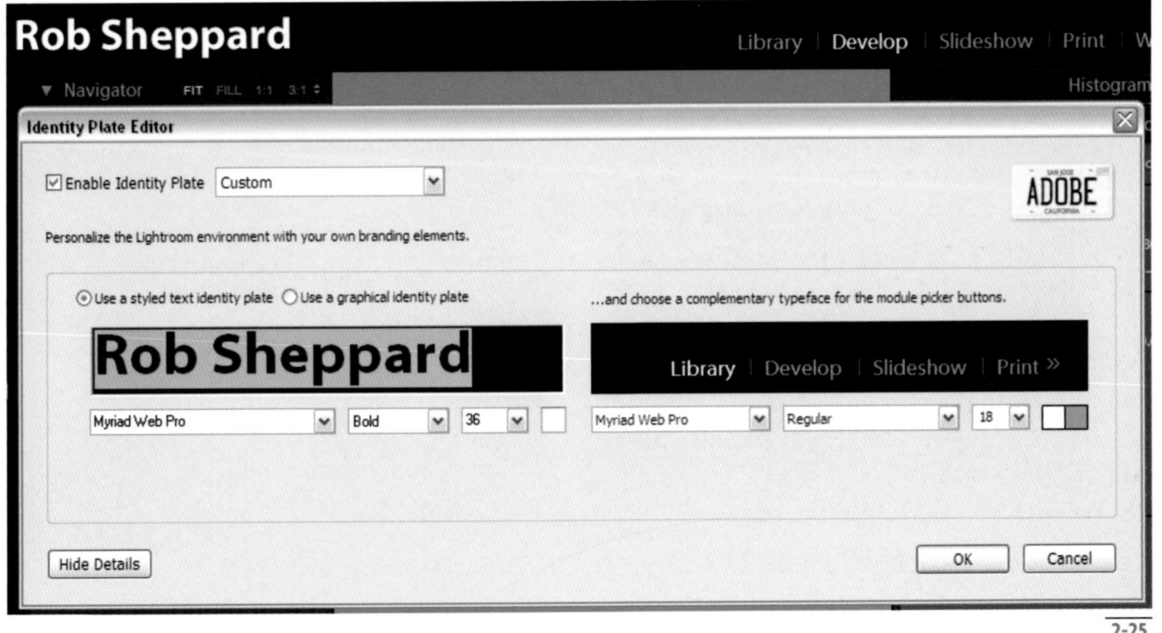
Rob Sheppard
Library
Develop
Slideshow
Print
Navigator
FIT FILL 1:1 3:1
Histogram
Identity Plate Editor
Enable Identity Plate
Custom
ADOBE
Personalize the Lightroom environment with your own branding elements.
Use a styled text identity plate
Use a graphical identity plate
...and choose a complementary typeface for the module picker buttons.
Rob Sheppard
Library | Develop | Slideshow | Print »
Myriad Web Pro
Bold
36
Myriad Web Pro
Regular
18
Hide Details
OK
Cancel

2-25

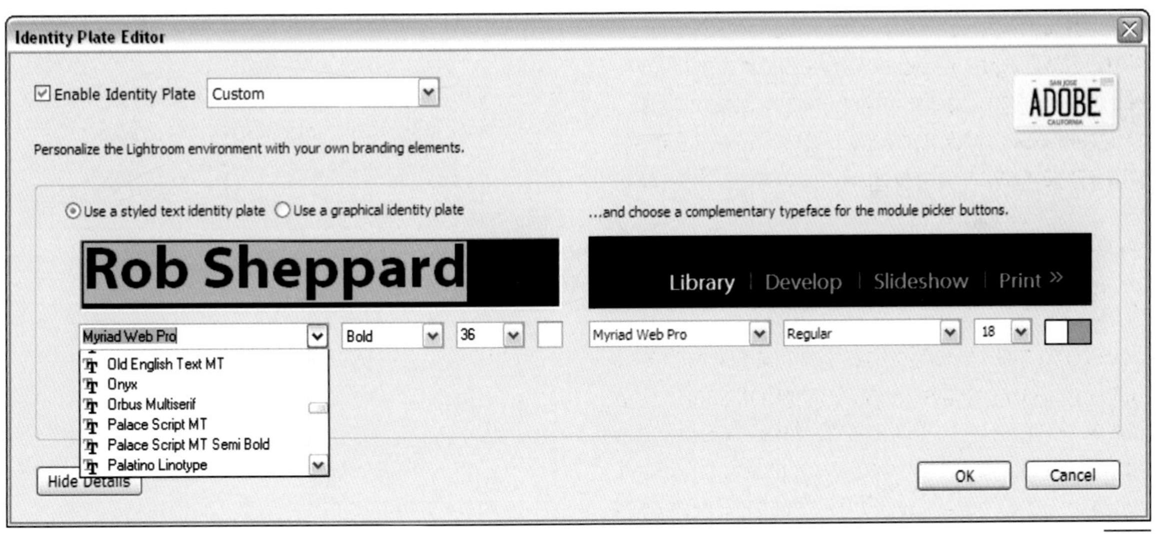
Identity Plate Editor
Enable Identity Plate
Custom
ADOBE
Personalize the Lightroom environment with your own branding elements.
Use a styled text identity plate
Use a graphical identity plate
...and choose a complementary typeface for the module picker buttons.
Rob Sheppard
Library | Develop | Slideshow | Print »
Myriad Web Pro
Bold
36
Myriad Web Pro
Regular
18
Old English Text MT
Onyx
Orbus Multiserif
Palace Script MT
Palace Script MT Semi Bold
Palatino Linotype
OK
Cancel

2-26

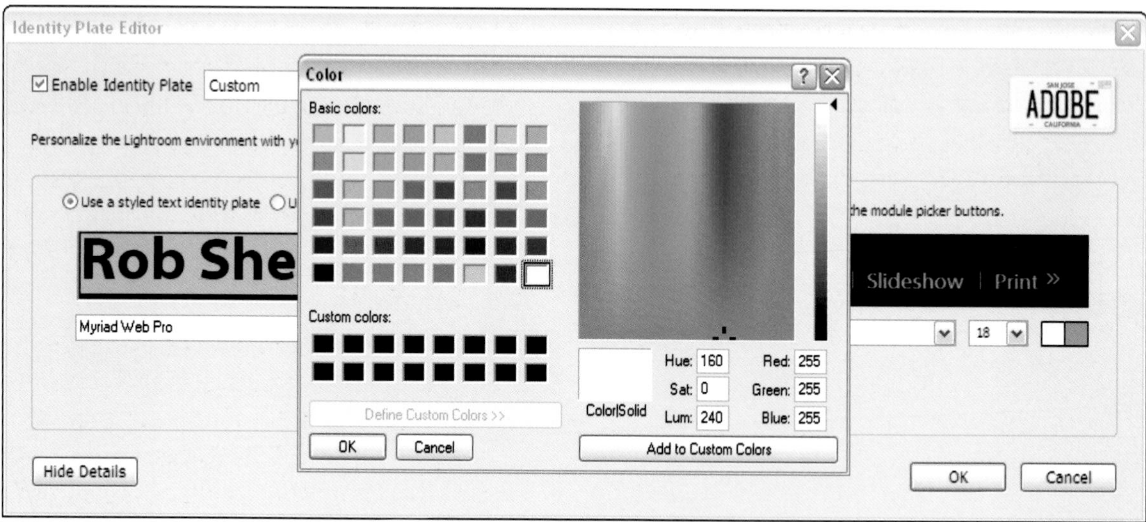

2-27

To enhance your Identity Plate and make it more graphic, you can even select parts of the name and change just that font and color, as shown in figure 2-28. This gives the Lightroom interface a very custom look.

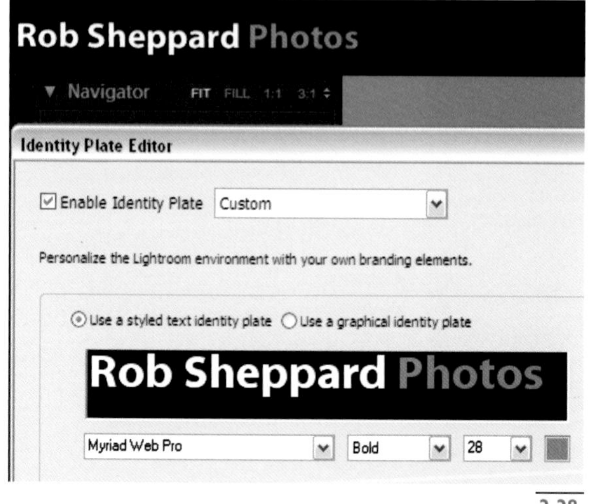

2-28

The ability to add your name and change fonts and colors gives you a lot of personalization capabilities, but if you have a studio with a graphic, you can add that, too, after you have sized it up to a maximum 60 pixels high (that is all Lightroom can use). Simply select the Use a graphical identity plate option and click the Locate File button that appears in order to navigate directly to the image you need. The result is the Lightroom interface with a custom logo.

CAUTION

A caution on the Identity Plate. Watch your colors and bold logos. They can be distracting from your actual photos. This can be a real problem when working with the Develop module because strong colors outside of your photo, for example, can affect how you see colors in the image you are processing. Notice that Lightroom has an overall very neutral interface — this was done for just that reason, to avoid color and tonal distractions.

Preferences

While Lightroom has a few preferences to set, I have found that using Lightroom with most of its default preferences, rather than going in and setting new ones, is fine for my use, and I suspect this is true for many other photographers. However, you should know where Preferences are and how to set them.

Preferences are found in the main menu. Choose Edit ➪ Preferences in Windows, and Lightroom ➪ Preferences on a Mac. This gives you the dialog box shown in figure 2-29, with General preferences as the first tab on the left. Here are the key settings for you to check:

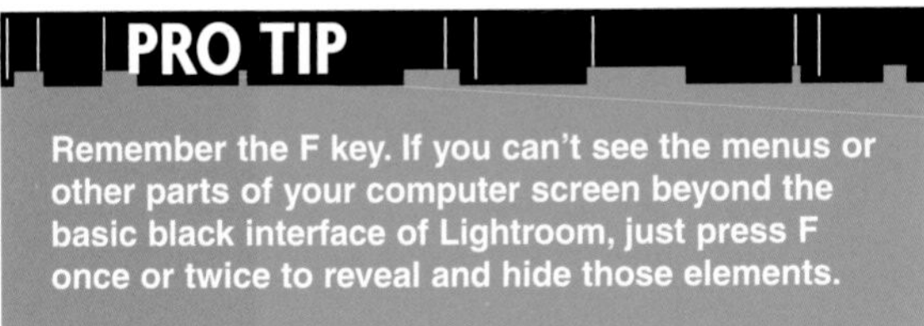

PRO TIP
Remember the F key. If you can't see the menus or other parts of your computer screen beyond the basic black interface of Lightroom, just press F once or twice to reveal and hide those elements.

> **General.** Mostly, the settings and choices are set up to work well with photographers' needs, so you can leave most of them as is. If you don't like seeing a brief splash screen as Lightroom starts up, deselect that setting. Many photographers don't like their computer to go to the Internet and check for updates to Lightroom, so they leave that setting deselected.

The next option is whether you use the default catalog or not. Some photographers set up multiple catalogs of images based on the type of shooting that they do. If you do this, then you need to tell Lightroom which catalog to start with.

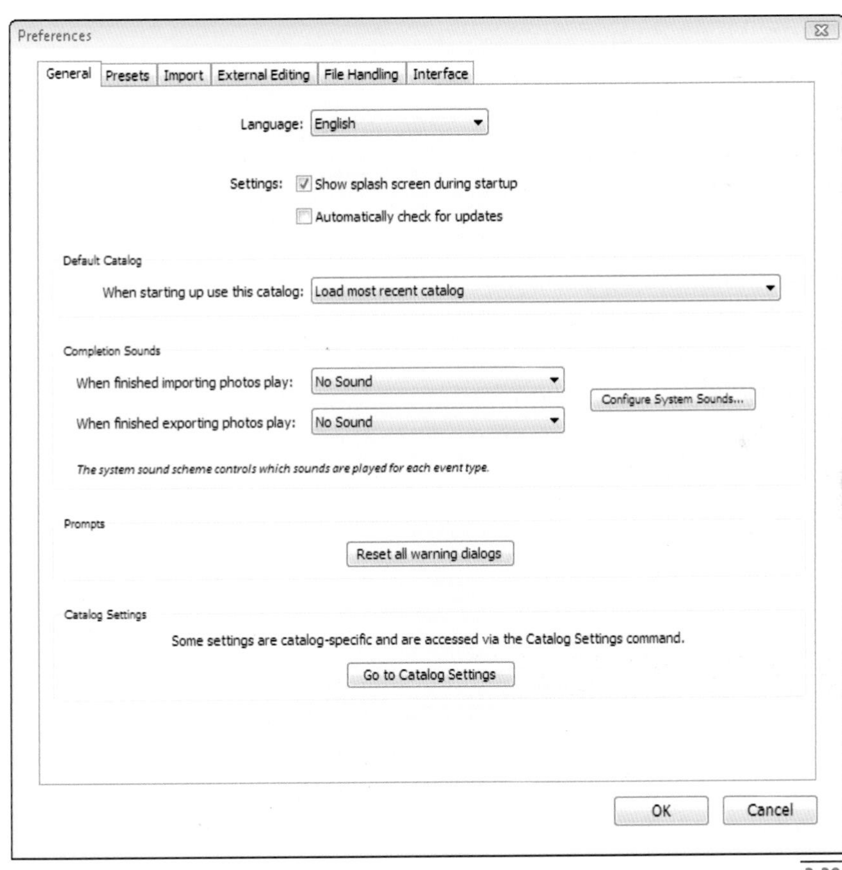

2-29

Completion Sounds are simply alerts to tell you when certain processes are complete. Some people like their computers to beep when certain actions occur, some don't. Your choices are to hear no sound or to hear a variety of beeps, chirps, and so on, depending on your operating system. You can also reset all prompts and presets if you find you are missing things after working in the program for a while.

The last option in General preferences is simply a link to another menu option for changing catalog settings, as shown in figure 2-30. You can also get directly to the catalog settings in the Edit (PC) or Lightroom (Mac) menu. This is where you can tell Lightroom how often to back up the catalog — it is important to keep your catalog backed up in a location separate from your main hard drive. You also have the ability to optimize a large Catalog if it starts to run too slowly. The File Handling tab of Catalog Settings enables you to change the preview size of your images as displayed in Lightroom. The Metadata tab allows you to change how Lightroom treats metadata.

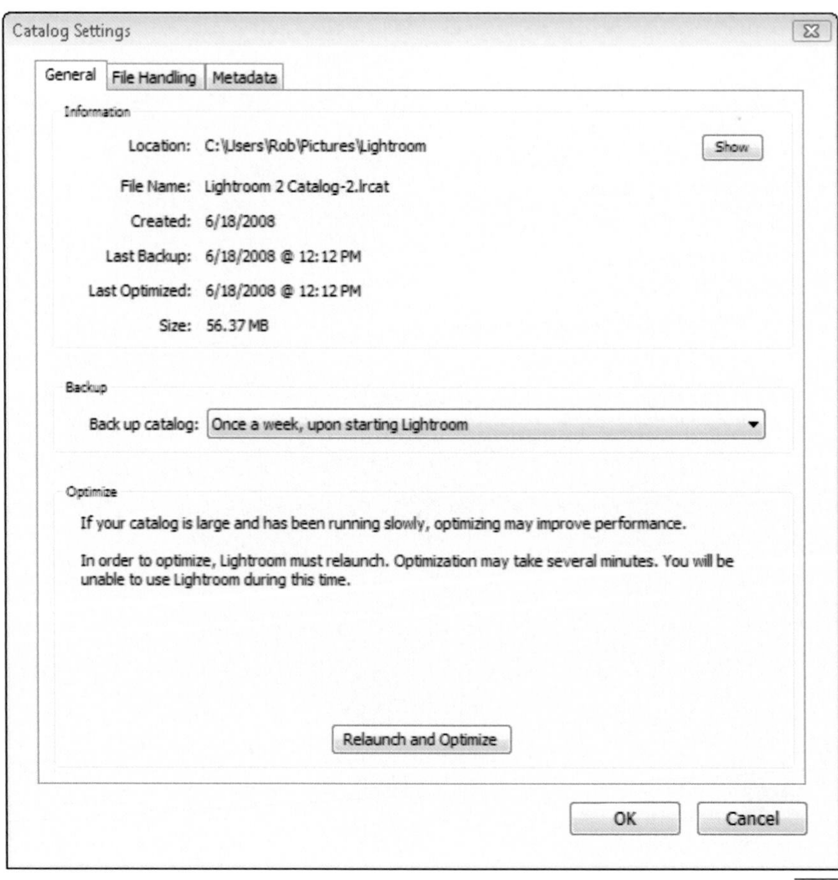

2-30

> **Presets.** Presets is a section that allows you to change the default Develop settings, as shown in figure 2-31. You will see later in this book why I am not fond of applying auto tone adjustments. If you are in an organization that is using multiple cameras, it can be helpful to make defaults specific to cameras. The rest of the presets are pretty much self-explanatory.

> **Import.** This is an important preference to review, as shown in figure 2-32. If you want to use Lightroom to help you import photos from a memory card, be sure to select the first option, Show import dialog when a memory card is detected. Most photographers can leave the rest pretty much at the defaults. The second option on ignoring camera-generated folder names is important only if you are importing exactly those folders from a memory card. The option for treating JPEG files is an interesting one. I shoot RAW+JPEG because there are certain benefits to shooting both formats. However, I don't need to see the JPEG files right next to the RAW files, as they just take up space on the screen. The last section on DNG (digital negative) creation is simply to set the defaults for how you would create a DNG file (personally, I think that while this is a good file format, it is a waste of storage space to change all of your image files into DNG files when importing them).

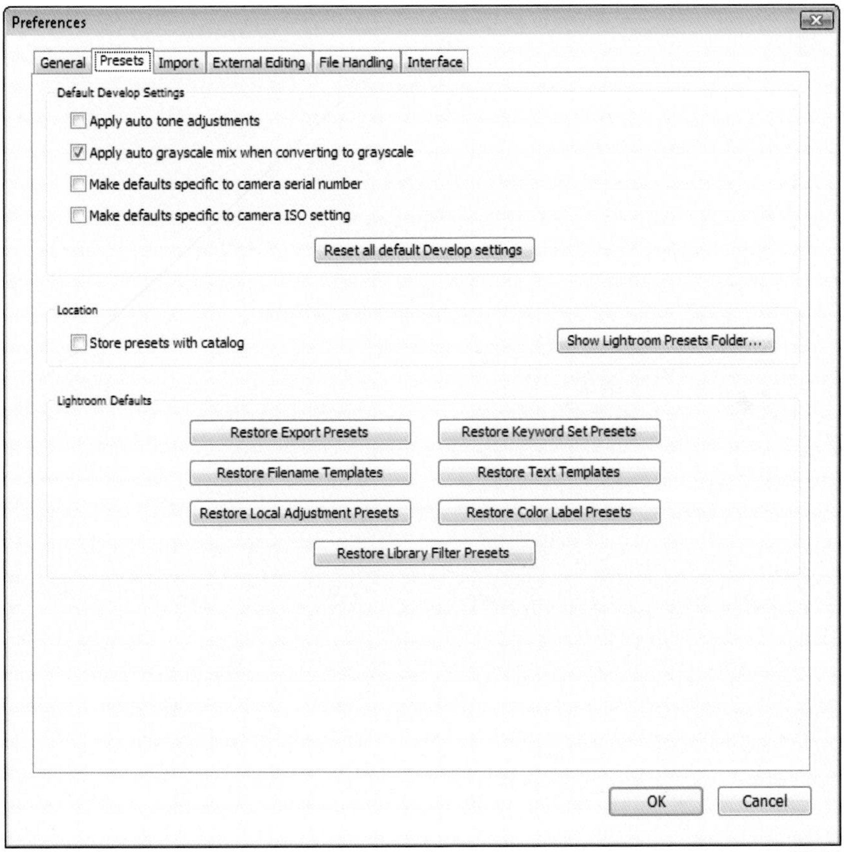

Preferences

General | Presets | Import | External Editing | File Handling | Interface

Default Develop Settings

- [ ] Apply auto tone adjustments
- [x] Apply auto grayscale mix when converting to grayscale
- [ ] Make defaults specific to camera serial number
- [ ] Make defaults specific to camera ISO setting

Reset all default Develop settings

Location

- [ ] Store presets with catalog

Show Lightroom Presets Folder...

Lightroom Defaults

Restore Export Presets | Restore Keyword Set Presets
Restore Filename Templates | Restore Text Templates
Restore Local Adjustment Presets | Restore Color Label Presets
Restore Library Filter Presets

OK | Cancel

2-31

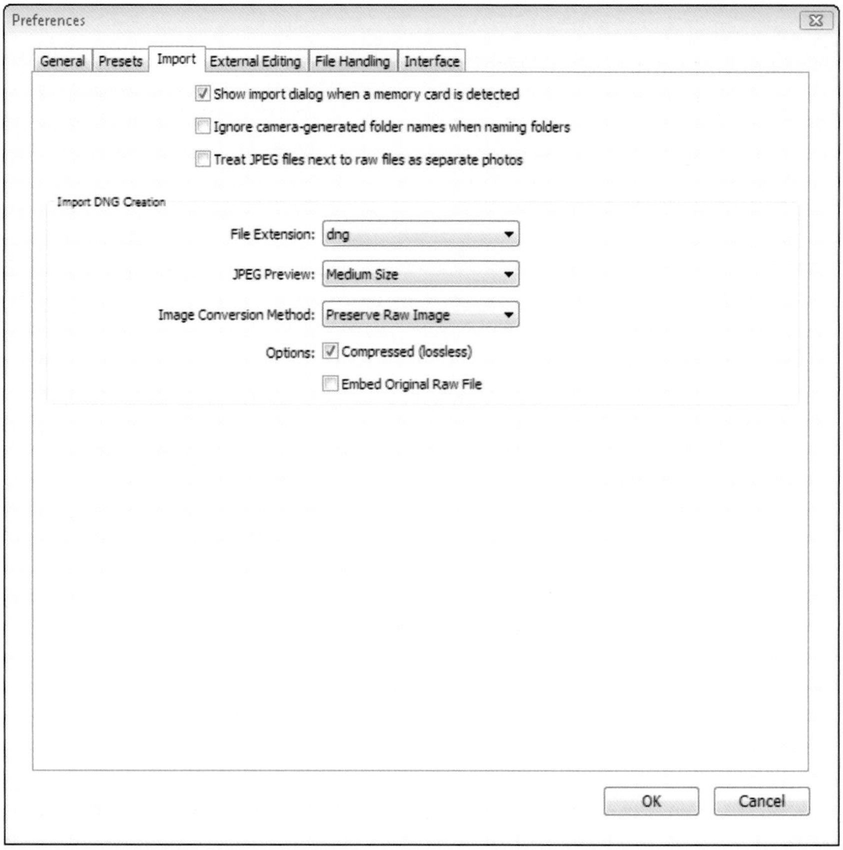

2-32

- **External Editing.** For External Editing, shown in figure 2-33, you set up how images are sent to Photoshop in terms of file format, color space, bit depth, and resolution. For most photographers, I recommend PSD or TIFF, AdobeRGB (1998), 16 bits, and 240, respectively. You can see that the Adobe engineers have included a paragraph about these choices — the information in it is true, but I think it is overly negative (as they had to use full disclosure) and not all that helpful. There are a number of people who are using ProPhoto RGB as a color space, and it is true that it has a bigger color space that represents what Lightroom is capable of. However, it can be a little misleading, because most printed images, whether in a publication or done with an inkjet printer, cannot display everything in this color space. Adobe RGB is still an excellent color space for photographers. Note that any of these choices only apply when you select the command Edit in Adobe Photoshop. When you export a picture using the Export command, you will choose all of these things at that time.

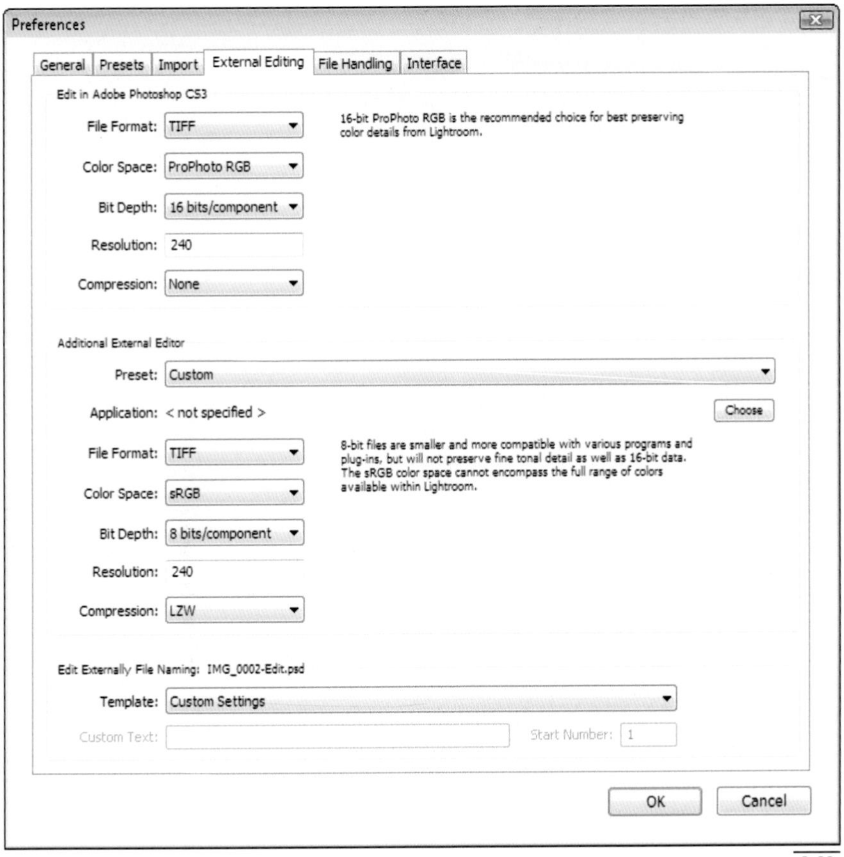

Preferences

General | Presets | Import | External Editing | File Handling | Interface

Edit in Adobe Photoshop CS3

File Format: TIFF

Color Space: ProPhoto RGB

Bit Depth: 16 bits/component

Resolution: 240

Compression: None

16-bit ProPhoto RGB is the recommended choice for best preserving color details from Lightroom.

Additional External Editor

Preset: Custom

Application: < not specified >

Choose

File Format: TIFF

Color Space: sRGB

Bit Depth: 8 bits/component

Resolution: 240

Compression: LZW

8-bit files are smaller and more compatible with various programs and plug-ins, but will not preserve fine tonal detail as well as 16-bit data. The sRGB color space cannot encompass the full range of colors available within Lightroom.

Edit Externally File Naming: IMG_0002-Edit.psd

Template: Custom Settings

Custom Text:

Start Number: 1

OK | Cancel

2-33

In the Additional External Editor, you can select whatever other image-processing software you might use. Click Choose to navigate to that application and select it, then choose the format, color space, and so on.

> **File Handling.** This is a rather specialized area that affects how Lightroom reads metadata and deals with file names. Most photographers will probably leave these at their defaults.

> **Interface.** In the Interface tab, shown in figure 2-34, you can generally leave all these settings at their default settings, too, although this is an area for some interesting personalization. For Panels, you can decide if you want to keep the decorative flourish below the last controls in any panel (Panel End Mark). Personally, I think this little design touch gives Lightroom some personality, but you can turn it off. Panel Font Size makes the fonts larger and easier to read, but that changes the spacing of the panels (this can be helpful on high-resolution monitors where the fonts can be hard to see).

In the Lights Out section, you can change how dark the dimming level is and its color (when you press L). I can see making it a little brighter, but I

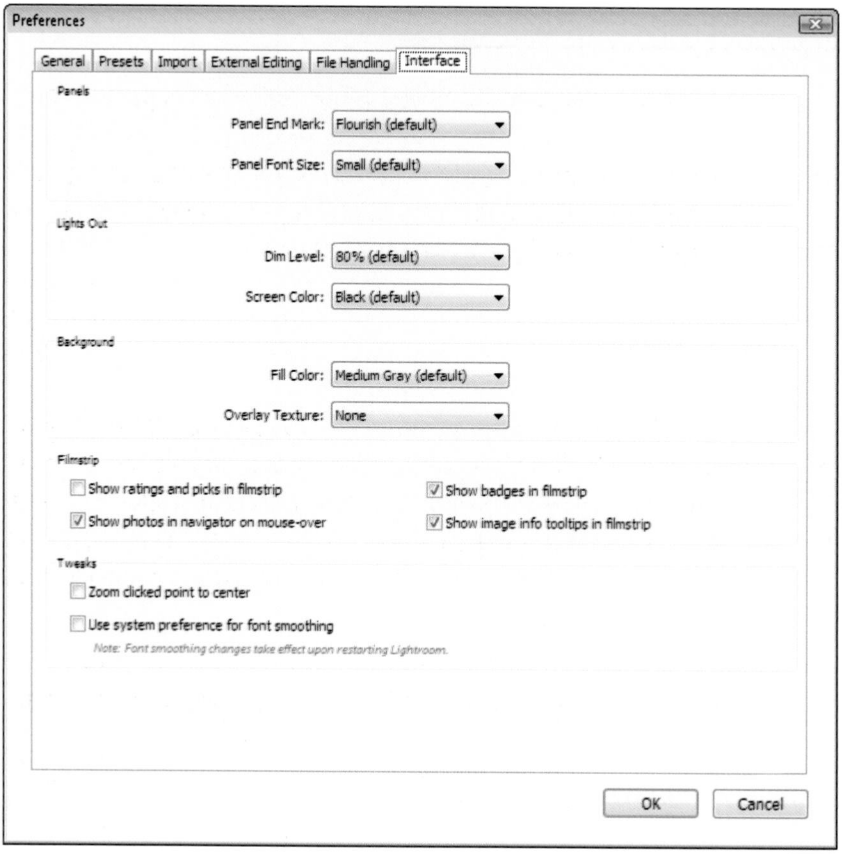

2-34

would not suggest other colors unless you have a specialized need. Other colors affect how you see colors in the image itself. I'd be wary of making Background changes, too, unless you have a very specific need for that. The Filmstrip section affects how you work with the Filmstrip. While it can be nice to see ratings and picks in the Filmstrip, those markings can also obscure part of each image. I do like showing photos in the Navigator on mouse-over, but these choices are all really rather personal. The Tweaks section simply adjusts how certain actions occur in the interface.

Q & A

What if I don't use all the modules? Can I turn any off in order to simplify the program even more?

That's an interesting idea, though at the moment, all five modules are always available. Adobe has promised to make it possible for independent developers to create new modules (sort of like plug-ins for Photoshop), but the company has not given users the flexibility to turn modules on or off.

The templates/presets browsers seem like an interesting way to apply standard effects to an image. They seem like they might be similar to Actions in Photoshop. Are they? And can I create my own?

That is very perceptive. You might consider Photoshop Actions to be the inspiration for these templates and presets. They basically set up the controls in Lightroom to create certain effects or do typical adjustments in standard, repeatable ways. These are not auto functions like auto functions in Photoshop — those examine an image through program algorithms and apply changes based on them. Presets and templates are like Actions because they use a precise set of adjustments to create an *effect*, a set that will always be duplicated once you choose that template or preset.

As you will see later in the book, you can indeed set up your own presets. This can make your own work in Lightroom more efficient and let you consistently apply adjustments that you need all the time.

There seem to be an awful lot of options for setting up how you work with Lightroom. I thought this was supposed to be a simple program. How can I know which functions to use, or turn on or off?

That is true. Lightroom has a lot of adaptability. The Adobe program designers knew that photographers tend to be an independent lot who have very specific ways of working that often don't match other photographers' choices. They wanted to make a program that would adapt to these needs.

You really have to play with the program a while. That is, perhaps, one reason why Adobe designers suggest you enjoy the process and that you experiment with the program. Find what works for you. You may or may not do everything the way I do, or the way any other photographer does, but if it works for you, then that is the best way to handle Lightroom. But that takes a bit of time working with it. You will know which functions work best for you after you have worked in the program for a little while.

Part II

USING LIGHTROOM MODULES

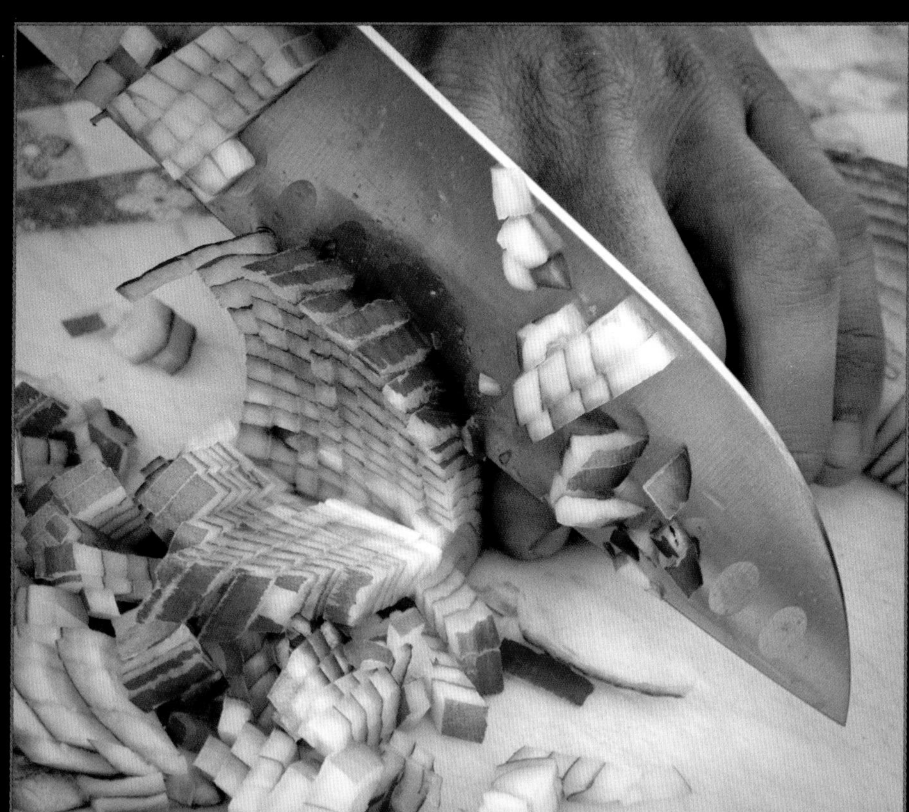

Chapter 3

LIBRARY MODULE BASICS

Improvements to the Library module in Adobe Photoshop Lightroom 2 have been substantial and welcome. This is a key module for Lightroom. It helps you import, sort, delete, rank, and organize your files, whether you have 100 or 10,000 or more. It is also designed to make your work go faster and more efficiently. That is very important for so many digital photographers who want to spend less time at the computer and more time behind the camera lens.

You will find some excellent tools here to help you edit and catalog your photos. It is important to keep in mind that every organization program has certain ways it works best, and that is true of Lightroom. In this chapter, you learn what the basic capabilities of Library are. The next chapter walks you through actually using Lightroom's Library with specific examples.

An Overview of Library

In figure 3-1, you can see how Library is structured. When you see all of the things you can do in Lightroom, it is easy to get overwhelmed. This diagram simplifies some of the main things you can do in Lightroom. What you may notice right away is all the arrows. You can easily move from one function to another, which helps give Lightroom its speed and efficiency.

Library has three main functions:

- **Import.** Lightroom does not recognize your photos until you tell it where they are by importing them into its view. This does not mean files change places, though this can happen if you tell Lightroom to move the files. You can import photos from a memory card or camera to your hard drive through Lightroom, which gives you some distinct organizing advantages.
- **Edit/Sort/Delete.** Traditionally, photographers would have just called this the editing function and been done with it. They edited their slides on a lightbox or their prints by going through them. Unfortunately, the computer folks working on image-processing software decided to call that software *image-editing software* because users could edit, or change, the elements of a single photo. So while Library truly does allow you to edit photos in the traditional sense, image editing has changed to mean something else in the computer world. Library is where you sort and delete your photos by marking, rating, and comparing them, among other things.
- **Organize.** By organizing your photos in some way, you will be better able to find them later. Lightroom offers you several ways to organize images, including using keywords, collections, and searches.

You are editing and organizing your photos for one main reason — to keep your photos in an order that helps you find them later. Lightroom is set up with several functions that allow you to search for and find photos, as shown in figure 3-2.

Basically, all search functions can be categorized as either visual browsing or a search for specific data:

- *Visual browsing* means you are finding images strictly by what you see. Images are grouped in ways that make this type of searching easier. The Grid view in Lightroom, your folder structure, and the creation of specific collections are all ways you are able to visually browse your work. This can be a very fast and intuitive way to view images, but you also can overlook seeing all the images; and if there are a lot of images in any specific group, visual browsing can become unwieldy.

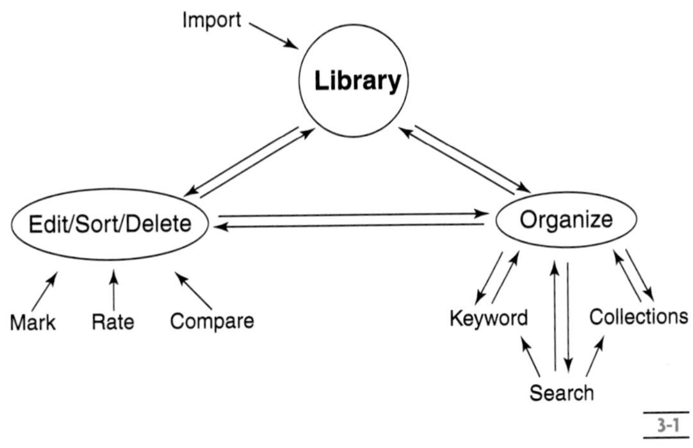
Photoshop Lightroom
Import
Library
Edit/Sort/Delete
Organize
Mark
Rate
Compare
Keyword
Collections
Search
3-1

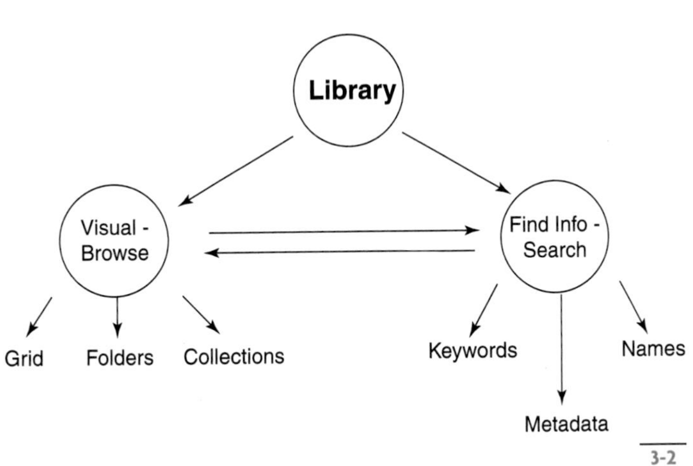
Ways to Find Photos
Library
Visual - Browse
Find Info - Search
Grid
Folders
Collections
Keywords
Names
Metadata
3-2

- A *search for specific data* means that you tell Lightroom to look for something based on criteria you have set up; although in the case of Lightroom 2, this search now uses "filters" to limit displayed images to these criteria, based on a specific group (folder or collection). Criteria can include keywords, image file metadata, and file names. This is not as fast as visual browsing when you are looking for a general sort of photo, but it is very fast and accurate when you are looking for something specific.

In figure 3-3, I have collapsed all the categories to their names on the left and right panels so that you only see these categories in Library.

Import is represented by a single button that appears at the bottom left (Export is similar) of figure 3-3, but don't let it fool you. It actually has a lot of power, as you'll see later in the chapter.

You sort and delete images (traditional editing) in the central area, using the toolbar below and the filmstrip at the bottom. A lot of things you do are based on simple keystrokes, which once again keeps Lightroom

3-3

fast and efficient. You organize your photos primarily from the left and right panels.

On the left side, you will find:

> Catalog

> Folders

> Collections (and Smart Collections)

> Navigator, while at the top of the organizing function list, is not an organization function, which is why you don't see it in figure 3-2 or listed as part of the organizing functions.

At the top of the main work area, you will find a toolbar for searching when you are in the Grid mode:

> Library Filter

On the right side, you will find:

> Keywording

> Keyword List

> Metadata

> Histogram and Quick Develop. I list these last because I rarely use these types of controls in Library.

It is important to understand that Lightroom's organizing capabilities are simply tools for image organization, not requirements for your workflow. Some photographers will use more tools than others, and they will use each function differently. Use Lightroom in ways that work for you. It really is designed to be flexible.

You use the central work or viewing area to view, edit, compare, and review photos. The Navigator part of the left panel, shown expanded in figure 3-4, is a key control that affects how images are viewed in the central viewing area, and it allows you to find a specific location on an image when it is enlarged. It offers four quick-access magnifications of the image (Fit, Fill, 1:1, and 3:1), as well as a drop-down menu for additional

3-4

PRO TIP

All of the categories in the panels can be confusing to use if they are open simultaneously. A good way to use them is to set them to Solo mode. This mode only allows one category in a panel to be open at a time, so when one is open and you click on a new one, the open one will close as the new category opens. You set this by right-clicking on any category in a panel and using the context-sensitive menu. While you can use Ctrl+click for the Mac, a right-click mouse is far quicker and easier to use.

choices. When you have an image enlarged in the central area, you can move the view around by clicking or clicking and dragging the white box over the image in the Navigator. It is also part of the Develop panel.

A toolbar below this area affects how you see images displayed in the image work area. There are a series of important commands you can access by clicking the appropriate icon on the toolbar or by using a keyboard command:

> **Grid.** Click this gridlike icon, or press G, and your images show up as a grid in the central work area, as shown in figure 3-5.

> **Sort.** This denotes a drop-down list that changes the order of your images in Grid view.

> **Loupe.** Click this single-image icon and you change the screen to show one image in the work area (shown in figure 3-6), which can be magnified (like when you use a magnifier or loupe) by clicking the image or pressing the space bar. You can also press E to get into the Loupe view.

> **Compare.** This X/Y icon takes you to a comparison view — you see a selected image (Select) that you want to compare to another (Candidate) for precise editing of your photos, as shown in figure 3-7. Pressing the letter C also gets you into this view. You can choose two or more images from the Filmstrip or Grid view (Ctrl/⌘+click to select), but only two show at once. As you click the X at the lower right, images are deselected from the group. Magnify images here by clicking the photo or using the Zoom control on the toolbar. If the images do not line up right, click the lock icon to unlock the connection between them; then you can move each image so it lines up with the other as needed, and lock them together again to keep the joint movement locked.

3-5

3-6

3-7

3-8

> **Survey.** The icon for this control looks like a group of images, and its function is to change the screen to a comparison mode similar to Compare, though this time you can compare two or more images at once, as shown in figure 3-8. You can remove any of the images from consideration by clicking an X that appears when you move the cursor over the photo. These photos cannot be enlarged as they can be in Compare. Press the letter N to enter this mode.

PRO TIP

Lightroom offers a whole range of keyboard commands for using its controls and accessing different parts of the interface. It is hard to remember them all. You can quickly see a set of keyboard commands for each module by pressing Ctrl/⌘+/ when you are in that module.

When you look at the overall Library interface, you can see it is pretty simple and laid out in such a way that you can easily and quickly find things. You can leave any of the panels and their controls collapsed so there is not a distracting set of choices that you don't need at any given time. When you Ctrl/⌘+click on any control category in a panel, all of the controls will collapse to the basic panel view with just the control categories visible. In addition, always think about using keyboard commands that let you access controls, panels, and more, quickly and easily.

X-REF

Most of these views in Lightroom allow you to rate the images, color-code them, or flag them for sorting. This is explained further in Chapter 4.

IMPORTING PHOTOS

Of course, to use all of the organizing and other features of Library, you need photos. At the bottom of the left panel are Import and Export buttons, as shown in figure 3-9. These are essential to Lightroom, as they enable you to bring photos into the Lightroom's view (Import) and send them out for use outside the program (Export). In addition, you can have Lightroom handle downloading your images from your memory card. To do that, you need to tell Lightroom to look for memory cards in the program's Import tab in Preferences (on the Mac, this is under the Lightroom menu; in Windows, this is in the Edit menu), as shown in figure 3-10. The Import Photos dialog box is identical either way you bring photos into the program's view.

3-9

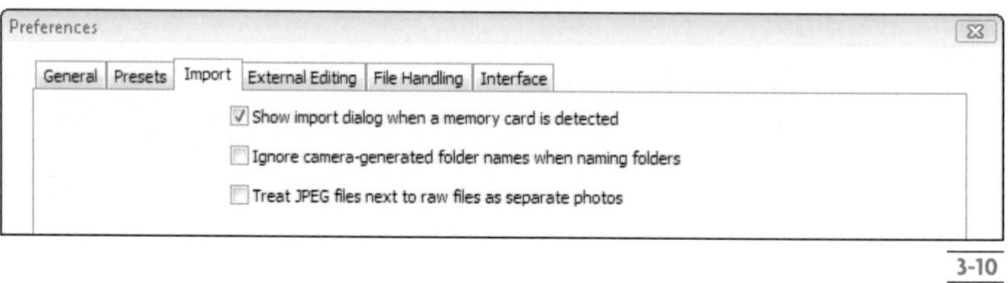

3-10

Click Import and you immediately begin the process of importing photos into Lightroom. Your operating system's Import Photos or Lightroom Catalog dialog box appears, as shown in figure 3-11. After finding the folder with your photos (that you have already downloaded to your hard drive), click the Import All Photos in Selected Folder button for Windows or click Choose for Mac (you can also select individual photos by opening folders and clicking the ones you want).

The Import Photos dialog box, shown in figure 3-12, appears. This is an important dialog box to understand, as it offers you a number of capabilities that give you more flexibility in handling your files, plus it makes organizing and sorting photos easier. This dialog box also shows up when you are importing from a memory card — the only thing you will likely change is the file handling. Let's take a look at the options.

3

Library Module Basics

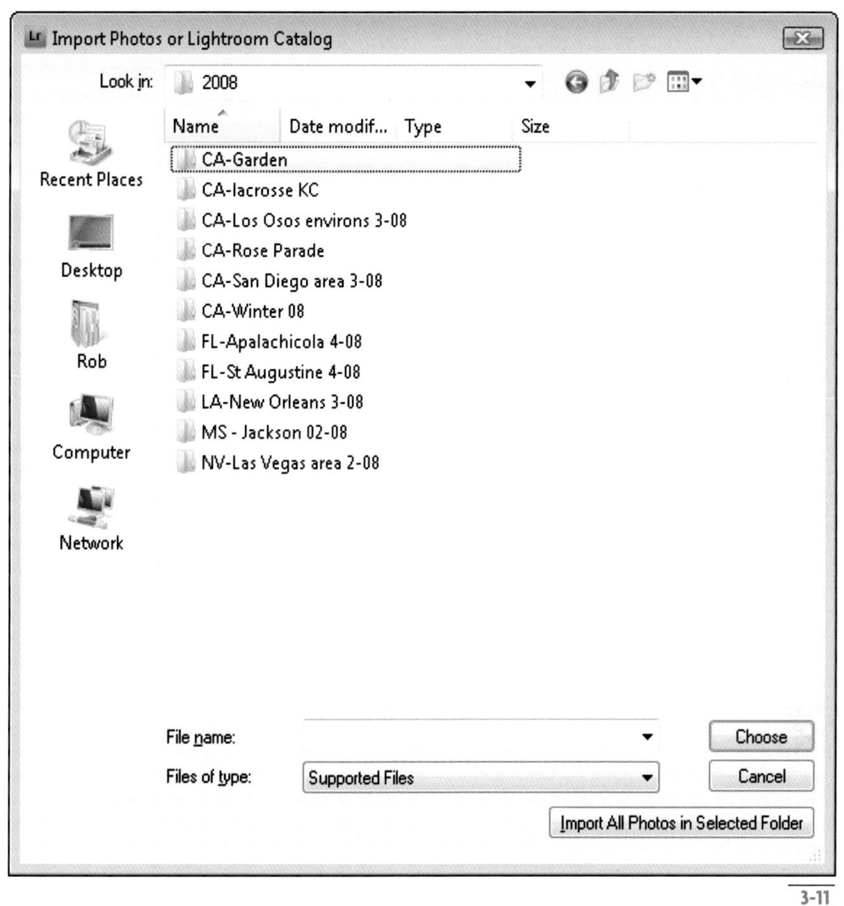

3-11

- **File Handling.** At the top, you have several choices available from the File Handling drop-down menu, as shown in figure 3-13, starting with Add photos to catalog without moving. The next three choices place files into a new location, which Lightroom sets up and controls either by copying or moving files, on your hard drive.

  If my photos are already on my hard drive, I choose Add photos to catalog without moving. If I am getting new photos from a memory card, then I choose Copy photos to a new location and add to catalog. In the latter case, you will get a new line that says, Copy to: [a location on your hard drive], as shown in figure 3-14. You can change that by clicking Choose and even creating a new folder for your photos, which is something I usually do for brand-new images from a camera's memory card.

  Otherwise, I really don't need the same photos in multiple locations, so copying has no appeal. Moving doesn't help me because it messes up my filing structure. Finally, although there are some good reasons to copy important images as DNG files (Adobe's RAW file format), doing an entire import this way wastes hard drive space. The only advantage that I can see to doing all of this is if you want to place image files into one location on the hard drive. If that appeals to you, then choose a copy or move option.

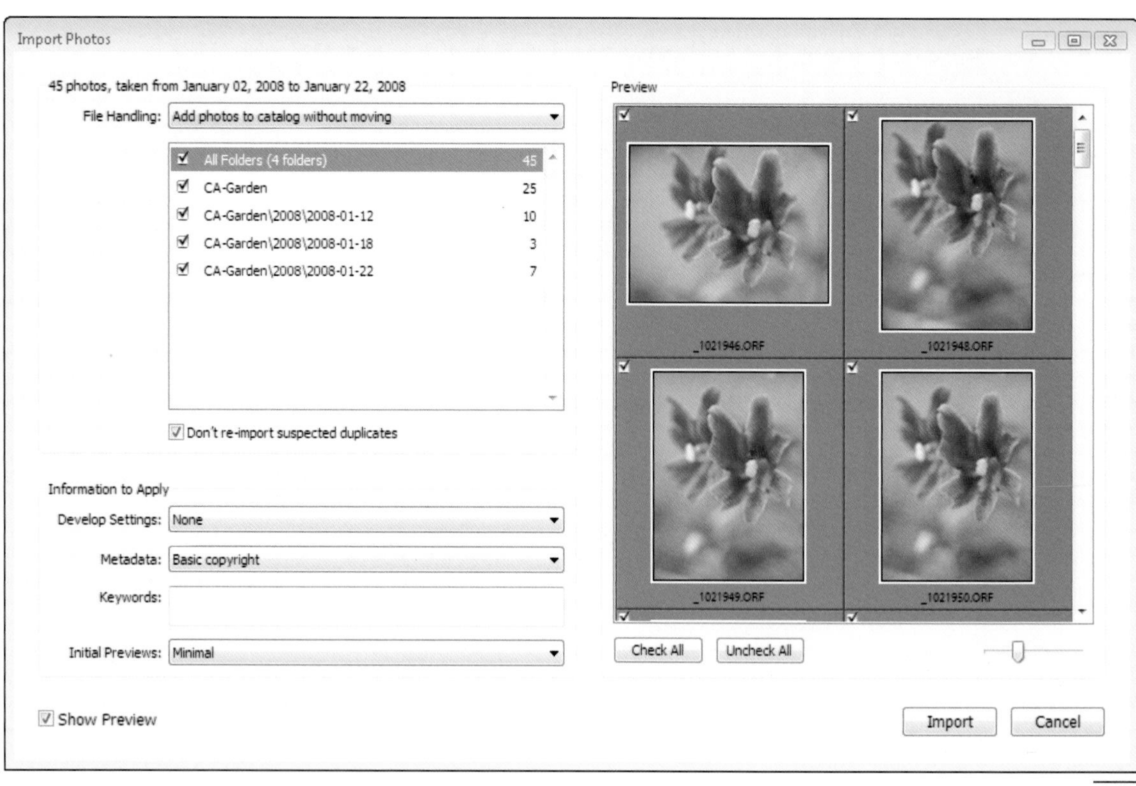

3-12

Import Photos

45 photos, taken from January 02, 2008 to January 22, 2008

File Handling: Add photos to catalog without moving

✓ Add photos to catalog without moving

Copy photos to a new location and add to catalog

Move photos to a new location and add to catalog

Copy photos as Digital Negative (DNG) and add to catalog

3-13

If you choose a copy or move files option from the drop-down menu, an additional section for file naming appears in the dialog box. You choose a naming template from the Template box and follow the template requirements that appear. Use whatever name works for you.

The next section of the file handling area deals with how the files are separated into groups when they're brought into Lightroom. Lightroom segments folders by default, so if you have subfolders in a folder, your photos are separated by those subfolders. If you want everything in a folder to come in en masse, then deselect the selected check boxes that define this by your subfolders, as seen in figure 3-12. If you are importing from a memory card, click the Organize drop-down arrow for a number of choices, as shown in figure 3-14. I generally use Into one folder.

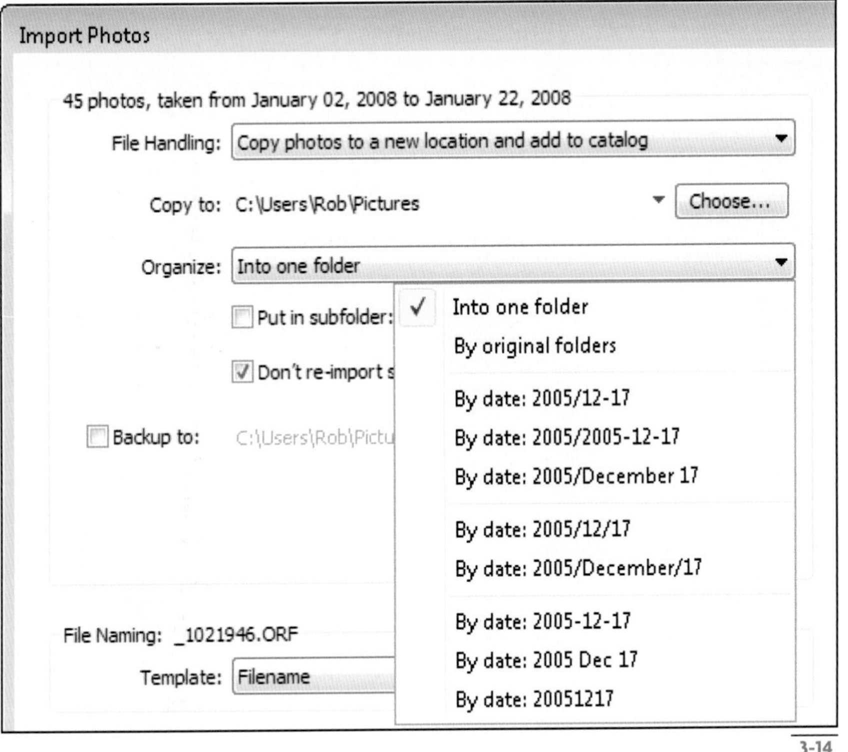

3-14

- **Information to Apply.** The Information to Apply section is next and is great if you are a working photographer because it lets you add important metadata to all photos as they move into Lightroom control.
  - The Develop Settings, shown in figure 3-15, are based on Develop module presets, which are covered in Chapters 5 and 6. However, this is really a specialized use of Import. For studio and commercial photography where the image type, exposure, light, and so forth do not change, this can be useful. For most other photography, it is rare that you would apply the

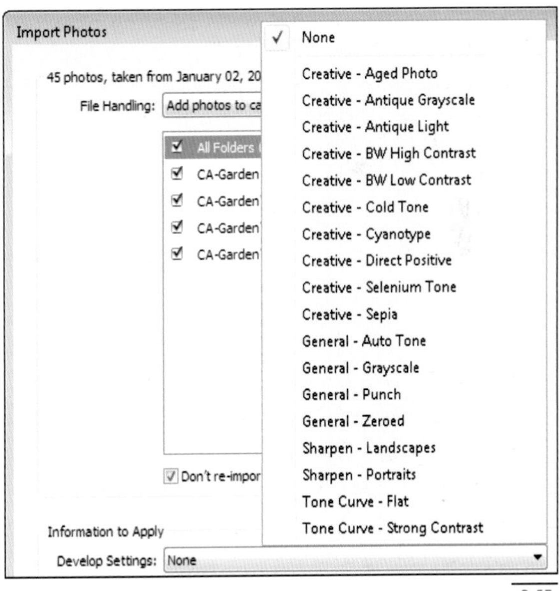

3-15

same adjustments to all images as you import them. However, there are certain cases when this can be useful. A friend of mine shoots infrared and uses a preset to get rid of the false color that comes from RAW files.

> From the Metadata drop-down menu, you can apply preset metadata information (such as copyright) or choose to create a new metadata preset, as shown in figure 3-16. If you choose New from the menu, the New Metadata Preset dialog box, shown in figure 3-17, appears. You

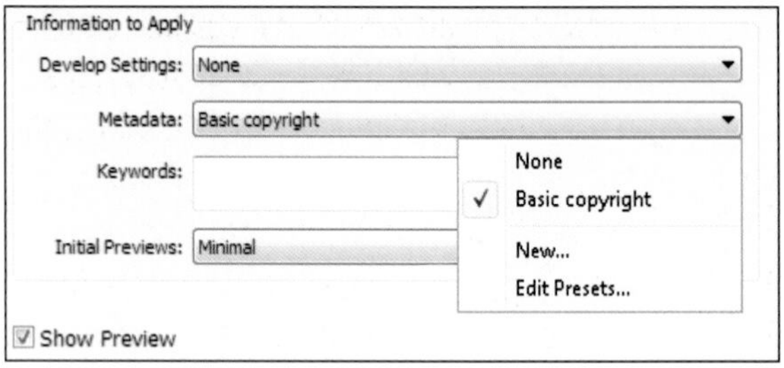

3-16

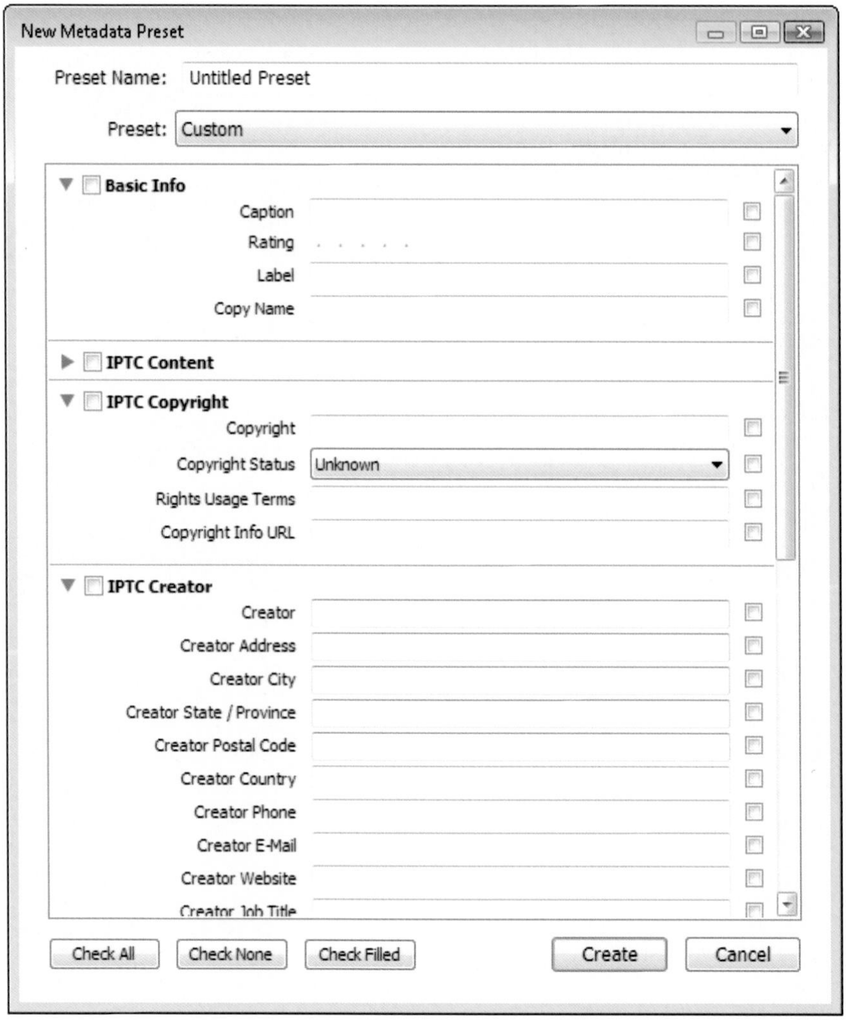

3-17

can add information in all of the blank areas (scroll down in your dialog box to see all the options), and the information is attached to the metadata of each imported image. If you are doing a regular series of shoots related to a specific client, for example, you can type the client's name in the Preset Name box, and then fill out the form so it's specific to that client and the work for them. This way you always have a unique set of information automatically connected with all the photos from your shoots (as long as you select that preset).

Because of the book and magazine work that I do, I have a preset called Basic copyright that is shown in figure 3-18. This allows me to put copyright and contact information on every image that leaves Lightroom.

> Below the Metadata field is the Keywords field, shown in figure 3-19. This is an important and helpful area to use as it will immediately associate keywords with your photos as they are imported. You can add keywords here that are specific to the imported images, such as client,

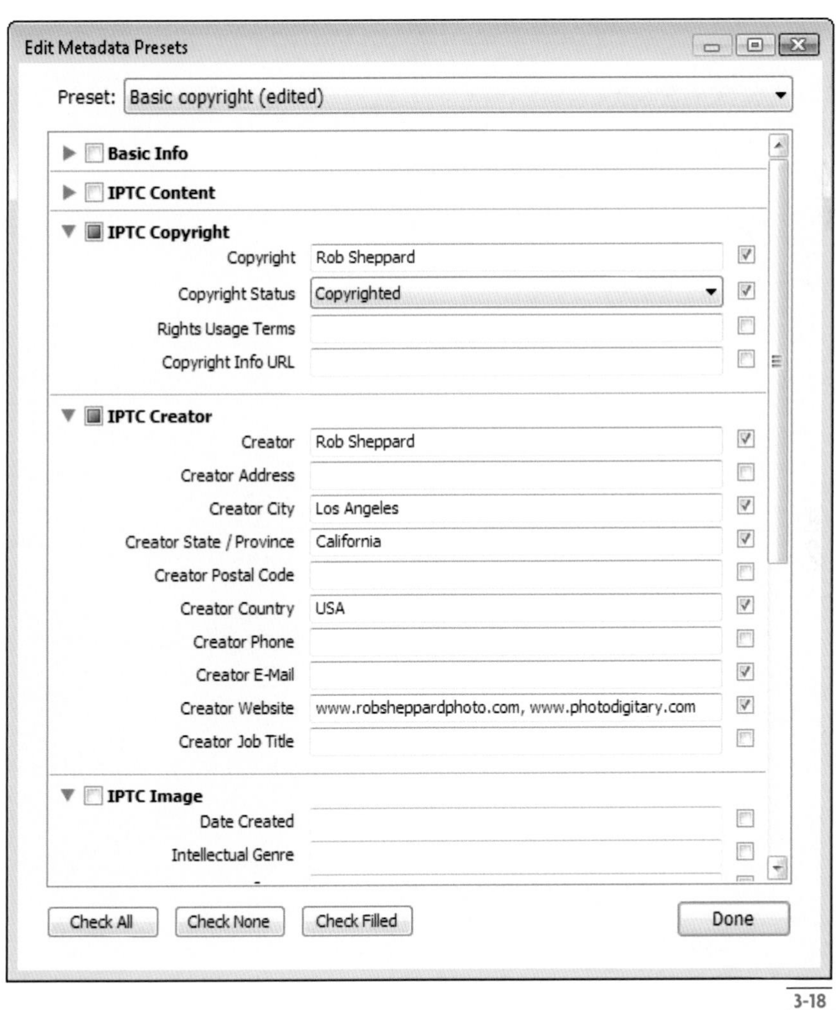

3-18

subject, location, and so forth, and these keywords are automatically applied to all the photos being imported. If your shoot is very specific and is basically all about one subject, then you can be as detailed as you want. However, if you have a variety of subjects, then you are likely to have fewer keywords that fit all the photos.

> The last field of this section is Initial Previews. Lightroom creates small JPEG previews so that photos load quickly into the interface. While larger images are nice, they will definitely slow down your importing. Lightroom will create whatever previews it needs as it goes, so you may find the default Minimal to be fine as this only affects the initial previews. You have to see how building previews affects your workflow.

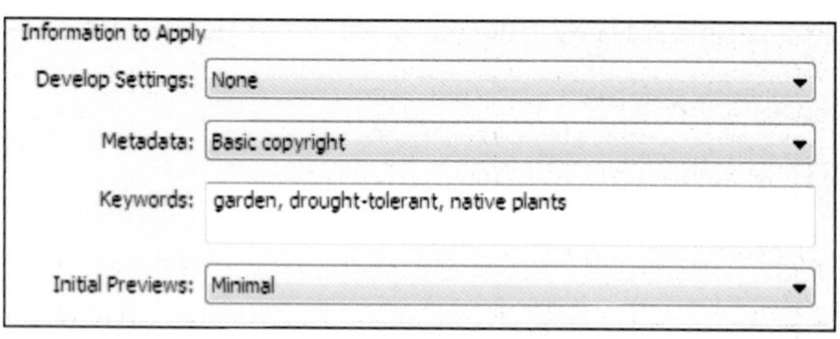

3-19

> **Show Preview.** You can quickly review (as well as select or unselect) all the images in a preview image at the right of the Import Photos interface by selecting the Show Preview check box, shown in figure 3-20. The selection part of this can be very useful. If you have a memory card with a mix of images on it, you may decide that you want to import them in groups with different metadata, keywords, and file handling. Then you can click

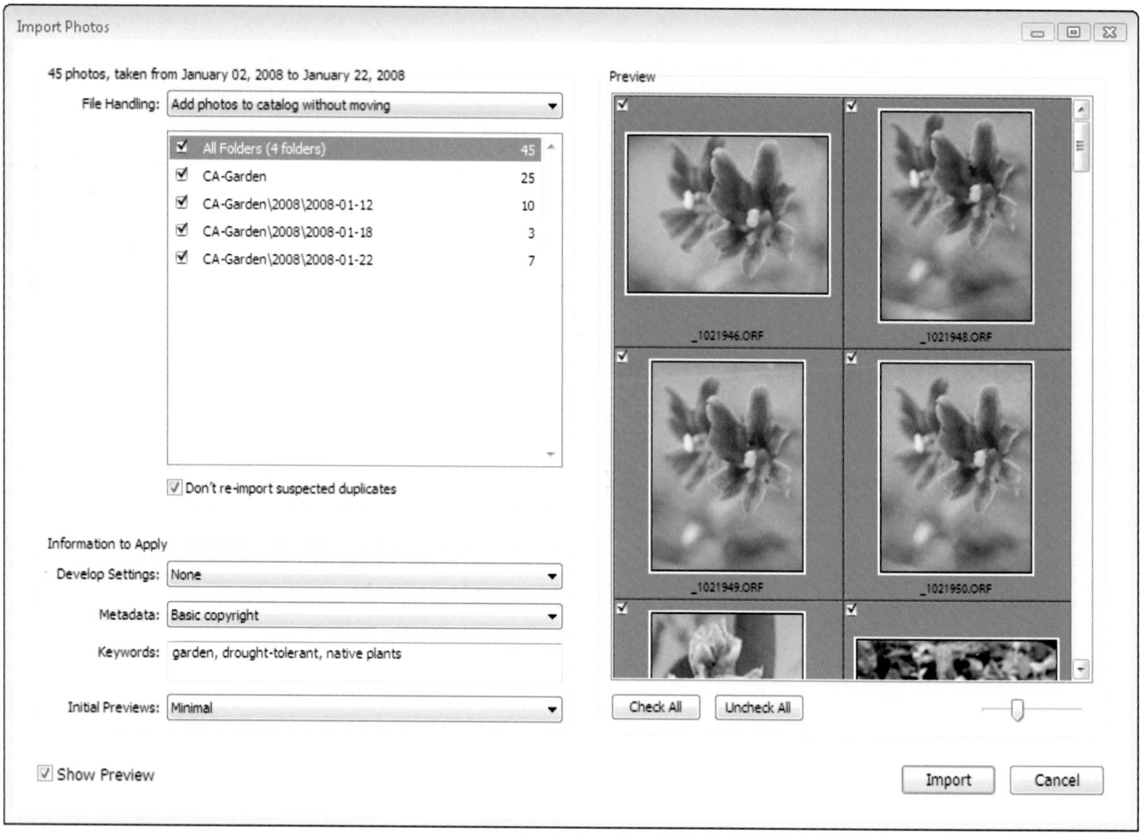

3-20

Uncheck All so that none will be imported and then select the ones that should be. The little slider under the preview window enlarges or reduces the size of the preview thumbnails.

Now just click the Import button in the dialog box and Lightroom imports all of the photos into its system and lists them in the Folders area. It may take Lightroom a little time to do its thing, depending on the power of your computer and the size of your import.

Two Monitors for More Display Options

Lightroom 2 now gives you the opportunity to use two monitors. This is a tremendous tool because you can now see different displays on two monitors, as shown in figure 3-21.

Both Windows and Mac operating systems allow for two monitors. You do need that capability in your computer, however. Most Mac's have this capability from the start. For Windows systems, you must have a computer that includes output for two monitors. If yours doesn't, you can usually add a relatively inexpensive video board that will give two outputs.

You don't need to have matching monitors as you will not be displaying the same thing on both; however, matching monitors can better help you get displays that match in color and tone. Still, if you do a little color calibration with two good monitors that don't match, you will usually get what you need. Not everyone has space for two large monitors, yet adding a smaller, second monitor definitely makes certain work easier.

Throughout this book, you will see one monitor, but realize that you can always set up a second display that can be beneficial to your work. For example, you might want to see a Grid view of a whole group of

3-21

photos as you are working on one photo in Develop. Or you might want to keep an enlarged area of an image in Loupe on the second monitor as you do overall work on that same image in Develop.

Putting a display from Lightroom onto a second monitor is very easy. You simply click the second monitor icon at the top-left corner, above the Filmstrip, as shown in figure 3-22.

There are several things you can display on the second monitor, all of which you choose by clicking the appropriate words at the top left of the second monitor screen, as shown in figure 3-23. They include the same Grid, Loupe, Compare, and Survey views you access in Library from the toolbar. In addition, Slideshow is available, which is set up in the Slideshow module. I explain Slideshow in Chapter 7.

3-22

Grid | Loupe | Compare | Survey | Slideshow

3-23

The Left Library Panel Revealed

In figure 3-24, I hid the right panel and the Filmstrip. Now the left panel is emphasized with its functional categories, plus a lot more space is dedicated to the images themselves. This setup can be very useful when you are editing images and need to see a lot of them at once. That can almost be a necessity if you are working on a laptop or a smaller monitor. Having more space on a bigger monitor that allows more space for display of the Lightroom interface makes it easier to leave all the panels in view.

PRO TIP

Remember you can hide panels at any time by clicking the small arrows at the far edge of each panel, but an easier way to do this is to use your computer's function keys. I do this all the time to quickly give me the work area I need. Use F6 for the Filmstrip, F7 for the left panel, and F8 for the right panel. You bring any panel back temporarily by moving your cursor over the edge where the panel would be, or bring it back on by clicking the arrow again.

Here's what those left-side functions do (open any category by clicking it):

> **Navigator.** This controls how images are viewed in the central viewing area. It will also display photos other than your selected image when you move your cursor over them in the Filmstrip.

> **Catalog.** This gives you a quick overview of all images that have been brought into Lightroom. It contains three options, as shown in figure 3-25.

> > **All Photographs.** This view shows you every single photo you have in your collection that you have assigned to Lightroom to track. Use

3-24

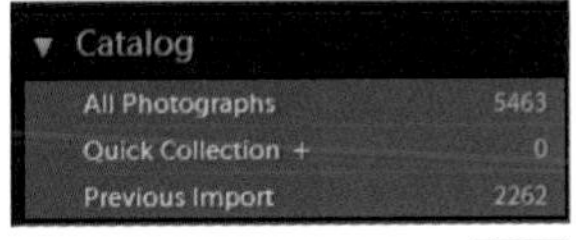

3-25

this function whenever you need to access all images that Lightroom is handling, especially when you are using a specific keyword search that needs to go across the entire catalog of images. Be aware that if you have a large volume of images, this view can take a long time to load unless you have a very powerful computer with a lot of RAM.

> **Quick Collection.** This grouping of photos is a useful way of very quickly making a selection of images that you want to separate from all the rest for a slide show, some prints, a Web gallery, or maybe selects for a client. You simply select a group of photos (Ctrl/⌘+click them or click the first one in a series and then

Shift+click the last one) and drag them over this category. You can also just press B. Then every time you click Quick Collection, you only see those photos. You can also instantly put images into Quick Collection through the Filmstrip. If you run your cursor over an image there, you see a faint circle appear. Click on that circle and the image is put into Quick Collection.

> **Previous Import.** This view is a way for you to quickly go to the last group of images you brought into Lightroom.

> **Folders.** Lightroom references all imported groups of images as Folders, as shown in figure 3-26. These folders are directly related to the location that your images are actually stored in on your computer (or accessed by your computer) and Lightroom also includes the hard drive or other overriding storage device here. This means the Lightroom Folder references the actual folder where you have placed your images on your hard drive.

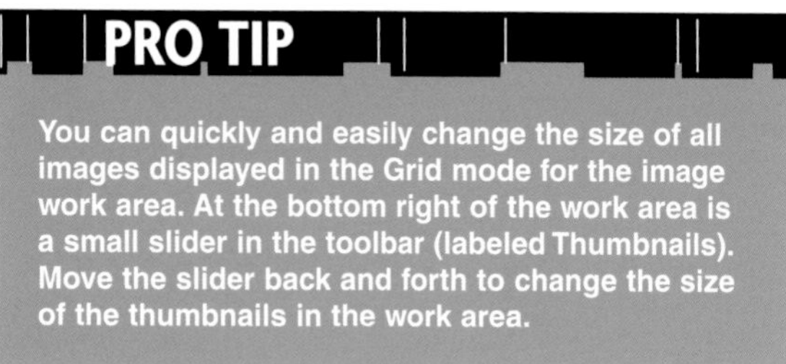

PRO TIP

You can quickly and easily change the size of all images displayed in the Grid mode for the image work area. At the bottom right of the work area is a small slider in the toolbar (labeled Thumbnails). Move the slider back and forth to change the size of the thumbnails in the work area.

You can rename any folder whatever you would like at any time by right-clicking the name and typing in something else in the dialog box that opens. (I would be very careful about keeping names consistent with whatever system you are using to organize your photos on your hard drive — Collections and Keywords are better places to

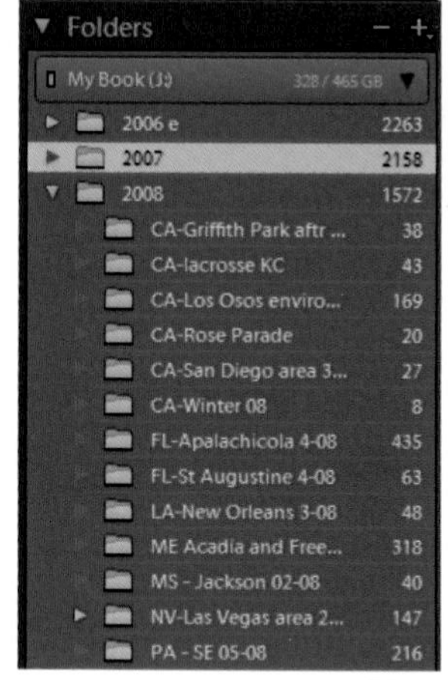

3-26

use unique names to classify and organize your photos.) The minus and plus signs allow you to quickly add or subtract folders from the list; however, minus does not remove photos from your hard drive, just from Lightroom's view.

> **Collections.** Collections is where the real organization of Lightroom begins. You get to pick your photo categories here, as shown in figure 3-27. (The list you see is just a simple illustration of what is possible.) You use Collections for any sort of category that enables you to group common types of photos together across multiple folders. You can pick anything that fits your interests and needs, from client-based subjects such as ABC Corporation Warehouses to personal themes such as family members. Imagine the various collections on diverse photographers' computers — there are bound to be some very interesting groupings!

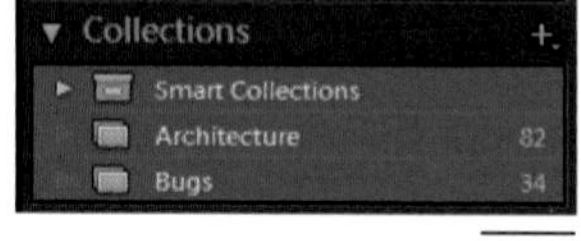

3-27

The Collections area is very easy to use. You set up a collection by clicking the plus sign at the right of Collections to get a drop-down menu, choosing Create Collection, and giving the new collection a name. (You can also create subgroups of collections by using Collection Set.) Next you select a group of photos from a folder (Ctrl/⌘+click them or Shift+click through a series) and drag those photos onto the collection name. Click and drag on the light gray navigation bar directly to the left of the collections to move the panel groupings up and down as you get increased numbers of folders and collections. (You will often want both categories open as you create collections so you can go between folders.)

Lightroom 2 has added a new element to Collections: Smart Collections. This is a really cool feature for Collections. It allows you to set up a collection based on some sort of criterion or set of criteria. This could range from a rating for photos to a range of dates they were shot to specific subjects. A collection is then automatically created based on those criteria. The really cool part is it will update itself as you import new photos with those criteria. To set this up, click Create Smart Collection after you click the plus sign for Collections to get the drop-down menu.

A really useful way of using this is to link certain keywords to your Smart Collection, as shown in figure 3-28. I have been photographing things related to fire ecology, so all such images have the keyword *fire*. As soon as I add *fire* as a keyword to any new group of photos, they are automatically added to the Smart Collection called Fire, as shown in figure 3-29.

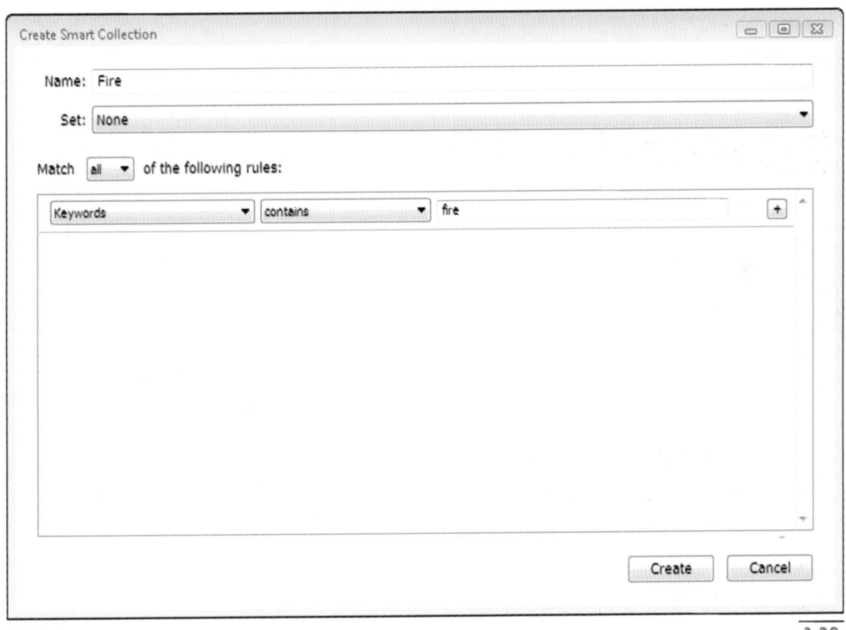

3-28

3-29

PRO TIP

You can expand or collapse all the panel categories at once by pressing and holding Ctrl/⌘ as you click any panel category (as long as it is not Navigator). You can also hide any category you don't need by right-clicking on any category in a given panel and using the drop-down menu to check which categories are visible and which are not.

Viewing Images in Library

Lightroom gives you a lot of power when you are browsing, editing, and reviewing your photos. I like to start by hiding the side panels and the Filmstrip by using Shift+Tab to get to what you see in figure 3-30. (You can also hide the toolbar by pressing T.) This makes Lightroom act like a light table used for editing slides.

I really like this form of Lightroom for editing photos, because it truly lets the photographer focus on the photos for editing. You don't think about making collections or processing them at this point.

There are several important things that you can do with your photos in this full-screen image mode. First, you will want to rotate all verticals to vertical. Many cameras include information in the metadata about a shot being vertical, and Lightroom will recognize this. But some shots just aren't recognized as verticals. Correct this by hovering your cursor over an image; rotate arrows appear at the lower left and right of the image. Click the arrow pointing in the direction you need to rotate the shot. You can do multiples by Ctrl/⌘+clicking the images and then clicking the rotate icon again.

Next, you can remove the shots you don't like, either just from Lightroom or from your hard drive as well. How you approach this editing phase is very personal. One way to do this is to click (or Ctrl/⌘+click for multiple selections) anything you don't like in Lightroom, and then press Delete. A Confirm dialog box appears that asks if you want to delete the file from the hard drive or just from Lightroom.

I like to use the Mark as Rejected command, the letter X. I quickly mark those obvious problem images in the Grid mode. Then I go to the Loupe view by

3-30

double-clicking the image (go back to Grid view by pressing G or Esc). By placing my left hand at the X key and my right hand at the arrow keys, I can quickly go through a lot of images, marking each rejected image with X, which labels it Set as Rejected, adds a little black flag below the image, as shown in figure 3-31, and grays out the photo in the Filmstrip. If I mark one with an X by mistake, I just press the letter U to remove the flag. You can also press the letter P to put a special Pick white flag with the photo, but I find using the keyboard from X to P or arrows to P to be very awkward, so I don't do it.

PRO TIP

You can display many things with each image in Grid mode. Each image has a default rating bar that includes a set of dots that you can use to give the photo one- to five-star rankings by clicking on a dot. In addition, if you right-click on the image, you will get a context menu that allows you to display all sorts of things with the image, such as setting Flags, Rating Colors, and Star Ratings. This, once again, is another reason why Mac users need to have a right-button mouse.

3-31

Once you have gone through a group of images, you can quickly get rid of your rejects. Press Ctrl+Backspace (Windows) or ⌘+Delete (Mac) and you will see all of the images grouped together along with a message asking you to confirm removing them from Lightroom or from your hard drive, as shown in figure 3-32. If you decide you want to keep some, you can click Cancel, sort your photos to just the rejected ones with the X flag by using the X flag icon in the Library Filter bar (which will be covered later in the chapter) and remove flags as needed.

Confirm

Delete the 78 rejected master photos from disk, or just remove them from Lightroom?

Delete moves the files to Explorer's Recycle Bin, removes them from Lightroom, and cannot be undone.

Delete from Disk | Remove | Cancel

3-32

You can also rate images from one to five stars according to whether you like an image or not (and how much), as shown in figure 3-33. Simply select an image, and then click on the little dots below it for the appropriate star rating. Or use the keyboard numbers 1 through 5 for the number of stars rating; use 0 to remove all ratings. You can go through a lot of images very quickly this way. In addition, you can mark images with colors, although I find they are not very obvious. You can select colors with keyboard numbers 6 through 9 or by right-clicking the image and choosing Set Color Label.

You will often want to match up specific photos with each other to see how the composition or focus compares. This is the purpose of the Compare and Survey modes. You can select two or more photos and click the Compare icon (X/Y) on the toolbar to give you the screen shown in figure 3-34. Click on either photo to enlarge both in tandem (or use the zoom bar on the toolbar), then click and drag in the

Library Filter :
Text
Attribute
Metadata
None
Custom Filter
Attribute
Flag
Rating
Color
Copy Status
Sort:
Rating
Thumbnails

3-33

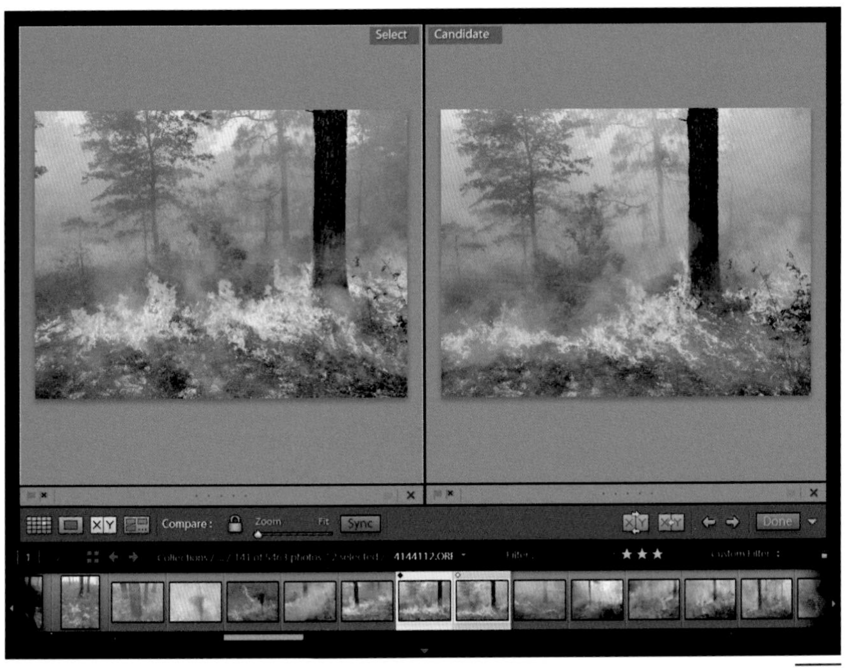
Select
Candidate
Compare :
Zoom
Fit
Sync
Done
4144112.ORF

3-34

photo to move around in both. If your photos need to have something line up, you can click the lock icon to unlock the connection between the two photos, and then move them individually. You can see that it is really helpful to keep the side panels hidden when using the Compare mode.

If you select a few images in the Filmstrip, you can also click the Survey icon and use the Survey mode shown in figure 3-35. Double-click any image, and it goes to the magnified Loupe view. Double-click again and you return to the Survey mode. The Compare mode is useful when checking critical focus, but often the Survey view mode is best to isolate and review several images at a time.

Navigating the Filmstrip

The Filmstrip is a very useful tool for finding and acting on images. You will find it an increasingly important resource as you work through Lightroom's adjustments, controls, and other features in all of its modules.

Navigating this strip is pretty easy and important for you to understand. The main slider underneath the images (shown in figure 3-36) moves the whole Filmstrip back and forth so you can find the photos you need. At the left and right sides of the strip are small arrows. Clicking either arrow moves the images in that direction to allow you to see more on the Filmstrip. You can use the arrow keys to do the same thing. If you click and hold, the images move continuously as if you really were watching a filmstrip in action — helping you get to photos faster.

3-35

3-36

3-37

Right above the Filmstrip is a set of controls related to image organization, shown in figure 3-37. At the far left are the monitor controls (which indicate what is shown or not shown). You can go to the Library grid at any time by clicking the last icon to the left before the monitor controls. The arrows are used to toggle back and forth between the view you are looking at and your last view. Next in line on the Filmstrip is a section showing you where the image is located along with its file name. Then you have sorting filters based on flags or on star or color ratings.

The Right Library Panel Revealed

The right panel, shown in figure 3-38, includes some specific things you can do to single images or groups if multiple photos are selected in the multi-image views and the changes are synced. If you need to do some quick developing work on multiple photos or apply keywording to a specific group of images, it is helpful to hide the left panel so that you have a larger area for the Grid mode. This arrangement lets you work more easily with many images at once when you are using the controls of the right panel.

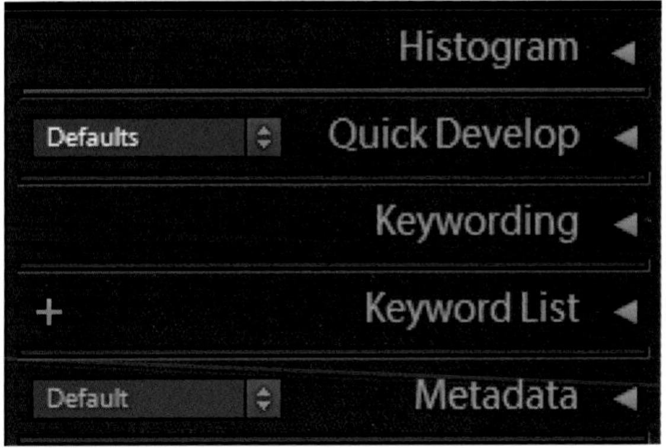

3-38

Here's what those right-side functions do:

> **Histogram.** At the top of the right panel are key bits of information about the photo. You can see a combined luminance and RGB histogram of the image and some important metadata for the shot (ISO setting, focal length, f-stop, and shutter speed), as shown in figure 3-39. This is mostly helpful, but RGB histograms are harder to read than simple brightness or luminance histograms (and the addition of the luminance histogram only makes it more confusing), and to use them fully, you have to know more about color channels than most photographers actually need to know. While it gives you some added information when you are deciding on picking a certain image or not, I keep it closed for the most part because I don't find it that useful in Library.

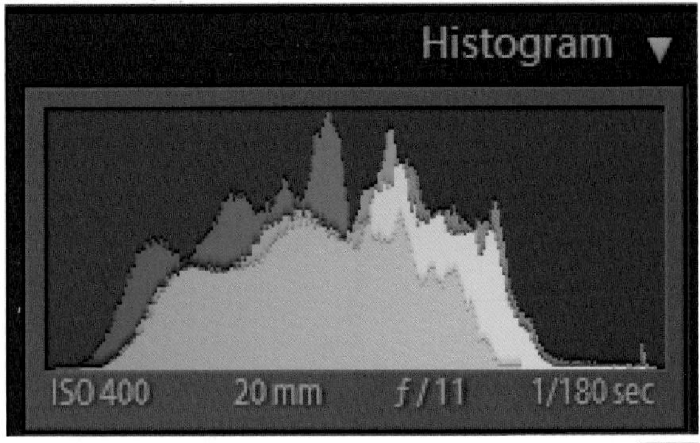

3-39

> **Quick Develop.** This set of options, shown in figure 3-40, is an add-in to the Library that really has little to do with Library functions. Given what this program is supposed to do for advanced photographers, I am a little puzzled at why this is even necessary. While it enables you to do some quick processing of images, the controls are quite limited compared to the power of the fully realized controls in the Develop module. Plus, you can really use Develop quite quickly if needed. However, Quick Develop does allow you to adjust white balance, change the exposure, adjust clarity, and enhance vibrance of the image by clicking the arrows to either side of the controls.

3-40

> **Keywording.** Keywords are a common way of tagging photos so that you can search for them using specific topics. The Keywording category, shown in figure 3-41, is a very useful part of the right panel and one you will quickly become very familiar with if you want better ways to find and organize your images. It includes three sections: Keyword Tags, Keyword Suggestions, and Keyword Set.

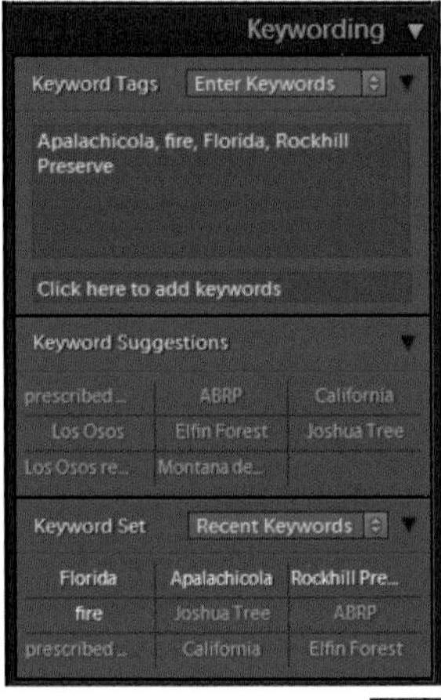

3-41

3 Library Module Basics

X-REF

Because all of the controls in the Quick Develop options are repeated in expanded form in the Develop module, they are explained in Chapter 6, where the Develop module is covered.

In Keyword Tags, you describe elements of your photographs so you can find those photographs again later. You can add keywords to individual images or to a selection of them in the Grid mode. You can also click any keywords in the Keyword Suggestions section below to add them to the images. In the next section, Keyword Set, you can use preset keywords. In figure 3-41 this area appears as Recent Keywords; however, Lightroom does include additional preset keywords you can find if you click on keywords or the arrow to the right of Recent Keywords to access a drop-down menu. Any existing keywords on an image show up in this category, too.

Photographers use keywords in very different ways. Some photographers heavily implant a lot of keywords with every image. Then when they perform a search by keywords, it locates those photos almost instantly. On the other hand, it takes time to put in a lot of keywords, so other photographers just use a minimal number. (I admit that I am not the hardcore keywording type, though I do understand its value — doing lots of keywords is just a bit too tedious for my personality.)

Lightroom has made adding keywords to a photo very easy: You can click and drag the photo (or photos) onto the word in the Keyword List to give it that keyword, click a keyword as needed, type in keywords in the Keyword Tags box (Lightroom will even finish commonly used words), or use the Painter icon (spray can). This way you don't have to do a lot of typing. Lightroom also lets you add keywords to photos as they are imported through the Import dialog box.

- **Keyword List.** This section of the right panel shows you all of your keywords. By right-clicking any of them, you get a menu that allows you to do certain things with them, including creating hierarchies of keywords. You can also filter them to a specific few to make organization easier.
- **Metadata.** *Metadata* is data about data or information about your image file. This information is searchable, too, like it is with keywords. You actually have several choices as to what is displayed here. The data shown in figure 3-42 are the defaults, but some entries can be changed, such as Caption. The areas that can be changed display as a slightly darker box. Click the box and you can add information, such as the caption shown in

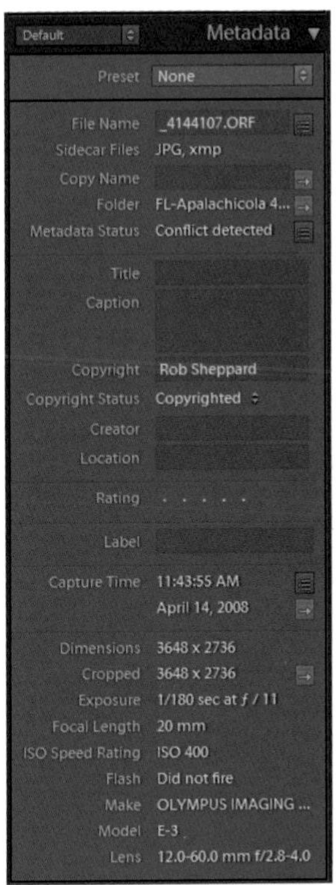

3-42

figure 3-43. If you click the Default drop-down arrow, you get a whole range of choices for metadata. A lot of this is for very specific purposes, and if you need it, you will know what it is about. This metadata is pretty straightforward, anyway, so you can go through the options and see if any of it would help you. You can check camera settings in the EXIF data or you can input IPTC data. IPTC stands for International Press Telecommunications Council, and IPTC data is a standard used by newspapers and news magazines for attaching specific, contextual information about a photograph.

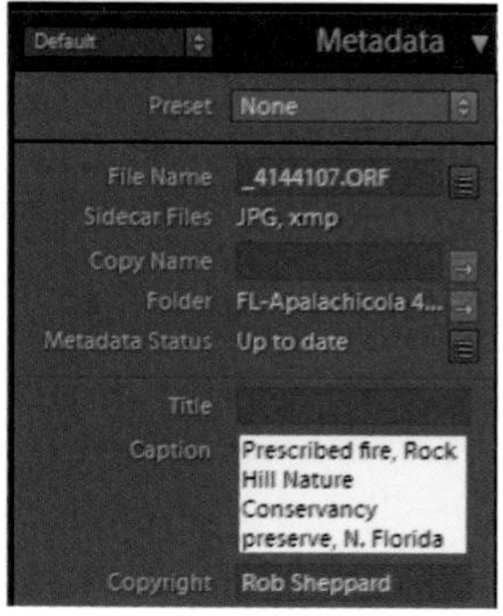

3-43

An important note: Metadata is stored with the photo but only in the Lightroom database. It will be written to the file when an image is exported from Lightroom. If you want a file to have this earlier, then you must go to the Metadata menu and choose Save Metadata to File. This will save all metadata, including keywords, to your file so it can be read outside of Lightroom.

> **Sync Settings and Sync Metadata.** Sync Settings and Sync Metadata buttons appear at the bottom of the right panel, as shown in figure 3-44. You use them when you have multiple images selected and you want to make processing adjustments or metadata details consistent across all of them. When you click either button, you get a self-explanatory dialog box asking you what you want to sync among the images. The Sync Metadata button can be very helpful for copying data you have for one image onto others. For example, you might have an important caption and realize that it fits other photos.

3-44

PRO TIP

Use the Painter spray can for keywords. The spray can icon in the toolbar represents a really neat and easy way of adding keywords. When you click the icon, you get an active area to type in keywords. Then you simply click your images in Grid to add the keywords. Click again and you remove them. You can also select a whole group of photos and click once to add the keywords to the entire group. Painter can also be used to add other data, such as metadata or ratings, to photos.

Searching for Photos: Library Filters

Filtering your photos is a way of searching for specific images. By using a set of filters based on specific criteria, you can narrow down the images displayed. Lightroom 2 has increased its filtering capabilities substantially since the first version. The filters are now based in a filter bar at the top of the work area, as shown in figure 3-45. Before you start filtering, though, you need to tell Lightroom where to do this work. You do this by choosing a Folder or a Collection from the left panel. You can also choose All Photographs in the Catalog group.

You can filter (or search) your images based on the following criteria:

> **Text.** As you can see in figure 3-46, you can search for text based on such things as the file name, caption, keywords, metadata, and more. Once you choose a category, you move to the Contains All drop-down menu. It restricts how the words are examined in your photos before filtering, such as containing all words chosen, or containing any, none, and so on. In the last box, you can type in your words and Lightroom immediately filters your photos to them. The important thing to remember is that Lightroom can only filter to words that are attached to your photos. If you have not put in specific keywords, for example, you cannot search for those words. If you want to consistently use certain criteria for searching for your photos, you need to attach specific information to your images by using keywords or metadata that include such criteria.

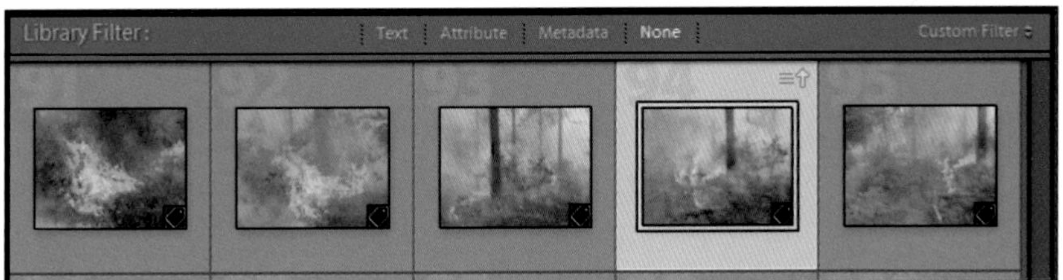

3-45

3-46

- **Attribute.** Filtering by attribute is simply identifying images by ratings, flags, colors, and virtual copies, as shown in figure 3-47. While you can do this in the Filmstrip, the advantage of doing it here is that you can do multiple filtering. For example, you could filter by a word (or set of words), then by an attribute to help you narrow down your images.
- **Metadata.** This is an interesting filter. Here you are not searching for text in the metadata; that comes from Text. In this section, as shown in figure 3-48, you search based on four criteria found in the metadata of the group of photos you are filtering: date, camera, lens, and label. These criteria will have a hierarchy (such as date from year to day) based on the metadata. This can be very useful in finding, for example, a specific image from a certain day.
- **None.** Click here to remove all filters and get back to your original complete group of photos. You can also remove filters by pressing Ctrl/⌘+L.
- **Custom Filter.** This gives some unique combinations of the other filters and even allows you to set up your own preset filter based on filters you regularly use. You simply set up the filters and then choose Save current settings as new preset under the Custom Filter drop-down menu.

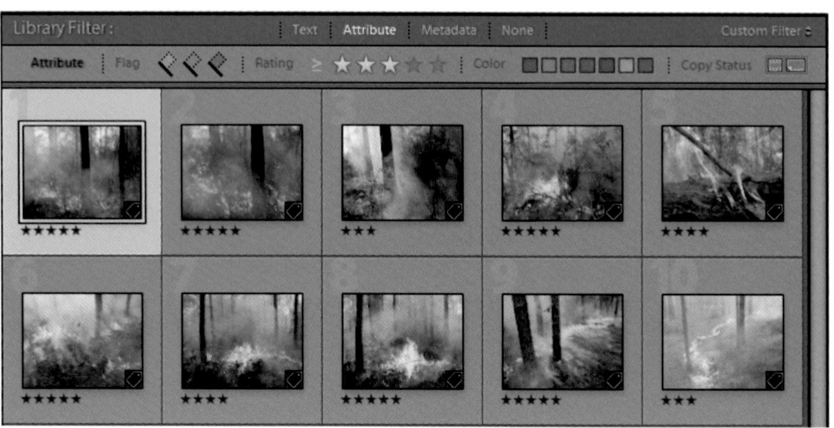

3-47

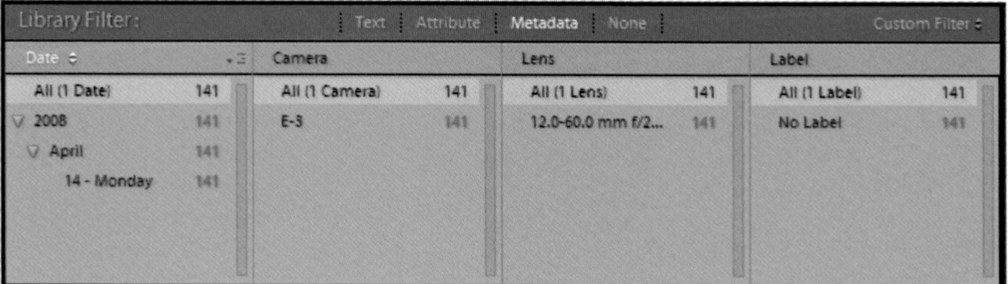

3-48

Exporting Photos

Export is the second button at the bottom of the left panel, shown in figure 3-49. Using the Export feature in Lightroom is fairly straightforward. It simply structures the traditional Save As command found in most programs for exporting one or more images. You cannot save over your original files in Lightroom (unless you really work to beat Lightroom with a TIFF or JPEG file, and you cannot affect a RAW file), so Export always acts like Save As.

Click the Export button to open the Export dialog box, shown in figure 3-50. You can also export by right-clicking an image and choosing Export in the context menu that appears. Here's what you find in the Export dialog box:

3-49

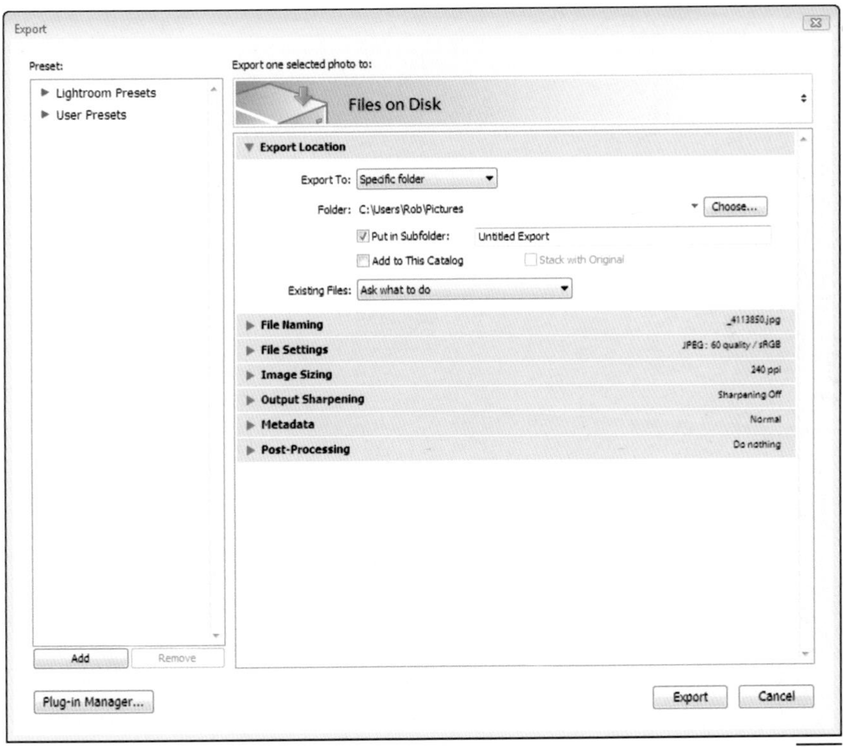

3-50

> **Preset.** This menu choice has some preset options for how you might want to export images as DNG RAW files or e-mail sized files; for example, in Lightroom presets, as shown in figure 3-51, you can add your own presets after setting up the right side of Export and clicking Add at the bottom of the Preset area.

3-51

> **Export Location.** This is simply the folder you want to put the photo into, shown in figure 3-52. Clicking Choose gives you a traditional file structure dialog box. You can also create and put this image into a subfolder by selecting Put in Subfolder.

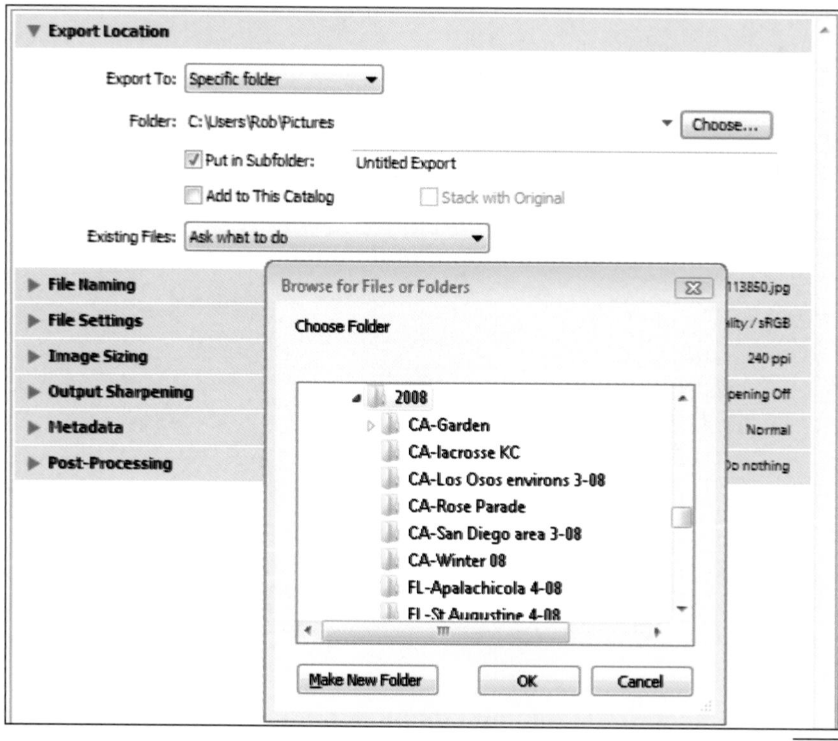

3-52

- **File Naming.** This section gives you a number of choices in the Template box, shown in figure 3-53. Each choice gives you unique options for naming your image or images if you have selected a group of them.
- **File Settings.** This important section has options for format and quality, shown in figure 3-54. From the Format drop-down menu, you can choose JPEG, PSD, TIFF, DNG, or Original, as appropriate to your needs. You can also choose a Color Space (sRGB, AdobeRGB [1998], or ProPhoto RGB and Bit Depth [8 or 16]). For most photographers, AdobeRGB and 8-bit will work fine most of the time. Use sRGB for photos going to the Web. Using 16-bit will add file size that will affect processing in Photoshop and storage, and if you do most of your processing in Lightroom, it is rarely needed. However, if you intend to do a lot more processing outside of Lightroom, use 16-bit.
- **Image Sizing.** This section, shown in figure 3-55, simply sizes your photos and sets resolution. Lightroom has a very good sizing algorithm for resizing both bigger and smaller. When Resize to Fit is selected, you can tell Lightroom how to size photos and their dimensions. Usually you will use Width & Height, as shown in figure 3-55, but this is a little confusing. It actually means your photo will be sized without changing its proportions up to the width or height of the longest side. You can then put in the same dimensions in W (width) and H (height) when enlarging either vertical or horizontal images and have them come out the same basic size. You can put in a number for Resolution appropriate to your end use, such as 240 pixels per inch (ppi) for a print or 300 ppi for a publication.

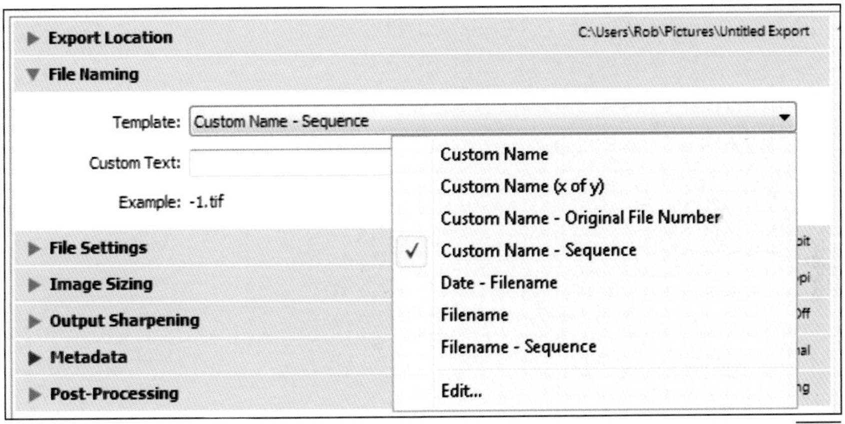

3-53

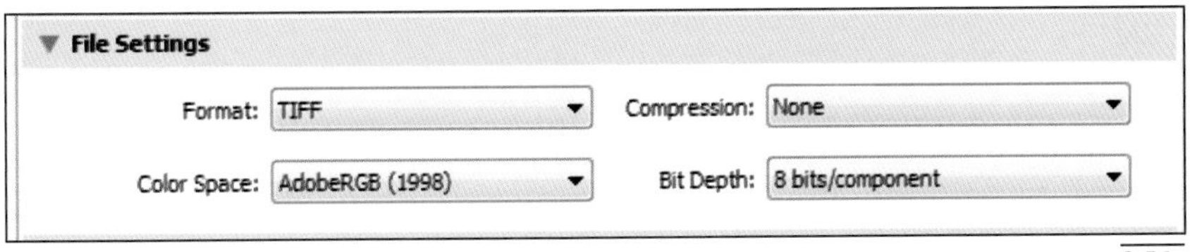

3-54

> **Output Sharpening.** This is new to Lightroom 2. Lightroom sharpens the photo based on its original captured file as I explain in Chapters 5 and 6 about the Develop module. However, as an image is processed for export, especially if it is resized, it may need to be sharpened again for a specific purpose, such as a paper type for printing, as shown in figure 3-55. This is further discussed in Chapter 9 on printing.

> **Metadata.** This section includes several functions that will not be used by all photographers (most could use the default settings). Minimize Embedded Metadata simply attaches a minimum amount of metadata to the file rather than everything possible in the IPTC and EXIF data. Write Keywords as Lightroom Hierarchy simply writes keywords to the file using the same hierarchy as used in Lightroom (if a hierarchy is used). Add Copyright Watermark embeds a watermark with your copyright into the image.

> **Post-Processing.** Here you can decide what you want to do with your file after it is exported, as shown in figure 3-56. For many images, you will simply choose Do nothing. However, you might want to do a little post-processing in Photoshop; in this case you would select Open in Adobe Photoshop CS3.

When you have selected all the appropriate conditions for your file, click Export and the photo is saved to your hard drive.

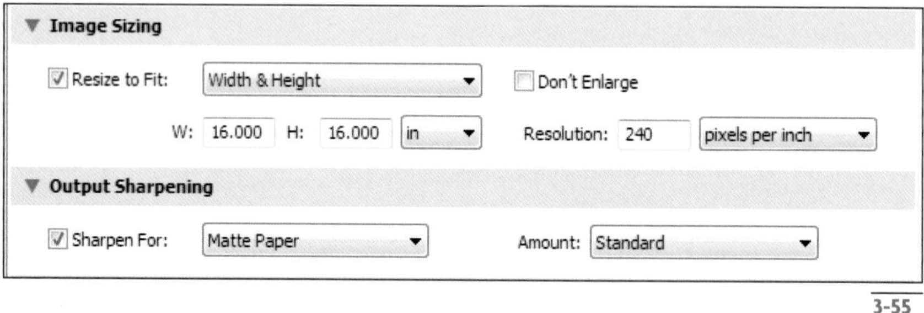

3-55

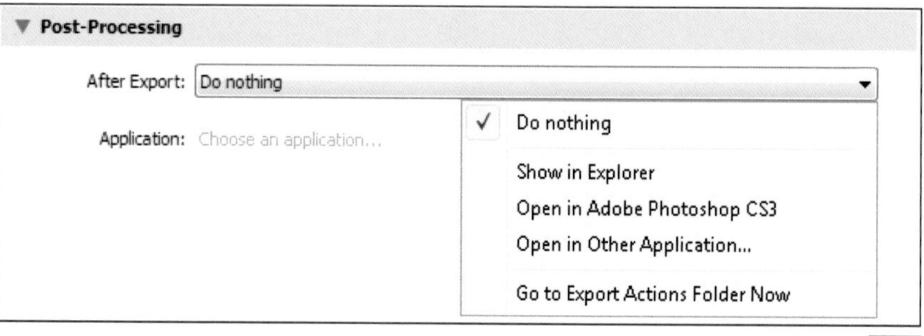

3-56

Q & A

I am not sure I follow this Export concept. In Photoshop, you just save a photo. How is Export different from Save or Save As in Photoshop?

Once an image is in Lightroom, it is never actually changed at a pixel level, and no layers are added to it. Everything that is done to an image is done by only adding instructions, making the adjustments "nondestructive" in that nothing is actually changed. Lightroom's database automatically records the instructions for the images.

In Photoshop, on the other hand, as soon as you make adjustments, something changes in that file. Even if you use an adjustment layer, which is nondestructive to pixels, you change that file with that addition of a layer. None of those changes are recorded to the Photoshop file unless you save them.

So, in order to make adjustment instructions in Lightroom "stick" to an image, or become permanent, you have to process the image file and save it as a new file. That is essentially what exporting does. With Photoshop, any changes to the file have already occurred while that image was inside Photoshop, so the file does not need to be processed, only saved. You can simply save the file as it is. It is basically just a difference in the way the two programs handle the preservation of changes in an image.

How do I choose to export with 16-bit or 8-bit color depth?

This is a good question because 16-bit files hold a lot more color and tonal information than 8-bit files. However, that information cannot actually be seen by the human eye. You cannot see the difference between an 8-bit and 16-bit file. The added information only helps when you need to do extensive processing. All processing inside Lightroom is done at the 16-bit level, so if you do most or all of your processing there, you will have little need for the larger file size of 16-bit outside of Lightroom. (It will double your storage needs.)

However, if you feel you will be doing a lot of additional processing in Photoshop or another program later, then you need to export as 16-bit to gain that advantage of extra information. Some photographers always export at 16-bit because they feel they need the "security" of its extra information, while others nearly always export at 8-bit because they only export what they feel they need, and they want to minimize stress on the computer's processor and storage space.

Chapter 4

ORGANIZING IMAGES IN THE LIBRARY MODULE

Lightroom's Library module has some easy-to-use features that are quite powerful as you saw in the last chapter. I find that they are definitely speeding up the way I work with my photos. I used to dread putting caption information on all the photos of a shoot, yet some of my projects and clients required that. Now, I can do it in a hurry and it isn't painful, either! I like the way Lightroom's Library helps me organize my images, but using those features in your workflow requires a bit of thought and work on your part. You need to decide how best to deal with organizing images. Lightroom provides a place; it's up to you to determine how to use that place.

One major issue among photographers today is what the best way is to file and organize digital images. There is a multitude of experts promoting their way to work as the best approach. In a sense, they are all right. When it comes to handling image files, different photographers respond differently to what is best for them, so there will be multiple "bests."

So, as a photographer, how do you know which approach is best for you? How can you use Lightroom optimally for your purposes? In this chapter, I offer some ideas on doing just that.

Managing Physical Image Files in the Past

It is important to first look at how you filed photos in the past because that can help you better work out a system for filing images on your computer. You may hear the argument from some computer gurus that how you filed in the past is dead and gone. You should be working "the new way," and paying attention to your old habits simply computerizes old, and perhaps outdated, habits.

There is good logic to that. After all, the computer does provide capabilities that one could not even imagine as recently as a few years ago. It is a waste to not use a computer's modern capabilities to gain new possibilities in working with images.

However, I have found that if photographers ignore how they worked with images in the past and simply adopt a new system because someone else says it is "best," they struggle with it; at best, they will not use it to its full capabilities, and at worst, they use it in a minimal and superficial (and not very helpful) way. On the other hand, if photographers look a bit at how they filed images in the past, and what worked or didn't work for them, they can apply some of those ideas to image file management in the computer, creating a system that is more appropriate for their specific needs.

With film, you had to have a physical place for the photos, as shown in figure 4-1. For many amateurs (and even a few pros I knew who did not shoot stock images), old images were filed by sticking them into boxes and tucking them away in some storage space — the old "shoebox in the closet" method. This was never a very efficient way of dealing with photos, but it did store them for potential (albeit difficult) access at some point. These boxes were organized, in a way, because they were kept in bags or boxes that related to a trip, a job, or, possibly, just a date. You could search for an image if you had an idea of where or when you took the picture.

However, photographers who shot stock needed a much more organized system. They needed to find specific photos to fill requests for images from potential clients. Typically, they would use many filing cabinets with categorized drawers, then further refine categories for folders or binders (the actual physical "holder" varied), and then even further refine information on specific images based on the filing names for them.

Photographers who shot commercial work (such as annual reports or advertising images) used something similar, but they had very specific needs based on clients. They would have the same sort of filing cabinets, but the drawers and folders would be organized first around clients, next by shoots for that client, usually in chronological order (often with the most recent at the front of the drawer), and then labeled by specific elements of a job (such as subject, selects, and so forth).

Photojournalists had somewhat different needs (whether they personally filed their images or their publication did). They needed to find photos specific to news events, sports competitions, unique days, and so forth. Still, they needed a place for these images and a way of accessing them in folders, cabinets, and other filing places.

In all of these situations, photographers were not even consistent within a specific group. This is actually a very important element of image filing to take note of, because it often revealed some things that were core to how a photographer worked and thought. Some photographers filed very broadly, for example, and simply took all images from a specific shoot, put them into a folder labeled by that shoot, and then did nothing else other than place that folder into the appropriate file cabinet or box.

Other photographers filed to a far greater extent. They would document very specific information about each and every photograph, including labels for slides that had tiny type that challenged even young eyes but had everything you needed to know about those images. Typically, this sort of filing would include very specific, detailed file names that affected how the images were organized.

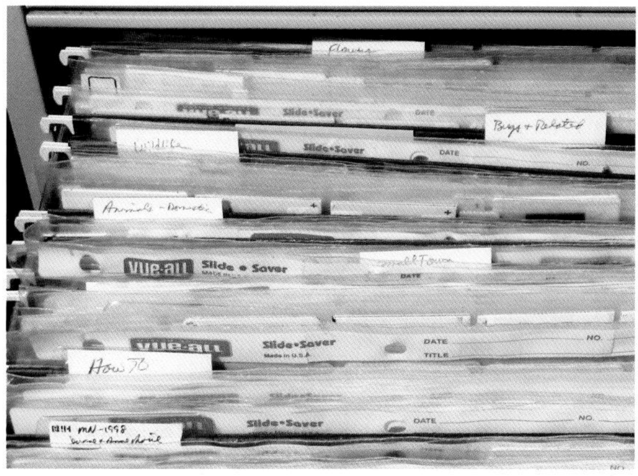

4-1

How one filed physical slides or other photographs is conceptually not that different from working on the computer to file photos there. You will find managing files on your computer to work best when it is based on how you file anything.

Managing Files on Your Computer

Many photographers get into trouble with image filing on the computer when they figure out they have to forget all they learned about their likes and dislikes regarding image filing of film. The computer seems so alien and different from filing cabinets and folders. It offers none of the physical contact that film filing does.

To make the most of Lightroom and your computer, you have to see the Library module as a way of accessing file cabinets, drawers, and folders. While they aren't physical locations, they act the same way — they are simply places to hold your photos. Look at figures 4-2 and 4-3. You see two different things, a filing cabinet and some of the folders recognized by my version of

4-2

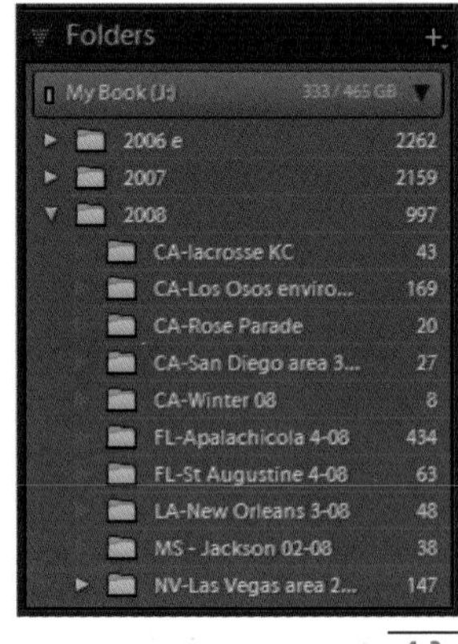

4-3

Lightroom, yet they truly do represent the same things. If you can hold that idea when working with managing image files, you can use many of the ideas you had in the past, and then modify them to better use the capabilities of the computer.

Using Lightroom's Library module really can be the same as filing slides in a cabinet. The better organized your cabinet filing system (based on your needs) was, the easier it was to find photos. The better you set up and manage your filing system with Lightroom, the easier it is to find your digital images.

I want to reemphasize, though, that I do not advocate any one way of setting up these files. I am offering you some ideas and possibilities to consider, but you must look at how you have worked over the years and determine what seems to best fit your personality as well as your professional and personal needs for filing and image access.

Lightroom, File Cabinets, and Such

In Chapter 3, you learned how Library was set up and organized. If you compare it to a traditional filing cabinet, I believe you will get good ideas on how best to use this module.

Your computer's hard drive is basically your room full of filing cabinets, as shown in figure 4-4. Lightroom can put images directly into that room if you download them through the program.

Or you can put the photos directly into folders in those "filing cabinets" yourself (before you import to Lightroom). This is what happens when you download a shoot into a folder on the hard drive. The folder sits inside other folders (organized by months or years, clients, location, and so on), which can be seen as the equivalent of drawers and cabinets in that hard drive "room."

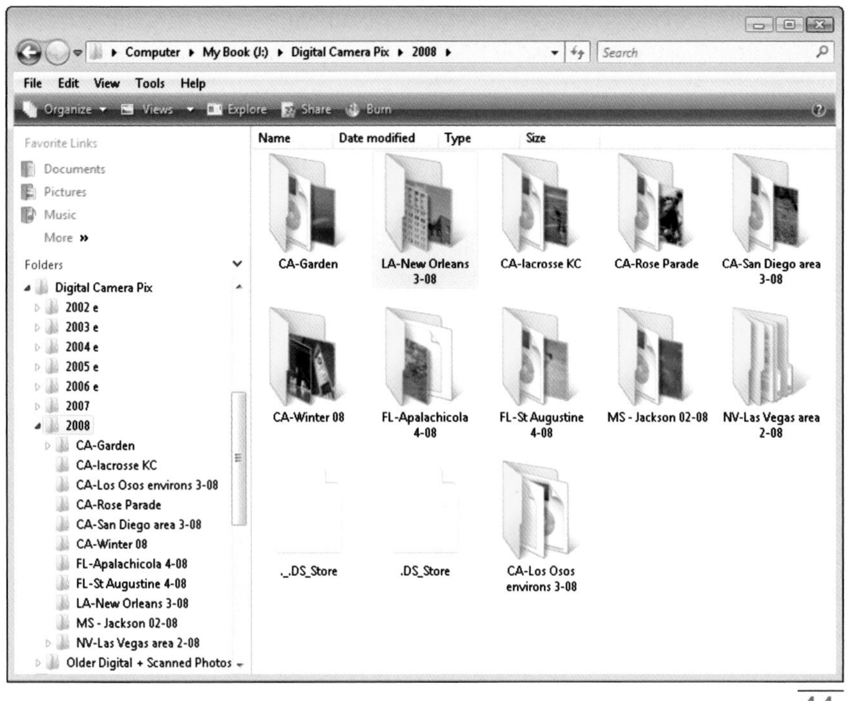

4-4

Lightroom then sets up its own virtual file folders in its own cabinets (its database) to reference your folders on the hard drive. One "cabinet" is the Folders section. There, it recognizes all of your images as folders based on a specific shoot or download. It does this with references to the images in their original locations — it doesn't move the actual images. In the Collections section, unique groups of images are collected and referenced into new groups based on special categories commonly used and labeled by you, with your specific needs based on how and what you photograph.

Photos are assigned additional organizational capabilities based on such things as how they are named, the caption information associated with them in the metadata, and keywords. The naming process is the same as the one you might have used to name film images; metadata and keywords convey the information that often went into little labels on the slide mount. A big deal for all this extra information is that you can quickly and easily search (using the Library Filter function) all images with the power of the computer. It is like having a Harry Potteresque assistant who can quickly go through all your cabinets, folders, and labels to find you exactly the photos you need.

Setting Up an Organization System

The power of a digital search is what makes the computer so helpful in dealing with image files. You can find photos faster than you ever could with a physical filing system.

However, the analogy of the physical system is very applicable here. If you did not put your slides, for example, into the "right" folders (that is, ones with appropriate names), you would never find those images. You might have the world's greatest photo of an American bald eagle catching a fish in the river, but if you filed it in the Travel cabinet in the Mississippi River folder and not in some bird folder, it might be difficult to find. The same thing happens in Lightroom. You might have a stunning photo of a young soccer player, but if you have filed it under an obscure shoot, such as Trip to Cleveland, and have not included it in a soccer collection or connected it to keywords such as soccer, youth, and goalkeeper, you might never find this photo again.

To avoid problems finding filed images and to enable you to make the best use of your photographs, you need to do some preplanning to decide on a consistent way to name your folders and collections, plus determine some conventions on how you will apply names, keywords, and captions to the photos. Use your personality, personal preferences, and past experiences with film to determine what and how much information to include in each area, but it is worth making some consistent choices to set up a system that works well for you.

It's important to be consistent because if you keep changing the way you name images, for example, you increase your work, complicate your workflow (because you have to figure out a new system every time), and make the images harder to search for and find successfully. Plus, if you don't have a consistent set of terms to use for keywords, the search process is frustrating: What do you search for? Baby, babies, newborns? Eagle, birds of prey, symbol of America? Sure, you could include all of these, but most people don't. You are best served with a list that you can use again and again, and to search images based on that list as well.

Keywords, folder names, and so forth are going to be personal, unique choices for each photographer. Photographers who work for a stock photo agency may find that the agency asks you to use a specific list. Otherwise, you need to create a list of words that work for you and that you can use in a consistent way. For example, a nature photographer might have categories broken down like this:

Birds

>Specific categories of birds (shorebirds, hawks, owls, thrushes, and so on)

>Locations for birds (northeast birds, southeast birds, Midwest birds, and so on)

Flowers

>Specific categories of flowers (sunflower family, lily family, mint family, rose family, and so on)

>Timing of flowering (spring flowers, summer flowers, fall flowers, winter flowers)

>Locations for flowers (northeast flowers, southeast flowers, Midwest flowers, and so on)

It is important to remember that you need to find what kind of keywords and other labels work best for you, or if they even work with your workflow.

All this organization work might seem a bit overwhelming — after all, Lightroom offers a lot of power to do this — but I want to emphasize again that you need to choose and use what works for you and your image needs. To be honest, I often get a bit overwhelmed by the projects I am involved with and don't have time to follow all the ideas I discuss here. That doesn't make those ideas less valid; it's just that realistically, life sometimes gets in the way of optimum organization. Plus, some folks are more detail oriented than I am and can sit down for hours and fill in keywords, whereas I get tired of it long before that.

Still, it helps to envision an ideal way of working. I'm going to explain an approach that I use. It works, but I recognize it doesn't work for everyone. Use it to stimulate your own methods for using your computer and Lightroom to file and organize your images.

Bringing Images into the Computer

I like to set up folders in preparation for receiving digital images. This fits the Lightroom workflow quite well, even though this portion is not done in Lightroom. I set up my hard drive so that there is a specific folder for digital images (this is like a filing cabinet). Then I create main folders in the digital images folder for each year (these are like cabinet drawers). I do all this separately from actually setting up folders for a specific shoot, though, usually, I set up a new year folder when I have the first shoot from the year. You can see how this might look on your computer in figure 4-5.

Before I really recognized the power of importing images through Lightroom, I would then open the year folder and create a new folder for that shoot every time I had a new shoot. Now I don't do that; I combine Lightroom with this file structure. When I put a memory card into my memory card reader, the Import Photos dialog box shown in figure 4-6 opens. I choose Copy photos to a new location and add to catalog from the drop-down menu for File Handling.

Next, and this is an important step for me, I tell Lightroom where to copy these photos to by clicking the Choose button, as shown in figure 4-6. This brings up the file system used by your computer. I navigate to the year folder and then click the Make New Folder button, shown in figure 4-7, to add a new folder specifically for this shoot. Put some thought into how you name these folders. They should represent your photography and how you shoot. Given I do a lot of travel and nature photography, I mostly name these folders based on location by state (or country) and month (the location fits both my travel and nature needs). If I go to a specific location many times, then I simply set up new folders for the same location but for different months.

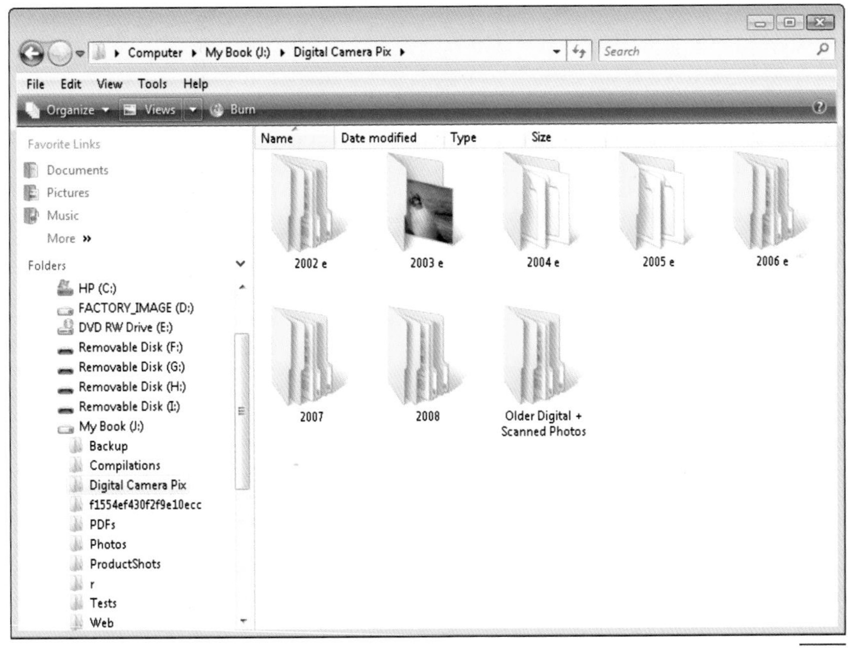

4-5

Import Photos

Importing 38 images that were all taken on May 13, 2008.

File Handling: Copy photos to a new location and add to catalog

Copy to: C:\Users\Rob\Pictures Choose...

Organize: By original folders

DCIM\325OLYMP 38

Don't re-import suspected duplicates

Backup to: C:\Users\Rob\Pictures\Lightroom\Download Backups Choose...

File Naming: _5134823.ORF

Template: Filename

Information to Apply

Develop Settings: None

Metadata: Basic copyright

Keywords:

Initial Previews: Minimal

Show Preview

Preview

Check All Uncheck All

Import Cancel

4-6

4-7

Copy to: J:\Digital Came...\CA-Griffith Park aftr fire 05-08 Choose...

Organize: Into one folder

Put in subfolder: Untitled Import

Don't re-import suspected duplicates

4-8

I then select Into one folder from the Organize drop-down menu, as shown in figure 4-8. You can also select By original folders, which is the default. Because most memory cards have multiple folders that have little real relation to any organizational structure, that option is not too useful to me. You can also organize folders into subfolders by date or unique subfolders within a folder you have already created.

Finally, I make sure my Basic Copyright metadata template is selected and I add some keywords, as shown in figure 4-9. It can be very helpful to add keywords at this point, even if they cannot be overly specific for a lot of photos. This can help get these images into a Smart Collection, too, if that collection is based on certain keywords. I click Import and all of these organizational aids are added to the files as they enter Lightroom.

Information to Apply

Develop Settings: None

Metadata: Basic copyright

Keywords: Griffith Park, chaparral, fire

Initial Previews: Minimal

4-9

PRO TIP

You can download images to your computer either from the camera or from a memory card reader. I highly recommend a card reader. With the camera, you have some distinct problems: You have to find a place to put the camera, the camera must have a fully charged battery (or be plugged into an AC adapter), and you need to keep track of your camera cord. If the camera runs out of power while the card is being downloaded, you can lose your image files. With the memory card reader, you have some definite advantages: It's usually faster than the camera, it requires no additional power, you can keep it attached to the computer, it has a very small footprint, and you can keep it plugged in and in place, ready for use.

Organizing the Images

I recommend keeping your folders on your hard drive solidly grounded in the same approach you use to file your images. Lightroom's Folders will reflect how your images are filed on your hard drive. Like most photographers, when I get certain shoots that don't fit the norm, I create special Folders for them.

However, you can also use Folders as a way of organizing distinct groupings of your photography, such as by client. You can create a folder that is a client name directly in Lightroom, and then import all jobs for that client into that folder, so each job shows up as a subset of the overriding Folder category. Do this by clicking the + button to the right of Folders. When the drop-down menu appears, select Add New Root Folder. The Browse for Files or Folders dialog box appears, as shown in figure 4-10. Find the folder you want to create a subfolder within, and then click Make New Folder. This is a way of keeping the Folder section a bit tighter when you have a lot of individual folders that still belong to a larger grouping.

All this can be necessary if you need to know exactly where certain files are for a client. In most cases, though, you will find that you can more easily use Collections for this purpose. I will typically use definite folders for tracking specific shoots, which goes back to the file cabinet analogy, but I use them from when I first import photos into Lightroom. I consider the Folders category as my file drawer and use the subfolder based on a shoot within it. I do tend to use Collections more for subject matter that cuts across folders.

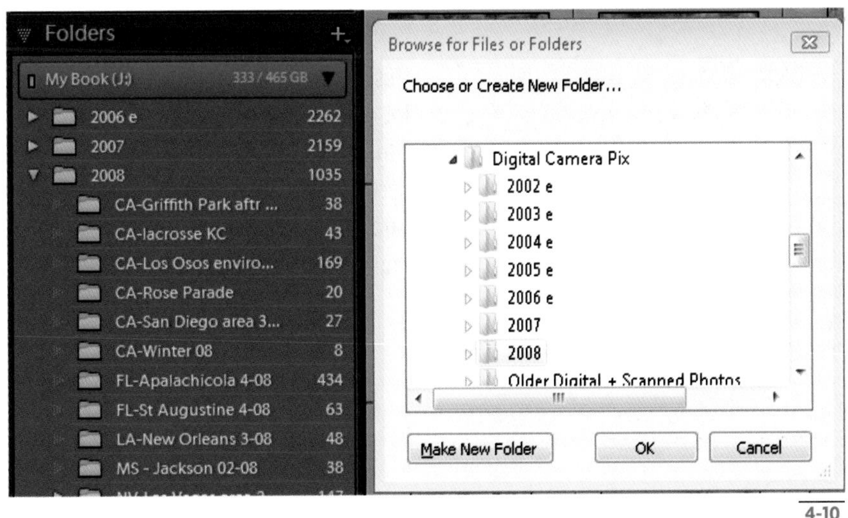

4-10

Renaming Images

After the initial edit, you may find it helpful to rename digital images to something related to a specific shoot — at least something that makes more sense than the names that come directly from the camera, such as IMG00982. You can rename files in Lightroom very easily. Simply select the photos you want to rename and press the F2 function key. The Rename Photos dialog box, shown in figure 4-11, appears (you will see a specific number of photos being renamed based on how many you have selected). If you click the File Naming drop-down arrow at the far right, you see a series of choices for renaming, as shown in figure 4-12.

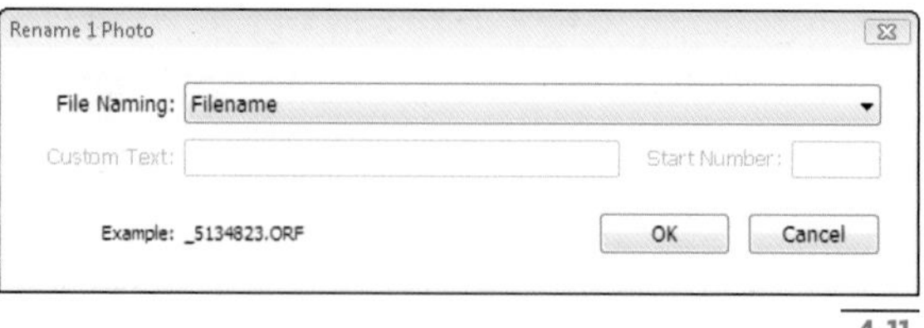

4-11

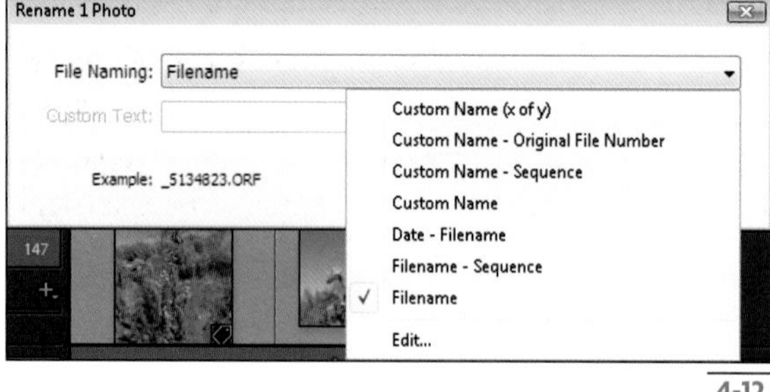

4-12

Another option for naming is to name your files when you export photos from Lightroom. That is what I do, but not for an organizational reason. I shoot RAW + JPEG, so I need to keep the original pair of images together. To do that, I need the original file name so I do not rename these photos before exporting. I could add more information here, but the names get unwieldy.

If I were only shooting RAW or JPEG, I would rename photos at this point because I would not need the original file name to reference both file types. This would give you another set of criteria (i.e., file name) that could be used for searching.

But how do you actually name your files, whether now or when you export?

This is an extremely personal thing. I believe you must create some sort of naming convention that works for you and gives you information you need. You want to create a way of naming so that you can look at a file name and learn something about it without even seeing the photo. You don't want to overdo this, though, as really long names can be very unwieldy and won't always display properly when you are looking for them.

I like to create a file name based on the File Naming template, Custom Name – Sequence, that works out something like this: CA-GriffithPark-after fire-1.ORF, as shown in figure 4-13.

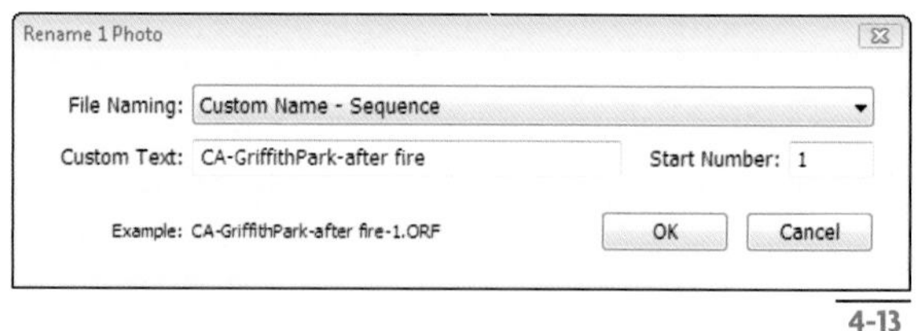

4-13

My chosen name translates as follows and may give you some ideas:

- **State or country.** Given most of my images are based on locations, I start with the two-letter state abbreviation or something similar for a country. The sample file name was a shot from California.

- **Specific shoot info.** I then add some abbreviated information that usually refines the location; this photo was taken in Griffith Park. And it might also refer to a specific subject matter I was shooting; this example shows images from a burned area of chaparral as the plants come back.
- **Sequence.** This just adds consecutive numbers to the file names.

PRO TIP

At some point when you're filing and organizing images, you need to back up your images. This is extremely critical. I have several external drives that duplicate all of my photo files, and as I bring new shoots into the computer, I also copy them onto the back-up drives. I use automated back-up software called Save-N-Sync from Peer Software for my Windows computer and Déjà Vu for my Mac, but there are others that do equally well. The important thing is to do it.

Using Collections

At this point in my Lightroom workflow, I can start using Collections and Keywords, which provide more ways to organize your photos. I can use Keywords when the images are imported into Lightroom, but it's only very generic at that point.

Collections are a great way of grouping images from many shoots into categories that you use regularly. You can add categories as you go, but use Collections for large numbers of images with subjects that go across folders. For me, that includes things such as spring or summer flowers, regional landscapes, bugs, travel scenes such as architecture, and so on, as shown in figure 4-14.

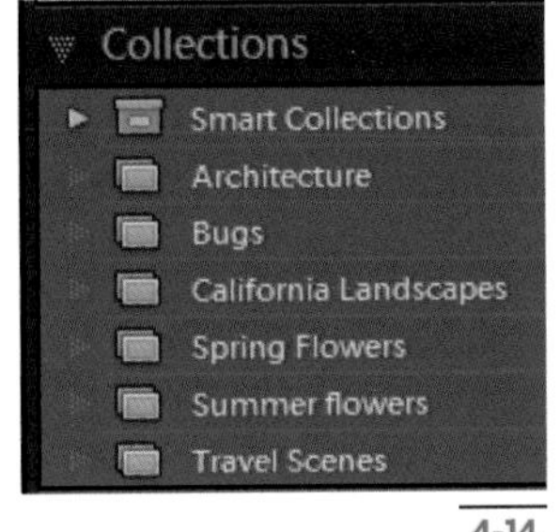

4-14

You can create both overall collections and subcollections within a larger group. This is a little different than in Lightroom 1.0. Now you create Collection Sets. A *set* is an overriding collection that includes a number of subcollections. To create a Collection Set, click on Collection, and then click the + button, which gives you a simple drop-down menu. Choose Create Collection Set and give it a name as needed in the resulting dialog box. You can then click and drag collections into this set.

You can also create Smart Collections that constantly update as you change information about your photographs. Click the + button next to Collections and choose Create Smart Collection from the drop-down menu. That gives you the dialog box shown in figure 4-15. Then you need to choose criteria as described in Chapter 3. Click on the arrow to the right of Rating to get the menu shown in figure 4-16. The easiest way to use a Smart Collection is with keywords as the criteria, but you can see you have many choices. If you are putting location information in the metadata, for example, you could have a Smart Collection based on location.

Once I have done my basic editing of a shoot and am satisfied with the organization of my Collections, I go through the new images in Grid mode with thumbnails that are pretty small. I have already seen the images

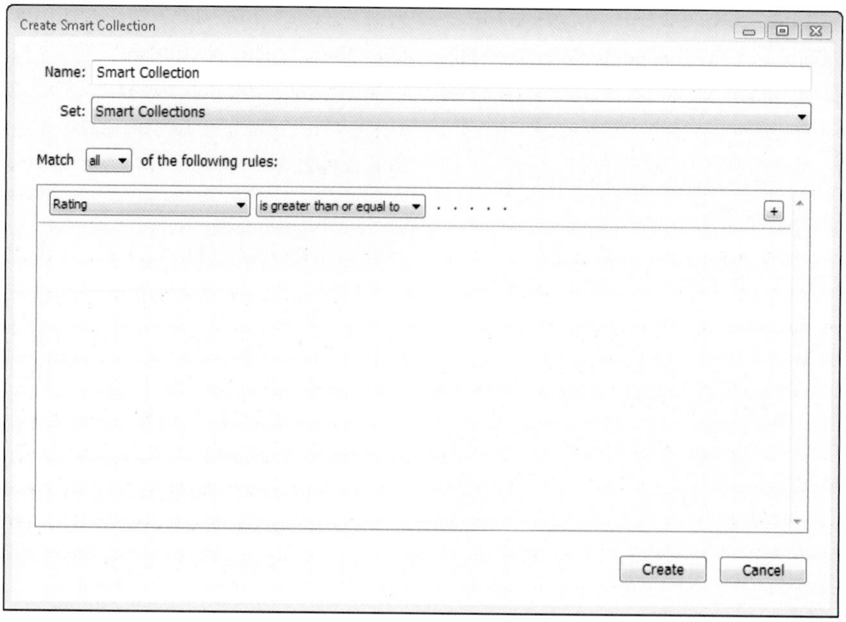

4-15

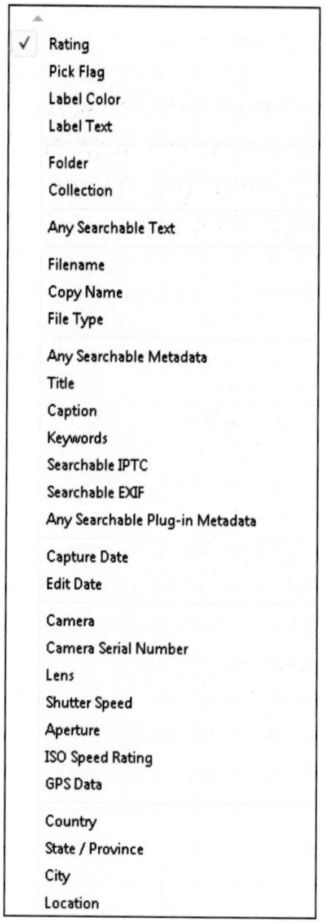

4-16

in a larger format when I was editing the shoot (enlarging as needed with Loupe), but, usually, seeing the big version doesn't matter for Collections. If you can't see the photo subject clearly when it's small, then use the Loupe view as needed. If you stay in Grid mode as much as possible, the organizing process is much faster.

In the Grid view, I select images in groups by Ctrl/⌘+clicking each, and then dragging the images onto the collection name.

How Collections and Keywords Are Different

Since you can create a Smart Collection based on keywords, you might wonder how they are different and why you should bother? Basically, keywords allow you to drill down into very specific names or descriptive terms for a photo so you can find a narrow selection of photos that meet the criteria for those specific names. You can really create a very tight search for photos by putting in a number of keywords.

Collections are designed to give you visual groupings of images, vast collections that you can browse, but not specific photos for a specific need. I like collections for a lot of my work because they allow me to put large groups of photos with similar subject matter together. If I need an image of an insect, but not a specific insect, I can use the Bugs collection. (A side note: Bugs are technically not all insects, but since most people call little critters bugs, I just use the term for all small invertebrates. Maybe this is not scientifically accurate, but it works for me – this is just a specific example of why it is important for you to find your own way of working within Lightroom.)

Quick Collection's Value

I constantly use the Quick Collection in the Catalog part of the left panel of Library, as shown in figure 4-17. What you actually see in the figure is a Quick Collection I created for working in the Web module of Lightroom and is seen in Chapter 11. The Quick Collection is simply a temporary "storage bin" for selected photos. I will use it for the output modules of Slideshow, Print, and Web because I can keep the number of images to a workable number appropriate to my needs for those modules by using this collection. I will also use it for specific assignments as I can collect photos from multiple shoots (or Folders) into one location, Quick Collection.

Here is how to gather images into Quick Collection:

- Click on the Quick Collection icon to add a photo to Quick Collection. Go to Grid and move through images very quickly. As you hover your cursor over an image, a small circle will appear at its upper right as shown in figure 4-18. Click on that and the photo goes to Quick Collection. You can do the same thing with the Filmstrip photos whenever the Filmstrip is visible.
- Select a group of photos in Grid and press B. You can "grab" a group of photos in the Grid by Ctrl/⌘+clicking them, then press the letter B to put them into the Quick Collection.
- Remove photos from the Quick Collection by clicking the Quick Collection circle icon again or by selecting the photo and pressing B. You can remove a group (or even all) of the photos by selecting them first.

4-17

4-18

If you want to keep all of your photos together in a more permanent collection, you can create a new collection in Collections for them. Then select all of the photos in the Quick Collection by pressing Ctrl/⌘+A and dragging them onto the new Collection name in Collections.

You can also set up a specific Collection to act as a Quick Collection called a Target Collection. Then instead of going to the Quick Collection, a photo will go to the Target Collection when you press B or click the icon. You can create a Collection for a slide show or Web site, label it for that purpose, then set it as a Target Collection. The easiest way to make a Target Collection is to right-click any collection and use the contextual menu that appears — select Set as Target Collection.

Saving and Exporting Catalogs

Lightroom does all of its magic with a special file called its catalog. It has .lrcat as the file extension at the end of its name, which is Lightroom 2 by default. This is a very important file, which is why you have a number of backup options in Lightroom Preferences (under the Lightroom menu on a Mac and the Edit menu in Windows). Be sure you do back up the file regularly to a drive different than your main hard drive, because if your main drive fails, you want to be able to access this file. This is also described in Chapter 2.

Many photographers are now using laptops in the field and want to work on images there, then bring the same work back to their main computer at their office or home. It is possible to do exactly that, but there are several things you must do:

1. Create a file structure for your saved photos that is identical on both computers. You can follow some of the guidelines I have given in this chapter and Chapter 3. Lightroom needs to be able to follow some sort of structure. If your photos are organized differently on your laptop than on your desktop computer, you will have a problem getting Lightroom to recognize them without starting a whole new catalog. The catalog is based on how images are filed in different folders.
2. Export your catalog. Go to File ➪ Export as Catalog. You will get a dialog box similar to that seen in figure 4-19 for Windows Vista. At the bottom, you will see what is actually being exported. Type in a name that is appropriate for your work, then find a location on your drive for this catalog and click Save. I would also suggest you name this file so that it is different than the original catalog file in your desktop computer.

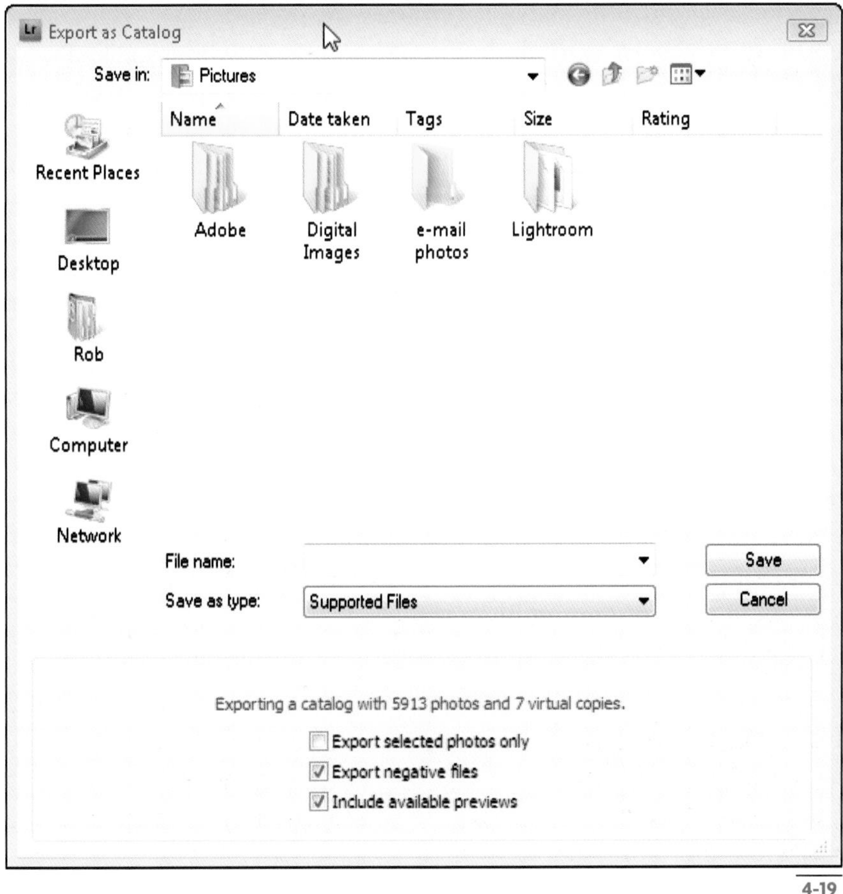

4-19

You can also copy your catalog as an alternative. The Lightroom catalog is located in the Pictures folder of Mac and Windows Vista (My Pictures for other versions) in a Lightroom folder. You will see the .lrcat extension if you have your computer set to display them (this makes it easier to find this folder). Note: When you copy your catalog, you are only copying Lightroom's data about your photos, not the photos themselves.

Copy your exported catalog to a drive (such as a jump drive) so you can transport it to a new computer (you can also copy this to the same drive used to transfer your photos, although I like keeping it separate so it is easy to find).

3. Copy your photos to move to the main computer. Use a portable hard drive.
4. Copy your photos to your desktop computer, using the same file structure (for example, a hierarchy of folders such as Digital Photos ➪ 2008 ➪ Location), then copy your Lightroom catalog to the same folder as it came from your laptop.
5. You can now use this catalog as a separate catalog for Lightroom by going to File ➪ Open Catalog or follow the instructions in Step 6.

6. Use your original catalog on your desktop, but now import the photos by importing based on the laptop catalog. Open Catalog in the left panel, then right-click on All Photographs. You will then see an option saying, Import Photos from Catalog. This will take you to a File Open dialog box that you will use to find your catalog.

You can even create multiple catalogs and load them the same way. To create a new catalog, perhaps for a second photographer using your computer, go to File ➪ New Catalog and create a new catalog named and placed appropriately. You can simply place the new catalog in the same location as your original catalog (by default, the New Catalog command opens the Picture folder ready for a new catalog named however you want – you may also find that it is in a folder called Lightroom in the Pictures folder), or you can navigate to a completely different location (such as a portable hard drive used by another photographer).

Q & A

I am not sure your approach to keywords will work for me. I have a staff that sometimes has to find images, and just going on a visual search doesn't necessarily work for them. You're the expert, so should I try to simplify my use of keywords?

No, not at all! You have to always translate an "expert's" advice so that it fits your unique needs. My way of working with images was used for an example. I know that my use of keywords simply doesn't work for photographers who have a staff who must find images or for photographers who shoot a lot of stock images. They need to be able to locate very specific images related to a subject or topic. In this case, having an extensive set of keywords really helps. It takes time to do all that keywording, but in the long run, it actually cuts time. It certainly helps prevent a lot of headaches from the wrong images being selected.

But you do need to understand that this is a very personal thing. Some photographers have hundreds of keywords and spend a lot of time giving very detailed keyword data for their photos. There is no question that this makes searches highly efficient.

For me, special keywords for unique subjects do help me find them. But often my work requires me to make a selection of an image from a variety of photos — I need the variety that keywords often won't give me. So doing a lot with keywords, which can take a lot of time, is not efficient for me. I love Collections because I can visually search through a group of related images and find what I need very quickly. I don't need the keywords in that case because the visual impression itself is so important.

I really find it hard to see the images in the Grid mode for editing purposes. What would you suggest to help?

First, I would recommend you use as large a monitor as you can afford. Monitors are pretty affordable today and are well worth the cost because they are really your vision into your files. I would recommend a 19-inch LCD as the minimum size. This allows you to display your whole interface larger.

Next, you can go to the Loupe view and simply go from photo to photo there by using the arrow keys. You can set your image ratings in Loupe view as well as in Grid view. This gives you a large image, but you can only see one at a time. You can keep the Filmstrip displayed so you can see how images show up in the order shot. I think that seeing images in the order of the shoot is important so you can better make comparisons. Use the Compare view as needed to see two large photos displayed at once.

Chapter 5

BASIC WORKFLOW IN THE DEVELOP MODULE

The Develop module of Lightroom 2 brings me back to the traditional darkroom. Finally, I feel that photographers have a true digital darkroom that provides the total control of a darkroom plus a whole lot more. Based on Ansel Adams' classic books, *The Negative* and *The Print*, I believe this is the program that Adams would have felt at home with.

Develop is truly designed to be photographer-friendly. Adobe Photoshop (all versions) is designed for working with photographs, but not for photographers. You can always see that whenever you open the program. Develop is designed both for photographers and for working with photographs. This is evident when you start processing an image. In Photoshop, you have to open each control separately, and there is no easy flow among them. In Lightroom, all of your controls are readily accessible so that you can go through them as needed, quickly and efficiently. In addition, Lightroom 2 now offers true local corrections like Adams always used, and you don't need to learn layers or layer masks to use them!

Adobe Camera Raw (the RAW conversion program that is a companion to Photoshop) and Photoshop Lightroom have a lot in common. They both use the same underlying processing engine, and both have the same basic controls. Develop, though, goes much farther than Camera Raw in dealing with image processing, plus its setup gives you a much more efficient way of working.

The most significant difference between Lightroom and Camera Raw is that Lightroom totally integrates RAW conversion and processing capabilities with every other part of its program, which Camera Raw has no possibilities of doing. As shown in figure 5-1,

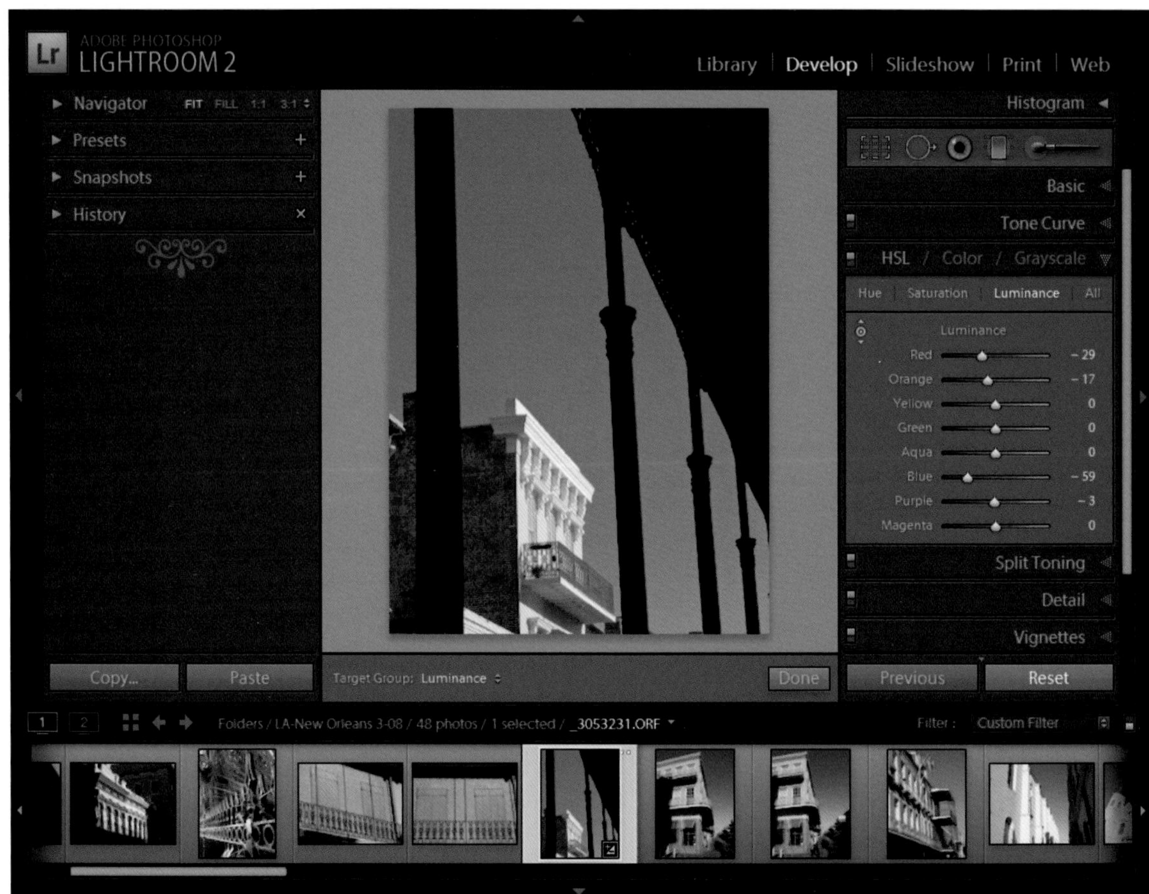

5-1

even though you are in Develop at one moment working on the color of a photo, you can click on any module to leave it, instantly go to print it, or go to Library to add a keyword in the metadata, and then go back to work on the color again. This gives you a lot of flexibility and makes your workflow more fluid.

In this chapter, I take you through the key global controls of Develop, following a workflow that I know works for photographers. *Global controls* are the overall controls that affect everything in a photograph. *Local controls* are those that affect only portions or local areas of a photograph.

An Overview of Develop

If you look at the controls on the right side of Develop, as shown in figure 5-2, you see a great layout for photographers. Everything you need to optimize your photo is readily accessible right there:

- At the top is a color RGB histogram that shows you a bit about the relationship of your tones across the whole range of tones possible in a photograph.
- Below that is a toolbar with controls such as crop and local brush tools.
- In Basic, you get color correction and tonal adjustment settings.
- Tone Curve gives you a lot of control over the tones in your photograph that hold detail (midtones and more).
- HSL/Color/Grayscale affect individual colors in your photograph.
- Split Toning allows you to change the color cast of dark and light parts of a photograph.
- Detail offers you control over noise and sharpness.
- Vignettes affects the darkness or brightness of a photo's edges.
- Camera Calibration includes some specialized color controls that some photographers use to calibrate a camera.

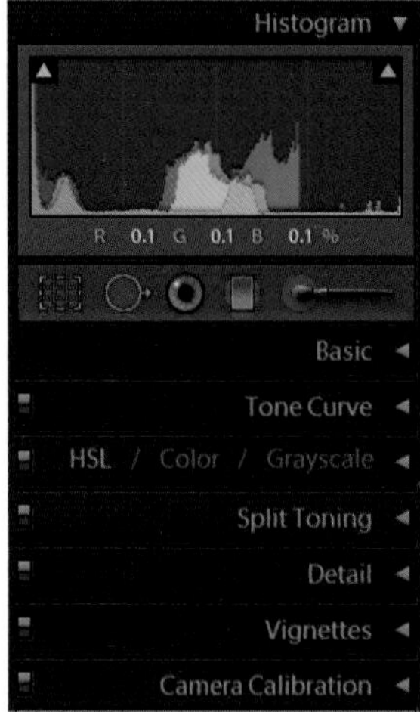

5-2

I find that these tools are organized better and are more appropriate for the photographer than any other Adobe product. I also find they have better controls and organization than the tools in any other RAW program on the market today (of course, that is very subjective and will depend on one's experience in using other programs).

The right side of Develop is essentially the digital darkroom for Lightroom. The order of the control groups from top to bottom is even an okay order to follow for a standard photographic workflow (although I find it less than ideal to follow exactly in this order, as you will see in this book). Still, you can skip around in these controls quite easily as needed.

At the bottom of the right side are two buttons, shown in figure 5-1. Previous takes you back to the most recent adjustments made on the image. Reset does what it says: It resets the Develop module back to defaults for the active image. (In general, I don't find either of these particularly useful — there are better ways to handle such changes, as you will learn in this chapter.) If you have several images selected, these buttons change to allow you to synchronize adjustments among those photos.

The left side of the Develop module, shown in figure 5-3, holds the image preview (Navigator) showing you what the whole image looks like, even when you have magnified the main image, and includes a box to show you where the magnified portion of the image is in relationship to the whole photo. (This operates the same as Navigator in Library.)

There are also three rather unique lists. Presets is simply a list of preset adjustments that affect your image in predefined ways for specific effects. You can quickly and easily see what each preset will do in the preview by running your cursor over the names of the presets, as shown in figure 5-4 (don't click the mouse or it will be applied).

Snapshots literally creates a snapshot of your processing that you can go back to later. Any Snapshot (captured by clicking the plus button) will remember exactly all of the adjustments on a photo at a particular point in your changes to the image. You can create multiple Snapshots to help you go back to multiple places in your development of the photo.

History is a unique way of remembering what you are doing. Rather than tracking every change you make, as you make it (as Photoshop does in the History palette), History only remembers the "condition" of a photo at a given point in the process (it is like a History State in Photoshop), which you can always go

5-3

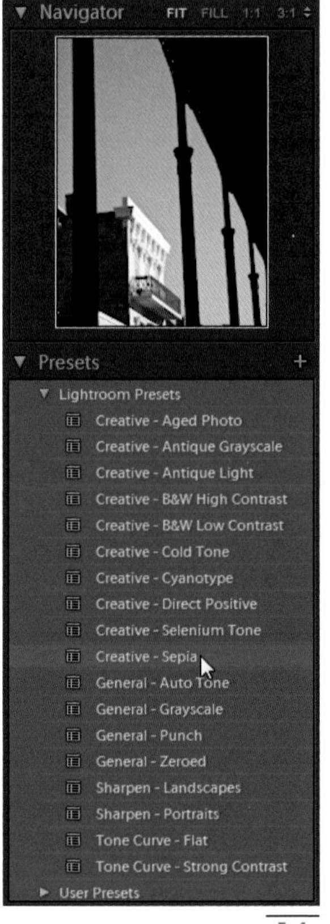

5-4

back to (even if you stop working on a photo, close Lightroom, and come back to it another day). I discuss History at the end of this chapter and cover the presets of this module in Chapter 6.

PRO TIP

The Filmstrip is very helpful as you are working in Develop. It allows you to move back and forth in your image processing from one photo to another. You can change the height of the Filmstrip, making it smaller to show more of the Develop interface, or making it larger to make your photos easier to see. Simply move your cursor to the top of the Filmstrip until it turns into a double-ended arrow. Then click and drag the Filmstrip smaller or larger as needed.

Two buttons appear at the bottom of the left side (shown in figure 5-1): Copy and Paste. These allow you to copy settings from any adjusted image and apply them (paste) to another photo by selecting another image on the Filmstrip.

Below the image in the central work area is a simple toolbar (which you can also turn on and off, as you do in Library, by using T), shown in figure 5-5. From left, this includes buttons for the full view of the image (Loupe view) and a comparison view (showing before and after). These controls are context sensitive and not always visible. Clicking specific adjustments in the right panel changes what appears.

5-5

Using Crop and Straighten

One of the first things I like to do with an image is to crop and straighten it. I try to be careful, but often I get images that are a little crooked. I go here first to remove distractions — technically, I cannot remove anything in Lightroom as the adjustments are nondestructive; however, cropping does then show an image that features only the important parts of the image. I don't want to have to continue to look at a crooked photo as I go along, nor do I want to be adjusting parts of a photo that are unimportant or just annoying. All of that takes you away from your actual work.

You do the actual cropping of an image by clicking the Crop Overlay button (you can also use the letter R) located at the left in the toolbar in the right panel, as shown in figure 5-6. This is a simple function to use, but it is different from most crop tools you may be used to. After you click the Crop Overlay button, immediately a bounding box shows up around the photo. You can click and drag any side, from any point, or the corners to crop the image. In order to make your cropped area fit the photo, you have to move the cursor into the frame and click and drag the image directly. The cropped out area shows up as a dimmed part of the photo, as shown in figure 5-7. As

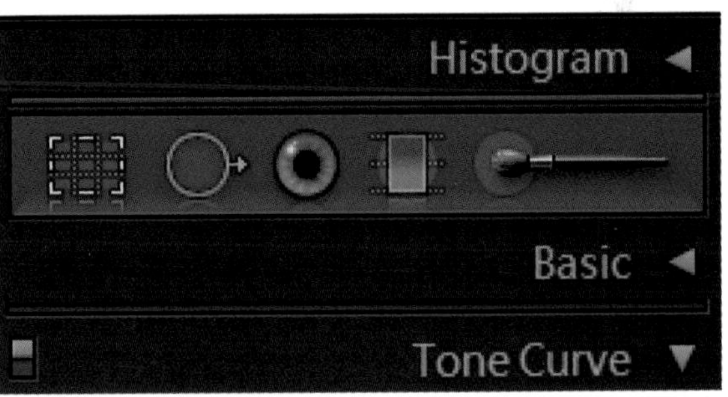

5-6

you move the edges, you see that a faint grid overlays the image. This is based on the classic "rule of thirds" for composition and can help you better define where the crop should be.

Once you engage the Crop Overlay tool, you get a new set of controls appearing on the right panel, as shown in figure 5-7. You can click on the Crop tool to allow you to click-and-drag a cropped area on the image. Aspect forces the tool to crop to a specific aspect ratio by using the drop-down menu that appears when you click the word before the lock icon. Clicking the lock icon locks your Crop tool to the original aspect ratio of the image; otherwise you are free to crop at any aspect ratio.

Press Enter/Return or double-click inside the cropped area and you will only see your cropped version displaying in all modules of Lightroom as well as the Filmstrip. A little square, black symbol also appears on the image in the Filmstrip to show that a crop has been made. You can go back to the original by using the History palette or by clicking the Crop Overlay button, and then clicking Reset.

You can also move your cursor outside of the box to rotate the cropped area when the Crop Overlay tool is active. When you do this, the cursor changes to a curved cursor with arrows at both ends. A grid shows up over the image so you can better line up parts of the image as you rotate it, as shown in figure 5-8. This can be a quick and easy way to fix a crooked photo.

Once you rotate an image, you see a number for the angle of change appear over the Straighten slider. You can move that slider to straighten more (the grid reappears), but a more accurate way of straightening

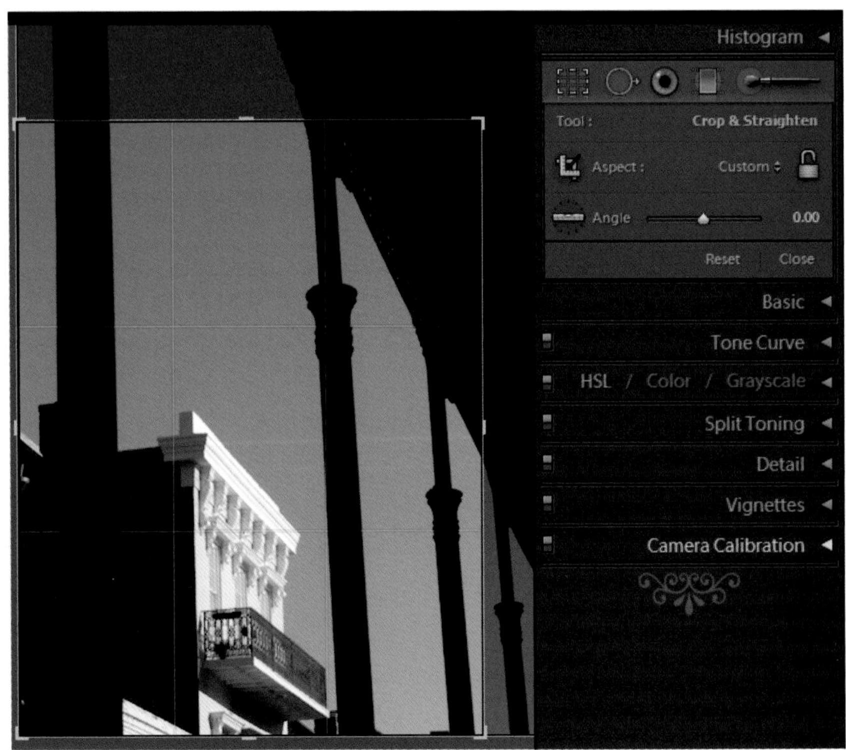

5-7

5-8

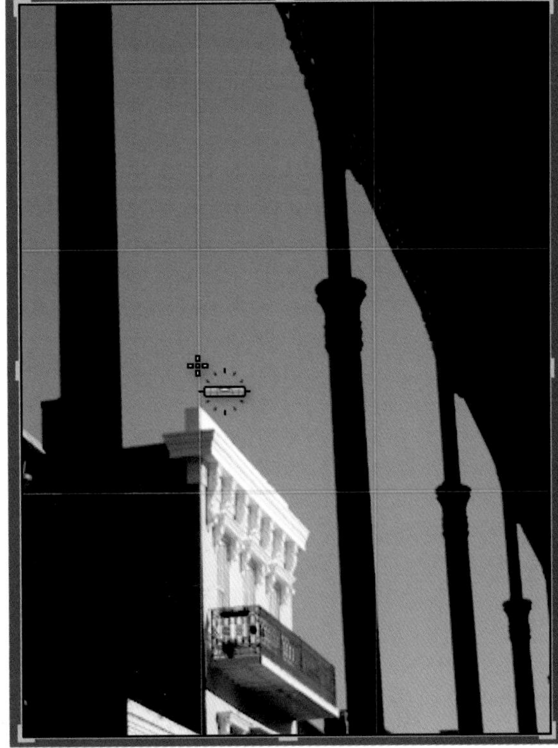

5-9

a photo is to use the Straightening tool. Click the tool that looks like a carpenter's level and your cursor changes to that icon along with cross hairs, as shown in figure 5-9, that show exactly where you will click the image. Now you can click and drag a line across something that should be horizontal or vertical and Lightroom automatically rotates the image to match.

If you want a specific crop setting, you can accomplish that quite easily by clicking the arrows to the right of Original in the toolbar (Original shows up when you first click the Crop Overlay button; Custom shows up when you make a cropping adjustment) to get the Crop Settings menu. There is a set of preset dimensions you can use or you can set your own at Enter Custom. When you choose a specific size, your cropping only fits the proportion you chose.

To get out of the crop mode, simply press the Escape key (Esc) or click again on the Crop Overlay button in the toolbar.

PRO TIP

If you forget any of this, that's no problem because, unlike Photoshop, Lightroom doesn't actually make the crop at this point. You can change it at any time. Lightroom only remembers the instructions for the crop and makes it permanent only when the photo is exported from the program.

The Importance of Black and White

This isn't a section about how to work with monochrome images. If you are familiar with my books and articles, you know how important I think properly setting black and white points is to the photographer. With a good, solid black in the image and a carefully chosen white, a number of key things happen to your photograph, as illustrated by figure 5-10:

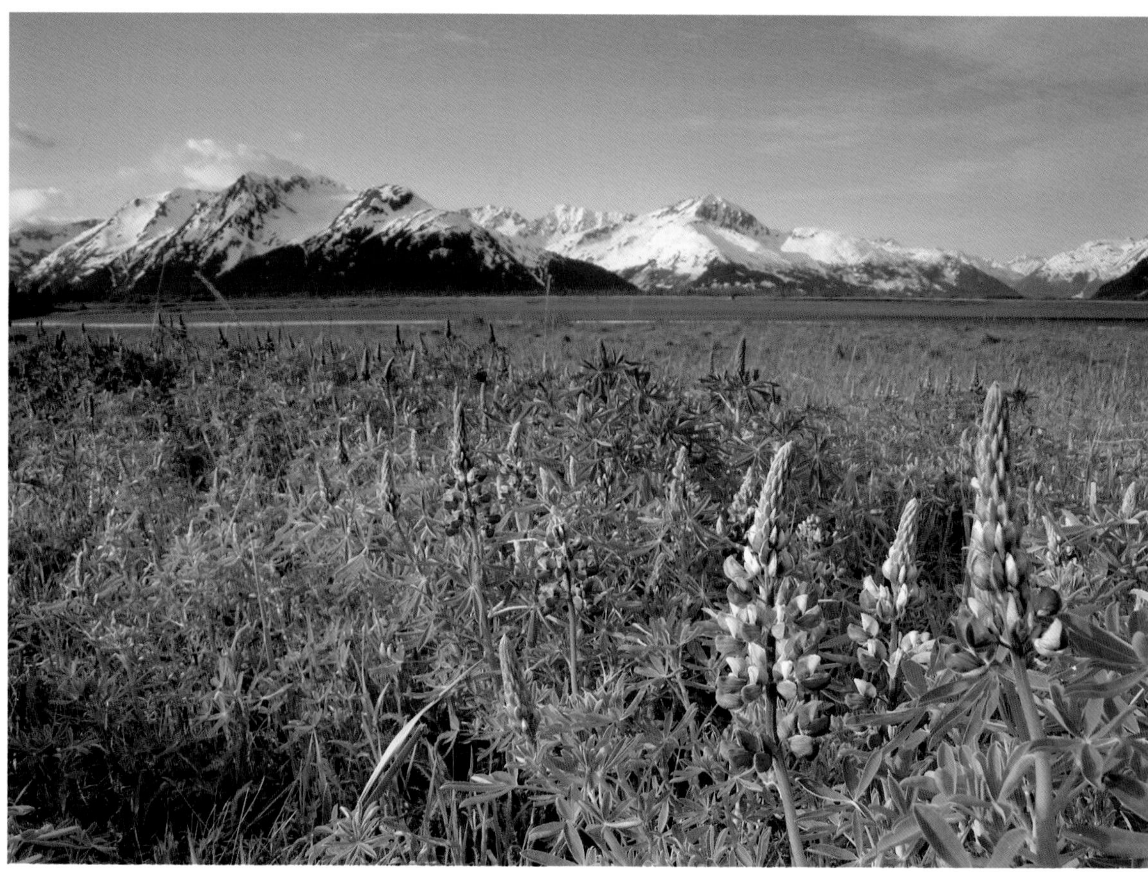

5-10

- Good contrast starts with something in the image that is pure black and something that is pure white (unless you are shooting a fog, which will not need either).
- Good color comes from having a solid black and a key white in the image.
- Midtones are set best when played against carefully chosen black and white.
- A good print starts with the proper black and white.

Consider this: Your printer, your monitor, and a published page all have the capability of showing off a range of tones from black to white. If your image does not match that, your image cannot look its best because it is using less than the output medium or device offers. This would be like expecting a car to go from 0 to 60 mph in four seconds, but only pushing the gas pedal down part way.

Your camera typically will not capture blacks optimally for your scene. Why? Because the engineers who designed your camera developed a compromise for capturing tonality that would allow the photographer more options for controlling dark tones; that is, brighter dark tones. Very often cameras will not capture a pure black from a scene because of that, which results in an image with weaker contrast and color than one would expect from a photograph. You see this all the time from photographers who think that they are "purists" by not adjusting their images, when, in fact, they are "adjusting" their images by using adjustments set up by engineers in Japan (mostly) who have never seen their subjects!

Lightroom, just like Photoshop and Camera Raw, gives you some excellent tools for setting black and white points. I often refer to this as "setting blacks and whites." I know this is not grammatically correct as there is only one black and one white, but I believe this is a good way to think about black and white in a photo. If you think about setting the "blacks," that is, the multiple small areas in a photo that should be black, you think differently about the photograph than if you think about setting a black point. In fact, Lightroom uses this very term.

PRO TIP

For much of your work in the Develop module, you may find it best to hide the left panel of Presets and the Filmstrip. This gives you a larger image space for your central work area, plus it removes distractions from the processing. You get a cleaner image of the photo you are working on.

Getting a good black is not an either/or option. It is a choice based on craft (how you work a photo), subject and composition influences (both affect what should be black), your personal taste, the needs of the end user of your photo, and creativity (your personal approach to an image). If you think about setting the blacks, your mind is more fluid and, I believe, more likely to see the whole idea of black differently. I have found from my workshops that photographers seem to respond better to the idea of "setting the blacks" versus setting a black point.

Setting Blacks and Whites

Once you have selected the proper image in Library, or from the filmstrip at the bottom, click the Basic group of controls in Develop to open them, as shown in figure 5-11. There are 13 different controls here. I recommend you start with the controls that affect blacks and whites first, because they affect everything else.

5-11

Start with Blacks in the Tone group, which, logically, adjusts the blacks, then go to Exposure, which adjusts whites (not so logically). I set my blacks first because setting blacks is more flexible and subjective than setting most whites, plus it can have a huge effect right away on your photo.

1. **Hold down the Alt/Option key and click and drag the Blacks slider to the right to start.** The white screen that appears (shown in figure 5-12) is the black threshold screen showing where blacks are beginning to appear (colors are simply where color channels have reached their maximum darkness). Read this by watching where the blacks appear and comparing that to the actual image (release Alt/Option). Don't worry if the actual image looks dark at this point.

PRO TIP

You can't be a slave to this technique for setting blacks and whites (or anything else in Lightroom if it doesn't work for you). If blacks are too strong for a subject, the photo will look heavy and flat in the dark areas. In some photos, you naturally have bright areas that are blown out (without detail), and that is okay. You just want to be sure that bright areas that need detail have detail.

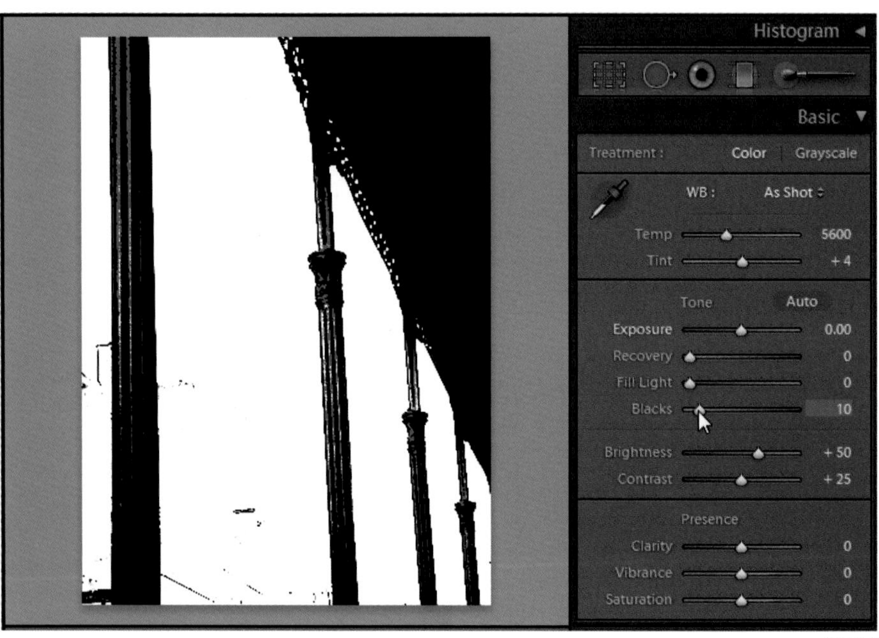

5-12

5 Basic Workflow in the Develop Module

2. **Tweak the blacks by going back and forth from the threshold display to color (alternately pressing and releasing Alt/Option) and seeing what is happening to the image.** How much to bring the blacks in is totally dependent on what you expect from the photo and your style. There is no absolute.

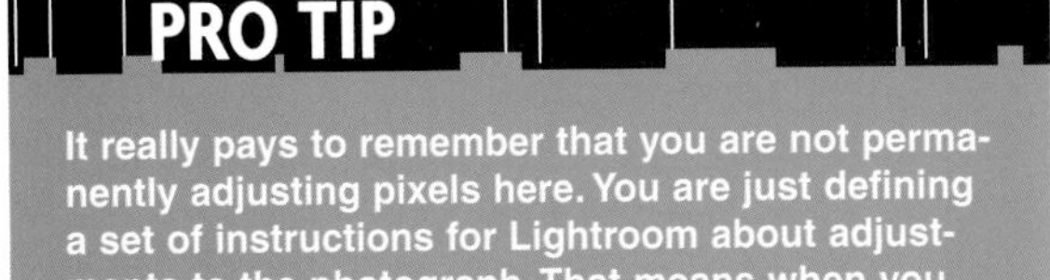

PRO TIP

It really pays to remember that you are not permanently adjusting pixels here. You are just defining a set of instructions for Lightroom about adjustments to the photograph. That means when you have made other adjustments that make your blacks look wrong, for example, you can go back and readjust the blacks at any time.

3. **Now work the whites.** Hold down the Alt/Option key and click and drag the Exposure slider to the left or right to bring in the white. The black screen that appears is the white threshold screen (shown in figure 5-13) showing where whites are beginning to appear. (Colors are simply where color channels have reached their brightest.) White adjustment is very sensitive, much more sensitive than blacks. In most photos, I suggest moving the slider until the screen is mostly black and the whites (or colors) just barely begin to appear, such as you see in figure 5-13. This will probably be too strong. Back off that adjustment until the photo looks right. Still, this is subjective, and you have to decide what the photo needs. Lightroom is also quite good at bringing detail out of bright areas, so you might be able to use both Exposure and Recovery to get the whites right.

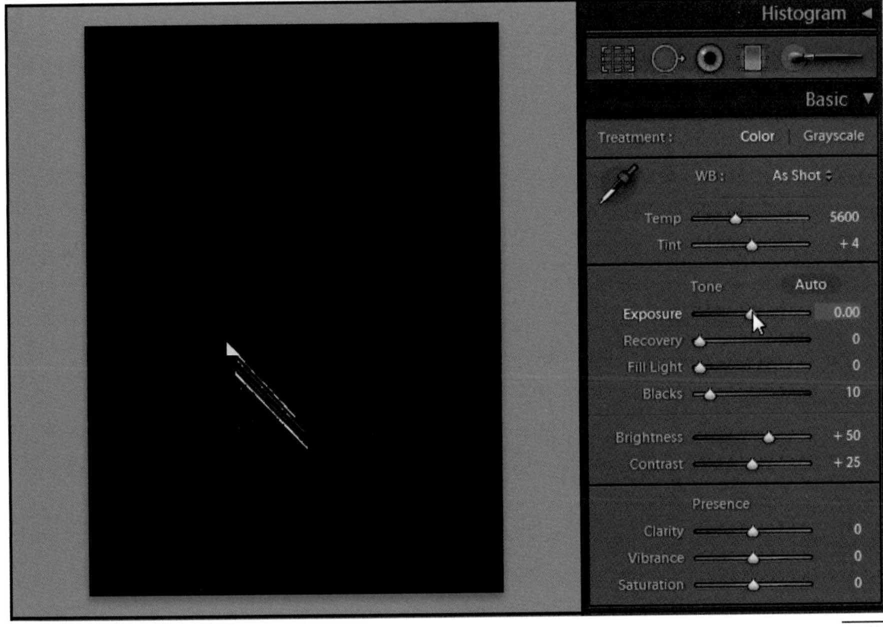

5-13

Recovery and Fill Light

Recovery and Fill Light are two extremely useful controls in Develop. They affect the highlight and shadow tones, respectively, and can really make a difference in gaining detail in those areas. They are quite easy to use.

Start with Fill Light as it will have the most important effect on most photographs. Increasing Fill Light values pulls out detail from the darkest areas of the image without affecting anything else or making pure blacks gray. This can be a very useful way of opening up dark areas in an image, as shown in figure 5-14.

Fill Light is an interesting control. I often use it to lift the brightness of the dark areas and give them a little more life. Yet, increasing Fill Light too much makes an image look unnatural and instantly tells your viewer that you "did something" to the photo. Try boosting Fill Light to 100 and you can see what I mean. You can't just use lower numbers, either, as they can make certain images look just as odd. The actual amount is dependent on the photo. Also, as you work with Fill Light, you may want to recheck your blacks to be sure they are still where you want them to be.

Increasing the Recovery values works to pull out added detail from the brightest areas of the image without affecting anything else and without making pure whites gray. I recommend enlarging the photo by going to Loupe view and clicking the image in an area where you want to find more highlight detail, as shown in figure 5-15. This slider is not going to create miracles with an overexposed photo, but you will find it helpful to gain more definition in bright areas.

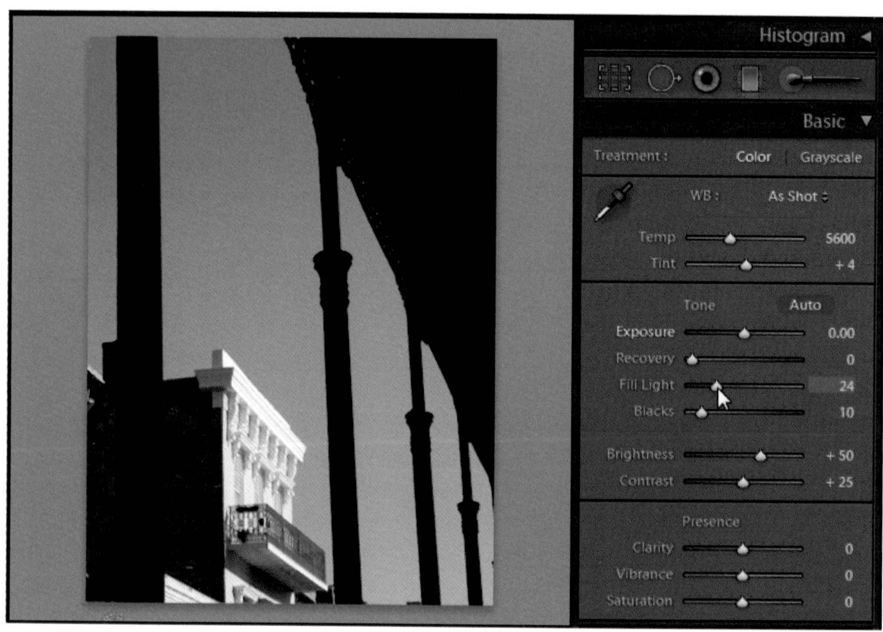

5-14

5-15

Adjusting Midtones

Once you have your blacks and whites set (including the darkest and brightest tones with Fill Light and Recovery), you need to adjust midtones. This is really a broader group of tones than purely the middle value tones in a photo, but you adjust them with the same control. They include every tonality between black and white. They are often grouped into sections according to brightness, from shadow to middle tones to highlight tones. Midtone adjustments affect the overall brightness or darkness to an image, especially in specific tonalities, and therefore, the colors of the image, plus the contrast. Setting blacks and whites does affect contrast and color, too, which is why you need to do that first.

You can set midtones in the following ways: Recovery and Fill Light for the brightest tones, Brightness and Contrast for simple adjustments (they work well together), and the Tone Curve. Brightness and Contrast are better than Brightness/Contrast in Photoshop, but still not my preference for midtones. They are a little too coarse for my taste, but I do use them for simple, quick adjustments to an image that doesn't need a lot of midtone change at this point or later in the process after I've made some local adjustments and just need a bit of overall brightness or contrast affected.

For most midtone adjustments, use the Tone Curve.

PRO TIP

Most controls in Lightroom are "scrubbable," especially in Develop. What this means is that if you put your cursor over the numbers box for a control, it turns into an adjustment cursor (you see it change to a double arrow with a hand), and then you can click and drag the control directly without typing in numbers or clicking exactly on the slider.

Tone Curve Work

Lightroom 1.0 brought a totally new approach to using curves (in the Tone Curve section of the right panel) that was, to that point, unlike anything seen before in Photoshop or Camera Raw. It looks more complex than the traditional Curves of Photoshop, as shown in figure 5-16, but I believe these changes have made this control far easier to use for photographers. The curve graph also includes an overlay of the image luminance histogram for photographers who like to use it.

The Tone Curve uses what are called *parametric sliders* to help adjust the curve. These are very intuitive for photographers as they are based on specific parameters of tonal adjustment, including highlights, lights, darks, and shadows. You simply click and drag a slider to both change that tonality as well as move the curve appropriately. These sliders are also limited in the range they can adjust to keep the results more photographic.

Most of the time I work directly with the parametric sliders. Sliders include Highlights, Lights, Darks, and Shadows. One thing that is really cool about these sliders is how their area of adjustment shows up on the Tone Curve. As soon as your cursor moves over one of these controls, a shaded area showing where it works appears on the Tone Curve graph, as shown in figure 5-17. That makes this so much easier to understand, as you can see immediately where the control is going to change the curve. Here are tips on using these four sliders:

> **Choose a slider to work with based on the photo.** If the highlights seem to be the biggest issue, start with them. If the light midtones mainly need brightening, work the lights first. If the dark midtones really are the challenge, go to that slider. If the shadows could be darker or lighter to better affect the look of the image, go with them. However, you can't go wrong with any of them, as you can always readjust as you go.

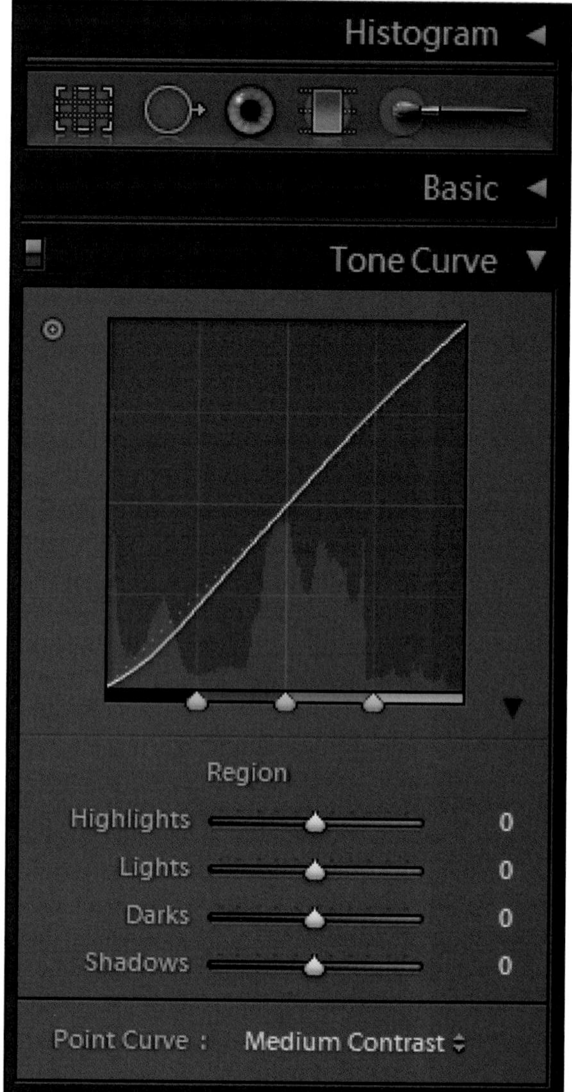

5-16

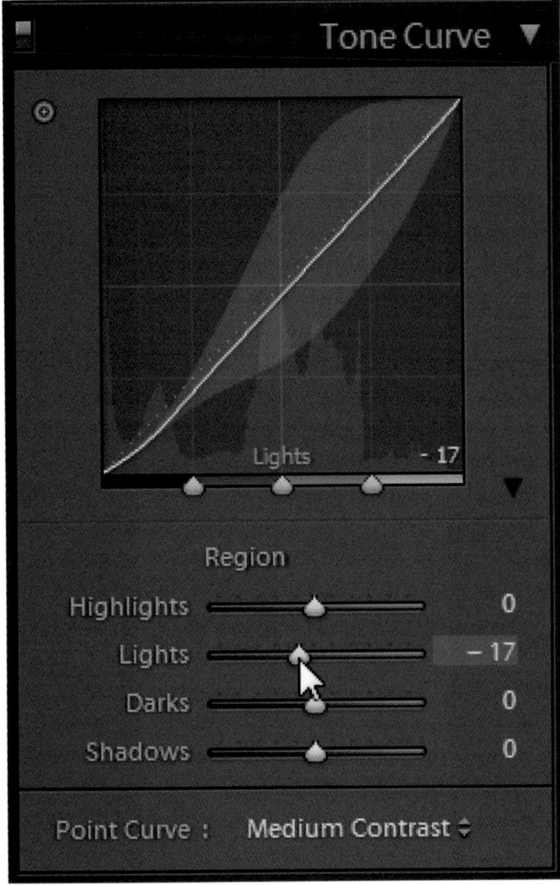

5-17

PRO TIP

To reset any individual setting in Develop, double-click on the name of that setting to the left of a slider or on the slider pointer itself. That resets it to zero. If you make a change in an adjustment and only want to reverse that change, simply use the traditional Undo command of Ctrl/⌘+Z. To reset a section of Develop, press Alt/Option and you will see a Reset button appear. Click it.

> **Go directly to the curve if you are familiar with traditional Curves.** As you move your cursor along the curve, you see the same shaded areas for adjustment showing up, plus you see the terms — Highlights, Lights, Darks, and Shadows — appear at the bottom of the graph. You can click and drag the curve at any point, though adjustments will be "parametric," by the parameters listed.

> **Use preset curves.** Below the curve, you will find something called Point Curve. This includes a menu that bends the Tone Curve in specific ways — you can use these as a start, and then make further adjustments based on what you see. When you click on the words to the right of Point Curve, you get these choices:

> > **Linear.** This is the standard, straight-line curve of Photoshop. It gives a flatter look to the image than the default does, and may be what you need for your image. I find that it is often a little too flat as a final adjustment, but it comes in handy for more contrasty images and when skin tones of portraits look harsh. I use it to get the curve back to a straight line when working the curve more intensely, as described in the next section.

> > **Medium Contrast.** This has a very slight adjustment to the curve, dropping the darkest tones somewhat and raising the light tones slightly. This gives a nice increase to the contrast of many photos and can be a good place to start.

> > **Strong Contrast.** This increases the effect of Medium Contrast, dropping the dark tones a little more and brightening the light tones a bit. Its increase in contrast is great for low-contrast scenes.

Adjusting the Tone Curve by Dragging in the Photo

My favorite part of the Tone Curve in Develop, and this is really a very cool new way of dealing with image curves, is to move the cursor directly over the photo and click and drag to change the curve shape from there. That's right! You can change the curve by going into the photo, to the areas that need the adjustment. This has never been possible before and makes this control much more photographic rather than technical.

You do this using the Targeted Adjustment tool. The name is dorky (obviously not named by a photographer), but it is really easy to use. Click on the small bull's-eye at the top left of the Tone Curve area to access this control. In figure 5-18, you see the cursor has changed its form, and the Tone Curve now has an area highlighted appropriate to the part of the photo that the cursor is on. Just below the photo, you also see new words appear in the toolbar, Target Group: Tone Curve. Now when you click and drag the cursor on the actual image in the exact part of the tones and colors you want to adjust, the Tone Curve changes with it, moving up as you move the cursor toward the top of the photo, and down as you move the cursor down in the photo, as shown in figure 5-19. Finally, if you make an adjustment in one area, and then move the cursor to another tonality in the photo, the Tone Curve immediately updates and allows you to adjust there as well, as shown in figure 5-20.

I believe this part of Tone Curve is a revolutionary way of dealing with midtones and is well worth spending some time trying it out. For me, it truly is highly photographic because you are going directly into the photo to deal with the midtones as you move your cursor around rather than adjusting a curve that is separate (and visually very different) from the image itself. You simply go through the photo clicking and dragging up or down wherever you need a tone brightened or darkened.

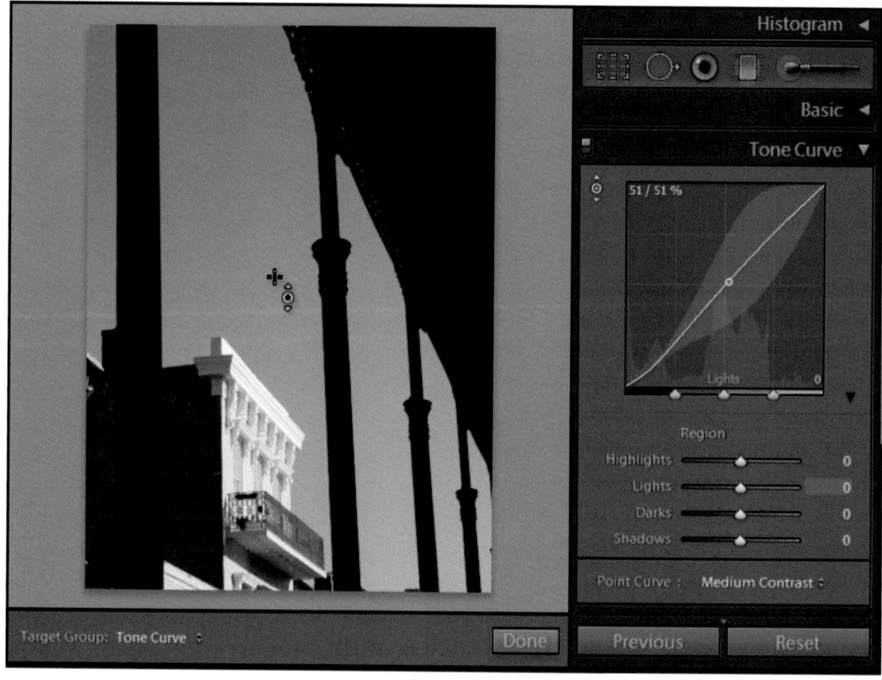

5-18

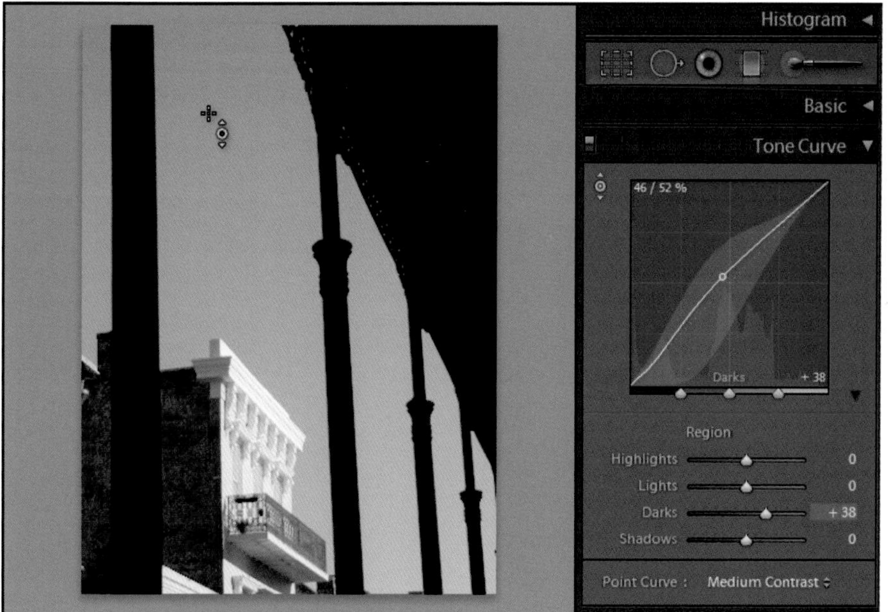
Histogram
Basic
Tone Curve
46 / 52 %
Darks + 38
Region
Highlights 0
Lights 0
Darks + 38
Shadows 0
Point Curve : Medium Contrast

5-19

Histogram
Basic
Tone Curve
12 / 15 %
Shadows + 25
Region
Highlights 0
Lights 0
Darks + 38
Shadows + 25
Point Curve : Medium Contrast

5-20

Using Clarity to Define Midtones

Clarity came into Lightroom in the first version, but was not there when the program was first introduced. It is a helpful addition to the program as it affects midtone details in a specific way.

Some Photoshop users often used a special technique with Unsharp Mask, not for sharpening, but for enhancing differences in midtone detail. To do this, they would use a very high Radius setting (40–60) and a low sharpness (20). This brought out the differences among tones in the middle range of details in an image.

Clarity does something very similar. It looks for differences in tonalities and gives them more contrast so they stand out. In Lightroom 2, the Clarity slider got a negative adjustment as well as a positive adjustment. Now you can both increase and decrease these detail tonal differences. You can see what this control does to the building details in figures 5-21, 5-22, and 5-23, which show no adjustment, full positive adjustment, and full negative adjustment, respectively.

In most photos with some important midtone detail, I find Clarity works well at around 30–50 points. For nature, travel, and architectural photos, I almost always use it to some degree, but I watch out for how small areas of tonality change. For portraits, you need to be careful because increasing Clarity can make skin tones look harsh. You may even need to use a negative amount of Clarity for people photos.

5-21

Histogram
Basic
Treatment :
Color
Grayscale
WB :
As Shot
Temp
5600
Tint
+ 4
Tone
Auto
Exposure
0.00
Recovery
25
Fill Light
23
Blacks
10
Brightness
+ 50
Contrast
+ 25
Presence
Clarity
+ 100
Vibrance
0
Saturation
0

5-22

Histogram
Basic
Treatment :
Color
Grayscale
WB :
As Shot
Temp
5600
Tint
+ 4
Tone
Auto
Exposure
0.00
Recovery
25
Fill Light
23
Blacks
10
Brightness
+ 50
Contrast
+ 25
Presence
Clarity
– 100
Vibrance
0
Saturation
0

5-23

Histogram

At the top of the right panel in Develop is a color histogram, shown in figure 5-24. For photographers who understand it, it can be a useful tool, although I am not convinced most photographers need it to use Lightroom effectively.

5-24

Basically it shows you where brightness values in a photograph are from black at the left to white at the right. Because it is a color RGB histogram, it shows this graphed in color, using three separate graphs for the red, green, and blue channels (other colors appear when these overlap). When these values are cut off at either side, the image loses detail because the blacks (left) or whites (right) are clipped. That means no detail is possible (it is clipped off) beyond those edges.

You can get a visual representation of this clipping by hovering your cursor over the arrows at the top-right and -left corners of the histogram, as shown in figure 5-25. Clipped shadows show up as blue; highlights appear as red. Figure 5-25 is correctly adjusted to gain strong, graphic blacks in the shadows. I rarely use this because, for me, the colors are so strong that they distract from the adjustments I am doing. You can see that in figure 5-25. You can also click on the arrows to keep these clipping warnings on, but I find this even more distracting.

That said, the histogram itself can be useful. In general, you do not want to have big gaps at either side. Adjusting blacks and whites as described earlier in this chapter will usually prevent that. But when you have big gaps and you want to quickly deal with them, you can click and drag in the histogram to adjust Blacks and Fill Light (left side) plus Exposure and Recovery (right side). As soon as you move your cursor over the histogram, you will see the appropriate adjustment name appear at the bottom, as shown in figure 5-26. You can even hold down the Alt/Option key to see threshold screens, which are much better than the blue and red clipping warnings.

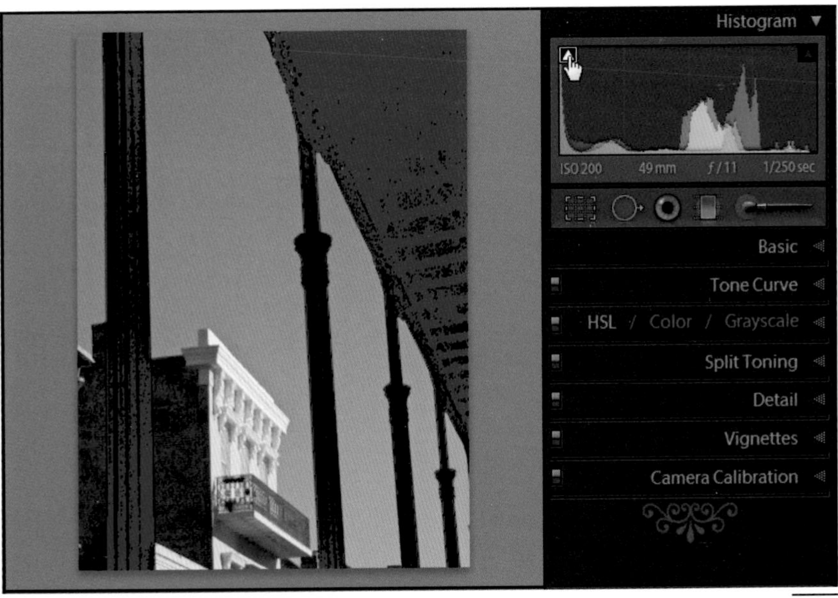

5-25

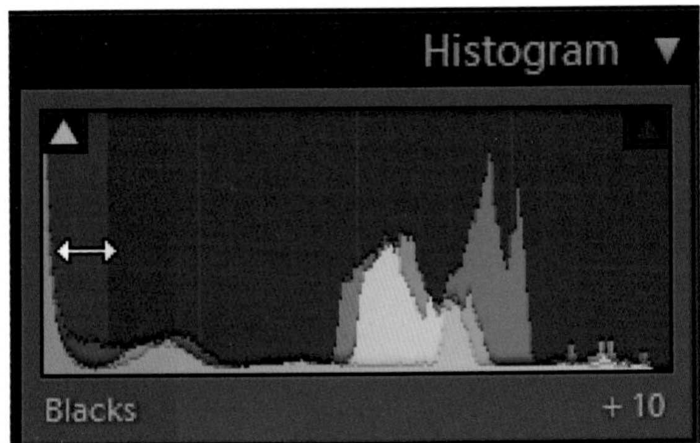

5-26

Color Settings

It is easy to look at Lightroom, Photoshop, or Camera Raw and consider color to be a separate function from tonal adjustments simply because there are separate color controls. However, it is really important to understand that color is tightly associated with tonalities in a photo. If your blacks and whites are not set properly, then colors do not have the right snap and vibrancy. If midtones are not adjusted well, colors never look quite right.

This has been a real problem in nature photography, especially when photographers made the transition to digital. Many photographers wanted the look of Velvia slide film and would try to do this by using saturation alone. That is not the best approach and typically gives garish rather than saturated color. A different misinterpretation of digital came from photojournalists who thought that cameras captured color accurately so they thought they were being pure by not adjusting color. That also is not the best approach because it often gave inaccurate colors based on an arbitrary interpretation of a scene by the camera.

All photography is interpretation — pick up three different camera models, point them at the same scene, and you will get slightly different results. In addition, camera engineers must create sensors and camera electronics that give a somewhat bland interpretation of the world so that they work for all photographers. (It is easier to adjust a bland set of colors and tones than to tweak something that has a lot of strong color or tonality.)

I believe good color starts with blacks and whites, period. Once they are set and midtones are adjusted for the image, then you can work on color. Lightroom offers you multiple ways to adjust color in your photo. Each is valuable in its own way. First I discuss what your choices are, and then I go into specifics on how you can best use them. Lightroom has these color controls on the right side of the Develop module:

NOTE

Lightroom color controls are not grouped in one location but are found in the Basic, HSL/Color/Grayscale, Split Toning, and Camera Calibration groups.

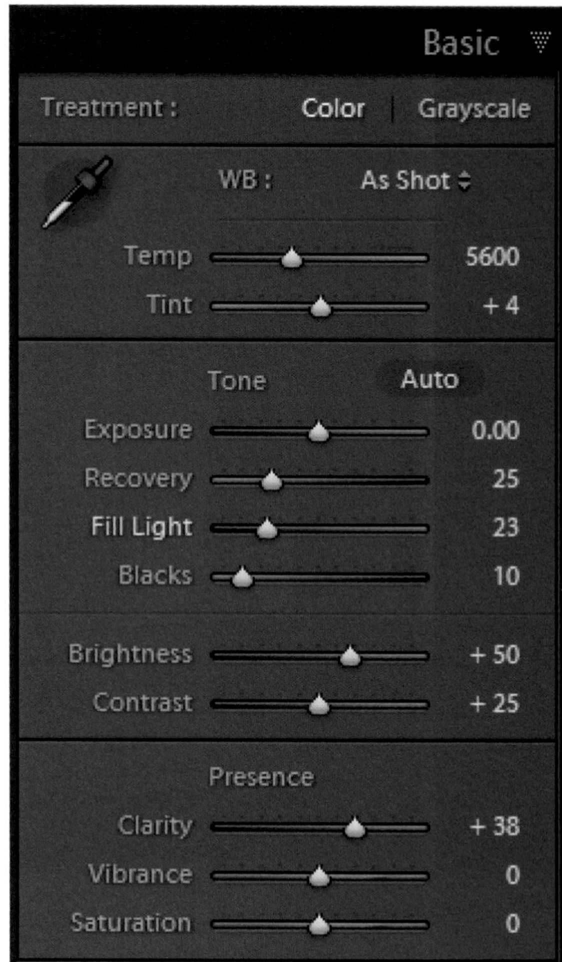

5-27

- **White Balance Selector.** This is an eyedropper in the Basic section, shown in figure 5-27, that lets you quickly color-correct images.
- **Color in the Basic Group.** This includes White Balance (WB), Temp, Tint, Vibrance, and Saturation, as shown in figure 5-27. Temp and Tint are really subsets of White Balance. You can also change a photo to black and white here by using the Grayscale button.
- **HSL Color Tuning.** This is a wonderful color section that offers a huge amount of control. It is a part of Lightroom that I think every photographer must master. I discuss it in Chapter 6.
- **Split Toning.** While this control was originally designed for black and white images, it offers some interesting controls for color photos, too. Not every photographer will find it useful, though. I discuss it in Chapter 6.
- **Camera Calibration.** This control comes directly from Camera Raw. While it can help refine the colors of an image and allow you to calibrate a camera to a degree, I find that it is not that useful for most photographers. I discuss it in Chapter 6.

PRO TIP

Sometimes it can be confusing if all adjustment sections of the Develop right side panel are open. You can make Lightroom only open one section at a time by using Solo mode, which actually works with all panels. Right-click one of the section headings and use the menu to find Solo mode. You will also note that you can turn off sections you don't use by clicking the check marks.

White Balance Color Adjustments

White Balance is a terrific tool for the digital photographer. It is one of the truly digital innovations that makes photography better. It wasn't that long ago that any photographer had some serious challenges making colors look just right in conditions that weren't optimum for the film. Slide film, especially, had a very low tolerance for out-of-whack lighting colors. The term was color balance for film, but White Balance does the same thing. White balance simply refers to making white and neutral tones neutral.

With White Balance controls, both in the camera and in the computer, problem colors under normal lighting are largely a thing of the past. Any photographer who has shot under fluorescent lighting, for example, will remember how hard it was to get good color. Now you can easily get natural color in situations that would have required a great deal of work in the past with color filtration over the lens, color temperature meters, film tests, and so on.

There are two basic ways to deal with the color balance of an image in Lightroom:

> **NOTE**
>
> I have to qualify the idea that White Balance controls can give good color under any light. Limited spectrum lighting, such as that from sodium vapor lamps, cannot be fully corrected because the camera doesn't capture a full range of color from it. And when lighting conditions are mixed, such as incandescent combined with window light from the sky, you will usually need to adjust individual colors in a photo differently. While some of that can be done with Lightroom's new local adjustments, often you need to go to Photoshop with its capability to use adjustment layers and layer masks.

- **Quick-and-easy.** Use the White Balance Selector tool in the Basic group.
- **Ultimate control.** Use the White Balance controls in the same group.

Quick-and-Easy Color Correction

The White Balance Selector tool acts like similar tools in Camera Raw and Photoshop. You simply click something in the photo and the program adjusts the image so that whatever you clicked becomes a neutral tone and everything else in the image adjusts accordingly. Here's how to use it:

1. **Select the White Balance Selector tool by clicking the icon or pressing W.** The White Balance Selector tool is that giant eyedropper icon in the Basic group, shown in figure 5-28. Well, maybe not giant, but it really is large and not in proportion with the rest of the settings. Check the toolbar under the photo and deselect Auto Dismiss, as shown in figure 5-29. Be sure Show Loupe is selected. Auto Dismiss parks the White Balance Selector tool back where it started when you click on the photo. Show Loupe gives the block of colors explained next.

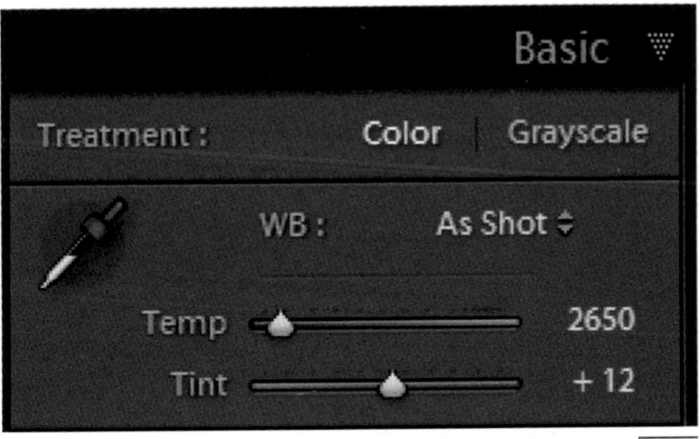

5-28

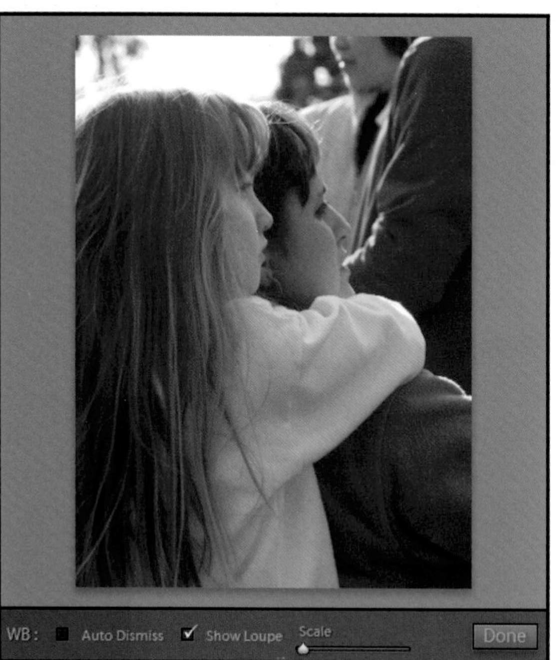

5-29

2. **Move the cursor over the image.** It is now an eyedropper. You see a block of colors appear next to it (this is from Show Loupe and can be changed with the Scale slider), as shown in figure 5-30. This shows you the color pixels that the White Balance Selector tool is looking at so you can look for something that should be a neutral white, gray, or black without color cast. The center pixel is the actual one that the control uses for adjustment.

3. **Watch the Navigator for overall color changes.** As you move the cursor over the image, the potential change is reflected in the Navigator preview, as shown in figure 5-30. The change does not occur on the image until you actually click the mouse.

5-30

4. **Find what might work best and click that tone.** The whole image shifts in color, as shown in figure 5-31. If it looks good (or close), click Done or click the eyedropper back in its parking spot. You can now tweak that color slightly using the other WB (white balance) controls in the Basic group.

5. **If the image color does not appear to be corrected properly or even looks really bad, just try clicking a different spot.** Sometimes you have to click multiple locations for this to work its best. (This is why it is a good idea to deselect Auto Dismiss.)

Keep going if a click or two doesn't give you the results you want. Do remember where you click because you might get a good, though not perfect, result that you want to go back to.

NOTE

If you select Auto Dismiss at the bottom of the center panel, you can only click once; the image changes and the Selector tool disappears. I don't find this very useful.

Very often the White Balance Selector tool gives you excellent results all by itself. Other times you have to do more adjusting with the white balance adjustments of Basic.

White Balance Controls in Basic

The White Balance section of Basic starts with actual white balance settings based on how your camera shot the scene. You could have shot this with the camera on Auto or a preset such as Sun or Cloudy. The first choice that appears to the right of White

5-31

Balance is always As Shot. Even if you used Auto, the camera still makes a choice as to how to deal with the color of the light.

Here's how to use the White Balance controls (shown in figure 5-32):

1. **If the color balance of your photo looks pretty good, leave the White Balance choices alone.** Going through them can quickly increase your work time when you don't need them.
2. **If you are not sure about the overall color of the image, try the White Balance Selector tool first.** If you click the arrows to the right of Custom, you see Auto as a choice. You can always try it to see if it helps, but I rarely use it because it can be rather arbitrary.
3. **Try the WB menu.** If you click on Custom or As Shot, you will get a menu of choices that look like the white balance settings from your camera. They are not the same as the settings on your camera; they are Adobe's interpretations of these settings, but they can give you a start in adjusting the color of a photo.

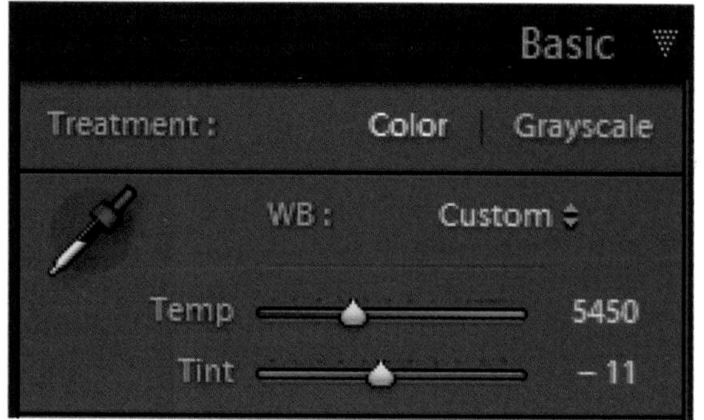

5-32

4. **If the photo seems a little too cold (cool) or warm, use Temp to change that.** The photo gets bluer when you move the slider to the left and more amber when you move it to the right. This can also be a creative control to make a photo warmer or colder (cooler) than it was actually shot.
5. **Tint affects a different continuum of color, from green at the left of the slider to magenta to the right.** Unless you have some idea for wacky creative color, normally, you will use this in small amounts. A very common use of this slider is to add magenta to get rid of a greenish cast to the photo.

Vibrance and Saturation Adjustments

Adobe purchased the very nicely done RawShooter software technology during its development of Lightroom. RawShooter always had a better saturation adjustment than Photoshop in its Vibrance control. Lightroom developers have now included both Vibrance and Saturation under the Presence section in Basic, as shown in figure 5-33.

Equate the Saturation slider with caution. There is a tendency among photographers, especially nature photographers, to boost this saturation control way too much. This is a pretty heavy-handed way of dealing with color. Too much use of this slider can easily result in gaudy, unattractive colors at worst, and out of place colors at best. Because of this, I rarely use it.

The gaudy bit often comes from photographers adding a little saturation, then a little more, and a little more, until the whole thing gets out of hand. Another way it happens is when an image has one color that has been recorded poorly; to compensate, the photographer boosts the Saturation control for that color, making the others look bad. If they don't look bad, then they often look out of place: A color that is not central to the subject (or the composition) gets boosted too much, drawing the eye of the viewer away from what is really important in the image.

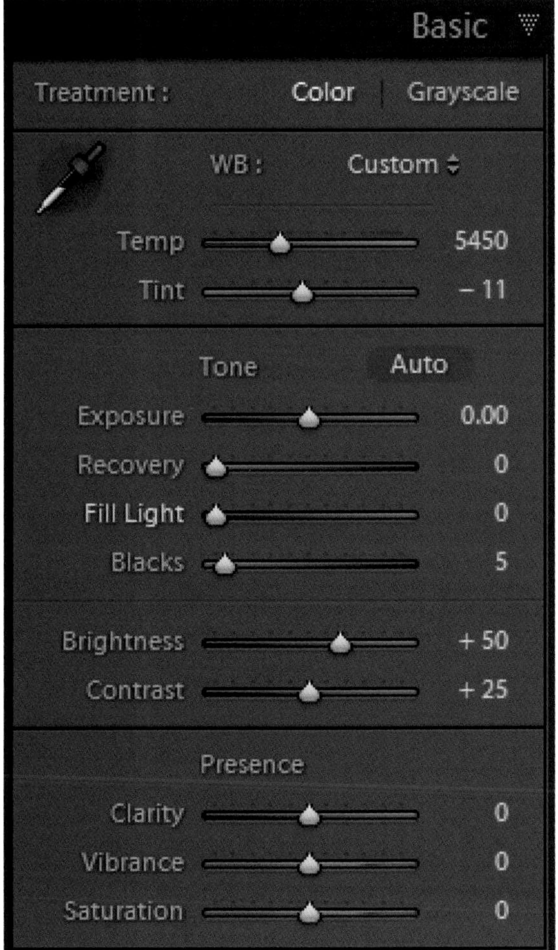

5-33

Vibrance is a better tool for overall saturation control. Colors look richer and detail does not block up as much when using it. It does not saturate everything equally the way that Saturation does. It tends to increase the saturation of less saturated colors more than highly saturated colors. Still, use both sparingly. Keep the Vibrance control in the 0 to 35 range when increasing saturation, and unless you are after some special effect, keep the actual Saturation slider in the 0 to 15 range.

Processing Multiple Images: Using Sync, Copy, and Paste

One of the big benefits of using Lightroom to process a group of photos is that it is so easy to use for that purpose. No, correct that. It is not simply easy; it is a fantastic tool that really speeds up your work. This has become such a part of my workflow that I would really miss it if I had to go back to Photoshop or Camera Raw to process multiple images at the same time.

Frequently, you will have a set of images of a similar subject in the same conditions. If you adjust one photo correctly, you then can adjust them all. This allows you to, in essence, batch-process groups of photos. All of the adjustments in the right-side groups of Develop can be synced to any other images you want. Most of the time, you are largely syncing the core exposure, contrast, and color settings I discuss in this chapter.

Lightroom offers several ways of doing this, but here's what works for me, and it really speeds up my work:

1. **Process one image of a group of similar shots as best as you can.** I like to focus on that image without being distracted by others, as shown in figure 5-34.

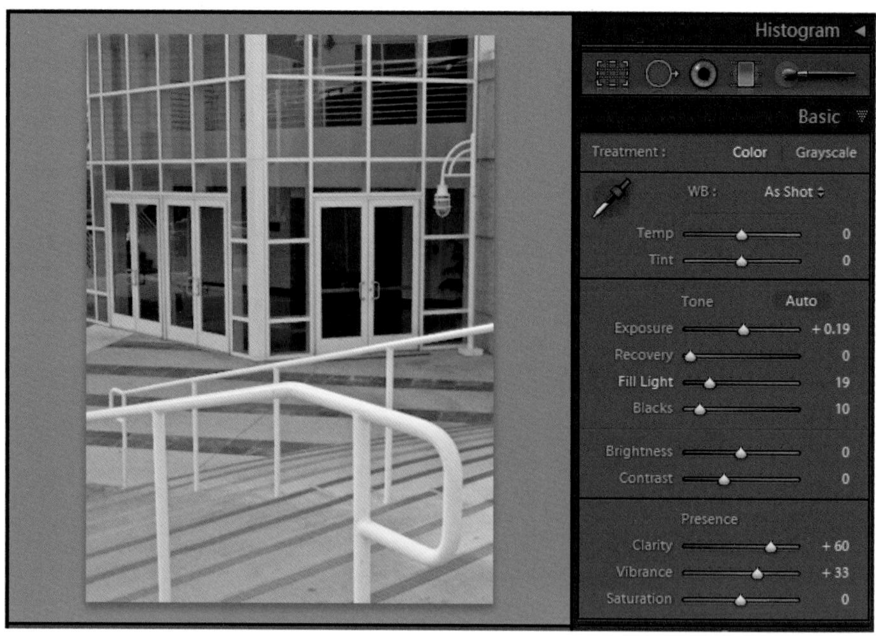

5-34

2. **Go to the Filmstrip and select additional, similar shots by Ctrl/⌘+clicking them.** Your original image is still selected and has a slightly different selected look, as shown in figure 5-35. It is called the First Selected.

5-35

3. **A new button, Sync, appears at the bottom of the right panel, also shown in figure 5-35.** Click it to get the Synchronize Settings dialog box shown in figure 5-36.
4. **Choose as many or as few adjustments as you want to sync.** Nearly everything in Develop is sync-able. Everything you choose will then be applied from the First Selected to the others.
5. **These adjustments are totally changeable.** You can then click your individual photos to be sure the synced adjustments work for each. (You will have to deselect the group by either clicking outside of the group or using Ctrl/⌘+D.)

I find this ability to sync photos a huge benefit to my workflow. And whether you are syncing 2 or 20 photos, the benefits of a more efficient workflow truly come from this button. I do feel that it is important

5-36

to check your photos to be sure you like the adjustments, particularly if the synced photos are not identical. You can also Auto Sync images as you go by Ctrl/⌘+clicking on Sync, but that doesn't work for my process. I like to focus on a single image and deal with the rest after that first one is complete.

The buttons at the bottom of the left panel, Copy and Paste, shown in figure 5-37, do something similar.

Clicking Copy results in the same dialog box, Synchronize Settings, that comes from clicking Sync, and is shown in figure 5-36. This lets you tell Lightroom to copy the adjustments from the active photo. Then you select another photo (or photos) in the Filmstrip and click Paste. That applies the adjustments to those selected images.

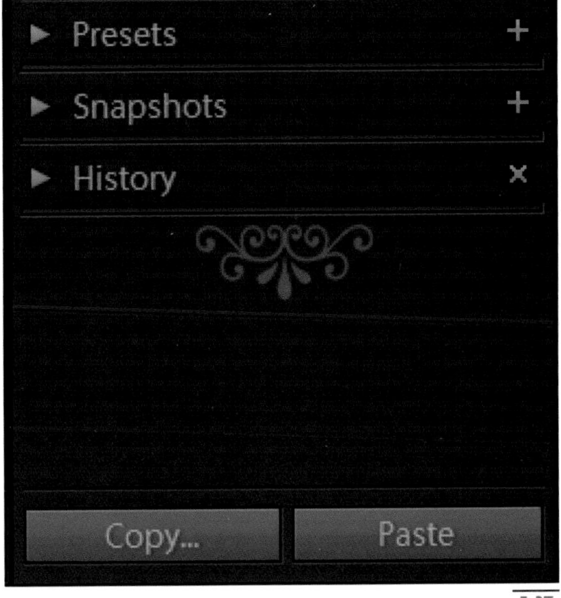

5-37

Working with Sharpening

Skip down to the Detail group in Develop, shown in figure 5-38, and you find some important controls for sharpening and noise reduction. The Sharpening group was a big surprise to everyone working with Lightroom, as it appeared after Lightroom was introduced. This means none of the Lightroom 1.0 books included it, for example. This was an unusual move by Adobe, but the sharpening controls that they added are very good.

You have probably heard the admonition not to sharpen an image until you are done working on it. This is because when you are working directly with pixels, some adjustments can affect the quality of sharpening if you do the sharpening too early in the process. In Lightroom, no adjustments affect any pixels until you export the photo from the program; therefore, theoretically, you could sharpen at any time. In fact, as a default, Lightroom applies sharpening instructions to all photos, as shown in figure 5-38.

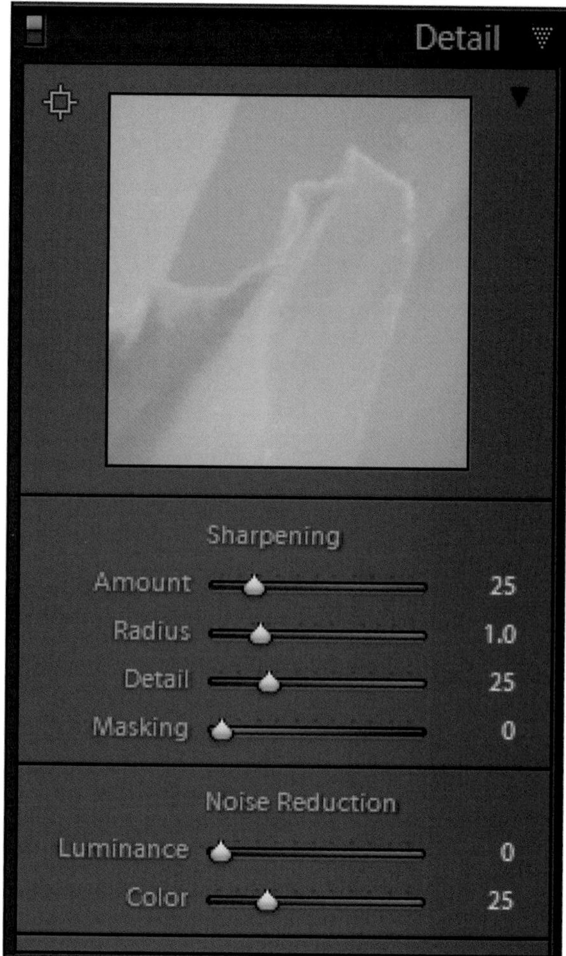

5-38

The Sharpening sliders use more advanced algorithms than Unsharp Mask in Photoshop and have absolutely nothing in common with the Sharpen filter in Photoshop. It is a subjective tool, though. What one photographer considers too little, another thinks is just right, and both photographers will be correct for their particular subjects and uses of the image.

Here's how to use the Sharpening group of sliders:

1. **Pick a detail that should be sharp for the preview in the Detail section of the panel.** Do this by clicking the target icon in the upper-left corner of the Details section, as shown in Figure 5-39, then clicking a spot in the photograph. This places that location at 100% pixel view into the preview.
2. **Enlarge your photo to 100% by clicking in a part of the photo that is sharp, as shown in figure 5-40.**
3. **Start with Amount.** Move the slider to the right until the image looks sharp but details still retain their smoothness, as shown in figure 5-41 (too much sharpening can make the photo look harsh). Amount is the intensity of sharpening. There is a lot of debate as to what is "right" for Amount. This is going to depend on the subject, camera, lens, and personal taste. I find that for my work, 50–70 works well. If colors get distracting, you can change this view to a black-and-white view by pressing Alt/Option as you move the slider.

5-39

5-40

4. **Adjust Radius.** Radius affects how fine details are dealt with by the sharpening algorithms. A higher radius will bring out detail in flatter tones like that shown in figure 5-42, but can hurt small detail. Radius in Lightroom does not act the same as Radius in Photoshop. If you adjust Radius high (and it is high in figure 5-42), you may find you have to reduce Amount. Pressing Alt/Option will momentarily remove color.

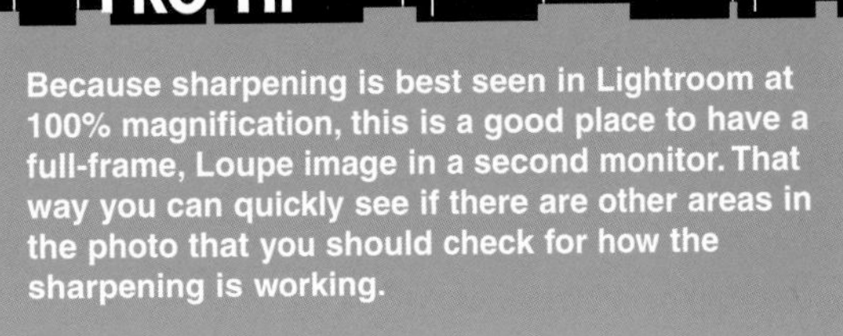

PRO TIP

Because sharpening is best seen in Lightroom at 100% magnification, this is a good place to have a full-frame, Loupe image in a second monitor. That way you can quickly see if there are other areas in the photo that you should check for how the sharpening is working.

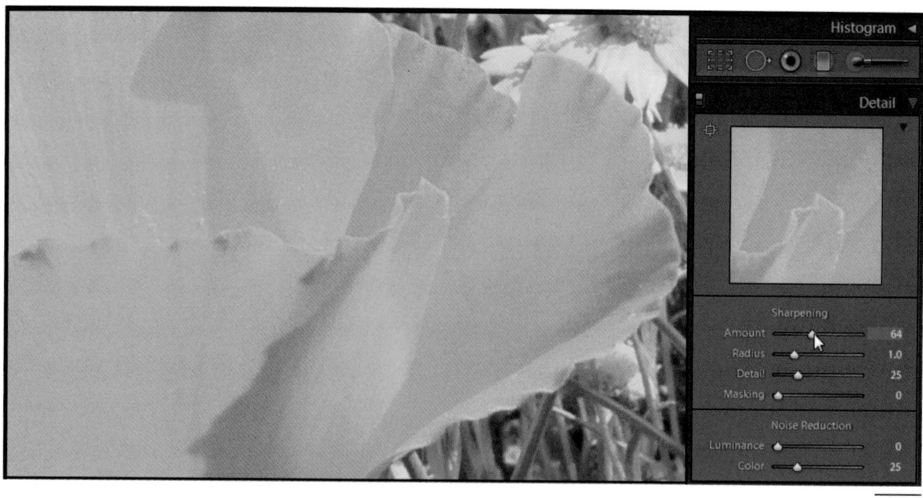

5-41

5-42

5. **Use the Detail slider.** Detail affects the very small detail in an image and interacts with Radius to affect how Radius is applied. You have to watch your photo and its small detail to know what is right, as shown in figure 5-43 (and the Alt/Option key acts the same, too). Photos with broad areas of tone such as in the poppy shown here can start to show too much noise if Detail is too high, yet that same high Detail may be perfect for a photo with a lot of small detail in it.

6. **Try out Masking.** Masking does not do any sharpening. It is a control that allows you to limit sharpening to edges. It must be used as you press Alt/Option, as shown in figure 5-44. (This shows an extreme use of Masking for illustration.) The white areas are sharpened, while the black areas are blocked from being sharpened. This can prevent artifacts such as noise being overly sharpened.

5-43

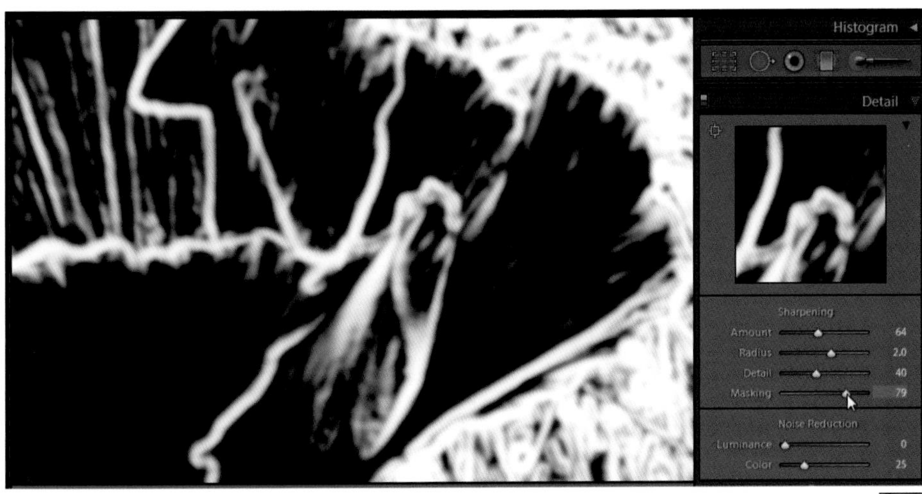

5-44

Be careful not to sharpen too much. One consistent problem among pros and amateurs is that if a photo is not quite as sharp as it should be, these photographers apply a large amount of sharpening, which is usually oversharpening. While it is true that certain subjects, such as a tack-sharp architectural photo or an expansive rocky landscape, can handle more sharpening, others, such as people or soft-focus flowers, can't. You have to decide what is appropriate for your image, but be careful about oversharpening that leads to a harsh quality to fine tonalities. Sharpening in Lightroom is harder to overuse to the degree that Unsharp Mask is, but it still can be overdone.

Working with Noise Reduction

Below Sharpening in Detail, you find Noise Reduction, as shown in figure 5-45. Be especially wary about how you use Noise Reduction sliders. While both can reduce the appearance of noise in an image, they both can remove some of the fine detail in your photo as well if you push the sliders too far to the right. If you have serious noise problems in your photo, I recommend exporting to Photoshop, and then using a specially designed noise reduction plug-in such as Nik Software Dfine. I find that Dfine does an amazing job of removing noise without hurting picture detail.

However, the Detail group of controls does help when your image has a small to moderate amount of noise. Luminance works on general luminance noise (this looks like sand on your image), while Color works strongly on color or chroma noise (this looks like color speckles on your image). Luminance has only a minor effect on color noise and Color has little effect on luminance noise. Look for noise in underexposed photos, images shot with high ISO settings, big areas of a solid tone, and dark areas of a picture.

I recommend you keep Luminance to less than 40 or you can significantly reduce the appearance of sharpness of small details. You may discover, however, that keeping some noise makes your photo look sharper. (This is an old retouching technique — add grain or noise to a slightly out-of-focus image and it looks sharper because the grain or noise is sharp.)

I recommend keeping Color even lower: 20 or less, except when you have some strong color noise obscuring other detail. I usually keep it at 0. This control changes tiny color details to match their surroundings — exactly right for noise, but exactly wrong for the real color details in a subject.

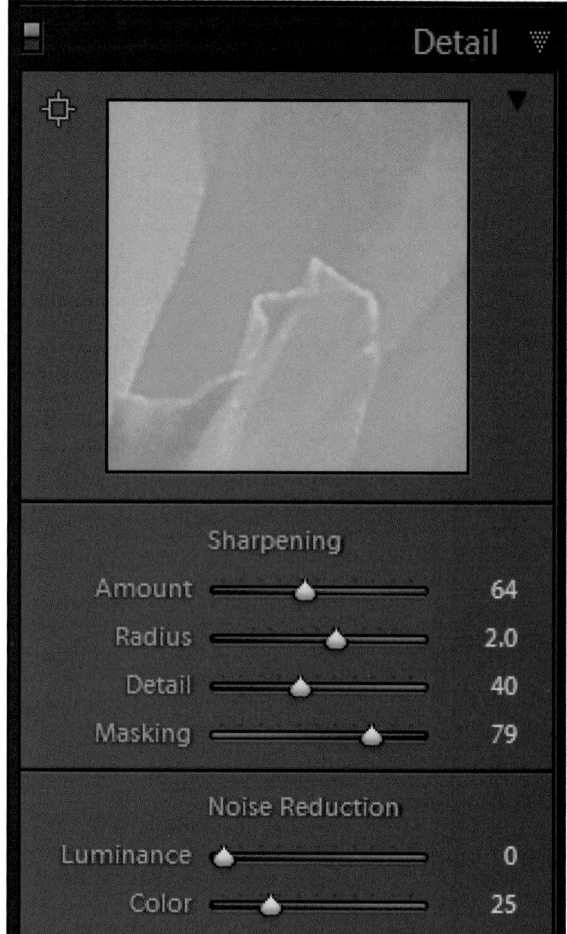

5-45

Using Chromatic Aberration Corrections

At the bottom of Detail is a group of adjustments that you might use often or never — Chromatic Aberration. It all depends on the lens itself, the lens/camera combination, how big you want your photo to be, and the subject. Some lens designs are superb for any use and never need correction. All lenses interact with the sensor in ways that change as

Capture Versus Output Sharpening

As you go through Lightroom, you will find several places where you can sharpen your photo beyond this section in Develop. A lot of photographers wonder what is up with that. The Adobe engineers are giving photographers two types of sharpening, capture and output sharpening. Some photographers feel these are critical and must always be used, while others are happy with one option.

Sharpening in Develop is capture sharpening. It applies sharpening to a photo to correct some of the inherent sharpness challenges that come from digital capture. The way digital works to capture an image with a sensor will create some built-in sharpening challenges that will mean an unsharpened photo will not give you the quality you would expect from your camera and lens. This sharpening is based on what is in the photo, the size of the sensor, and so forth. It optimizes an image from its original capture from the sensor.

Output sharpening (such as that in the Print module) sharpens a photo for a specific output media. Print media, for example, look best when an image is sharpened optimally for the specific media, such as matte or glossy. This is not about the original photo's needs, but about getting the best output for the medium you are working with.

you change megapixels. You may find that a certain lens works fine on one camera, but when you use that same lens on a higher megapixel camera, you start to see lens aberrations that weren't visible before. In addition, if your photo is used small, you may never see any lens issues; yet if that same picture is blown up to a big display print, you can see obvious defects along the edges of the composition.

Lens aberrations that need correction typically show up along the edges of the frame, especially where a dark object contrasts against something bright, such as the sky. Click your photo to enlarge it, and then move it around until you get to an edge, as shown in figure 5-46. An easy way to do that is to go to the Navigator image at the upper left and click inside the box showing where the magnified view comes from, and then drag it to an edge. Look for an edge with strong contrasting lines — this is where lens aberrations show up. You might see some color fringing along these edges (which could use correction) or none at all. The image in figure 5-46 is from a full-frame fisheye lens for a small-format digital camera and shows this color fringing at the far corners of the frame when high-contrast subjects are photographed.

If you see colors along the edges (or you just want to see if there are some there), go to Chromatic Aberration. For red or cyan fringing, use the Red/Cyan slider; for blue or yellow, use the Blue/Yellow slider, as shown in figure 5-47. Defringe has two choices: Highlight Edges or All Edges. In this case, it is the highlight edges that are the problem, so I used this option. The algorithms used for this correction are sophisticated and shift pixels when the image is exported to fix the problem. If moving the sliders around has no effect, then you have no aberration problems that Lightroom can affect.

Navigator
FIT
FILL
1:1
3:1
Presets
Snapshots
History

5-46

Histogram
Sharpening
Amount
25
Radius
1.0
Detail
25
Masking
0
Noise Reduction
Luminance
0
Color
25
Chromatic Aberration
Red / Cyan
– 17
Blue / Yellow
+ 38
Defringe :
Highlight Edges

5-47

A Specific Workflow in Lightroom

In this chapter, you've seen how a number of overall adjustments work in Lightroom. The order I have presented here is based on a specific workflow that I find works very well to get the best overall tonality and color from a photo. The chart in figure 5-48 shows this.

The flow goes from left to right, following the large, red arrows. You enter the Develop module, then go to tonal adjustments: blacks and whites, recovery and fill, and midtones. Then you move to color adjustments: color correction and white balance, Vibrance, and HSL (which will be covered in the next chapter). Finally, you go to Detail, where sharpness and noise are adjusted (plus occasionally lens problems).

This chart shows something else very important: the small, dotted-line arrows. Note that these go back to earlier steps and move freely among the adjustments. This is one thing that makes Lightroom both effective and efficient. It is so easy to move back and forth among adjustments.

History and Snapshots

To view History and Snapshots, you need to be sure your left panel is visible. History in the left panel, as shown in figure 5-49, is like the History palette in Photoshop. It remembers all the adjustments you do as you do them. You can go back to a specific adjustment, although remember, in Lightroom, you don't necessarily need to. All adjustments are non-destructive, so you can always go back and change anything without harming the quality of the image. Adjustments are only instructions until you export a photo.

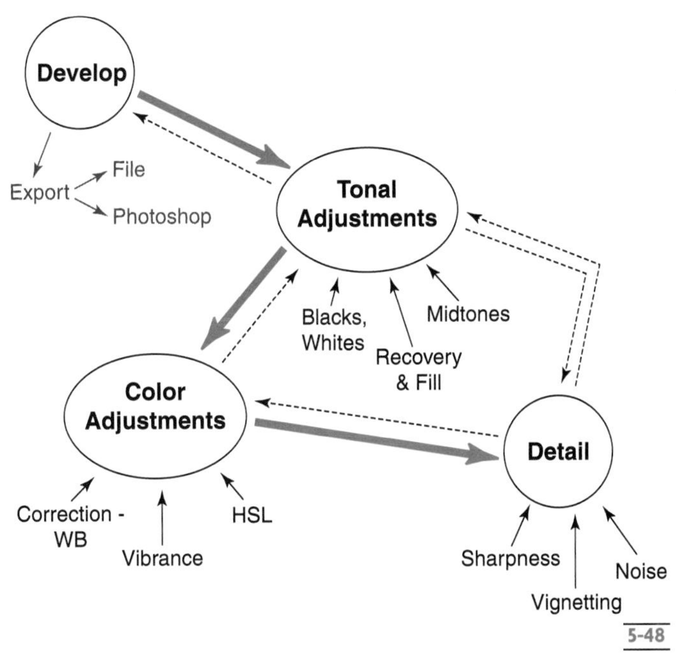

5-48

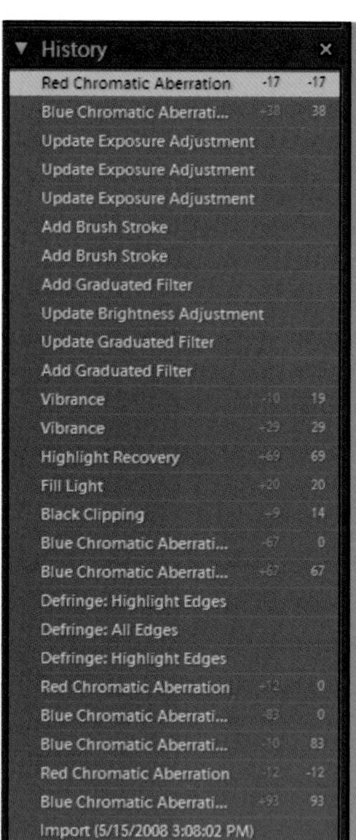

5-49

History can be helpful in returning to a certain point in your image work or to go back and see what a specific adjustment was. One thing that is quite different about Lightroom's History compared to the one in Photoshop is that Lightroom remembers the history of an image's adjustments so that any time you go back to a photo that has been adjusted, you can quickly check and see what was done. Clearing History removes the record of the adjustments, but the adjustments themselves are not affected.

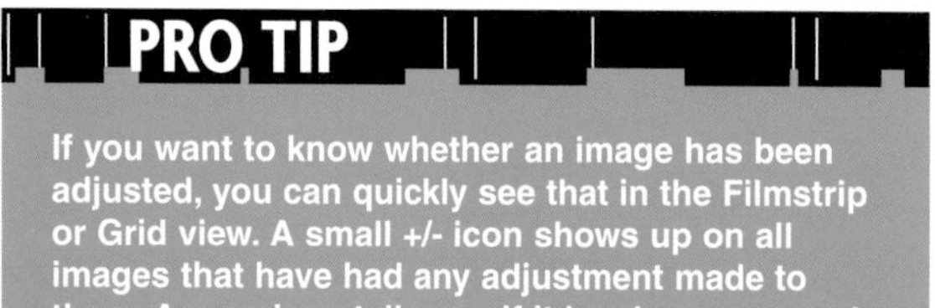

PRO TIP

If you want to know whether an image has been adjusted, you can quickly see that in the Filmstrip or Grid view. A small +/- icon shows up on all images that have had any adjustment made to them. A crop icon tells you if it has been cropped.

Snapshots, shown in figure 5-50, is a lot like the photo states in the History palette of Photoshop. It records or saves the state or condition of an image at certain points in your adjustments. You can record the snapshots of any image as it appears in the central work area. When you have reached a certain stage in the process that you want to remember, you can go back to the History, click on a certain point there, and record that adjustment as a snapshot.

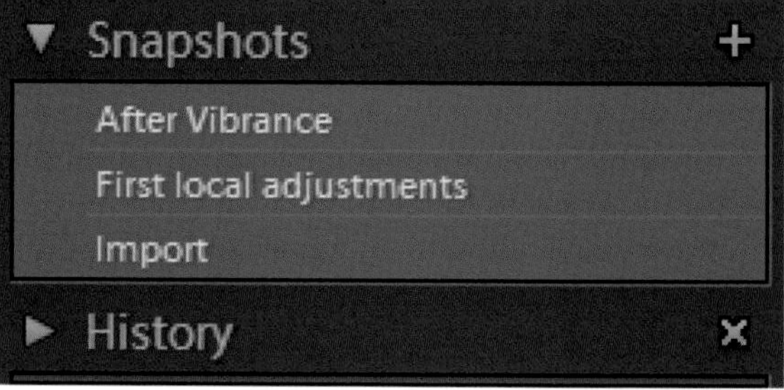

5-50

Snapshots is not just about remembering your adjustments. You can also use it as a very powerful tool to try out different adjustments on a photo and compare them. Here are some tips for doing that:

- **Once you've made an important adjustment, save it by adding it to Snapshots by clicking + and giving it a name in the dialog box that appears.**
- **Try an alternative adjustment to the original image.** Make your new changes, and then save that image to Snapshots.
- **You don't need to go in order.** This is an important and freeing concept when using History. Click any point in History that you want to use as a basis for a new snapshot.
- **Make multiple interpretations of an image, saving each one by adding it to Snapshots.** This is like having versions that can be used for a client, for your own experiments, and so on.

Q & A

I remember from earlier in the book that you can turn the panels of Lightroom on and off. What would you recommend for those choices in the Develop module?

That is absolutely right, but it is not a simple question to answer. This is a highly personal choice. Some photographers like seeing a certain part of the interface open, even if they aren't using it, just because it reminds them of things to do. Other photographers turn off whatever they can, thinking that what they are not using is just distracting.

For a lot of the work in Develop, you can certainly hide the bottom Filmstrip by clicking the bottom arrow. You don't really need to know what other photos are waiting for you (and maybe that is even a source of stress!). It is important to have the Filmstrip available if you want to sync images, but you can quickly go back to the Filmstrip by putting your cursor at the bottom of the screen or pressing F6.

In much of Develop, you don't need the preview at the left or the presets. The preview helps when you have the image magnified, but the value of keeping the left panel open or hidden really depends on the photographer. Hiding it does allow the center image to show more when it's magnified. Press F7 to do that.

You seem to lump highlights, midtones, and shadows all together as midtones as you control midtones with the Tone Curve. Why?

Traditionally in photography, black and white are considered differently than all the gray tones in an image (or equivalent in colors). You are adjusting black, white, and gray tones separately, so photographers will typically call all the gray tones midtones. The gray tones are between black and white; hence the name midtones.

Highlights in Lightroom are the lighter tones above middle gray, yet they include a little more than pure highlights and actually affect all tones above the middle grays to some degree. Shadows are the darker tones below middle gray, and they also affect brighter tones to some degree. This makes Highlights and Shadows midtone adjustments, no matter what Adobe calls them. Some photographers break up midtones into quarter tones, using such terms as *shadow quarter tones*, *mid-range quarter tones*, and *highlight quarter tones*, but still all of these are affected by midtone adjustments.

You don't seem to always follow the exact order of controls on the right side of Develop. I would think the order in Lightroom had a specific purpose.

It does. The controls are grouped by type of control from a Lightroom perspective. However, I am a firm believer in working an image based on its needs and teaching that philosophy rather than purely following the program. When working an image in the Develop module, I think photographers are best served by doing adjustments based on the very photographic approach:

> Set blacks
> Check whites
> Adjust midtones
> Correct color
> Enhance color

These are how a photographer looks at an image, but they do not exactly follow how Lightroom organizes the tools.

Chapter 6

LOCAL CONTROLS AND MORE IN THE DEVELOP MODULE

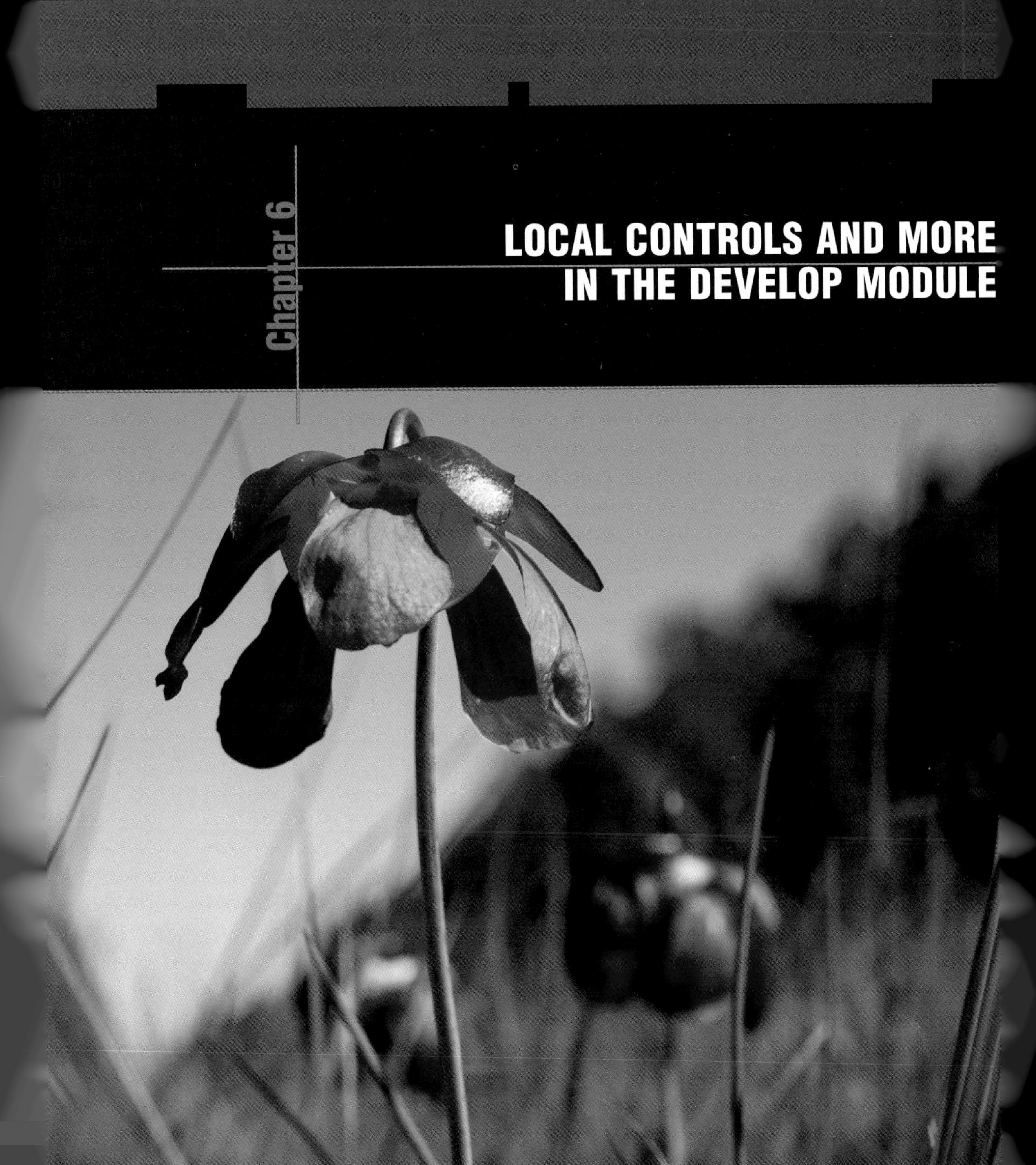

6-1

Overall adjustments are always a core part of "developing" a photograph, which Develop has done very nicely since the first version of Lightroom. Yet this does not give a true photographic experience based on the traditional darkroom. For that, you need local controls, adjustments that affect one part of the image and not others.

While Lightroom 1 had a few very limited local controls, Lightroom 2 changes that completely. After working with it for a while, I really feel like I have regained long-lost darkroom controls, as shown in figure 6-1. The wonderful control that photographers such as Ansel Adams and W. Eugene Smith had over the black-and-white image was never fully realized in the color darkroom. This was one reason Adams gave for never liking color photography (and why the only book of his color work came out only after he died).

Sure, you could do a lot of work in Photoshop, but local controls were neither simple nor easy for most of us. Lightroom 2 totally changes this. I believe that the program may even change the way photographers approach color photography. This chapter covers the new local controls as well as additional distinctive features beyond what you saw in Chapter 5 that can really help you get the most from your images. Also in this chapter, you learn about Lightroom's excellent black-and-white conversion capabilities that offer very high quality, black-and-white images.

Why Bother with Traditional Darkroom Controls?

A very legitimate question is "Why should the modern digital photographer bother with the idea of traditional darkroom controls?" Why, indeed! "Because that's what Ansel Adams and W. Eugene Smith did" is not a very satisfying answer. Their era was many years ago. I believe the answer is about control of the image, controlling how the viewer sees your subject and your interpretation of a scene.

Andreas Feininger was a *LIFE* photographer during its peak, and he wrote a lot of very popular books about photography during the 1960s and 1970s. His work influenced many of the professional photojournalists working today. Feininger said that an uncontrolled photograph lies, and that only by controlling the image can the photographer bring truth to a photo. What he meant is that a photo always limits how we see the world — it doesn't move, it is in two dimensions, there are no other senses other than vision involved, the frame of a composition arbitrarily cuts off the rest of the real world, and so on.

Because of those reasons and more, a photograph can never be an "objective" recording of reality, simply because it cannot capture reality, only an interpretation of it. If that interpretation is not controlled, Feininger felt, then the image could be very misleading about what is really in the world represented by that photograph. Of course, a photographer can also use control to deliberately mislead people, too.

Your camera sees the world in a very specific way, using an interpretation of a scene based on the sensor's capabilities and how camera engineers in Japan have decided to interpret the data coming from it. Some photographers have the impression that RAW files mean there is no interpretation of data, but in fact, that is not true. Data that represents a photo comes from the sensor as an analog signal that must be converted to digital. All manufacturers process that signal as it is converted to digital in what is called the A/D (analog to digital) converter. Some manufacturers even do some processing of the analog signal before it gets to that converter. They do this in order to create a digital image file that they believe is a quality interpretation of the world. But to be frank, they also do it because they know certain interpretations will sell cameras better to specific markets. So at this level, at least, I think you probably know a bit more about interpreting your subjects and scenes than the engineers in Japan do!

On another level, the camera sees the world in an entirely different way than we do. One of the things that a camera does is capture a scene very flatly in a visual sense. For example, if I were to look at you as part of a group of friends, my vision would see you as the star of the group. The rest of the group would certainly be here, but the area where my eyes were focused would be emphasized, as shown in figure 6-2. Photographing that same scene with a camera would then make everyone in the group equal, as seen in figure 6-3. You would not be the star or emphasized. This is why photographers will use flash, graduated neutral density filters, and other techniques to emphasize a part of a photograph over other parts.

That emphasis is exactly what traditional darkroom workers like Adams and Smith did. And this is exactly what the new local controls in Lightroom 2 give to photographers.

6-2

6-3

6-4

6-5

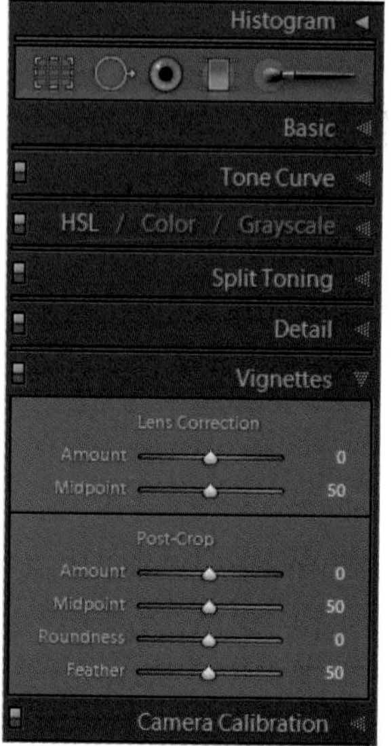

6-6

Using the Vignette Controls for Edge Burning

Most master printers of photographs know a neat little trick, *edge burning*. Ansel Adams even spent a bit of time talking about this in his book, *The Print*. Edge burning is darkening the outside edges of a photograph by adding light from the enlarger (called *burning in*). Adams explained the reasons for this rather well. He says that prints are generally mounted with something around them or nearby that is attractive in some way to the viewer's eye. The result is that the viewer's eye will stray to the edges of the photograph and even outside, without really seeing the subject and the composition as well as the person should. This is certainly true with photographs that are used in publications, on the Web, or just displayed on the monitor, unless you have a pure black room.

Darken the outside edges of your image, and you will find that the viewer is more likely to stay focused on the picture, and you'll often find that a picture becomes more dimensional in appearance. You can see the effect in figures 6-4 and 6-5. This strange flower is the blossom of a parrot pitcher plant in the panhandle of Florida. The effect is exaggerated a little bit in 6-5 compared to what you would normally use so that it will show up when printed in this book. Still, you can see how adding edge burning to 6-5 makes for a richer image, an image that keeps the viewer's eye on the parrot pitcher plant flower and that is more dimensional.

This is actually very easy to do in Lightroom 2 by using the Vignettes controls in the right panel of Develop, as shown in figure 6-6. When you first open Vignettes, you'll find two sections: Lens Correction and Post-Crop. The Post-Crop controls are the ones that give the edge-burning effect. Lens Correction is designed to remove edge darkening caused by lenses. This often occurs with very wide angle lenses and especially with wide-angle settings of extreme zooms. You will likely see it in sky, where it is really noticeable. You can use the Lens Correction section to correct for that effect; in this case, you are usually lightening an already dark edge. Obviously, darkening of an edge from a lens issue still darkens the edge and may be appropriate for certain photographs. The problem is that this occurs all the time with certain lenses and needs to be corrected, because you don't want it in your photographs all the time. In addition, edge darkening that comes from a lens occurs only with the full image area, so if you crop the photo, that darkening will disappear from whatever edges you crop.

You gain control over edge darkening in Post-Crop as this affects the photo regardless of whether it is cropped or not. (You can also brighten an edge with these same effects, though that is less common.) Here's how to use it:

1. **Set a starting Amount.** Amount affects how strong the edge darkening appears, as shown in figure 6-7. You will typically go back and modify this after setting some of the other controls, too, but you have to have some amount before you can use the rest.
2. **Change the Midpoint.** The Midpoint slider controls how far into the photograph the darkening goes, as shown in figure 6-8.
3. **Consider the Roundedness and Feather sliders.** You don't need to use these sliders all the time; however, they can add some nice finishing touches to the dark area around your subject. Roundness affects how round or oval shaped the vignette effect is. Feather changes how the edge blends from zero to its maximum.

Play with this effect with your photographs. I think that you will find you will start using it all the time. Some photographers like a gentle, subtle effect, while others like something more dramatic. Both work with the right subject and photograph.

6-7

6-8

PRO TIP

Remember that you can reset any slider back to its default position by double-clicking it or by double-clicking on the adjustment name.

Local Adjustments and the Graduated Filter

The local adjustments or local controls section of Develop is based in the toolbar between the Histogram and Basic. It includes five controls, as shown in figure 6-9: cropping, spot removal, red-eye removal, the graduated filter, and the adjustment brush. Click any one of these to open up its working menu. You learned a bit about cropping in the last chapter. Spot removal and red-eye removal will be covered later in this chapter.

The really amazing new part of Lightroom 2 comes from the local adjustments of the graduated filter and the adjustment brush. These two controls give you a huge amount of control over the image that is very much like working in a traditional darkroom. They are fast and easy to use. Both offer a variety of controls within their adjustment space: exposure, brightness, contrast, saturation, clarity, sharpness, and a color overlay, as shown in figure 6-10. They act just like the controls from the rest of the Develop module that they are named after (sharpness uses a unique sharpening algorithm, while color simply overlays a color over your photograph in a blended manner).

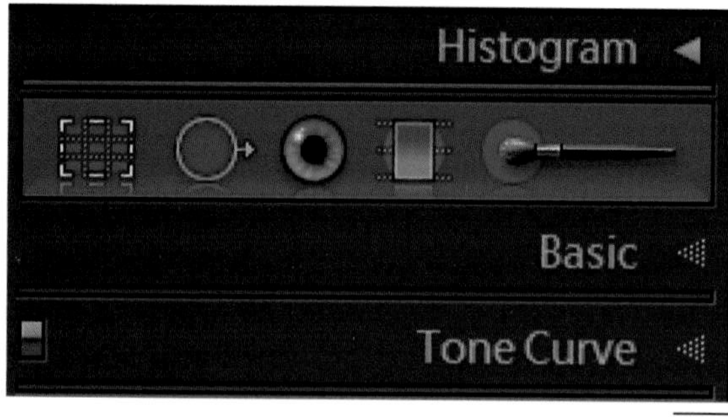

6-9

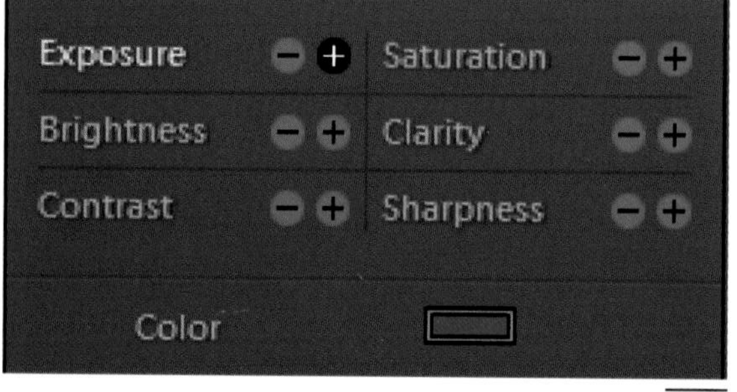

6-10

The graduated filter control is a good place to start. It acts indeed like a graduated filter used over your lens, but it includes a lot more controls. Here's how to use it:

1. **Select the graduated filter by clicking on the rectangular icon between the eye and brush icons in the toolbar below the Histogram, as shown in figure 6-9.** You can also press the letter M. To close the graduated filter, press M again or press Esc.
2. **Set the type of control you wish to use within the graduated filter (such as Exposure or Sharpness) by clicking the name of the control or the – or + signs to the right of the name (except for color, where you click on a color to select it to use as an overlay).** You can do one control at a time.
3. **Set an amount with the Amount slider.**
4. **Simply click and drag on the photo and the effect immediately appears, as shown in figure 6-11.** You move your cursor farther away from your original point and the gradient gets larger, and you rotate your movement of the cursor and the gradient also rotates. Three lines appear to show you how the gradient is being applied, although you will actually see its effects being applied as well. This scene is of the Apalachicola River in the Panhandle of Florida, and the image originally has a weak sky because of the limitations of exposing for the lower part of the photo.
5. **Press Escape or Enter/Return to complete the adjustment.** A white control point will appear and show you where the adjustment is in the photograph.
6. **Revise the adjustment by clicking on the white control point.** You can actually change your adjustment completely, both in amount and in where the gradient goes across the photograph.

You can set up multiple gradients across the photo to get your local brightness values adjusted as needed. In figure 6-12, you can see an additional darkening gradient being applied to the lower right of the photograph. To remove a control point, click on it and press Delete.

PRO TIP

You can get basic information about a photograph, including file name, date and time the image was shot, pixel size, and basic exposure settings, as an overlay across the top of the displayed photograph at any time by pressing I. This information cycles as you press I again.

6-11

6-12

There are lots of things that you can do with these gradients. Here are some ideas:

> **Exposure.** I like to use exposure when certain regions of a photograph are too dark. I find that exposure works very well for brightening a photograph and sometimes for darkening it, too.

> **Brightness.** My preference is to use Brightness for darkening. I like its effect because, for me, it better mimics the traditional darkening of burning in from the old darkroom. However, I don't like the way it lightens an image and prefer Exposure for that. I use Exposure and Brightness constantly in photographs (using the adjustment brush, too).

> **Contrast.** Contrast allows you to bring out (more contrast) or reduce (less contrast) details in an area.

> **Saturation.** This is a nice control that allows you to selectively change contrast within a photo. Often, that is the best way to deal with color, rather than making a change overall, especially with the overall saturation adjustment (which is pretty heavy handed).

> **Clarity.** Clarity is like a refined contrast adjustment and allows you to both enhance and reduce contrasts around fine detail in restricted areas.

> **Sharpness.** Sharpness is exactly what it seems to be, a control that allows you to increase or decrease sharpness in specific areas based on the gradient.

> **Color.** You can add color to an area or intensify a weak color with a gradient based on a specific color overlay; for example, building up the blue in a sky that recorded weakly. You choose the color by clicking the little color rectangle to get a Color Picker.

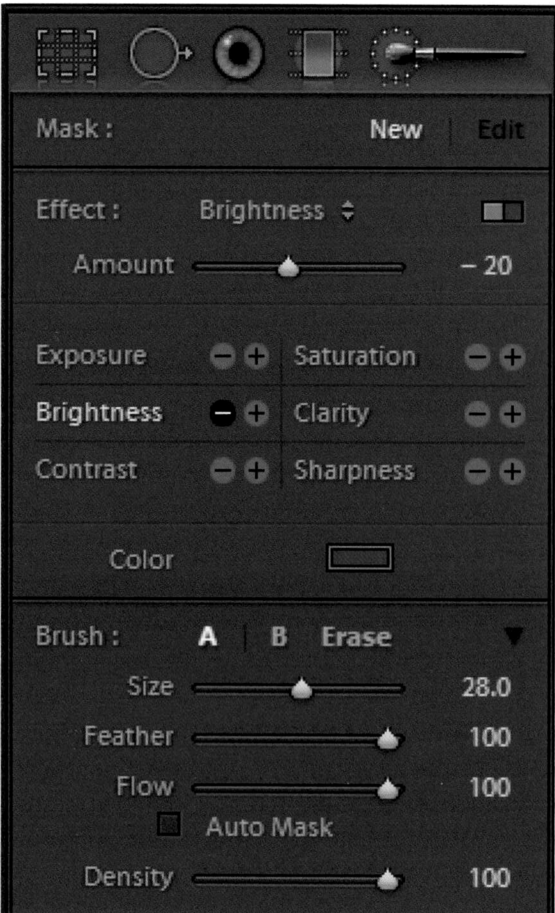

6-13

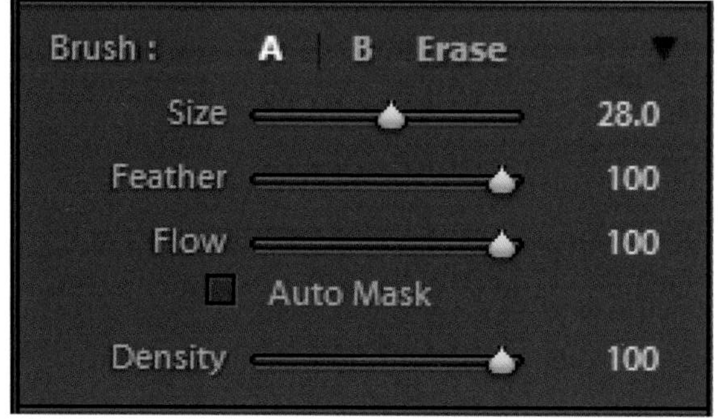

6-14

Local Adjustments and the Adjustment Brush

The adjustment brush uses the same controls as the graduated filter, as shown in figure 6-13, but you literally brush the effects on to the picture rather than dragging a gradient across it. This is a very fun tool to use. You can go over your picture and darken bright spots, brighten dark spots, give a line more contrast, paint in a little bit of color, and so forth.

You'll also notice in figure 6-13 that there are some additional items for this brush. There is a whole section that allows you to set up the brush itself, as highlighted in figure 6-14. First, you can set up two distinct brushes, A and B, chosen simply by setting the parameters after you click on A or B. Next, you can change the size of the brush, the feather or softness of the brush's edge, and the flow and density. (Flow and density affect how the effect is actually applied, but I find them a little confusing, and most photographers will do fine just using them at their defaults.) Frankly, the easiest way to use the brush is to leave the feather at 100 and change the brush size by using the bracket keys to the right of the letter P on your keyboard. Auto mask is a way for Lightroom to apply an effect to specific tones and not to others.

The adjustment brush applies its effects as you brush your cursor across the photograph as needed. You set it up similarly to the graduated filter; here's how:

1. **Select the adjustment brush tool by clicking on the brush icon below the Histogram.** You can also press the letter K. To close the graduated filter, press K again or press Esc.
2. **Set the type of control by clicking the name of the control or the – or + signs to the right of the name (except for color, where you click on a color to select a color to use as an overlay).** You can do one control at a time.
3. **Set an amount with the Amount slider.**

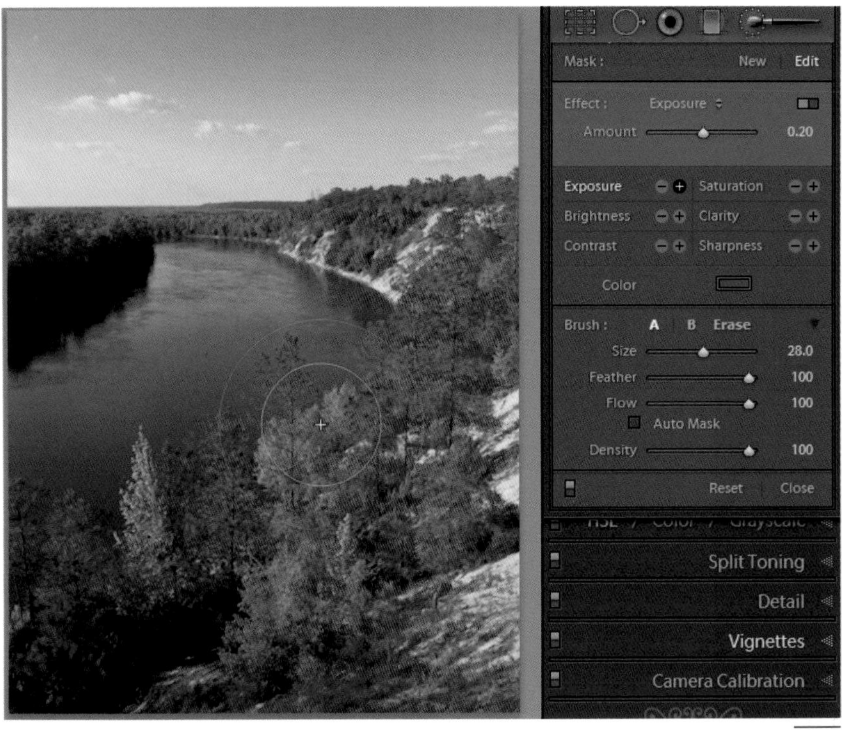

6-15

4. **Simply click and drag on the photo and the effect immediately appears, as shown in figure 6-15.** You can see the size of the effect in the concentric circles around your cursor. You can quickly change that size as I mentioned previously by using the bracket keys to the right on your keyboard ([is smaller,] is larger). Brush your cursor wherever you want and the effect is applied, but it is still just the same effect. If you hold down the Alt/Option key as you brush, you will remove the effect.

PRO TIP

Local adjustments can be used in a multiple adjustment mode. This chapter describes the easier-to-control single adjustment mode. Click on the black-and-gray rectangle to the far right of Effect: to open an interface with sliders for all of the adjustments available for the local controls. Change your effect with as many different adjustments as you want, all now applied at the same time.

5. **Press Escape or Enter/Return to complete the adjustment.** A white control point will appear and show you where the adjustment is in the photograph.

6. **Revise the adjustment by clicking the white control point.** You can again change your adjustment completely, both in amount and in where the brush is applied across the photograph.

You can set up multiple places for the adjustment brush across the photo to get your local values adjusted as needed. In figure 6-16, you can see an additional darkening brush being applied to the upper-left sky of the photograph. Remember that you can remove a control point by selecting the point and pressing Delete.

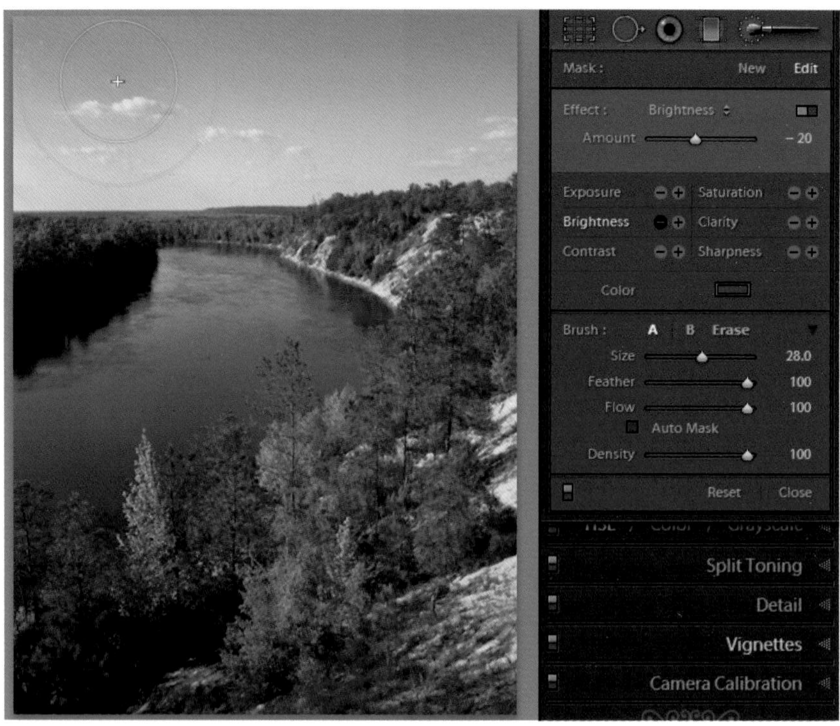

6-16

There are lots of things that you can do with the adjustment brush, and the tips I listed in the graduated filter section will give you some ideas. One thing to look for when working on local adjustments is the balance within a picture. Very often the photograph is not captured by the camera in a balanced way. Look for some of these things to adjust with the adjustment brush (use the graduated filter similarly):

> **Tones can be out of balance, where one part of the picture is too bright proportionally compared to another.** Brush in minus brightness to darken an area or plus exposure to brighten it.

> **Colors can be out of balance where certain colors have too much or too little saturation compared to others, because of the way the camera captured them, the light, or simply contrasts within the image.** Brush in plus or minus saturation as needed.

> **Individual pictorial elements can be out of balance.** This can happen if something is lit unevenly, for example. The adjustment brush is ideal to correct that by brushing in more or less brightness, by changing saturation, or even by adjusting clarity.

> **Emphasis is something that has always been important to photographers, but is difficult to do with color photos.** That is something W. Eugene Smith was a master of. Now you can be, too, with Lightroom's controls. You can try making a subject darker or lighter, and its surroundings the opposite, to make a subject stand out. You can also do this with saturation, clarity, and sharpness.

If you want some inspiration on how to use such controls, check out Ansel Adams' books, *The Print* and *Examples: The Making of 40 Photographs*. They are still in print, or you can probably find them at the library. While you won't find the discussion of chemicals and such things of use, Adams' descriptions of how and why he adjusted photos are just as valid and thought-provoking today as when he wrote his text. He even has before-and-after images in *The Print* along with notes on how he applied his "adjustments."

PRO TIP

Lightroom includes a lot of "drag-on-the-photo" features, including a nifty way of readjusting your adjustment brush change to the photo. You can click and drag on the control point to change the adjustment. This lets you watch the change directly on the photo rather than having to go to the controls on the right panel.

HSL/Color/Grayscale

HSL/Color/Grayscale is an important part of Lightroom that offers overall adjustments, specific color adjustments, and even some local controls. This section probably has the most variety of interrelated controls in Lightroom, let alone the Develop module. HSL/Color/Grayscale is shown in figure 6-17 with it open to show all of the HSL section. This is a key area to understand if you really want to affect color in an image. For nature photographers and others who love the saturated colors of Velvia and the old Kodachrome, this is the place to go. And for any photographers who need to correct specific colors that weren't captured properly by a digital camera (and that is pretty common), this is the place to make corrections. Here's how to use it:

> **HSL.** At first, HSL looks very complex because it can change the hue, saturation, and luminance (HSL) of eight different colors: red, orange, yellow, green, aqua, blue, purple, and magenta. When you click HSL in the Category bar, it becomes the active item. You see tabs for Hue, Saturation, Luminance, and All. Tabs for the first three each have sliders to control the eight colors. If you click the All tab, you see 24 different sliders because this view groups all the controls together (not all display in figure 6-17 because of the screen resolution used for this book; however, you will probably rarely use the All tab).

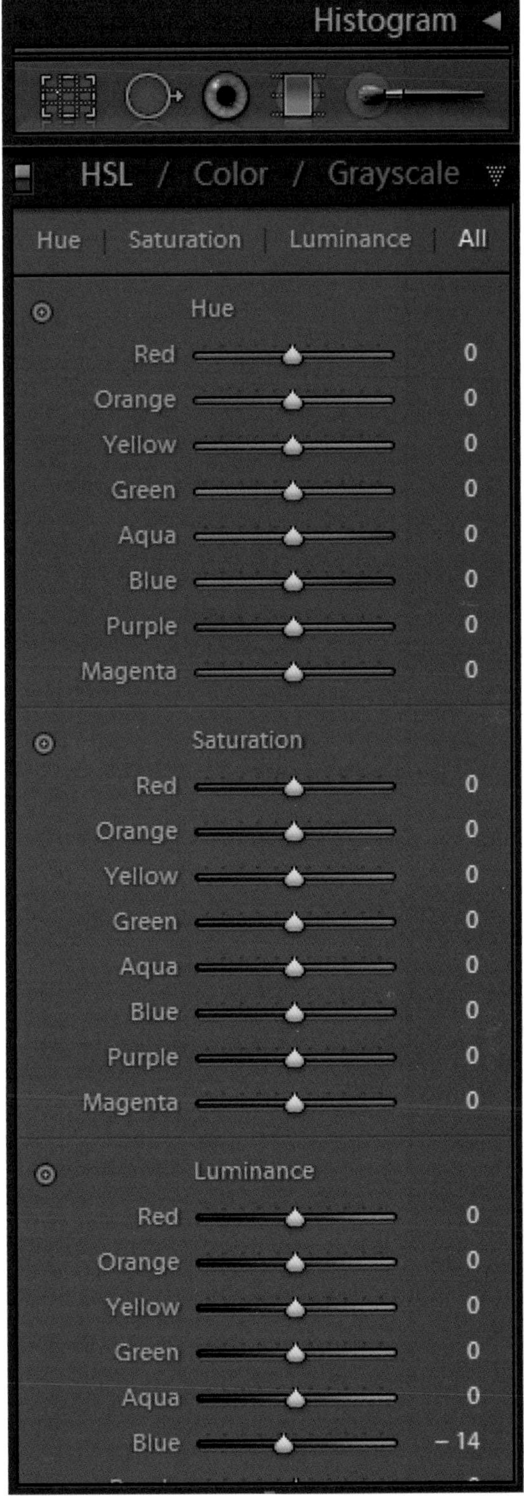

6-17

- **Color.** If you click Color instead of HSL in the Category bar, you get a new way of looking at the same Hue, Saturation, and Luminance controls, but now all three appear at once, as shown in figure 6-18. This option groups the controls by color rather than type of control. I prefer the HSL grouping that keeps hue, saturation, and luminance separate because it lets me do saturation changes, for example, on different colors all at one time.

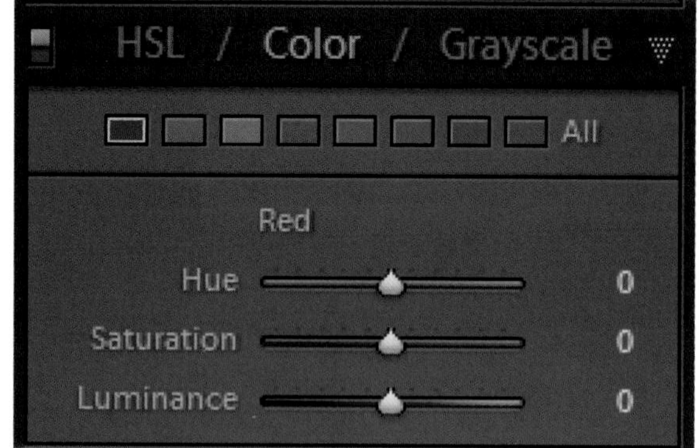

6-18

- **Grayscale.** The third part of this right-panel group in the Develop module is Grayscale. This changes an image to black-and-white and offers some quite powerful controls for better black-and-white conversions. I cover this later in the chapter.

Don't be intimidated by all of these controls. What HSL does is pretty simple — it changes specific ranges of color by the color itself (hue), the intensity of that color (saturation), and its brightness (luminance). What makes the controls complex are all the choices.

That said, if you know Photoshop, you can simplify how the HSL part of this group of controls works in a hurry. The Hue/Saturation control of Photoshop is a common way to adjust color. If you use it for specific colors rather than overall adjustment (in other words, use the drop-down menu of colors from Master and not adjust in Master), you have a great deal of control over the individual colors in a photo.

That is exactly what HSL offers, except with new and improved algorithms. Photoshop's Hue/Saturation has the same choices, but you don't see them all available at once like you do here. Having them all out in the open makes it easy to go from color to color, but it does mean you have to find your color amongst all these choices! And Lightroom actually makes it easy for you to do that as you will soon learn.

There is no step-by-step approach to using the HSL controls because the colors that need adjustment in your photo influence which specific sliders you use and how. Here are some ideas, though, that can help you master HSL:

- **Start by using your photo and subject as a guide.** What colors need tweaking in your photograph? What colors are not registering correctly? Are any inaccurate? Do any need intensifying to make them look better? Are any colors too intense, taking attention away from other colors?
- **Work one color at a time.** Look at your photo. So often photographers using Photoshop see a weak color and try to make it look better by increasing saturation of the whole image — not the best approach. This tool forces you to work each color separately, which is how it should be. Figure 6-19 shows saturation being adjusted only on the green leaves of the spring trees around the Apalachicola River in Florida's Panhandle. Such individual adjustment gives you so much more control, plus it complements how digital cameras really work, which is that they don't deal with colors equally in a way that would match what we see with our eyes.

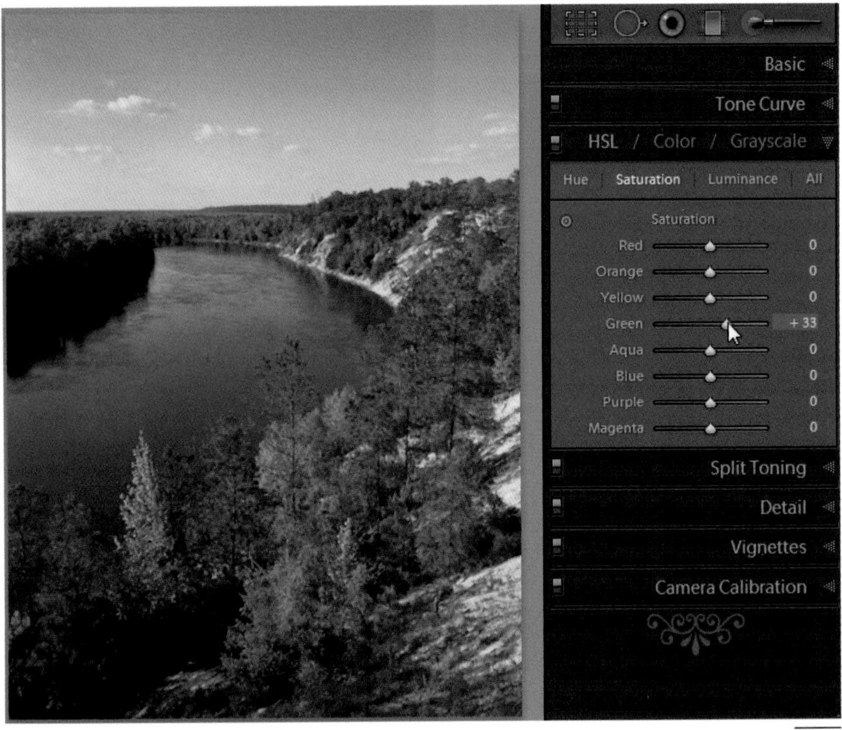

6-19

- **Fix inaccurate colors.** Certain colors cause problems for digital sensors. Consistently, certain blues and violets record inaccurately. This can be important for nature or documentary photographers who want to get a color right, and can be critical for advertising photographers who need to match a client's color needs.

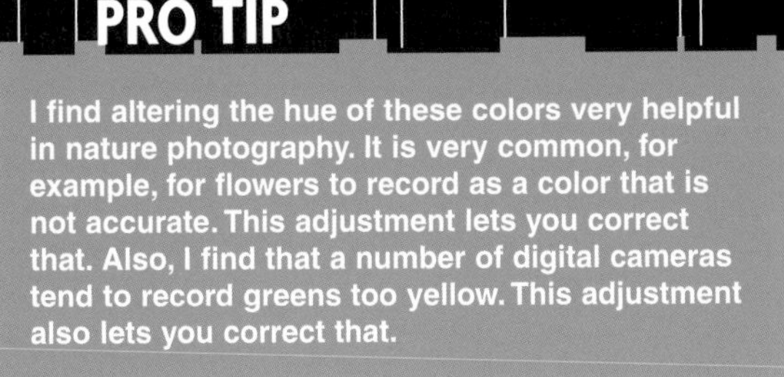

PRO TIP

I find altering the hue of these colors very helpful in nature photography. It is very common, for example, for flowers to record as a color that is not accurate. This adjustment lets you correct that. Also, I find that a number of digital cameras tend to record greens too yellow. This adjustment also lets you correct that.

- **Use Hue, Saturation, Luminance, in that order, for individual color correction.** Use Hue for your color if the color is off in its actual color (for example, a pure green looks blue-green) and needs correction. Once the "color of the color" or hue is right, go to Saturation to affect its intensity. Increase or decrease its intensity so that the color is optimized or enhanced for your composition and subject. Use Luminance to make the color brighter or darker.
- **Fix color imbalances.** It is very common in a photograph to have some colors record inappropriately compared to others. This is not the same as inaccurate colors — the colors can be accurate as to hue, for example, but record too saturated or too bright compared to another color. Reds are a good example of this — they are often out of balance from other colors. You can change this in HSL quite nicely.

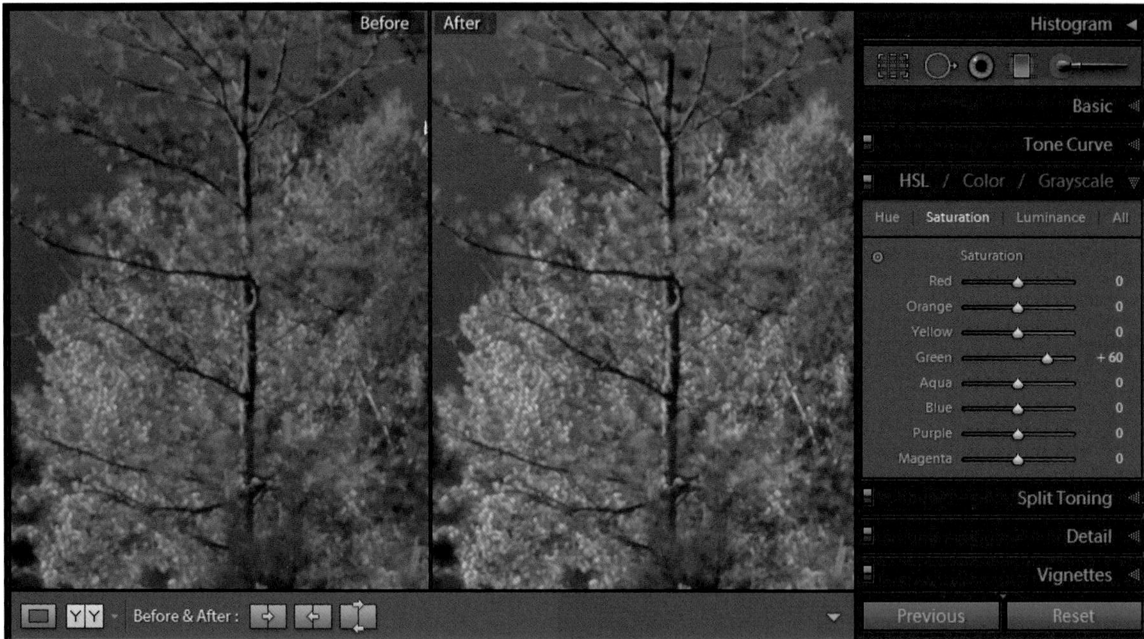

6-20

> **Use the Before & After views.** It is very easy to overenhance the saturation of a color by adjusting a little at a time while your eye adjusts to each change. If you have a reference (the Before), you are less likely to do that. Lightroom offers a great way of seeing before and after by clicking the Before & After view mode button in the toolbar, as shown in figure 6-20 (this enlarges the trees in figure 6-19, too). This button is the second from the left, under the central image. This view mode actually gives you multiple ways of seeing before and after images; figure 6-20 is just one of them. You can cycle through them by clicking the Before & After view mode button and see which ones you like best.

PRO TIP

To identify more precisely what color or colors need adjustment, find that color in the photo. How do you do that? One way is to use the Saturation tab. Click a color that you think might be correct and move the slider all the way to the left, removing its color. You then see gray in the photo. If that shows the right parts of the photo, you know you have the correct color. You can also click and drag in the photo after clicking the Targeted Adjustment button, clicking a color, and then dragging it to zero saturation. See if that shows the correct parts of the image; then you also know the correct color by looking at which one in the list changed. Undo either of these saturation removal changes by pressing Ctrl/⌘+Z or resetting the number to 0.

Click and Drag in the Photo for Color Control

A truly remarkable part of Lightroom is the ability to use the photo for direct color control. Just as in the Tone Curve, HSL can use your cursor to recognize and adjust color directly on the image. This is a very cool feature and makes the color adjustment responsive because you can simply click on the photo itself, and as you move your cursor, the photo changes immediately underneath your cursor. In addition, this gives HSL some direct, local control over colors.

You can, for example, click on the sky when the cursor is activated for Luminance and drag up to make the sky lighter, and down to make it darker. The Luminance control in Lightroom is excellent for this and is nothing like Luminance in Photoshop's Hue Saturation controls. You can easily control brightness this way in specific areas of the photo as long as you are able to "target" a color and only that color needs to be changed. Of course, you can also do this with Hue and Saturation.

Here's how to click and drag for color control:

1. **Click the button slightly above and to the left of the word Red to access this in the HSL area you want to affect (hue, saturation, luminance), as shown in figure 6-21.**

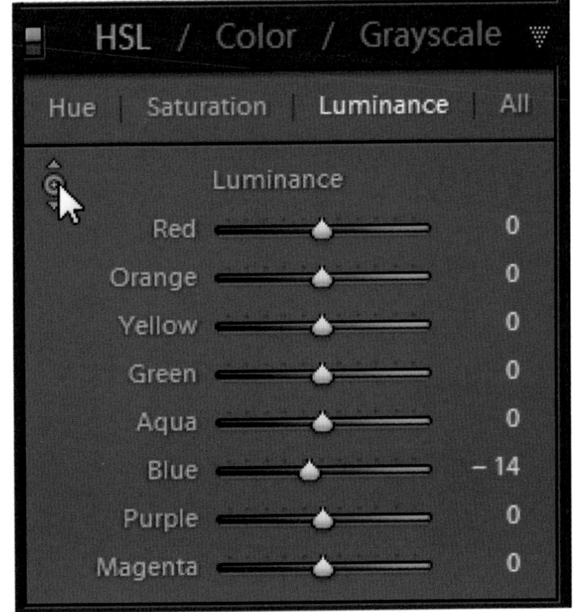

6-21

2. **Then click the color in the photo that you want to adjust, and drag the cursor up or down to adjust the color more or less, respectively.** Lightroom finds the right color and highlights it in the HSL panel, then automatically makes the appropriate adjustments to the sliders.

In figure 6-22, you can see the blue sky of this scene being adjusted.

6-22

This is very photographic. You don't have to guess what colors to adjust. Lightroom finds them for you. You just find something on your photo you want to adjust, and then click and drag on it. You can go through a photo very quickly this way: click, drag, click a new place, drag, and so on.

Camera Calibration

Camera Calibration was originally designed for Camera RAW to tweak how a camera sees colors (hence the name), but most photographers use it for other purposes, so the name seems misleading at first. With the HSL group, I find I rarely use Camera Calibration. Most photographers will never miss using it.

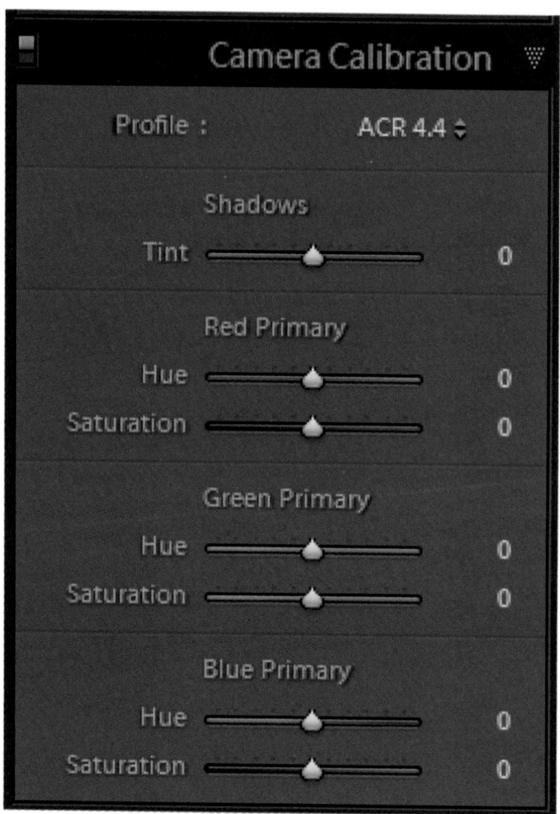

6-23

The camera sensor itself and the camera's A/D converter affect how that camera responds to color. Even camera models from the same manufacturer can have different responses to colors because the sensors are different. Camera Calibration was developed to enable you to affect this color response at a different level from simply changing white balance or saturation. You can adjust the hue and saturation of the primary computer colors of red, green, and blue to, in a sense, "calibrate" a camera for a better color response, as shown in figure 6-23. However, this is much more a computer thing than how photographers normally see pictures.

So, most photographers don't use this control for that purpose. They use it to tweak and affect colors based on a specific subject and scene. And indeed, this gives the photographer another way of working color in an image. Very often if a photograph needs more color saturation, this is a better place to do it than using Saturation in Basic. You can adjust red, green, and blue separately, which frequently gives better colors because you can respond to individual color needs rather than making an overall color adjustment that might help some colors, but might hurt others. However, I think that HSL is more intuitive for the photographer (plus it has that really great click-and-drag-on-the-image color adjustment).

Adobe has proposed creating specific camera calibration templates for this section that could be used to help a specific camera model give more neutral results. This could be useful for studio and commercial photographers who have some unique color requirements for their clients, but probably adds an unneeded layer of complexity for most photographers.

PRO TIP

Be cautious about overadjusting color saturation. Intense color has become very popular in everything from ads to snapshots. If you are doing purely documentary work, then obviously you need to be careful about making colors accurate and not overdone in saturation. Otherwise, increasing saturation is not a problem in and of itself — only when it is done blindly, just to "boost colors" without also watching to see how these colors really look in the image. It is, unfortunately, only a short step from vivid to garish.

Converting Color to Black-and-White

Black-and-white photography has seen a real surge in interest. When color began to dominate photography back in the 1970s, black-and-white was seen by many as old and antiquated. Photographers quit doing it, darkrooms were closed up, and black-and-white as a creative option was seen as an oddity and not something most photographers did.

In recent years, black-and-white has seen new popularity. Some people are even opening up old darkrooms. Black-and-white film is still being used. In addition, new photo printers make outstanding black-and-white prints with density ranges (the range from pure black to pure white) greater than traditional prints.

You don't have to shoot black-and-white in film or digital (in cameras that allow this). You can get very high quality, black-and-white images from color when you use Lightroom. Some photographers imply that somehow this is "cheating" and you lose the discipline of the craft of shooting black-and-white from the start. I would say that converting color to black-and-white still requires a disciplined approach in order to do it well, as shown in figures 6-24 and 6-25, plus it offers some excellent and versatile options in getting black and white tonalities that you can't get if you shoot black-and-white from the start.

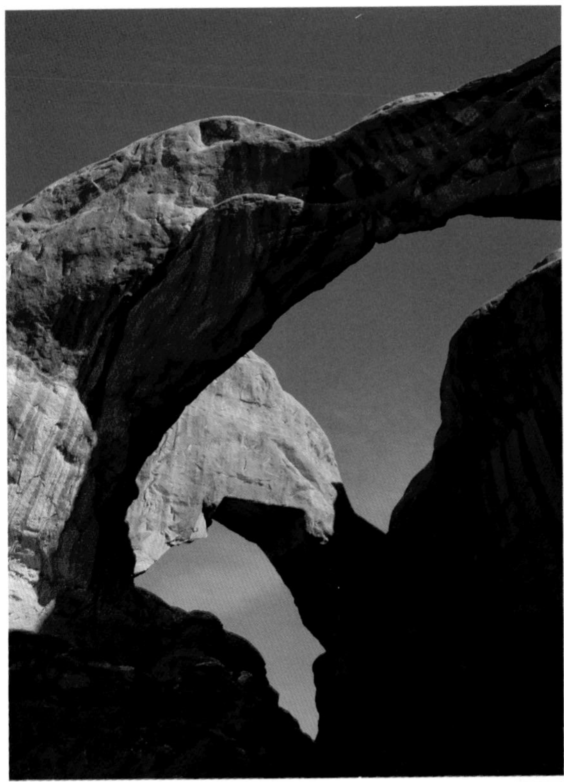

6-24

There is no question that some photographers have made a real art from photographing in black-and-white from the start. If this suits you, then go for it. All of the tonal controls in Develop (blacks, whites, and midtone adjustments) discussed in this chapter and in Chapter 5 apply to processing a pure black-and-white image.

For many photographers, though, shooting color and then converting to black-and-white presents a strongly creative workflow that offers added control options. When colors in the world are changed to black and white tones in the camera (whether you shoot film or digital), you are locked into those tones. When you shoot in color and translate colors to black and white tones in Lightroom, you have many more options on how they make that translation.

6-25

For example, if you shoot a red flower in black-and-white, you can, through the use of filters, translate the red color into a tone of gray from light to dark, but then you are stuck with that tone. If you shoot a red flower in color and then bring it into Lightroom for conversion to black-and-white, you can change it to a range of tones as needed. You are not limited to the tone as shot.

PRO TIP

Use Virtual Copies for black-and-white. You can create a virtual copy of any photo in Lightroom by right-clicking the image and choosing Create Virtual Copy. This creates a copy of information, but no actual pixels are copied. Use the virtual copy for your black-and-white conversions and keep the color image intact for other interpretations.

Using Grayscale in HSL/Color/Grayscale

Lightroom's primary way of changing color to black-and-white is Grayscale in the HSL/Color/Grayscale group on the right side of the Develop module. You can also convert to grayscale (black-and-white) in Basic, but I don't recommend this "auto black-and-white" option, except for very basic, down-and-dirty, black-and-white needs. It uses a similar set of changes to what you might get from the Grayscale mode in Photoshop.

How colors translate to tones of gray has a huge effect on the effectiveness of a black-and-white photo. Compare figure 6-26 with figure 6-25. This new translation is okay as a simple auto black-and-white conversion, but it is a harsher version that won't print as well.

Remember that ultimately, black-and-white is about color and how that color changes. If you remember that, Grayscale Mix, shown in figure 6-27, is fairly easy to use. (However, ease of use and mastery of use are different things — practice helps you master this control.) It is set up with sliders to affect how a particular color translates into gray. Moving any slider to the right makes that color a lighter gray in the photo. Moving a slider to the left makes that color a darker gray.

Black-and-white photography needs contrast, which comes from adjusting these sliders, or everything blends together with the same shades of gray. Yet if you get a group of photographers together who then convert the same scene to black-and-white, you usually find a set of very different interpretations. Some prefer high contrast; others like more subtle gradations and changes in tone. Black-and-white should be about interpretation — another reason why the standard Grayscale or auto option should be a limited choice for anyone serious about black-and-white images, although Grayscale is what appears first in Basic by default. Just don't stay there!

One of the best reasons for translating a black-and-white image in Develop and using the Grayscale sliders is that this is another area where you can activate the cursor for click-and-drag changes. This is really huge in helping photographers with their translations of color to gray. When you activate the cursor (same icon at the upper-left of the Grayscale panel section), it allows you to hover over anything in the photo, and Lightroom finds the color to adjust for you! It automatically gets highlighted in the sliders and in their values. Then if you click-and-drag the cursor up or down to make the adjustment, Lightroom actually recognizes the appropriate color (or colors) and changes how it translates into grayscale tones! I find that remarkable.

6-26

6-27

In figure 6-28, you can see the green trees of this scene being adjusted (Adobe engineers seem to like to call greens yellow, as can be seen in the sliders). This is one of the best ways of translating color into black-and-white tones that I know. This makes black-and-white far easier and intuitive than ever before. Photoshop CS3 does have a similar adjustment for black-and-white conversion, but it can't be used with RAW files.

Here are some ideas for you to consider when working with Grayscale in the Develop module:

> **Work multiple colors.** Almost always, I make one color lighter and a different color darker, as shown in figure 6-29. By clicking the activated cursor on several locations (you can see the colors that are affected when they are highlighted in the adjustment panel) or by using several sliders, you can control exactly which colors are affected. Keep in mind that colors in a scene are not always precise matches to specific slider colors, which you saw in figure 6-28. You may find when moving one slider that seems to be the right color that the adjustment doesn't work as well as you'd like. This is one reason why the activated "targeted adjustment" cursor works so well: It finds exactly the right color both in the photo and as defined by Adobe.

> **Don't be afraid to make big moves with these sliders, even maxing them out.** I like to make big moves because I like contrast in black-and-white. Some photographers like more subtle effects and never max out these sliders. My point is not that you have to max them out, but that you can do it as needed with no ill effects on the photograph. A caution, however: Sometimes you will find that strong adjustments with certain colors can increase the appearance of noise or tonal banding. This is especially true with skies. Watch for this, then tone down your adjustment or be prepared for using noise-reduction software outside of Lightroom.

> **Watch out for colors that have similar brightness.** Red and green are the classic examples of this. If you use Auto for a photo that has strong red and green colors, you typically end up with a plain gray photo with none of the contrast that the colors displayed. Work those colors in the Grayscale Mix so that they separate and appear as different tones.

> **Revise black-and-white conversions in Basic and Tone Curve.** You won't need to change every black-and-white conversion, but many times the black-and-white version of an image needs new black and white points, plus midtone contrast.

> **Turn on the Before and After views.** I find this is often very helpful because I can see where the colors are in the Before view. This way I can better decide which sliders to use to make them lighter or darker grays or where to click for direct color control by clicking and dragging.

PRO TIP

To get the most out of an image in black-and-white, you have to still pay attention to the blacks, whites, and midtones, as I discuss in Chapter 5. Simply converting an image to black-and-white without checking blacks and whites and setting midtones gives you less than the best results, and you can end up making unneeded adjustments in the Grayscale controls. Do your best with the color image, first, then check the blacks and whites again after making the Grayscale conversion.

Histogram
Basic
Tone Curve
HSL / Color / Grayscale
Grayscale Mix
Red − 11
Orange − 21
Yellow + 36
Green − 2
Aqua − 18
Blue − 32
Purple + 19
Magenta + 4
Auto
Split Toning
Detail

6-28

Histogram
Basic
Tone Curve
HSL / Color / Grayscale
Grayscale Mix
Red − 11
Orange − 21
Yellow + 80
Green + 19
Aqua − 20
Blue − 54
Purple + 19
Magenta + 4
Auto
Split Toning
Detail

6-29

Giving Black-and-White Some Color

A long tradition in classic black-and-white photography is *color toning*. It is done to give the image some color other than just neutral tones, and in many cases, the toning is done to increase the life of the print. Color toning gives black-and-white photos a different dimension. Some photographers prefer a purely neutral black-and-white image, but others find color toning gives their photos an added richness.

Color toning is very easy to do in Lightroom. Once you have a black-and-white conversion, go to Split Toning, which is just below HSL/Color/Grayscale, as shown in figure 6-30. Highlights now affect mainly the lighter tones in your photo, while Shadows color the darker tones. The Balance control affects how both deal with the entire image, including pure white and pure black. You can use this control with black-and-white like this:

6-30

1. **Get your best black-and-white conversion first.**
2. **Move Saturation of Highlights up to about 50 percent, as shown in figure 6-31.** This lets you see the color toning without it being too strong. You won't necessarily keep this setting, but it helps in first adjustments.
3. **Change the Highlights Hue until you like a color tone on your photo.** Warm colors give a sepia tone; bluish colors give a cool tone. You can also click the color box to the right of Highlights to get a Color Picker that you can use to choose a color.
4. **Refine the Saturation of Highlights.** Move it up or down until you like the effect, as shown in figure 6-32. If you like the overall color at this point, you don't have to go further — use it as is.
5. **Move Saturation of Shadows up to about 30 percent.** This lets you see its effect on color toning without it being too strong. You also won't necessarily keep this setting, but it helps in first adjustments.
6. **Change the Shadows Hue until you like a color tone on your photo.** Shadows and other dark areas of a black-and-white photo often look good with a slightly cool tone to them. However, you can also use a color similar to Highlights for a very rich effect as well.

Histogram
Basic
Tone Curve
HSL / Color / Grayscale
Split Toning
Highlights
Hue 0
Saturation 50
Balance 0
Shadows
Hue 0
Saturation 0
Detail
Vignettes
6-31

Histogram
Basic
Tone Curve
HSL / Color / Grayscale
Split Toning
Highlights
Hue 56
Saturation 36
Balance 0
Shadows
Hue 0
Saturation 0
Detail
Vignettes
6-32

6-33

7. **Refine the Saturation of Shadows.** Move it up or down until you like the effect. Usually, I find I like a lower saturation for the color in Shadows, as shown in figure 6-33.
8. **Finish with the Balance control to change how the color toning is applied to both shadows and highlights.**

You can also use Split Toning with color photos. Experiment with it to make highlights warm and shadows cool, for example, which mimics real-world highlights and shadows when the sun is low in the sky. However, it can be used in totally unexpected and creative ways as well, such as giving highlights a very strong color to contrast with the rest of the photo.

Develop Module Presets

Develop adds Presets to the left side panel that are pre-made controls for certain adjustments and effects that you can use directly with a single click. There are 18 presets that come with Lightroom, as shown in figure 6-34, plus you can add your own. You can quickly see what any look like by hovering your cursor over the preset (don't click) and watching the preview image above the presets, also shown in figure 6-34. You can apply the presets to the image by clicking any of them.

There are ten Creative presets that offer some very interesting ways of dealing with your photo, mostly black-and-white, but they go much further than simply adjusting the Grayscale sliders. The best way to see what they will do to your photo is to try them. Their effects look quite different from photo to photo. Some will fit your needs, some you will think are ugly. Use what works for you, and remember that none of these are permanent. As long as you are working in Lightroom, nothing is actually applied to the image until you export.

The eight other presets simply give you quick and easy overall adjustments to your photo. You may find them interesting to look at, especially if you try one and see what adjustments have actually been made. To get the most from the presets, consider them fast ways to make some adjustments to a photo, even as quick previews if you just run your cursor over them. I find this can generate some ideas on how I might approach a particular photo.

Then use the Preset adjustment as a starting point. If you like it, great, but you'll often find some additional tweaking helpful to get the most out of a photo. Consider that these preset adjustments can never "know" what your actual photo is; they can only offer interesting changes that work for many photos and photographers. Your interpretation of them can be very important in getting results that work for your images.

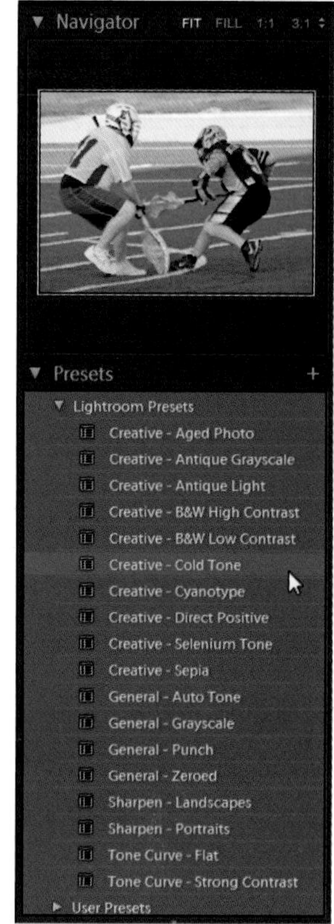

6-34

Making Your Own Presets

Lightroom makes it easy to create your own presets. It is a way to save adjustments that you use regularly and turn them into "presets" to use again and again. If you have certain types of photographs that need regular ways of processing, you may find that creating your own presets (or saved adjustments) for them speeds your workflow.

To create a preset, select a "standard" photo, one that works well for the adjustments you want to use in a preset. Adjust it optimally to create a consistent way to control images for this preset, as shown in figure 6-35.

6-35

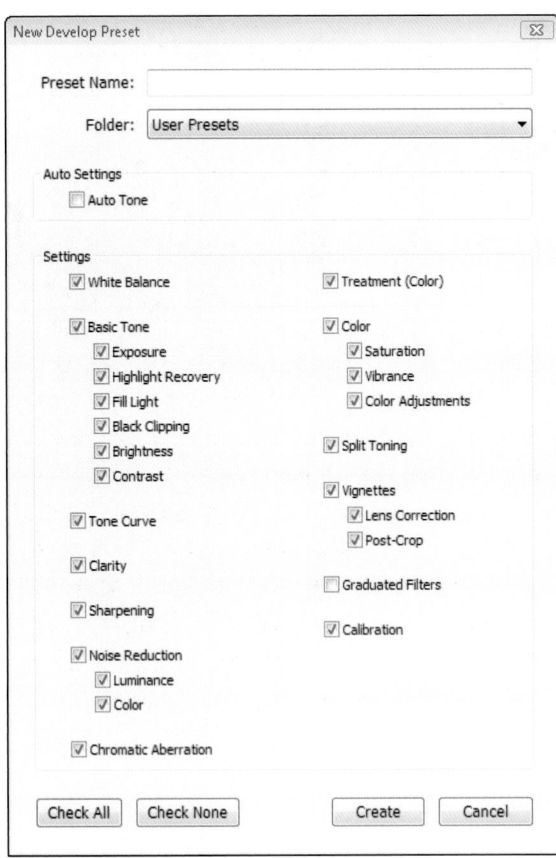

6-36

To save those adjustments and create your preset, do this:

1. **Click + at the right of Presets (you remove Presets by clicking first on a preset then on –).** A dialog box appears, as shown in figure 6-36, for a new preset that is similar to the one you saw for the Sync button. It includes nearly all of the adjustments on the right side of Develop.
2. **Choose the settings that you want to use for your preset.** You can simply use them all to match your photo exactly as adjusted. Or you can select just the key adjustments that create the effect you need for your preset.
3. **Type a name for your preset in the Preset Name box, and click Create.** The new Preset appears in your Presets list.

There are many ways you can use new presets, and you will get ideas for them as you gain experience working with images in Lightroom. However, here are some ideas that might help you get started:

> **Create black-and-white conversion presets.** You can set these up to make certain colors lighter or darker. For example, you can get a "red filter" preset by using Grayscale Mix and setting the red and magenta sliders far to the right to make reds lighter, then the blue and cyan sliders far to the left to make them darker. Or you can create a "foliage" filter for black-and-white by using Grayscale and moving the green and yellow filters pretty far to the right.

> **Create color enhancement presets.** Make a red enhancement preset by going to HSL Color Tuning and increasing the Red Saturation slider, and then going to Camera Calibration and moving the Red Saturation slider all the way to the right. Similarly, make green and blue enhancements by using the Green and Blue Saturation sliders in Camera Calibration.

> **Create unique desaturated looks for images.** The mostly black-and-white photo with a slight bit of color can be a very interesting look. Try using the HSL saturation controls to desaturate each color differently.

> **Create a high-contrast look with the Tone Curve.** Go to the Tone Curve and make a steep ascent from bottom to top by moving the lower section downward and the upper section toward the top of the graph.

When you are making a new preset, you can limit the adjustments to only specific changes by selecting the check boxes in the dialog box related to those changes. If your preset needs to use everything you have done to a photo, then be sure all the check boxes are selected.

Exporting Photos

You learned the basics of Exporting photos in Chapter 3 on the Library module because Library holds the Export button. However, I rarely export from Library; typically, I will export while I am in Develop, after I have worked on one or more images. It is rare for me to want to export images without doing at least some minimal processing. Because this processing is quick and easy to do in Lightroom, I find little excuse not to do it.

I do want to talk a little about the two basic ways that you can export photos from Lightroom: the Edit In and Export functions. Nearly always, I access these functions by right-clicking on my photo and choosing either function from the menu that appears, as shown in figure 6-37. I typically use the Export function, because the Edit In function doesn't fit my needs. However, I do understand that the Edit In function is perfect for other photographers.

In the Export method of getting images out of Lightroom, you can define a lot of parameters for those images, such as file type, file name, image size, file saved location, bit depth, and more, as described in Chapter 3. These parameters are important to me, as they fit my way of working with images for everything from assignment work to book projects.

In the Edit In option for exporting, you typically export the photo to a specific program, plus when you save the image, it is saved in the same file folder as your original. You can then work on that image, and those changes are saved back to the photo that has been added to Lightroom. My preference is to keep my processed images separate from my original photos, and to give them original names, which Edit In does not do, except as an added step in Photoshop. For photographers who like to keep these images together, however, this works well, but the photograph's name will be a variant of the original.

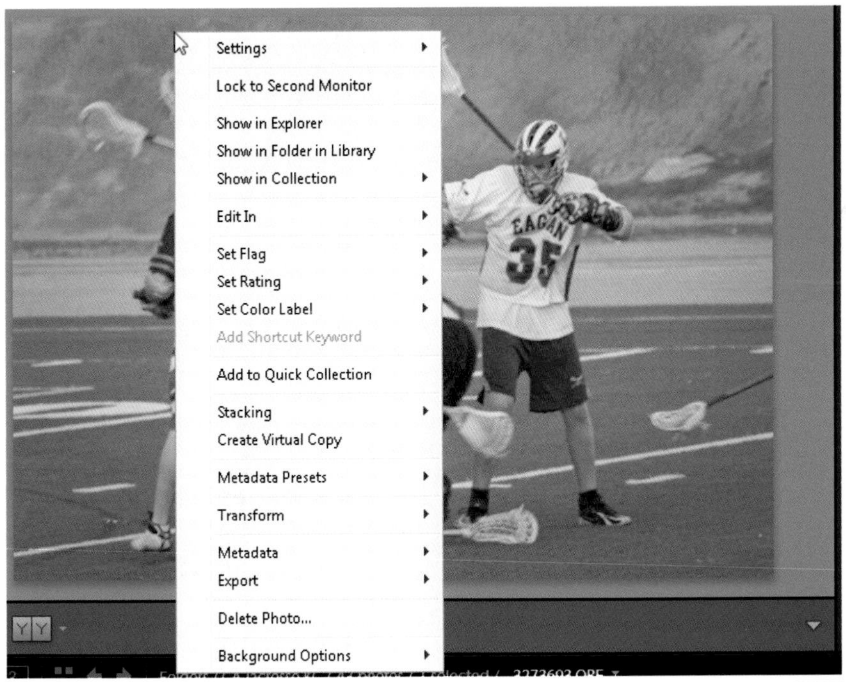

6-37

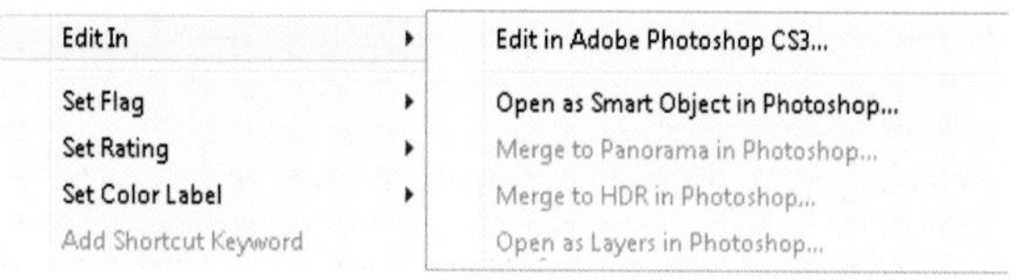

6-38

Edit In does offer some unique ways to export photos that can be important and useful for many photographers. As shown in figure 6-38, they are:

- **Edit in Adobe Photoshop CS3.** This option sends your photo directly to Photoshop. You can also send your photo to Photoshop through Export, but this option is a very simple way of going to Photoshop. Click it and the photo goes right to Photoshop without using any other dialog boxes. To gain the most out of Lightroom 2, though, you do need to have the latest version of Camera RAW installed with Photoshop.
- **Open as Smart Object in Photoshop**. This is a really interesting option that is used typically by photographers who are doing a lot of compositing. This creates a direct link between the photograph, as it appears in Photoshop, and what you can do to it in Lightroom. Smart Objects are a bit beyond the scope of this book. What they basically allow a photographer to do is have a photograph as a layer, for example, and then if that photograph needs to be adjusted, the photographer can go right back to Lightroom, make those adjustments, and have them reappear in that photograph all in the layer.
- **Merge to Panorama in Photoshop.** For photographers who do a lot of multi-image panoramic work, this can be a very useful way of editing images out of Lightroom. You can take multiple photos shot for a panoramic and adjust them in Lightroom so that they better match each other in tones and colors. Then you can select that group of photos and send them to Photoshop's panoramic function.
- **Merge to HDR in Photoshop.** Many photographers are discovering High Dynamic Range photography or HDR. This involves shooting the same scene with a variety of exposures, then using the computer to combine all those exposures to create a final image that has a far greater tonal range compared to what the camera and sensor can normally capture. In many cases, this gives you a scene that is closer to what can be seen with the eye than what the camera is capable of handling. This option allows you to do some work in Lightroom on all of these images before sending them to Photoshop for the HDR merging. I can't really recommend it because I am not fond of the Photoshop way of dealing with HDR. At the time I am writing this book, most photographers are using a program called Photomatix from HDR Soft (www.hdrsoft.com) for their HDR work.
- **Open as Layers in Photoshop.** This is a rather useful way of opening images if you are doing such techniques as *double processing* or *two-exposure blending*. You can have two different images, each with different processing, for example, and open those as layers in Photoshop so that one is right over the other. Double processing is typically used for images that have challenging highlights and shadows. With this technique, you create a virtual copy of your image, then process one copy for the highlights and one copy for the shadows. In Photoshop, you combine these two images for a better photograph than you would get from trying to process both highlights and shadows at once. Two-exposure blending allows you to capture widely divergent brightness levels within a scene by using different camera exposures, then combining them in Photoshop (HDR is now used a little more often).

Q & A

If you really want to use Camera Calibration to calibrate a camera, how could you do that?

On an engineering level, this is not the tool to use for that. There are programs on the market that can help you calibrate a camera, though I have not found any all that useful.

On a more photographic level, you can create a preset for a specific camera that uses Camera Calibration to adjust for that camera's biases in capturing color. You can go the scientific route and get a color checker chart, photograph it, then tweak how it looks in Lightroom with Camera Calibration, and save those settings as a preset. In addition, Adobe is working on specific camera profiles for common digital single lens reflex (SLR) cameras that will be able to be loaded into Camera Calibration. These may or may not work for you.

I tend to take a more subjective approach. I find that certain cameras have biases that directly affect the colors in subjects that I shoot. I have found some cameras, for example, make greens too yellow. I can then select a photo that has that subject and those colors, adjust it in Camera Calibration to make the colors look better, and then save that as a preset. In the green example just given, I can adjust the Hue and Saturation sliders for Green in Camera Calibration to get better greens, and then save that as a Green preset.

You don't talk much about the Color section of HSL/Color/Grayscale. I understand you don't like it, but it seems like it would be a good way of isolating adjustments to a specific color.

That's true on both counts! It can be a good way of isolating adjustments to a specific color, and I don't like it. That can be seen as a good example of how photographers really do respond to controls and tools in Lightroom differently. Just because I don't like the control does not mean it is not very useful to folks who like the way it separates colors.

One big limitation is the lack of the direct photo control. There is no button to select to allow you to click-and-drag on the photo to directly change the hue, saturation, and luminance of a color. I find that click-and-drag option to be very intuitive and helpful for the photographer.

Chapter 7

PRESENTATION POSSIBILITIES IN THE SLIDESHOW MODULE

Slide shows have always been a very important part of the way a photographer presents his or her work. I do slide shows all the time in presentations that I do for workshops and other programs around the country. Yet, in recent years, the traditional slide show has almost disappeared. Kodak even quit making the classic carousel projector. Few people still set up a slide projector and screen to show off their latest trip to Europe.

Luckily, the computer now fills this function. Anyone can project images as a "slide show" (even though there are no true slides in digital photography) that looks better than ever. Now you can do music, slides, and transitions, all from the camera, and never have a single image jam, have the music get out of sync, run out of slide tray space, or have the two slide projectors lose their sync.

Lightroom's Slideshow module offers a simple, yet quite elegant, way to assemble your images for a slide show presentation. You get to it by clicking Slideshow. When Lightroom first came out, I was disappointed in how simple the Slideshow option really was. There are some definite limitations to slide shows made in Lightroom. However, as I have used this program more and more, I have discovered that there are some very nice aspects to doing slide shows with Lightroom, including presenting some of the best color-managed slides for projection that I've seen. In this chapter, I give you the basics of using Lightroom tools to create a slide show.

The Slideshow Module Layout

Like all Lightroom modules, Slideshow uses the same organization of panels as the rest of Lightroom, as shown in figure 7-1. Here's an overview of the four main panels and their functions:

> **Center work area.** This holds the main photo, plus slide details like titles.

> **Right panel.** As in all other modules, this is the adjustment side of the module. It is where you change backgrounds and other features for how slides display, plus you can control the timing of the images and the use of music.

> **Bottom Filmstrip panel.** This is a key element of Slideshow. It is where you arrange your photos in the order needed for the slide show. While you often hide it in other modules, this is one module where you always need to keep it available.

> **Left panel.** This is where you find more "presets," though, in this case, they are called templates, plus a preview photo and a way to select images or "content."

In addition to the panels, there is once again a toolbar under the central photo that can be used to work on images, as shown in figure 7-2. It includes these tools:

> **Playback controls.** These are the four buttons at the left side of the toolbar. Play, at the right, plays your slide show from the image you have selected as a preview. The others affect how you move around within your slide show. The square at the left stops the slide show if it is playing or it takes you to the beginning of your show images. Next are two arrows: The left one steps you backward through the photos, while the arrow to the right steps you forward through the images. This can be very helpful for seeing how one photo goes against another.

> **Use: selector.** In the middle of the toolbar is a button labeled Use: You click the words to the right for a drop-down menu that allows you to select what photos to use in your slide show. There are three choices for content: All Filmstrip Photos (this choice simply uses all of the images in the Filmstrip), Selected Photos (if you decide that you want only certain images from the group in the Filmstrip, then you can select the ones you

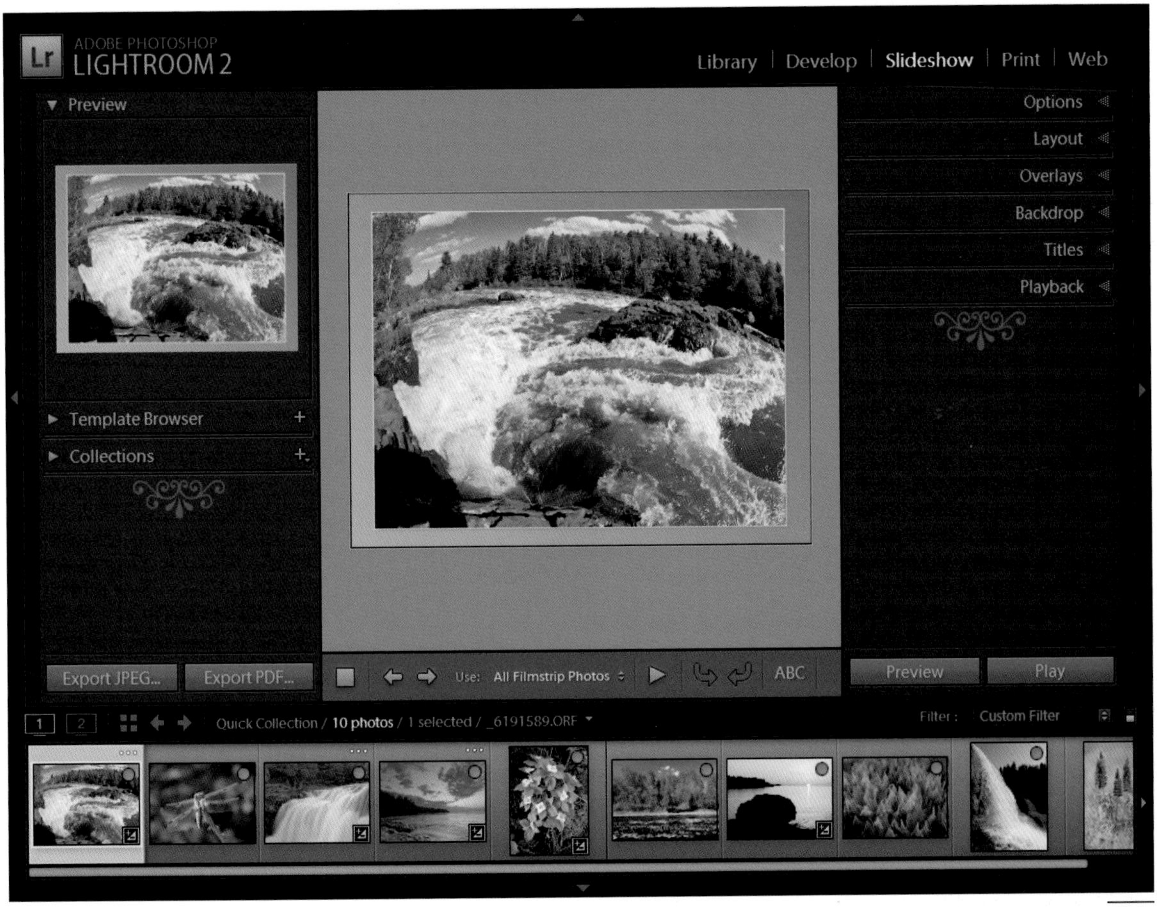

7-1

want by Ctrl/⌘+clicking them), and Flagged Photos (to flag images in your collection for use in a slide show, you need to go to the Library module and flag the images as discussed in the chapters about Library).

> **ABC button.** At the right of the toolbar is a button labeled ABC that you click to add text or titles to your photos in your slide show. (It adds this information to all photos.) When you click it, the Custom Text dialog box appears (which also gives options for automated text based on metadata). Otherwise, this box simply shows the numbers of your images in the slide show.

7-2

Slideshow Workflow

As with the workflow in any part of the digital process, every photographer will discover what works best when he or she uses the Slideshow module. However, there are some things about working with a slide show that affect how you might use this module.

Slide shows are about a group of images being shown consecutively. How they are edited and organized makes a big difference in your final show. Lightroom gives you a lot of choices for making your show look aesthetically interesting, but these choices can be a distraction if the organization of the show is not right. I am suggesting a workflow that works well for retaining the primary function of the show: that it is a group of images shown together in a particular sequence that creates an effect greater than any individual photo.

Here's a workflow that will get you started in creating an effective slide show:

1. **Set up a "basic" slide background to start your edit and organization process.** Do this by clicking Default in the Template Browser. Next, click on the Identity Plate (if one is displayed on the center photo) and delete it. Then click the file name (below the center photo) and delete it. Now press Ctrl/⌘+N and a new Template dialog box appears. Type **Basic** and it appears in the Template Browser. Now any time you click this, you get a simple, basic background for your slides. You only need to do this once and it is part of your Template Browser.
2. **Select a group of images in Library for your slide show, put them into Quick Collection, and then go to Slideshow.** You can also start sorting your images in the Grid view of Library, but I don't think this works nearly as well as putting your slides into the Quick Collection. You can also create a unique collection specifically for your slide show, then take your quick collection images and put them there. Following this simple process gives you a slide show very quickly.
3. **Set your "view" to a simple image of the photos in the center work area.** Use the custom basic setup in the Template Browser I describe in Step 1 and show in figure 7-3.
4. **Make your images, your "slides," small enough in the Filmstrip that at least ten or more show up in that work panel.** You can make the Filmstrip larger or smaller by clicking and dragging on the dividing line below the toolbar, as shown in figure 7-4. (Your cursor changes to the double arrow when you are in the right position.) Your thumbnails are small now, but you are not looking for details at this point. Make the thumbnails large enough that you are comfortable with what can be seen.
5. **Move slides around on the Filmstrip by clicking and dragging.** Give the slides an order that you think will work for a slide show. This is just like sorting slides on a real-world lightbox.
6. **Go through images one at a time by clicking the right-facing arrow in the Playback area.** See if you like the arrangement of the photos.
7. **Revise the image arrangement as needed.**
8. **Adjust the images' brightness, color, or contrast so they better fit the grouping of photos.** You often discover an image looks too bright or too dark when it is contrasted to another one that comes before or after it. One great thing about Lightroom is the ability to go back to Develop whenever you want and make a correction like this so an image (or images) better fits the sequence.
9. **Work out a look for your image presentation.** Start with the Template Browser — move your cursor over the choices to see what they might look like in the preview area above the browser, as shown in figure 7-5.

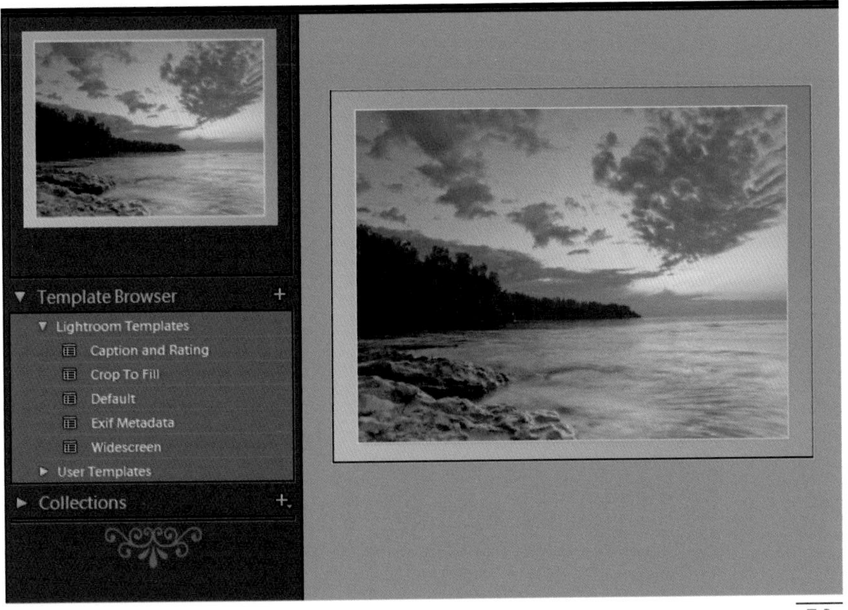

7-3

7-4

10. **Refine the look for your image presentation.** Use the adjustment controls on the right side of Slideshow to do that.

11. **Click Play to see how the photos actually look playing for a specific time and with a transition.**

12. **Refine the timing of your presentation.** Use Playback in the right panel to change the length of time each slide is on and transition timings.

13. **Add music (select Soundtrack in Playback).** Refine the timing of your presentation to match the music by changing slide duration, or adding and removing slides, or both.

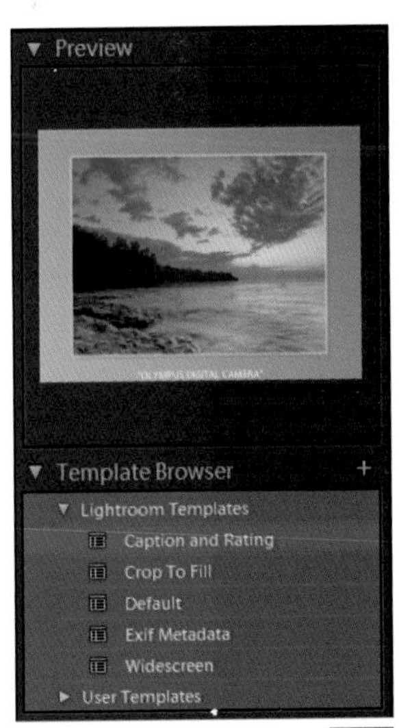

7-5

Selecting and Grouping Photos for a Slide Show

To produce a slide show, you need a set of images to work with. Lightroom offers you a number of ways of doing this, starting with the Library module. Allowing you to move among modules as you need their capabilities is another strength of Lightroom's modular design.

Here are several ways you can group images for a slide show:

> **Multiple selection.** You can open a Folder or Collection in Library and use the standard computer selection tools to select a group of photos. Click on an image to start the process, and then Shift+click another photo, and everything between is included. Or you can select as many individual photos as you want by going through the images and Ctrl/⌘+clicking the desired pictures.

> **Rate photos.** You can go into a Folder or Collection and use Lightroom's rating function to select a group of images. If you keep one rating specifically for slide shows (such as 5), you can use all other rating numbers for ranking and sorting photos for other purposes. You can sort to the rating and then select them all (Ctrl/⌘+A) or move them to Quick Collection. You can only work one Folder or Collection at a time for Slideshow.

7-6

> **Quick Collection.** For me, Quick Collection is the best way to start selecting images for a slide show. You can easily and simply select images to go instantly into the Quick Collection by clicking the small circle that appears over the top-right corner of an image in Grid or Filmstrip when you run your cursor over it (or press B), as shown in figure 7-6.

You can remove an image from Quick Collection by clicking again on the same circle or by pressing B again with the image selected. A big advantage of this technique is that you can add and subtract photos from diverse Folders or Collections continuously from Quick Collection. You then click Quick Collection in the Catalog category of the left panel of Library, as shown in figure 7-7, and go to Slideshow to use the photos. The disadvantage of Quick Collection is that it can only handle one group of images at a time.

> **New Collection.** Another great way to group photos for a slide show is to create a collection specifically for your show. You click + in Collections and give your new collection a name based on your slide show topic, as shown in figure 7-8; then you have a unique collection for the slide show. I think the easiest way to move images into this new collection is to use Quick Collection to gather the slides, then select them all while you are in Library and press Ctrl/⌘+N. Choose Include selected photos in the Create Collection dialog box, also shown in figure 7-8, and everything automatically goes to the new collection, as shown in figure 7-9. A nice thing about this approach is that you can always keep your group of photos together as a slide show. If you need to do special things to the images, you can also use Lightroom's virtual copy option to make copies that you can work with in this collection totally separate from anything else. You can add

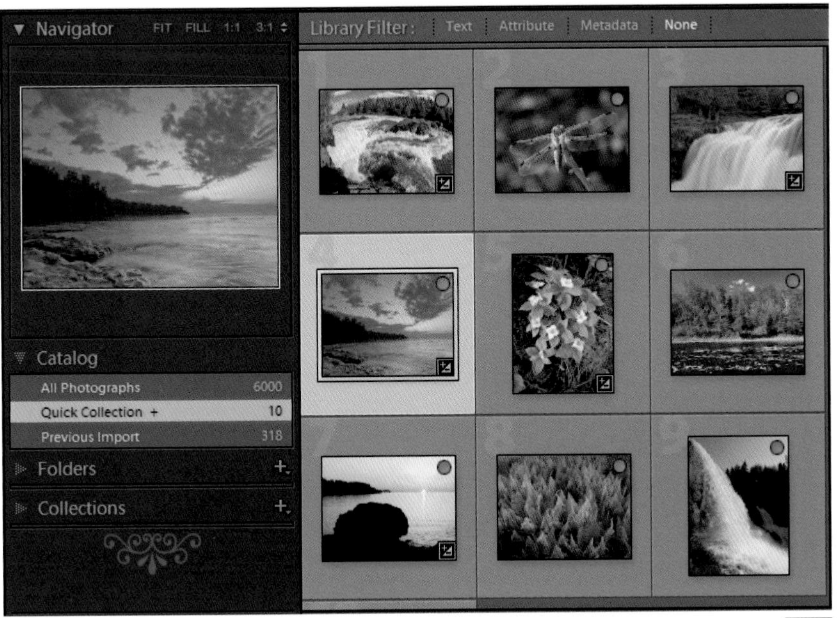

7-7

to your collection later or remove photos you no longer want. If you no longer need this collection, it is easy to delete, too (click the – sign). You can also group all slide show collections into one Slideshow Collection. Create the Slideshow Collection first. Then as you need new and specific slide show groups, click Slideshow first, and then +. When the dialog box appears, select Create as a Child of Slideshow.

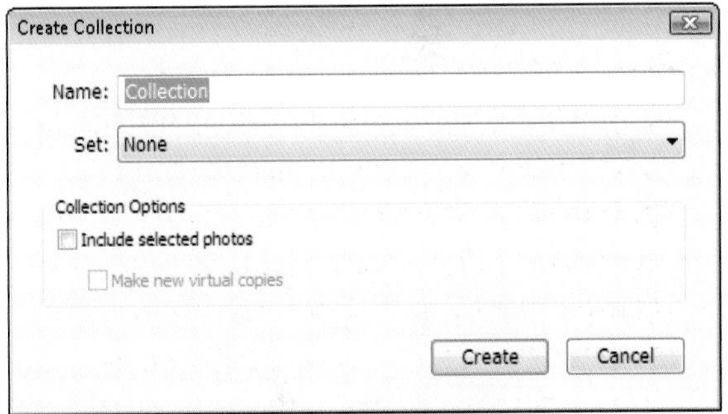

7-8

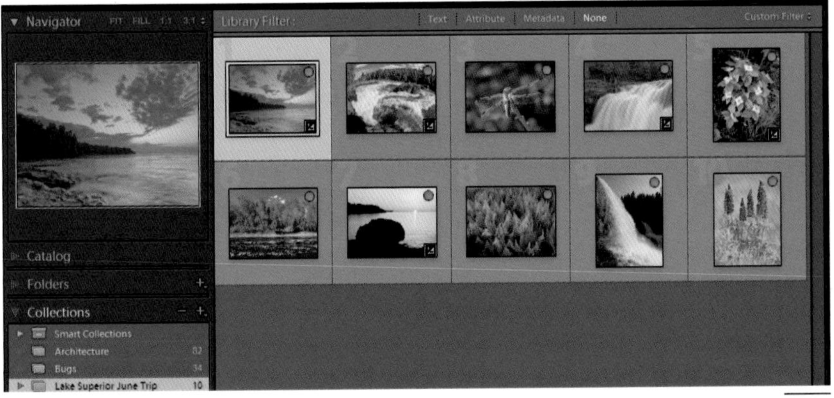

7-9

Organizing and Editing Your Images

After you have selected a group of photos, you can start organizing and reediting your photos for the show. You can do this in the Library Grid mode or on the Filmstrip. Either way, you are going to be changing the order of your images. This, for me, is a very important reason for having them in their own unique Collection. I don't like arbitrarily rearranging images in a Collection that is used for a different purpose (though you can always use the sorting capabilities of Lightroom).

I believe it is easier to start organizing in the Library Grid view before going to Slideshow. To get as much space as possible in the central work area for this job, try hiding all of the panels, as shown in figure 7-10. Yes, you can move images around in the filmstrip area while in the Slideshow mode, but you see less of the images there and you can only work with a linear arrangement.

This work area, as shown in figure 7-10, is excellent for doing a slide show. You need to see how the photos look together in order, and you need to see the organization of the show. As nice as Lightroom's display tools are for creating a look for each image, a slide show is about a group of images, a story from beginning to end, how one image relates to another, and so forth. Having a "slide table," or a large work area, allows you to see many, or even most, of your photos at once when they're sized appropriately. In addition, that large work area makes it a lot easier to drag images around to change their order.

You do, indeed, play with the slide show organization by dragging and dropping your photos into new places. And you remove photos from the collection by pressing the Backspace/Delete key. (Ctrl/⌘+Z brings it back through the Undo command.) This does not remove the photo from Lightroom, just from the Collection and your work area.

Here's how I like to work with this virtual slide table:

1. **Look at all the photos and get an idea of what topics or types of images should come first, which should come second, and which should be last.** In Chapter 8, I give more details on how you might do this.

7-10

Library Filter : Text Attribute Metadata None Custom Filter

7-11

2. **Start moving photos around to fit that order.** Click and drag an image to a new, better location for the slide show, as shown in figure 7-11 if you compare it to figure 7-10. Click directly on the image itself, not on the "mount," to drag it; also, you can select several images at once and drag them together to a new location. Delete photos that don't fit.
3. **Go to a single image in Slideshow at any place in your slide set and use the forward arrow to go through the photos.** Does the order make sense? Do images seem to go together?
4. **Go back to the Grid (just press g) and rearrange images as needed.** This takes you back into the Library module. As your show is developed, you can probably stick with Slideshow and refine your images in the Filmstrip rather than going back and forth to the Library Grid view.
5. **Be sure you have interesting beginning and ending slides in your group.**

Giving Your Show a Unique Look

At this point, it is time to give your show a graphic look. Turn the right and left panels back on, as shown in figure 7-12, so you can access the tools needed for this graphic look.

In this module, it helps to start with the Template Browser to get an idea of possible choices you have. With practice, you will probably not need to do this. You may even set up your own custom templates based on your slide show needs such as I suggested earlier in this chapter with the Basic template.

Lightroom allows you to control how large the photo is within the display area, the background behind it, drop shadows and borders for the images, and what text is included. You can really create a very elegant-looking slide show with these tools.

7-12

The Template Browser includes five default choices in the option called Lightroom Templates, as shown in figure 7-13. As you move your cursor over each template choice, the Navigator changes, but nothing is changed on your center image until you actually click the choice. Each one offers you ideas, as well as a change to the look of your show.

- **Caption and Rating.** This template reduces the size of the photo to allow a gray background and image effects (this template has a drop shadow and a thin white border), plus it includes the photo's Lightroom rating and any caption information associated with the image, as shown in figure 7-14.

7-13

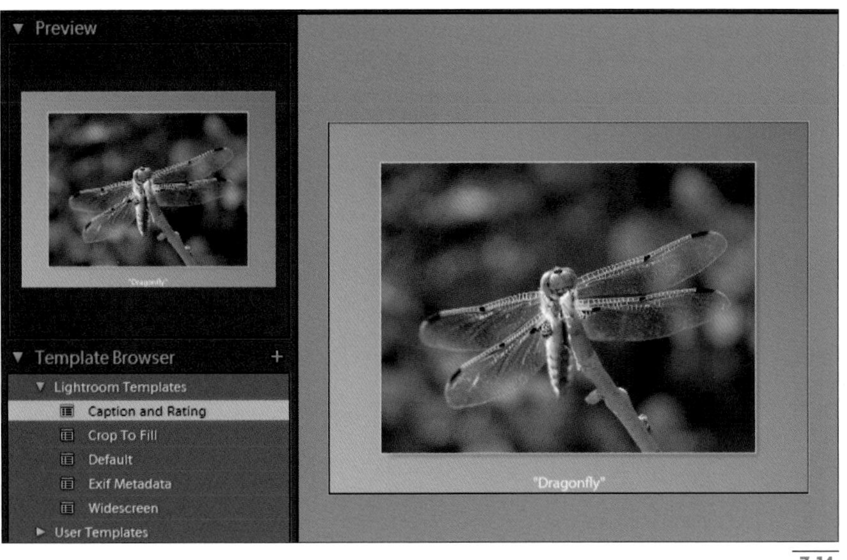

7-14

When you first look at this (or any other template), you may see a grid of white lines. They are guides only and can be turned off in Layout in the right panel by deselecting Show Guides.

- **Crop To Fill.** This option enables you to fill the screen with your photo, cropping the image if necessary so it fits without any gaps, as shown in figure 7-15. This is a way that you can show nothing but the photo. You can click and drag the photo within the frame to make it look its best for the crop. For horizontal photos, this may be fine and may even tighten up your composition. However, this option really destroys verticals. You shot a vertical for a specific reason, so it seems to me a mistake to now turn it into a horizontal by cropping it to fit the horizontal screen. Crop To Fill can be useful if all of your photos are standard-sized horizontals, but if you include verticals, I suggest another choice.
- **Default.** Here you get a slightly bigger image than Caption and Rating, plus the file name is displayed below the photo and your Identity Plate (if you created one under Edit ➪ Identity Plate Setup, which I explain fully in Chapter 2) at the top left. You can change either or both as desired. Default uses a black background, a small Identity Plate, and ratings (if present), as shown in figure 7-16.
- **Exif Metadata.** This template changes a lot of things. First, the image is now displayed as the same size as Default, but with a black background and white border, as shown in figure 7-17. Second, the image includes a lot of information. At the top left is an Identity Plate if you are using one, and at the top right, the date the photo was shot. Centered below the photo is the picture's title from the metadata. At the right is camera EXIF data including f-stop, ISO speed rating, and focal length used. (You can change this.)
- **Widescreen.** The name of this option is a little misleading. It seems to imply that your photo will be something like the 16:9 format of HD video widescreen television. Actually, what you get is "full frame" — you see the whole image and it fills the screen to its full height or width without cropping either, and then a black background fills any gaps. No borders or drop shadows are used, as shown in figure 7-18.

Preview
Template Browser
Lightroom Templates
Caption and Rating
Crop To Fill
Default
Exif Metadata
Widescreen
User Templates

7-15

Preview
Template Browser
Lightroom Templates
Caption and Rating
Crop To Fill
Default
Exif Metadata
Widescreen
User Templates
Lightroom

7-16

Preview
Template Browser
Lightroom Templates
Caption and Rating
Crop To Fill
Default
Exif Metadata
Widescreen
User Templates
Lightroom

7-17

Preview
Template Browser
Lightroom Templates
Caption and Rating
Crop To Fill
Default
Exif Metadata
Widescreen
User Templates

7-18

A slide show is a totally different animal than an individual photo or a print. Therefore, you have to treat it completely differently. You must see photos (plural) and not be stopped by a photo (singular). That is a very important distinction. Slideshows are never seen as individual pictures — they are always seen by viewers as a group of images. For a slideshow to be really effective, all of the images that go together in that show must work together as a whole.

Sometimes a photographer puts together a slide show that is basically a series of single unrelated images. For example, a photographer may need to do this when putting together a presentation for a client. Still, a slide show works best when there are connections between and among the photographs. While individual photos may offer something, such as size or the capability to show images in different locations, they rarely have the impact of a group of photographs working together.

In this chapter, you will learn more about working with slides to make an effective slide show. You learn to use Slideshow controls to make a group of images work as a group, to create something greater than just a simple showing of individual images, and to create a real show.

Starting the Organizing Process

The Grid view of Library is a great place to organize your images into a show, as you saw in Chapter 7. I want to put that organization into a different perspective: I am going to use some terms to describe the views that are not "official" Lightroom terms, but terms that I think are more descriptive of the process. You can use the work area in two ways to organize your photos:

- **Use the Overview view.** This is the Grid view with only the main work area and the Filmstrip visible, as shown in figure 8-1. It gives you an instant overview of images. In the specific view seen in this figure, I reduced the size of the thumbnails by using the Thumbnails slider at the bottom so all of the images in this short show appear. These images have also been edited somewhat from what you saw in Chapter 7. You can see which photos are together and which are not, and where images are within the whole show; and you can move the images from one area to another to find new relationships among them. In addition, I like to include the Filmstrip to get a linear look of the slides as well. The beginning, middle, and end of the show are quickly visible; and Grid view enables you to instantly look at the photos in front of and behind a selected photo in order, and then change the order by just clicking and dragging photos.

PRO TIP

Remember to make your work area as large as possible by hiding the other panels to the left, right, and top of the interface by using Shift+Tab. You can also click the arrows on each respective side to hide the panel, and press T to hide the toolbar. You can bring any of them back when you need them by clicking the arrows on each respective side again or by using Shift+Tab.

- **Use the Single Image Playback view.** This is the work area of Slideshow, as shown in figure 8-2. When you use it with the forward and backward controls below the work area, you can move from photo to photo as if you are actually viewing a slide show. This lets you see what happens when one photo changes to another. It also gives you the chance to actually view how a group of photos works together, seen one at a time.

ADOBE PHOTOSHOP
LIGHTROOM 2
Library
Develop
Slideshow
Print
Web
Navigator
FIT
FILL
1:1
3:1
Library Filter :
Text
Attribute
Metadata
None
Custom Filter
Catalog
Folders
Collections
Smart Collections
Architecture
82
Bugs
34
Lake Superior June Trip
25
Import...
Export...
Sort:
User Order
Thumbnails

8-1

ADOBE PHOTOSHOP
LIGHTROOM 2
Library
Develop
Slideshow
Print
Web
Preview
Template Browser
Collections
Smart Collections
Architecture
82
Bugs
34
Lake Superior June Trip
25
Options
Layout
Overlays
Backdrop
Titles
Playback
Export JPEG...
Export PDF...
Use:
All Filmstrip Photos
ABC
Preview
Play
Filter:
Custom Filter

8-2

It's important to know that you can integrate your use of "Single Image" and Filmstrip views. When photos seem to work together in a grouping in the Grid or Filmstrip view, you need to also see how they play against one another, one at a time, in the Single Image view. As you watch photos in the Single Image view, you will see awkward changes, so you need to go down to the Filmstrip, also shown in figure 8-2, and rearrange photos. With practice, you will find this works very quickly and easily.

Ways to Organize a Slide Show

There are many ways to organize a slide show, and you will develop unique groups and arrangements of your images that will provide a distinctive stamp of your vision as a photographer. I know, however, that many photographers are so used to working single images that they struggle a bit with producing a great slide show that brings images together into one entity.

I say this again, because it is key to doing a good slide show: Think of what the images form as a group and do not look at them as individuals. Again, I fully recognize that some photographers will use Lightroom simply as a way of presenting a PDF file of photos for a client, and the "group" is simply selections from a shoot. Still, it is worth remembering, even then, that images interact with each other. How you position them in relation to each other and how they sequence together affect the viewer's impression of both the overall group of photos and the individual shots. Putting some thought into organization and flow for even the simplest show can create a show that has more impact and effect on your audience.

First and foremost, a slide show should have a beginning, such as in figure 8-3, which shows a sunrise on Lake Superior at Gooseberry Falls State Park, and an end, such as in figure 8-4, a night shot of moonlight along the shore of Lake Superior (shot with a white balance setting to give it this golden color). Think carefully about which photo you want your audience to see first and which it will see last. I can tell you that many slide shows are weakened because the last slide didn't finish the show on a strong note, or worse, didn't seem to finish the show at all. Sometimes, that finish is simply your credits, and I will discuss creating text slides later in the chapter. Still, the last slide before those credits needs to provide some sort of closure for the viewer.

Another thing to keep in mind is that the overall show should have a flow. While it is important that the beginning and ending images lead the viewer through the start and finish of the program, there must be some sort of transition between images as the program moves through them. This does not have to be spelled out for the viewer, but the viewer needs to sense that there is a reason for the images used and the order in which they appear.

PRO TIP

Short sequences within the overall slide show can be helpful in building the whole show. A show will keep an audience's interest if there are changes within it, including short sequences that build up to mini-highlights or peaks of things like graphics, thoughts, or emotions, and then go to another sequence. You can apply all of the ideas in this section to both the whole show and short sequences within that show.

8-3

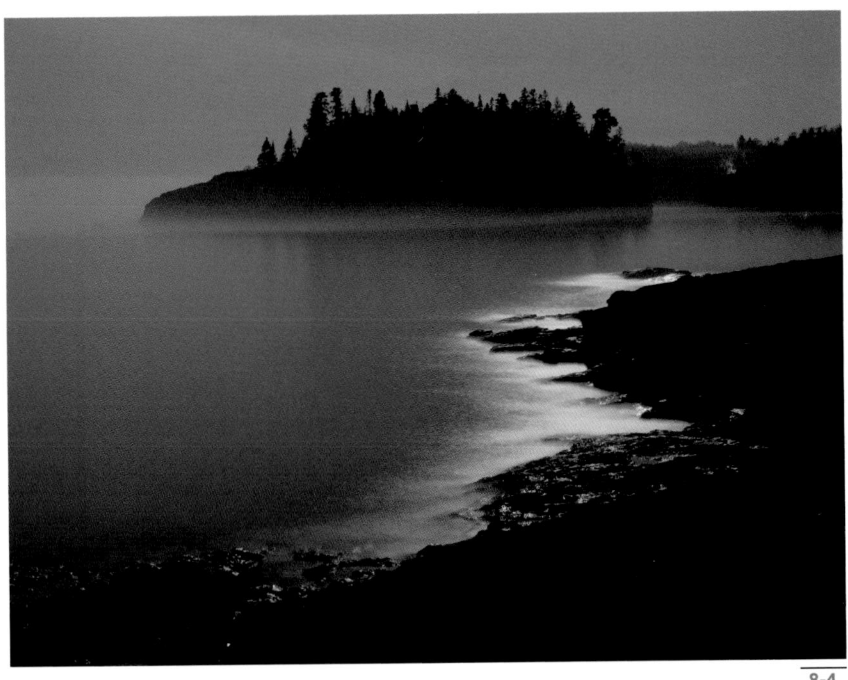

8-4

With those guidelines in mind, here are some ideas that may help you get started (unfortunately, these are hard to show in a book, but you can find many great examples of slide shows on the Web if you check the Web sites of newspapers — most major papers show off photos in slide shows):

- **Story.** Story is a classic technique for organizing anything that takes time for the viewer to see and understand it all, whether that is a novel, a movie, or a slide show. Story, at its most basic level, is something that has a beginning, middle, and ending. That means you look for slides that create a beginning to your show, find other slides that make a strong ending, and then fill in the rest with images that make sense as a transition from beginning to end. Story is not about what you studied in English class in high school; it is about organization in such a way that a "story" is created with your images, a sequence that keeps the audience interested as it builds from beginning to ending. It gives the audience something to follow, something to anticipate. You can also create little mini-stories within the overall story that can be especially helpful when you work with a long show.
- **Color.** Color can be a way of organizing photos, including working images against each other to give them more impact. Color can be used to group photos, as shown in figure 8-5, where color helps make transitions among them, and to create a sequence or "story" about color. It is rarely used as a basis for an overall story (that is, you start with one color and end with another), though it can be. Changing colors for the story usually is a technique used for small sequences. Colors can also be kept consistent through certain parts of a show to add impact to that particular color or to keep the audience's attention on the subject rather than on color changes. You can also use color to jar the viewer by changing dramatically from one color to another as sequences change within a show, as shown in figure 8-6. Be careful of this, however, because it can be so jarring that you lose your viewers for a moment as they try to track what is going on, plus dissolves between colors can give surprising and unwelcome results.
- **Tone.** Tone is another visual technique to bring images together. You can group photos by their overall tonalities (bright or dark, for example), by their tonal atmosphere (a crisp light versus a soft light, for example), and so on, as shown in figure 8-7. (These three images were shot at different times, but they definitely go together.) You can also use tonal changes (contrasting tones) to build a sequence or to create a visual exclamation point for the audience (like color, however, you have to use such contrasts carefully or you risk losing your audience). Color and tone are two major graphic elements that can link and build sequences in a slide show. You can use them to deal with images that are otherwise quite different in subject matter.
- **Subject matter.** The subject is, of course, the traditional way of organizing slide shows for teaching or informing an audience. I deliberately did not put it first because I think too often it is the only thing considered for a slide show. But even if the subject is the key to a particular show, you still need to organize it beyond lumping a bunch of photos together simply because their content applies to the same subject. This is where attention to color and tone can be extremely useful. The wrong colors and tones running into each other can jar viewers enough that they lose track for a moment of what you are telling them about the subject. Story can also help keep viewers on track by giving them something to follow and anticipate.

Collections / ... / 25 photos / 4 selected / _6201861.ORF

8-5

Collections / ... / 25 photos / 4 selected / _6191661.ORF

8-6

8-7

PRO TIP

You might have noticed that the figures of images here are shown using the Survey view of the Library mode. This is a good view to use when you want to compare just a few images with each other rather than seeing the whole slide show.

> **Chronological.** This is another traditional approach to a slide show, and when it is done right, it can be very effective. Chronology, just by definition, offers the story elements of a beginning, middle, and ending. But be careful not to be a slave to the timing of shots because that can put photos together that visually compete when they are shown. When working a chronological show, it is very helpful to watch for how colors and tones interact and to be especially careful that you guide the viewer and not annoy him or her because of jarring contrasts.

> **Context.** Almost always, a slide show, or at least elements within it, will have a context. Context is the setting for the images — environmental, psychological, geographical, sociological, historical, and so on. This can change through a show. If context is important to your message or the audience's appreciation of the photos, then you need to select photos and order them in such a way that context is preserved. This can be especially important for short sequences. Audiences get annoyed when they are happily viewing a context, say historical, make a transition to a new context for the images, say geographical, and then get a random historical image tossed at them.

> **Framing.** As you change the framing of a subject from wide shot to medium shot to close-up, you change the way a viewer looks at your photo, as shown in figure 8-8. This has a lot to do with composition, but it also has to do with the distance to

8-8

the subject, lens choice, and so on. You can organize photos by how they are framed. You can put a group together that is all framed the same, such as a group of close-ups, or you can group images based on how they change from close-up to wide shot. Making deliberate choices about how one image goes with another because of framing can pay off in smoother, more effective slide shows. If you don't pay attention to this, you may find viewers have trouble visually grasping a change from a wide shot to a close-up, for example.

> **Builds.** Building a sequence of images is totally unique to a slide show. You can take a series of photos from a distant wide shot to a close-up to help a viewer focus on details. You can build a sequence from a close-up to a wide shot to bring a viewer to a new view. You can show sequences of action, building to a climax. You can group images that come together to build a visual journey through an area. You can build a lighting effect, showing a subject gradually changing as the light changes on it. Builds, however, typically need to be shot for that effect when you take the photos in the first place. This is something to keep in mind as you photograph — can you take a few additional images to create some sort of build for a sequence?

> **Punctuation.** Punctuation in a slide show is just like punctuation in writing. It is something that allows the viewer to pause, separates parts of a show, helps a viewer better understand the show, and gives special attention to a specific image or sequence. Pauses, like commas, can come from simple, peaceful images or even black slides (which I explain later in this chapter). Exclamation points come from big changes, such as a jarring change in color or tone, and can wake an audience up (again, a warning — be careful how much you do this or you risk losing your audience). Question marks come from specific images that make a viewer think and wonder what is happening in the photo. A period comes from an image that is definitely an ending to a sequence.

You can use these ideas individually for organizing a slide show or combined in all sorts of ways to get the most out of your images. Any technique you use should be used to create a slide show that as a whole is much greater than the sum of its parts.

It is very important to realize that a slide show is not about putting photos in front of an audience. If you do that, your show becomes photographer-centric and you can lose your audience. Good communication, which is what an effective slide show is about, is not simply about what is "told" (or shown) to an audience. It is also much about what the audience actually "hears" (or sees) in that effort. Therefore, a good slide show is about creating something that affects and communicates with, not at, an audience.

PRO TIP

As you go through your images, you may notice that some look different than expected when you play them against specific photos before and after. They may look brighter or darker, have a different color balance, and so on. Lightroom makes it very easy to compensate for this. Just go back to Develop with any images that give you a problem and adjust them for the slide show. You might want to save your original adjustments by creating a snapshot in the Develop module, or you could use a Virtual Copy by right-clicking the photo and choosing Create Virtual Copy, then making the adjustments on it.

Timing a Slide Show

Once you have the basic organization for a show, give it some sort of timing as to how long each slide is on-screen and how long the transitions are between each image. This affects how the photos look together and gives a distinct mood or impression of the photos for your audience. As you change timing, you may find you need to readjust some of your photos. Two photos that looked good when you saw them quickly together might not work right if there is a long dissolve (or blending) of the images as they transition from one to the other.

You change the timing of your slide show in Playback. You can change the duration of slides (how long each one stays on-screen) from 0 to 20 seconds, as shown in figure 8-9. Twenty seconds is a very long time when you consider this is how long each image stays on the screen. That might be something to use for a slide show that is just a background to an event, however. Transitions between photos also range from 0 to 20 seconds — I am not sure what you would do with a slide show that had 20 seconds for each slide and 20 seconds of transition to change between them.

How long or short the slides stay on-screen and the length of transitions are very subjective. You need to preview your show and see how the timing feels, based on what you are trying to accomplish with the slide show. In addition, timing may be limited by your computer. Lightroom has to find and load each image from the hard drive as it plays a slide show. If your hard drive is slow, your RAM amount too small, or your processor speed too slow, you may find the show does not play properly at short duration times.

Here are some things affecting your timing choices that you might want to consider:

> **Setting for the show.** Where is the slide show going to be shown? What sort of place is it? Who will see it? Each of these affects how long images

need to stay on-screen. For a show with a group of art directors, you may want to go through images pretty quickly, as they are generally used to seeing photos quickly and will get tired of images that appear too long on-screen.

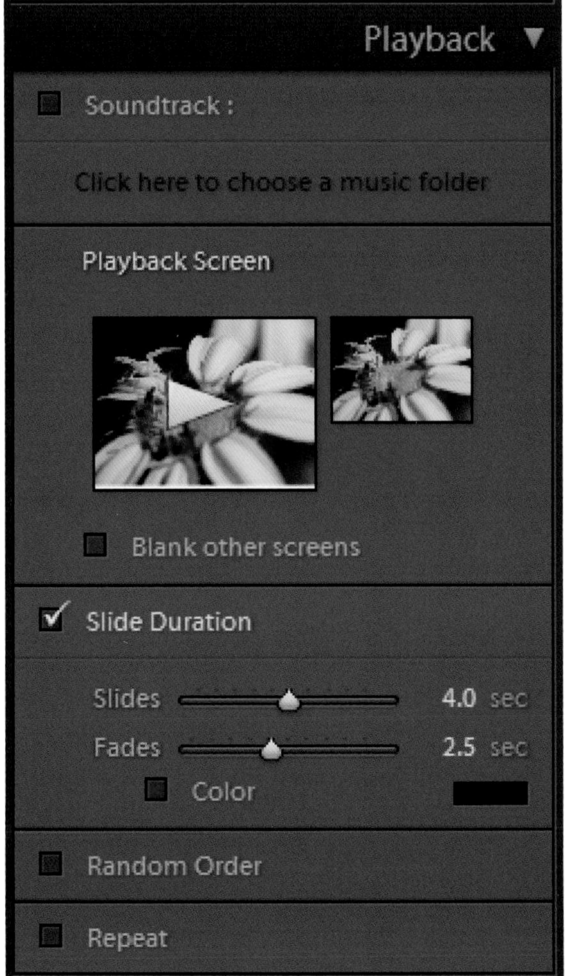

8-9

- **Use for the show.** How is the show being used? For example, you might be using a show for a marketing introduction, which would likely need an energetic, lively pace; or you might use a show for a community organization that will want to see images on-screen longer so the audience can look them over, finding things they recognize.
- **Images in the show.** The photos actually seen in the show can dictate the timing of the show. A slide show of detailed landscapes, such as in figure 8-10, needs some time for the audience to really look at each image. A show of sports action, such as in figure 8-11, might look best when the photos change quickly, giving an impression of lively action.
- **Music used.** A fast-paced music track looks silly with slowly changing photos, while a majestic orchestral fanfare will not work well with fast-changing photos. You need to play your music against the photos and see if the music and slide tempos complement or compete with each other.

Timing, and all of these ways of thinking about timing, affects your choice of how long a slide is on-screen as well as how long the transition is between two slides. Usually, you will combine short times for an image to appear on-screen with short transition times. Conversely, you will typically combine long times on-screen with longer transition times. There are no absolute rules about this, however. Try different settings with your images, click Preview, and see how they affect the show.

8-10

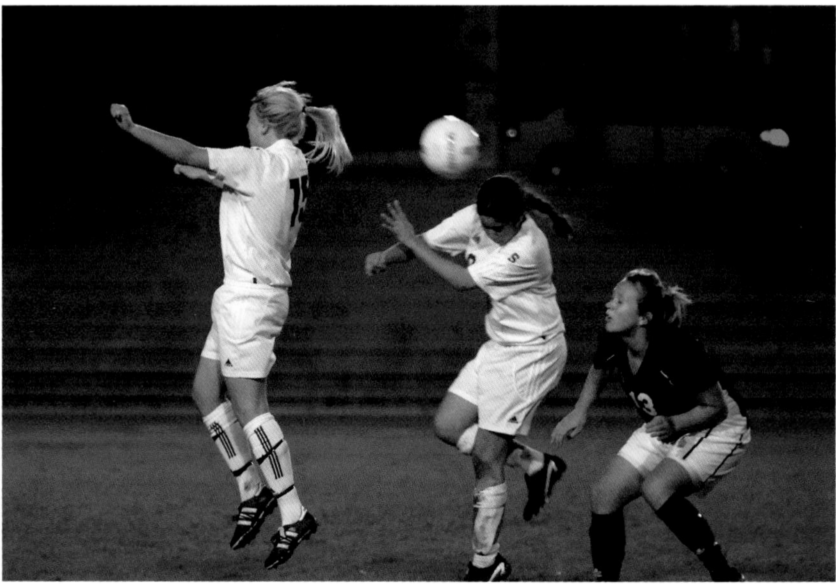

8-11

Working with Music

Music can be an important way to enhance a slide show (though obviously I can't show you examples of this in a book). Lightroom has very limited capabilities with music — it can only be used when a slide show is played directly from the Slideshow module. However, that doesn't mean you should take it lightly. Just the fact that you can add music at all increases the possibilities for your show.

In order to choose the best music for a slide show, it is worth considering how it might affect your images. Here are some things to consider:

> Music can set the right mood for your images.

> Music can affect and determine a pace that makes sense for the content and use of the show.

> Music gives your photos an emotional quality. With music, you can make a show happy, sad, moody, joyful, majestic, and so forth.

> Music can change the appearance of your images. It affects how an audience looks at, and, therefore, perceives, the photos in the show.

> Music changes the mood of the audience.

> Music can affect how long a show seems. You can actually take the same show with the same transitions and timing, play it with two different pieces of music, and the show seems to take different times to finish.

Because music has such a powerful effect on a slide show, it needs to fit the images and setting of the show. Picking some popular music just because you like it and attaching it to your images might actually change the show in a negative way if that popular music fights the images and their organization.

That brings up an important point: You cannot simply use any music with your slide show for any use of that show. Music is copyrighted material. If you use music from some album for a personal, private showing of images that you do not, in any way, charge for, you can generally use any music without getting permission. However, should you use that music for any show that is shown publicly, especially when money is involved in some way (a fee is charged for admission, a charge is made for the class, and so on), you are breaking the law. It is illegal to use copyrighted music for such purposes.

There are other sources of music. You could work with a friend who has a band (and we all know musicians in our circle of acquaintances who would love to have their music featured for a credit), buy royalty-free music, download music that has no rights restrictions, and so on.

PRO TIP

You can create your own music quite nicely with some computer programs that build music sequences for you (and at a specific length). One that is easy to use and has a lot of flexibility is Sonicfire from SmartSound Software. This program lets you pick types of music and then builds a unique soundtrack to a specific length that you can use with slide shows. Being able to get a specific length is extremely useful for serious slide show creators.

When You Need Black

Slide shows need black. They work best if they start with black and end with black. Lightroom does that for you automatically, but you have no control over it. You may need a longer opening (to allow some music to play first, for example), or you may want to make a transition between sections of your show or when the music changes. Going to black for a moment is a good way of telling your audience the subject is changing, as shown in figure 8-12 (though you have to be careful that you don't have dramatic music ending right as you go to black or the audience will think the show is done).

To add a black moment to your show, you need a black image. It is a good idea to have a collection set up specifically to hold black images. You can simply shoot a black, way-underexposed image the next time you are shooting by leaving the lens cap on, setting the camera to manual, and shooting at very small f-stops (such as f/16) with a very fast shutter (such as 1/1000 second). Shoot a bunch of these, and then put them into a collection for use as needed.

You can also create a pure black image in Photoshop and save it as a JPEG file. (This keeps it small and inconsequential on your hard drive — JPEG has no effect on a solid color of black.) You then import it into Lightroom and keep it in a collection (or you could just leave them in the Folder that they come in as).

You probably noticed that I said it is a good idea to have a collection of black images, yet I've talked about creating a single image. You do need "images" because you have to use a new black slide every time you need the effect. However, you can make a group of black images from a single image by simply using Lightroom's Virtual Copy capability. Right-click on the image and choose Create Virtual Copy from the menu that appears.

8-12

Title Slides

Lightroom gives you no easy way of doing title slides throughout a slideshow. In the new section of Slideshow called Titles, you can add simple title slides to the beginning and ending of your slide show, but you are very limited in what you can do for text. Title slides can be very important to a show. If you want a special title slide, you can go outside of Lightroom. Use any text program that lets you save TIFF or JPEG files. You can create titles in Photoshop by making a blank image about 1600 × 1200 with a background that complements the slide show background and then adding text. A neat way to do that is to take a photo from your show that will take a title well, right click it, and choose Edit in Photoshop. This creates a copy of the image and places it right by your original, as shown in figure 8-13.

Title slides can be an important addition to a slide show. They can help begin your show, giving it an actual title, along with any other important information (such as identifying the photographer). They are very useful as endings for a show, giving important credits or photographer contact information, and they can be quite helpful for setting apart sections of a show.

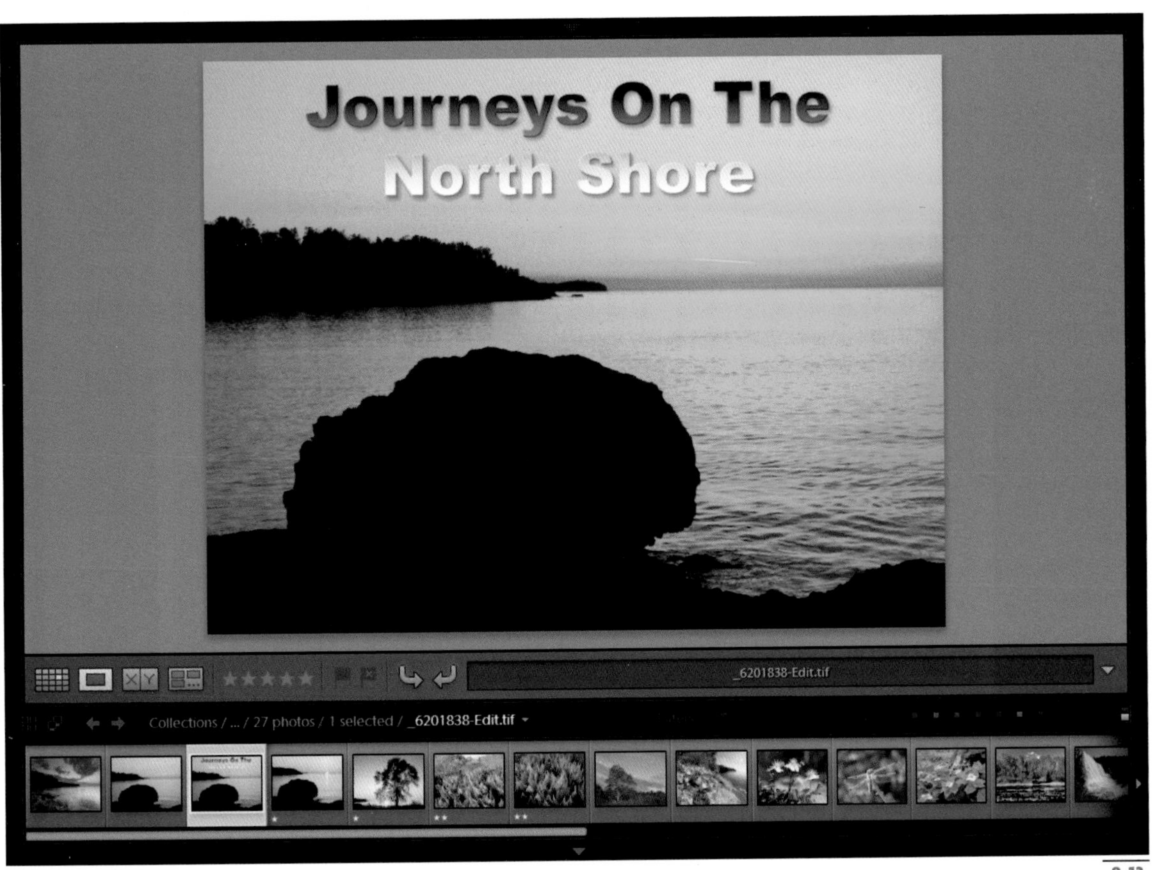

8-13

Working the Background of Your Slide Display

While I have put this section last in this chapter, you can alter the background — the image settings, layout, overlays, background settings, and so forth — at any time. I think it is best to do it after you have your basic organization and tone set to the slide show, as that affects the kind of "setting" each slide resides in as it plays on-screen.

Background includes more than just the backdrop of the photo display area. You learned the basics of Options, Layout, Overlays, and Backdrop in Chapter 7. Now, I give you some ideas on how you might integrate these tools into the production of an effective slide show.

8-14

8-15

Creating a Backdrop for Your Slides

I am going to skip down to Backdrop, which controls the background graphic or image behind your slides. I think it is good to start here because the colors, tones, or images you use in your backdrop affect the additional elements, such as Stroke and Shadow in Options, and image placement in Layout, that you use in the show.

The color of your backdrop greatly affects how the images appear to the audience. Neutral tones keep colors constant, while strong colors can change the appearance of colors in the image. When two colors come together, they interact visually, causing us to see them as changed colors — this is called *simultaneous contrast*. Compare figures 8-14 and 8-15 and you will see what I mean. The only difference in the photos is the color around them, yet the actual images look different.

Backdrop colors are sort of like a mat used around a photo when it is framed. They set off and complement the image. A very important difference, however, is that a mat typically appears with one photo. Your slide backdrop must work with all photos. This is why you need to be very careful about using colors, especially strong ones, for a background. A strong color might look good for a few images, but then can adversely affect the other images displayed. It can make your photos look less colorful or create unpleasing color interactions.

Here are some ideas you can use when choosing a backdrop color:

- **White.** White can look very elegant, especially when it is used with black and white images, as shown in figure 8-16. White, though, is obviously very bright, so it can quickly take the viewer's attention from the photo, especially as the area of white gets larger. The use of a black stroke border can help. Also, a shadow can add too much contrast that may take away from the images. White can make dark colors look even darker, even to the point of giving them less apparent saturation.
- **Black.** Black is a dramatic, rich background. It can make colors lively and bold, as shown in figure 8-17. It also reveals weaknesses in contrast in your photos, making any weak blacks look gray and dull. Try a white stroke border with it; a shadow won't show up.
- **Grays.** Grays are always a good, neutral color for a background. You've seen them throughout this and the previous chapters. You can use them from light to dark, gaining some of the characteristics of white or black while minimizing the problems. A light gray, for example, can still look quite elegant, yet it will have fewer problems with darker colors compared to pure white. A dark gray offers many benefits, such as lively, dramatic colors with less harshness than black.

8-16

- **Colors.** Colors in the backdrop can be very important if you use client colors, for example. You can also use color to set a tone for the slide show, though it is generally best to use colors that are not very intense. Dark, less saturated colors can give a rich look to the slide show without causing too many visual issues. Often it helps to use colors as part of something else, such as part of a Color Wash, as shown in figure 8-18.

I like Color Wash a lot. It is a classic technique, with an almost retro slide effect. A dark gray on top and light gray on the bottom of the backdrop give you a highly directional setting for your photos. You might want to experiment a bit with Angle to see what works best with your photos.

Other colors that work well together in a wash include dark blue and medium blue, dark violet and medium violet (both turned way down in saturation), light gray and white, and black with almost any dark color. Avoid strong reds (they always compete with your photo) and bright yellows (they attract the viewer's eye and create some strong color effects).

When you are projecting images from a digital projector, consider the environment where you will be showing your photos. A dark background will help your photos show up better if there are brighter areas around the projection screen, for example. Having some sort of neutral background between your photos and the surroundings can help when the surroundings are distracting.

8-17

8-18

Using Options Effectively

The main controls you will be using in Options are Stroke Border and Cast Shadows. Zoom to Fill Frame is too limiting, in my opinion, for serious photographic slide shows because it crops arbitrarily, plus it makes verticals into horizontals.

The choice of border and shadow settings is highly affected by both the color of the backdrop and the tonalities of the photos. Stroke tends to have the strongest visual effect on the photo because it puts a border all around the image. Most photographers find that either a white or black border gives a nice look for the photo. I find that in most slide shows such a border gives the images a more finished and polished look.

The choice of black or white is very personal and highly dependent on the photos and the background. If most of your photos are light in tone — the backdrop is light — a black border often looks nice and helps define the edge of the photo (if black looks too strong, try a dark gray). If your photos are mostly dark in tone — the background is dark — a white border can be a good addition to your photo. You have to try them (it is simply a few keystrokes to change) and see what looks best for your needs.

On some photos, such as an image with a bright sky against a light backdrop or a night photo with a dark sky against a dark backdrop, a border becomes a necessity. Without it, your viewers will have a hard time seeing the photo. Compare figure 8-19 and figure 8-20 to see what I mean.

Be wary of colors. A colored border can create some very undesirable interactions with the photos. That doesn't mean you can't use colors for Stroke Border, just use them carefully and deliberately. One place they would be appropriate is with a themed slide show, such as for the Fourth of July, where some strong colors are the norm.

8-19

8-20

Shadow size and density are very personal decisions. Photographers vary considerably in how strong they want this effect. The backdrop color and tone also affect how you set up a shadow. A dark background needs a darker, and often a sharper-edged, shadow. A light background with a soft, gentle shadow might make a photo look best. When you use a photo in the background, you often find that the shadow needs to be considerably darker and larger in order to work well.

Setting Up Layout Controls

The last step that I typically use for a slide show is to set how big the image is against the backdrop and where it is positioned in the frame. The default of Slideshow is to make the margins all equal and to move in and out together, as shown in figure 8-21. This keeps the actual space around the photo consistent, but not necessarily equal. If your photo is not cropped to match the working area, it cannot give equal space all around it. The best example of this is a vertical. If it fits between the top and bottom margins, there is no way it can have the same margins at the sides because you are working with a horizontal method of presentation — your computer screen or digital projector.

How big the margins need to be depends on how large the resulting slide show will be seen, text needs, the backdrop, and your personal tastes. With the margins sliders all selected (Link All), you can move the sliders all together to make your photo larger or smaller in the display space. You might also try deselecting the Bottom option and moving it up — this offers a traditional art presentation where the photo sits slightly high in the display area, as shown in figure 8-22. (This can be a very nice look.)

Having smaller photos in a large space is also an artistic way of presenting images (though it can look rather pretentious if the photos are too small, but again, some venues want small photos). That sort of layout needs to have a backdrop that complements the photos and space, plus the photos need to be displayed with good size, whether on a large monitor or with digital projection. Smaller photos are also needed if much text is used or if there is a large Identity Plate.

Images that nearly fill the display space can also look quite nice, especially with the right border and shadow. However, be careful about moving the photo edges too close to the display edges, as the images will then look cramped.

Layout
Show Guides
Left 128 px
Right 128 px
Top 128 px
Bottom 128 px
Link All
Overlays
Backdrop
Titles
Playback

8-21

Layout
Show Guides
Left 128 px
Right 128 px
Top 108 px
Bottom 161 px
Link All
Overlays
Backdrop
Titles
Playback

8-22

Q & A

You did not talk much about Overlays in this chapter, yet it is obviously important as noted in Chapter 7. How would you use it effectively?

That's a tough question for me to answer, because I don't find Overlay options all that useful for slide shows. There are occasions where having an Identity Plate can be helpful to give an identity to the show (especially if the show is being used for promotional reasons), but as soon as you add such a plate, you need to adjust the layout of the slide so the two look in balance on the screen.

I have no use for displaying Ratings. That is really a distraction, I feel, for a slide show. The viewer should be watching the show without thinking about how the images are ranked unless they truly are judging images (such as in a contest or client-based sorting usage). I do understand that some photographers find this useful for specialized presentations to clients, but most of the time, I can't see its value.

You talk about using black or titles as a way to break up parts of a show or add punctuation. Could you also use solid colors or even special images?

Absolutely. The advantage of black is that it is neutral and it recedes to the background. It is always a safe transition. As soon as you use something stronger, you get more attention from the audience, so you have to be able to use that attention wisely.

Title slides, which you create in Photoshop, can be effective transitions, and they can look good on many backgrounds. If you use a photo for a transition, you need something that doesn't compete with the rest of the show. This can be a good place for a gentle use of your business's or client's logo. You can also use an out-of-focus image with text over it, which offers a lot of dimension, too.

To me, it seems like music is really important. I can't understand why you can't keep music with the slides when a slide show is exported from Lightroom.

I totally agree. Unfortunately, Lightroom uses the PDF format for slide shows, and at present, that format does not save music with it. Lightroom is really great for creating portfolio presentation sorts of slide shows where the photographer talks about the images, but not so much for emotional slide shows with music.

If you really want music with your slides, you probably should check out the Pro Show Gold program from Photodex Software for Windows or FotoMagico by Boinx Software for Mac. Both allow all sorts of slide show effects and precise use of music.

Chapter 9

MAKING SENSE OF THE PRINT MODULE

When the traditional black-and-white darkroom was popular years ago, lots of photographers made their own prints. But then came the popularity of color photography, and printing your own images became a real challenge. Only a minority of photographers even tried, so most had their prints made at a lab. Everyone who used to try to get a good, custom print from a slide or negative knows what a challenge that could be. Sometimes it would take multiple visits to the lab when an image didn't print right and had to be reprinted. Or, you'd often just accept the print as is because it was "good enough" and any changes weren't worth going back and forth with the lab. You probably know what I am talking about.

One of the great joys coming from the change from shooting film to digital is the opportunity to get really great prints that are optimized for the subject and photographer, as shown in figure 9-1. Yet, setting up a program like Photoshop for printing could be daunting for a lot of photographers. Digital printing has great potential, but not everyone had realized this when they were using standard image-processing programs. Further, the expectation that digital could solve all photo problems led to disappointment with prints when they didn't quite measure up.

Lightroom takes digital printing and makes all of the settings much more accessible. The settings also make more sense to the photographer. The Print module offers some outstanding features to help you get the best prints from your photos, and it is the tight integration of this module with the rest of the program that enables you to go beyond making good prints to making great prints.

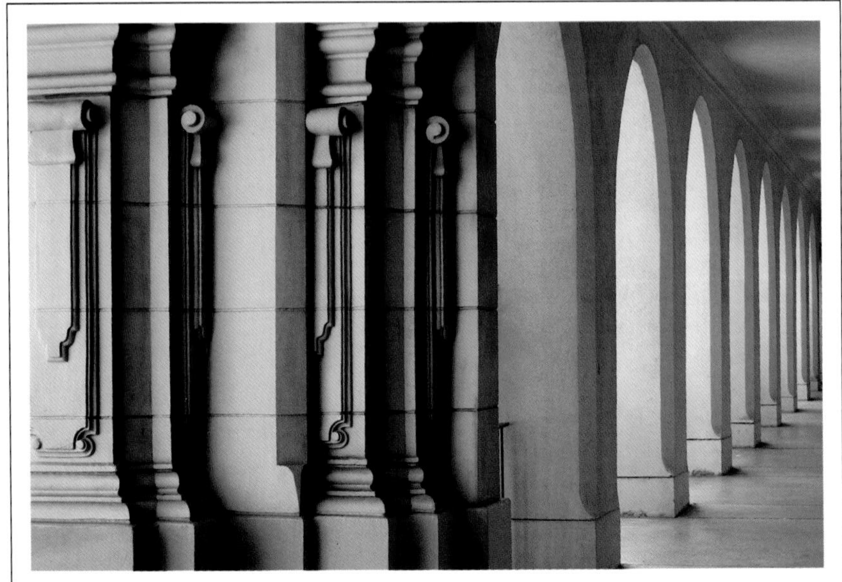

9-1

The Print Module Layout

The Print module is set up like every other module in Lightroom, as shown in figure 9-2. You should begin to see a consistency in what you can do based on what you know about other modules. Print has the same four-panel interface:

> **Center work area.** As usual, this holds the main photo. By default, it also includes rulers that show how the image is sized for printing and information about the print "job," including the number of pages, the printer, and the paper size in an Info Overlay (turn the [Info] Overlay off and on by pressing I on your keyboard). Also by default, this area displays everything as a vertical sheet of printing paper. You immediately see how your photo will appear on the paper, along with non-printing guides that show things such as margins and the active image area.

> **Right panel.** As in all other modules, the right side of Print is the adjustment side of the module. It is where you change how the photo prints on a page, the information that prints with it, the image resolution, and so forth.

> **Bottom Filmstrip.** This standard photo display area can be quite helpful in Print to allow you to quickly choose images for multiple prints or choose several images on a page.

9-2

> **Left panel.** Once again, you find presets here, which are like Slideshow in that they are called templates, plus a preview area that shows what the templates look like as you move your cursor over them. In addition, you have access here to Collections from the Library so you don't have to go back and forth to Library to make prints.

In addition to the panels, you see several features that are unique to the Print interface:

> **Workspace toolbar.** Just below the center work area is a very simple toolbar for printing, shown in figure 9-3. At the left is a square that takes you to the first page of a multipage printing job. You can go page to page by clicking the back and forward buttons, just right of the square (or by just using the left and right arrows on the keyboard). You can also jump to a new printing page by dragging on the box that says Page 1 of 1 in figure 9-3. The Use: option gives you a short menu for using selected photos, using all photos in the Filmstrip, or using flagged photos for printing.

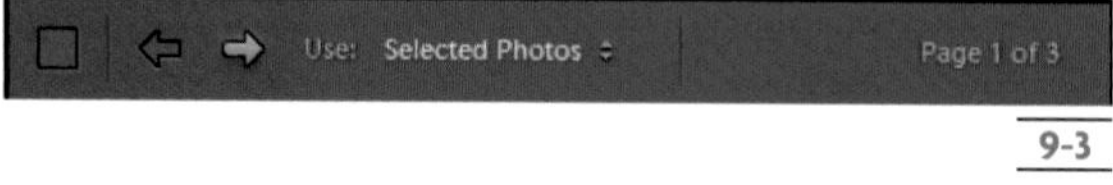

9-3

I find that all of the panels are so useful for printing that I go back and forth among them. Because of that, I tend to keep them all visible while I am in Print.

> **Page Setup button.** This button, located at the far left side of the Print toolbar, does slightly different things for Windows and Mac. In Windows, it takes you to your system's standard dialog box for choosing paper size, orientation of the photo (landscape/horizontal or portrait/vertical), and properties of the printer driver. On the Mac, it gives you the Page Setup dialog box that does not include access to the printer driver.

> **Print Settings button.** This button is meant to give you access to your printer driver to adjust things like the paper used and borderless printing, and to turn color management on and off. In Windows, this button opens the same dialog box that appears for Page Setup for Windows. When you click Properties, you actually get print settings. On the Mac, clicking the button opens the Print dialog box. Print settings include the type of paper used, bordered or borderless printing, and options for color management.

> **Print One button.** Click this button to print one copy of your photo without any further work.

> **Print button.** This button allows you to print your photo, though as a last check it brings up access to the printer driver again so you can change print numbers, for example.

One other thing to keep in mind about the Print module is that it creates an area called a *cell* for the photo to exist on a page. You will be adjusting such a cell to change how large the photo is on the printed page and its orientation.

The Print module makes printing easier and more intuitive for photographers. It presents key printing adjustments in a logical format.

Printing Workflow

There are a lot of excellent choices in the Print module. You will typically find that you use certain choices again and again, while you use others rarely. And if you have contact with other photographers, you'll quickly discover that these choices are quite variable, even to the point of argument over which is truly "best." My feeling is that the best settings are those that give you the results you want, regardless of how any other photographer might use Lightroom.

However, there are some things about printing through Lightroom that affect how you might use the Print module. The workflow described next is one that I find useful to start with. It is a good, standard workflow for printing from Lightroom. With experience, you may find you want to alter this for specific printing needs.

1. **Select an image in the Filmstrip or Library for printing.** Usually, this is an image you have finished adjusting in Develop, but you can print any image at any time.
2. **Turn off the rulers by pressing Ctrl/⌘+R and the Info Overlay with Ctrl/⌘+I if you find them distracting.** I usually turn the Info Overlay off in order to get a cleaner-looking interface, as shown in figure 9-4.
3. **Adjust Page Setup for the desired print size.**
4. **Choose Maximum Size in the Template browser.**
5. **Adjust the size of the photo in Image Settings and Layout until you have what you need.**
6. **Add any Overlays that are important.**
7. **Set your resolution, print sharpening, and color management in that order (the order in the panel) and as needed in Print Job.** This order is a good habit to use if you work in Photoshop, too. While the order has no effect on Lightroom adjustments (none are applied until you actually tell the program to print or export an image), the order definitely affects Photoshop adjustments. I like to stay consistent.
8. **Set up the printer driver for the right paper and adjustments using Print Settings.**
9. **Print the photo.**
10. **Evaluate the image as a print (not just how it compares to the monitor).** Use Develop to make adjustments and print again. Use a virtual copy if you need to make distinct printing changes but do not want to change the original photo. (This can be important if you are making a very small or very large print as they will often look quite different at their final sizes.)

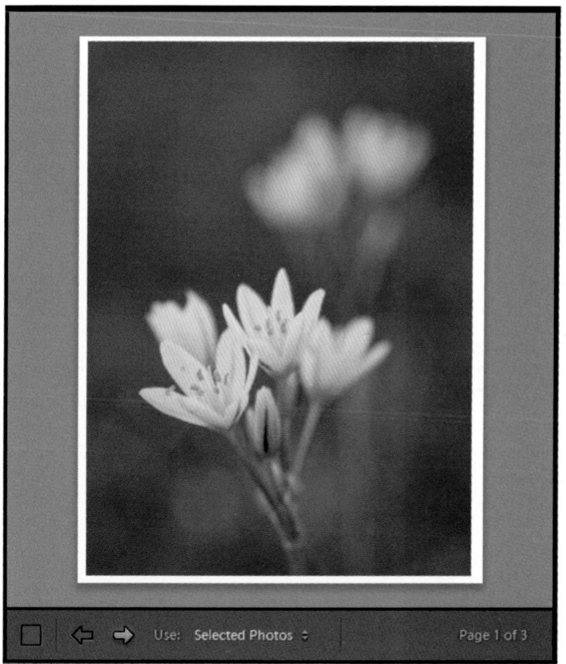

9-4

Selecting Photos for Printing

A great thing about Lightroom is how easy it is to go from any module to another. You can go through a whole range of photos in Library, select a photo (or a group of photos), and then go instantly to Print; or you can work on a photo in Develop and go right to Print with it, as shown in figures 9-5 and 9-6.

If you need to search a lot of photos in a shoot or collection for a print, then you are probably best off using Library for its Grid view and search capabilities. Many times, however, the Filmstrip will be an easy way to find photos for printing because it can be immediately accessible in Print. Filmstrip is also a convenient place to make multiple photo selections for making prints of them all.

Simply click any photo in Filmstrip to instantly load it into the Print work area. Then Ctrl/⌘+click other images in the Filmstrip to add them to a group for printing. These additional images do not appear directly in the Print work area; however, you know they are included because they become highlighted in the Filmstrip, and the page numbers at the bottom of the central work area change to reflect the added images, as shown in figure 9-7.

Page Setup Choices

After you click Page Setup, a very standard dialog box (shown in figure 9-8 for Windows and figure 9-9 for Mac) appears that you will recognize from Photoshop and most other programs that you print from. This is based on your operating system and is only accessed by Lightroom. This is one area that looks significantly different in Windows and Mac computers. Neither offers any real advantages here, but you need to know how your system deals with the choices for Page Setup.

9-5

9-6

9-7

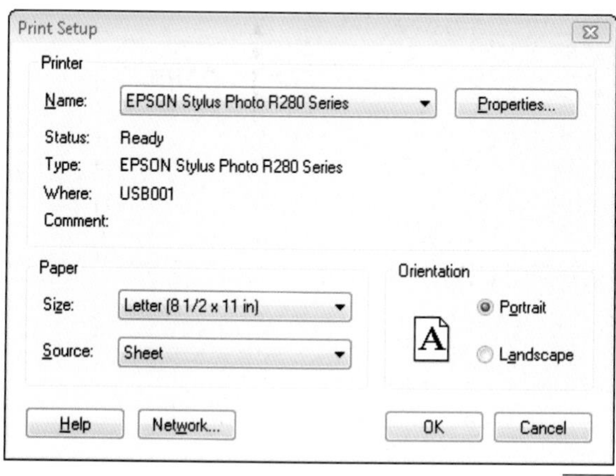

Print Setup

Printer

Name: EPSON Stylus Photo R280 Series — Properties...

Status: Ready

Type: EPSON Stylus Photo R280 Series

Where: USB001

Comment:

Paper

Size: Letter (8 1/2 x 11 in)

Source: Sheet

Orientation

Portrait

Landscape

Help — Network... — OK — Cancel

9-8

Page Setup

Settings: Page Attributes

Format for: EPSON Stylus Photo R2400

EPSON SP R2400 (1).

Paper Size: US Letter

8.50 by 11.00 inches

Orientation:

Scale: 100 %

Cancel — OK

9-9

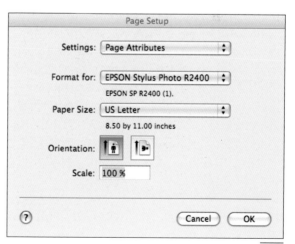

Choose your printer if it has not been selected for you automatically. This ensures that the paper size choices are limited to those that the printer can actually handle. The key settings you need to check in this dialog box are Paper Size and Orientation. Paper Size lets the computer (and Lightroom) know how big the paper is that you are using so it keeps those dimensions straight from Lightroom to printer software.

Orientation is, at its simplest, the way a photo is shown, either vertically or horizontally. However, it also affects how Lightroom places photos into certain templates and layouts of photos on a page. By default, Lightroom places your photo onto a vertical page in the display area when it is printed full size. If you use a multiphoto, per-page template, you may find your photo doesn't use the space orientation you prefer. If you want something different, change it here.

Leave the scale of the image in the Mac dialog box to its default of 100%. You can control sizing better, and with more efficiency and quality, if you do it within Lightroom and not here.

Preparing the Page for Printing

Print offers you six groups of controls on the right side of the interface, as shown in figure 9-10. These enable you to set up the page with your photo for printing so that it looks right and prints optimally. One of the problems photographers have with Photoshop is that the many printing controls are scattered throughout the program. The Lightroom designers sought to correct this by putting them all in one place in these six groups of controls. Don't be put off by the odd names (Layout Engine and Print Job) — the controls are quite straightforward and easy to use.

You have to start somewhere in order to use these controls. Lightroom uses the settings based on the Maximum Size template (shown in figure 9-11), which gives you an image centered on the page at the maximum size printable for most printers when borders are included. I recommend you start there. After you work a bit in Print, you may want to create your own templates as standards based on your most common printing sizes and use them as starting points for Print.

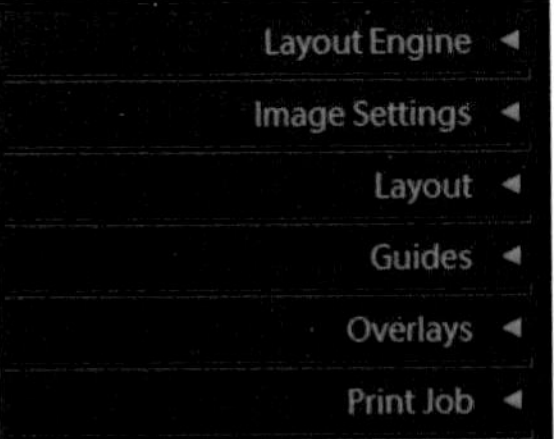

9-10

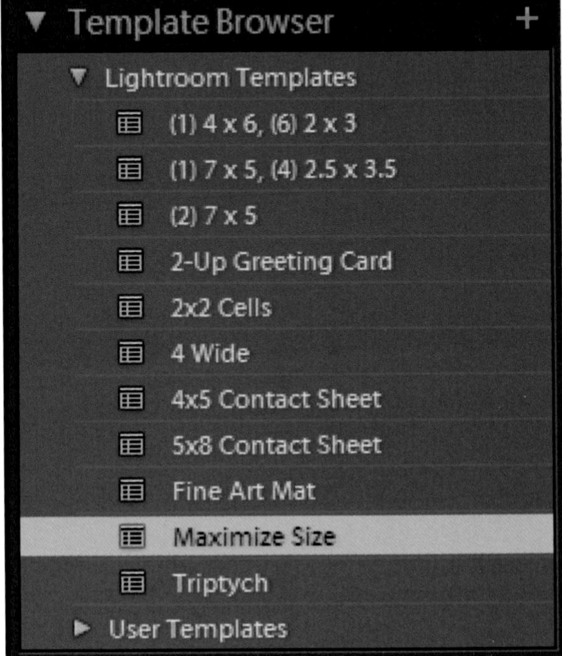

9-11

You can immediately print from any template and get good results. However, I think you'll find that you often want to be able to control the print more, creating a page that can be as unique as the photo, a page custom made for a client, or a page for any special needs that you have. That's when you need to go to the right-side controls.

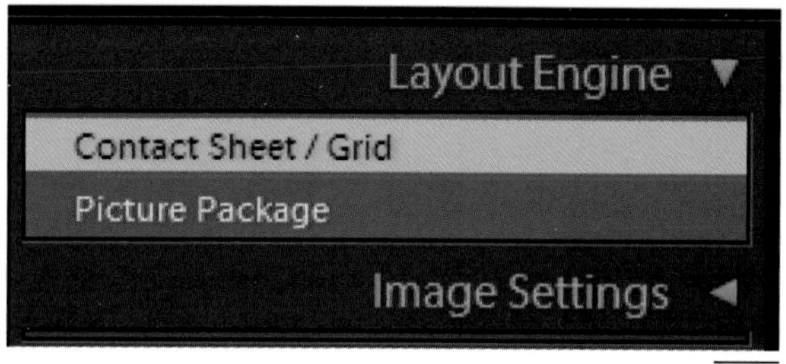

9-12

Using Image Settings and Layout Engine

Start with Image Settings, even though Layout Engine is first. Layout Engine is designed to quickly give you the controls needed to print a single photo and multiple same-sized photos (Contact Sheet/Grid) or a group of specially sized photos (Picture Package), as shown in figure 9-12. Choose Contact Sheet/Grid for straightforward printing as described here. The name, Contact Sheet/Grid seems an odd one for the single photo use you will use most of the time, but it refers to a 1 × 1 grid, or one photo. You'll learn more about working with several photos on a page in the next section.

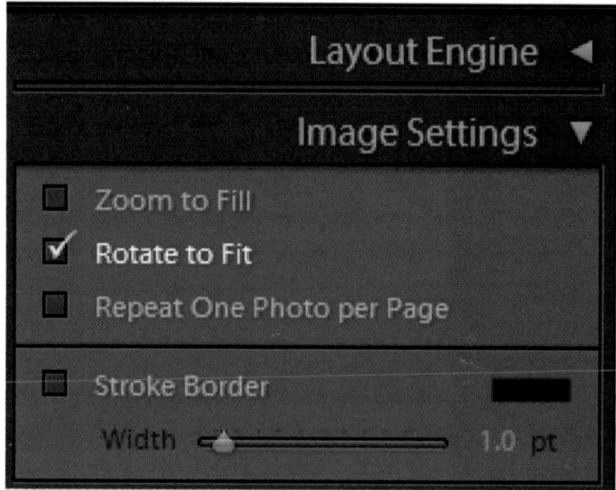

9-13

The Image Settings group of controls, shown in figure 9-13, gives you three simple options that you either turn on or off, plus a fourth, separate option that lets you add a border to the image when printed. They are important choices that greatly affect the look of your photo as printed.

Here's how to work with them:

> **Zoom to Fill.** Click this and Lightroom immediately fills the cell used for the photo, cropping the image to fit. That cell area is the portion of the printing page in between the margins. If you do not click this, the photo fills as much of that area as possible without being cropped, so there will be gaps on two sides unless the cell's proportions are exactly the same as your image.

When you select Zoom to Fill and the image is cropped to match the cell proportions, you can change where the cropping occurs. Move your cursor over the photo — it turns into a hand, as shown in figure 9-14 — and you can click and drag your photo to make it better fit the crop. Some photographers love this option, as it allows the printing paper to be more fully filled with the image; yet others hate it because it crops their photos and does not show the image as originally shot. Both are valid opinions; decide which works best for you and your photos.

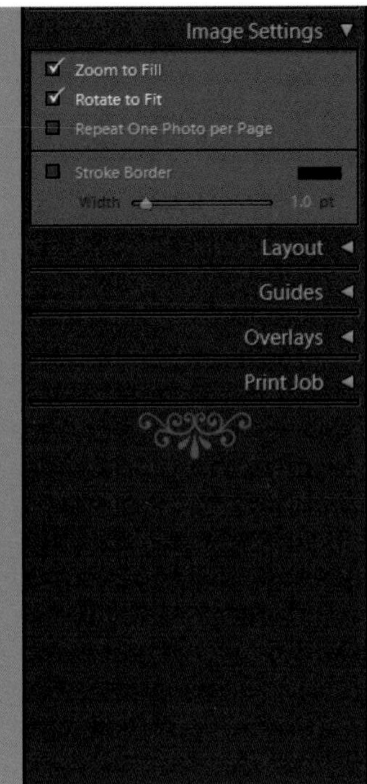

9-14

PRO TIP

You will often have the need to produce duplicate images to give to people who work with you on a shoot (professional reasons) or to family and friends (personal reasons). You can do this very quickly with the Repeat choice. Select multiple photos, choose a template with several cells (or make your own, as explained later in the chapter), select the check box for Repeat, and you will have as many pages as you have photos, each page showing one photo multiple times.

> **Rotate to Fit.** Most of the time you will likely leave this selected. This means that the image is rotated so that it fills the cell with the long side of the photo matching the long side of the cell, and the short side of photo matching the short side of the cell. This is the "best" use of the cell in terms of space used. However, there may be times that you want to rotate an image differently so that it fits the page overall with a certain orientation, regardless of the cell orientation. An example of that would be a horizontal photo placed onto a vertical page so that the page stays vertical and the photo is still oriented in its correct horizontal position. Then you would deselect this option.

> **Repeat One Photo per Page.** This option only works when you have multiple cells on a page, such as the 2 × 2 Cells template. With this choice, Print fills each cell with the same photo on a single page, as shown in figure 9-15. This is a great way to print duplicate images in a hurry.

> **Stroke Border.** This gives a very classy addition to a photo. It puts a fine line all the way around your image. This is an excellent look when you use a small width and a black line. Width is changed by the slider and affected by print size — larger

9-15

prints will need a larger border, but still, it should not be more than a few pixels. You can change the color by clicking the color rectangle to the right of Stroke Border to get a Color Picker. A border can be a necessity with very light images or photos that have bright areas that blend into the printing paper otherwise.

Positioning Your Photo with Layout and Guides

With those basic choices from Image Settings out of the way, you can move on to how the photo will appear on the overall printed page. I am putting Layout and Guides together because they are really quite integrated. It is hard to talk about one without discussing the other, even though once you have things set up, you may only use one of these panel sections. Layout allows you to set margins around your photo, set specific photo sizes (cell size), and decide how many photos appear on a page, as shown in figure 9-16. The flexibility of this part of the program can make for an overwhelming number of choices. Here's how I would suggest you use it (the order is not from top to bottom):

1. **Turn your guides on or off.** The Show Guides group in the Guides section of the right panel can help you judge the overall sizing of images, but they can be distracting when you are making a final evaluation of your photo and positioning it on the page. If you find them distracting, turn them all off by deselecting Show Guides, or you can turn off specific guides that you don't want to see by deselecting them one at a time.

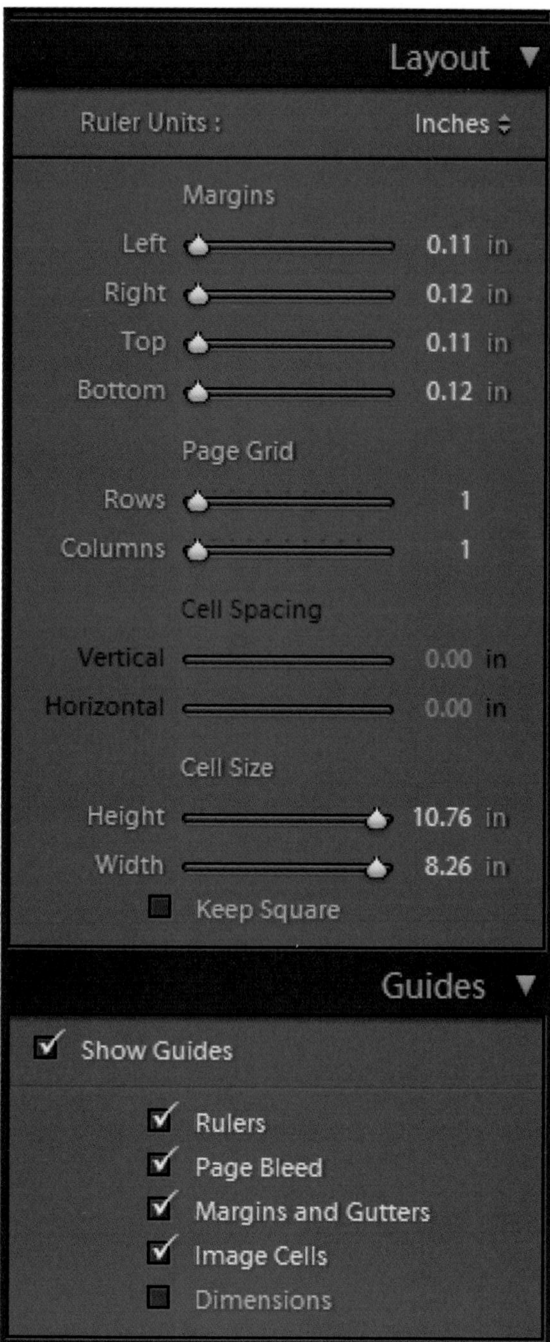

9-16

2. **Check the Cell Size.** This is the specific size that your image will be printed. You can change it by moving the Height and Width sliders or by clicking and dragging on the numbers themselves. A detail of what the cursor looks like when you click and drag directly on a number is shown in figure 9-17. All control numbers in Lightroom act this way. Photoshop CS versions also do this, but not everyone knows that. If you have never tried this, just click and drag on a number to see how it works.

If you want a group of prints that include both horizontal and vertical photos in the same location (for a portfolio presentation, for example), you might want to select Keep Square under Cell Size and be sure Zoom to Fill Frame from Image Settings is deselected. That keeps all of your photos the same proportion (they can only be as wide or as tall as the square) and centered in the same place. You can also use Keep Square with Zoom to Fill Frame to create square images on the page.

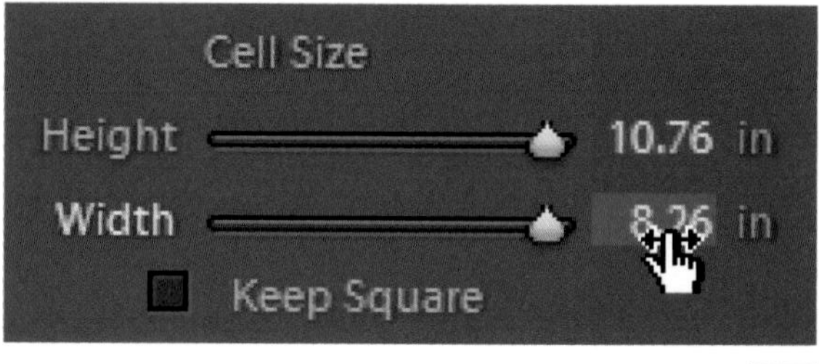

9-17

PRO TIP

You can change margins by either using the sliders in Page Layout Tools or by clicking the margin guides directly in the central work area and dragging them into place.

PRO TIP

Create a fine-art look by creating a margin at the bottom of the page that is larger than the margin at the top of the page. This makes the image sit higher on the page, giving that gallery mat look. The Fine Art Mat template also does this but with a specific cell size.

3. **Move the photo on the page.** Use the Margins sliders to move the image up, down, right, or left within the page. If your photo has room within the page, you can move it as needed and the cell size remains constant. If your photo does not have space, then the cell size changes as you change the margins. You can't miss this as the photo very obviously changes in size. If you need a certain image size on a specific size of paper, you may be limited as to where you move your margins. If not, you can move margins to create visual space as needed. If you leave Show Guides on, you can click and drag the guides to change margins.

Page Grid is used to control how many photos you want on a page. You simply drag the Rows and Columns sliders as needed to add multiple images to a page. This will give you equal-sized cells. Spacing between the cells is controlled by Cell Spacing. This control is only available when you are in Contact Sheet/Grid in the Layout Engine.

If you choose Picture Package in the Layout Engine, you get a whole new set of layout and cell controls, as shown in figure 9-18. These are predefined packages of "cells" or pictures on a page. New sections appear. Rulers, Grids & Guides simply gives you more control over the placement of cells in this multipicture page. Cells gives you a group of preset image sizes that you can add to your page, either manually or automatically by using Auto Layout. You can also tweak an individual cell with Adjust Selected Cell.

9-18

When to Use Overlays

For many, many photographs, you won't use Overlays, shown in figure 9-19, much. This is really a specialized group of print adjustments that can be extremely valuable if you need them, but they can also be choices that many photographers never use. It is worth knowing what this group of adjustments does for you and how you might best put them to use. Here's how to work them:

- **Identity Plate.** You've seen how Identity Plate can be used with the overall Lightroom interface in Chapter 2 and with slides in Chapter 7. It is something that clearly identifies your images with you, and, if you are a working pro, with your business. Attaching an identity plate to photos being submitted to a publication, for example, can be very important. Adding an identity plate to all of your prints can appear pretentious, so you need to think about how it adds or detracts from your photos.

  You add your identity plate by selecting Identity Plate, as shown in figure 9-20. At this point, you can choose from your standard graphic, or you can create a custom graphic by using the right drop-down menu accessed by clicking the Identity Plate preview, which brings you to the Identity Plate Editor, shown in figure 9-21. Change the Identity Plate's size and strength with Opacity and Scale (or you can just click and drag the anchor points around the Identity Plate, as shown in figure 9-20). Render behind image and Render on every image make the Identity Plate partially hidden by the image or appear on every photo, respectively. The Identity Plate is further explained in Chapter 2.

- **Page Options.** Select Page Options to include Page Numbers, Page Info, and Crop Marks on the printed page. Page Numbers and Page Info are rather specialized. Page Numbers is obvious, and you would only use it if you have a lot of images that you need to keep in certain order. Page Info gives information about how the page is set up for printing and can be used for testing prints and printers. Crop Marks can help you cut multiple photos from a page so that they come out even and correctly trimmed.

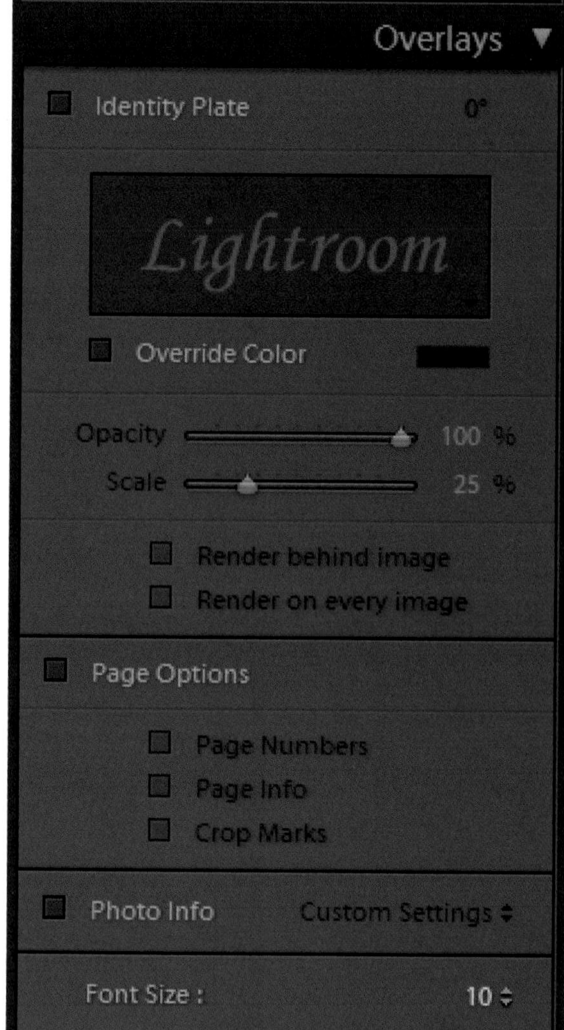

9-19

9 Making Sense of the Print Module

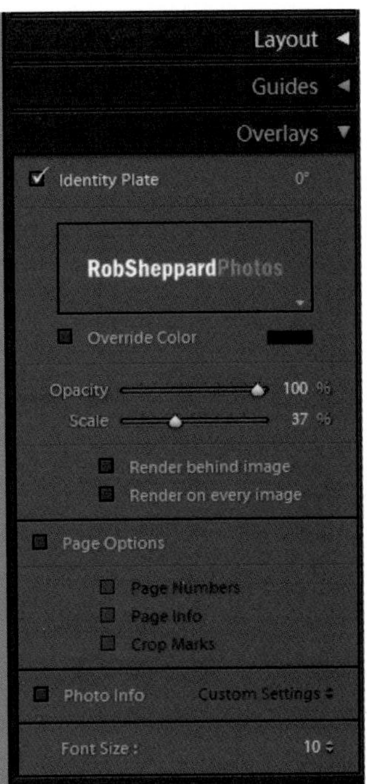

9-20

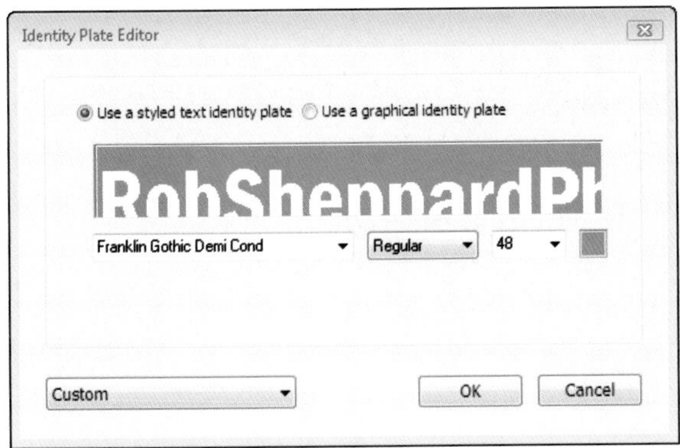

9-21

> **Photo Info.** You can add a number of standard bits of text based on the metadata of your image when this is selected. When Photo Info is active, you can click Custom Settings to the right to give you a number of choices, as shown in figure 9-22, including the image file name, date it was shot, exposure, equipment used, and more when you select Edit. You can change the size of the text by clicking the number to the right of Font Size and choosing a new size.

This information is fairly specialized for most photographers, though if it is needed, it is also critical. A pro submitting proofs to a client is very likely going to include the file name. Any photographer testing new equipment will want to choose Equipment and perhaps Exposure so prints can be compared. Because the information that you can add to a print is so specialized, it is difficult to offer any real guidelines.

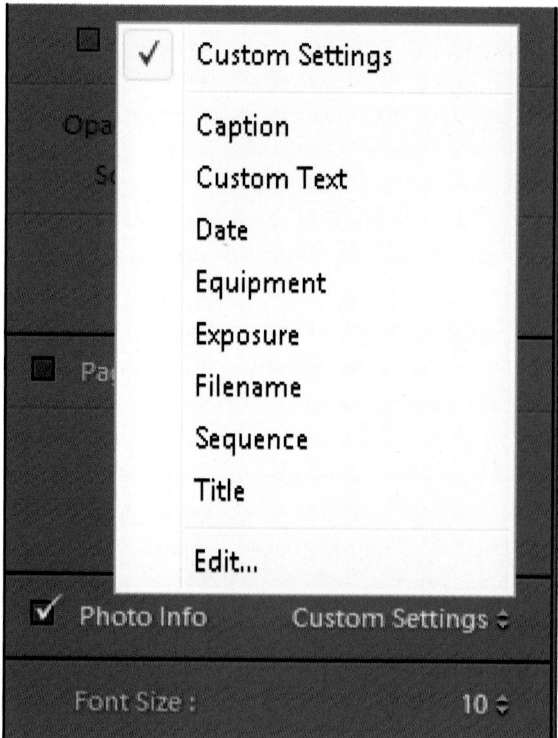

9-22

Print Job

The Print Job section is very important for getting an optimum print from Lightroom. It is where you tell the program how to communicate with the printer so that the two speak the same language and is shown in figure 9-23. Lightroom is designed to make the whole digital photography experience easier and not to have a lot of absolutes, so I give you some ideas here on how to use Print Job simply and effectively. Because the individual settings of Print Job are so important, I am giving them to you in separate sections. I am not going to spend much time with Draft Mode Printing, however. This is designed for very quick prints from the JPEG preview that Lightroom makes for viewing, rather than having Lightroom process the original file. Where this can be important is when you are printing multiple photos on a page as it can speed up the process considerably. It will not give you optimum quality for larger prints.

Choosing Print Resolution

Print Resolution is the resolution of your image as it is sent to the printer. It is very important to understand that this is not the printer resolution and has nothing to do with printer resolution. The default of 240 pixels per inch (ppi) is fine. You sometimes hear Photoshop users say that you should print at 360 ppi. That puts an unnecessary processing burden on your computer as your print file increases in size dramatically. An image at 360 ppi can add a huge amount of memory demand compared to 240 ppi. You can try printing at 240 ppi or even 200 ppi as your photos increase in size so that you keep the demands on memory lower.

On most printers, you see little difference between prints of 200 ppi and 360 ppi. There often is a minute difference that can be seen only if you put your nose to the print. Now if someone has to put their nose on your print to decide if you have a good image or not, something is wrong about our priorities as photographers. Some folks will also say they can see a difference with a magnifier, but who do you know who hands you a print, and then a magnifier to see it better?

Print Sharpening

Print Sharpening is a little confusing. After all, you sharpened in Develop, right? Actually, print sharpening does make a difference. Sharpening in Develop is what is called *capture* sharpening, meaning that it is designed to get the most from the original image as captured, to gain the best sharpness based on what your camera and lens actually saw as compared to what was recorded. Print sharpening is output sharpening, meaning that it sharpens specifically to deal with the sharpness needs of printing, and it really does work.

Lightroom sharpens differently than Photoshop and uses different algorithms than either Unsharp Mask or Smart Sharpen. You can't use any formulas you used to use for Photoshop here. Lightroom is sharpening the image as it comes from a linear gamma space. Okay, I admit, I am not an engineer and I can't explain exactly what that means, but I can tell you that it means you need new formulas for using Lightroom.

Sharpening is always a subjective thing. The subject itself, the size of the print, the mood of the image, and the personal preference of the photographer all influence what might be used for sharpening. Print Sharpening offers three choices when you click the drop-down menu arrow, as shown in figure 9-24: Low, Standard, and High. It also enables you to refine that sharpening for Media Type in Glossy or Matte (choose whichever best fits your paper type). I recommend you experiment with them using these guidelines:

- **Low.** This is often a good choice for images of people, especially women and young children. It is useful for soft-focus or selective-focus images. Moody, atmospheric photos usually need less sharpening, too.
- **Standard.** This is a good choice for many subjects: groups of people, men, athletes, flowers, gentle landscapes, and moody scenes with more detail.
- **High.** Reserve this for subjects that can handle it, such as architecture, landscapes with lots of textured rocks and other detail, dramatic abstract images, industrial scenes, and so on.

Working with Color Management

This is an important section that whole books have been written about. Lightroom is designed to be easy to use, however, so you really don't have to read a book about color management to use it well. One thing that I do recommend is that you ignore advice that makes you feel incompetent because you don't fully understand color management — you don't have to. Color management here is simply the way Lightroom communicates how it sees a photo to the printer.

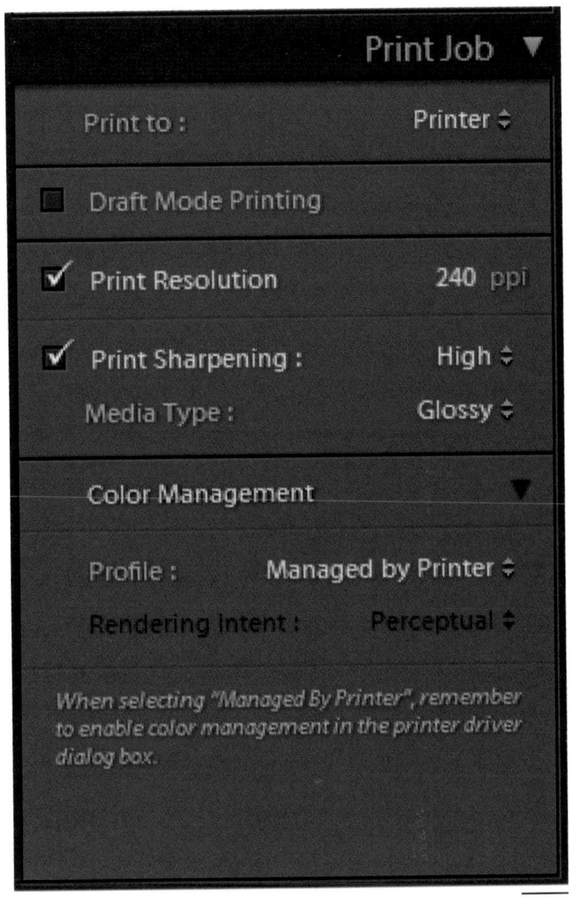

9-23

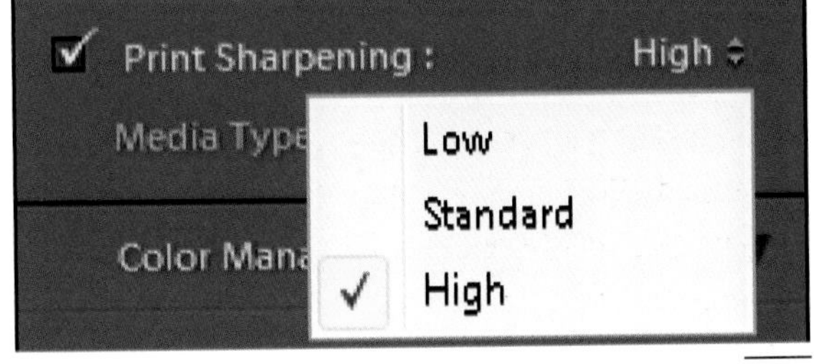

9-24

Color Management gives you two controls, Profile and Rendering Intent, as shown in figure 9-25. Both have two choices by default. Here's how to use them:

- **Profile.** This is the paper profile of the printer and defines how colors are translated from the computer space to a specific paper. You have two choices: Managed by Printer and Other, as shown in figure 9-26 (although once you choose a profile with Other, it will appear as a new choice). It used to be that Other generally worked best with advanced photo printers, but that is not so automatic anymore. You may find that your printer works better with Managed by Printer.

Color Management
Profile : Managed by Printer
Rendering Intent : Perceptual
When selecting "Managed By Printer", remember to enable color management in the printer driver dialog box.

9-25

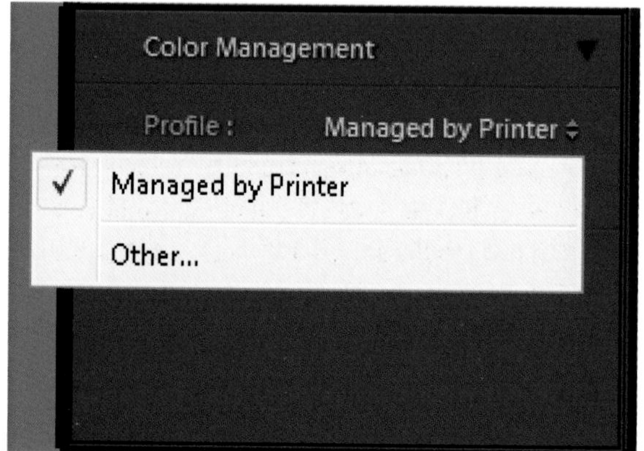

9-26

- **Profile: Managed by Printer.** Many Photoshop users often downplay this choice. Years ago, it was rarely the best choice. However, printers today are very, very good. Printer manufacturers want you to have a good experience printing. It is to their benefit when the printer software handles the paper profile automatically if the resulting prints are good. I find that this choice works well with the Hewlett Packard photo printers as well as the simpler and more mass-market photo inkjet printers of all brands. In addition, photographers occasionally find that no matter what they do, they cannot get the results they want with a paper profile on a particular printer. Yet if they select this option and let the printer take control, they often do. It can be worth trying a sheet of paper to see how it does.
- **Profile: Other.** Other gives you choices in paper profiles, as shown in figure 9-27. You simply select the profile that matches the paper you are using. When you choose a profile, the word "other" changes to the profile you have selected. Choosing a paper profile is frequently the best way to go with high-end inkjet printers designed for pros. These profiles have been very carefully developed by the printer or paper manufacturer. They either come with your printer when you install it or you can add them later by downloading profiles from a paper or printer company Web site.
- **Rendering Intent.** You have two choices when a profile is chosen: Perceptual and Relative. Both refer to the way Lightroom renders colors, but both work, and the choices are really quite subjective as to which you might prefer. Some photographers will chose one and stick with it based on their needs, paper used, and final use of the print. Others will change this regularly. There is no absolute and it is hard to give a specific recommendation.

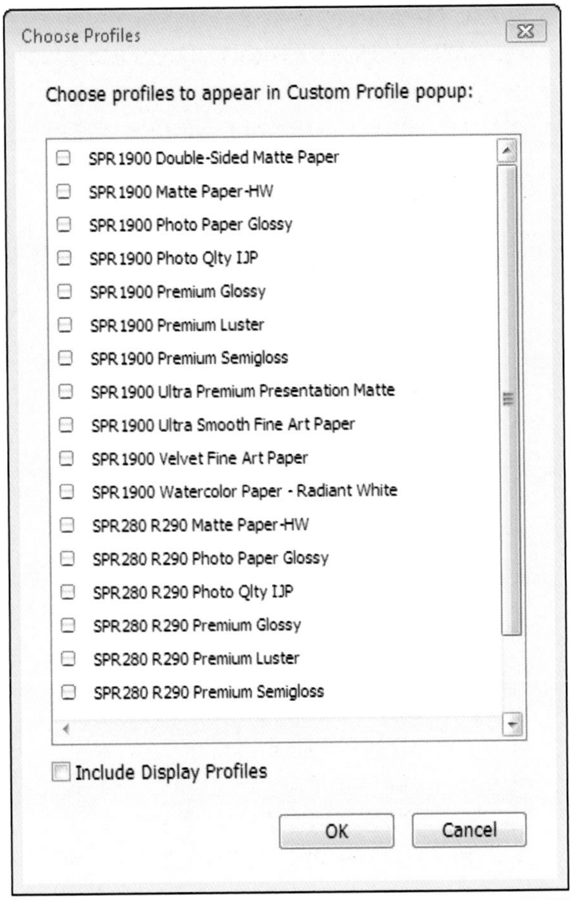

Choose Profiles

Choose profiles to appear in Custom Profile popup:

- SPR 1900 Double-Sided Matte Paper
- SPR 1900 Matte Paper-HW
- SPR 1900 Photo Paper Glossy
- SPR 1900 Photo Qlty IJP
- SPR 1900 Premium Glossy
- SPR 1900 Premium Luster
- SPR 1900 Premium Semigloss
- SPR 1900 Ultra Premium Presentation Matte
- SPR 1900 Ultra Smooth Fine Art Paper
- SPR 1900 Velvet Fine Art Paper
- SPR 1900 Watercolor Paper - Radiant White
- SPR280 R290 Matte Paper-HW
- SPR280 R290 Photo Paper Glossy
- SPR280 R290 Photo Qlty IJP
- SPR280 R290 Premium Glossy
- SPR280 R290 Premium Luster
- SPR280 R290 Premium Semigloss

Include Display Profiles

OK Cancel

9-27

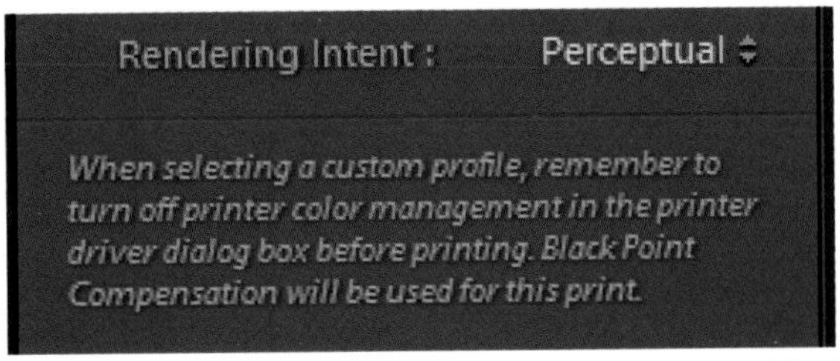

Rendering Intent : Perceptual

When selecting a custom profile, remember to turn off printer color management in the printer driver dialog box before printing. Black Point Compensation will be used for this print.

9-28

> **Warnings.** Immediately to the right of Color Management is a dark arrow. Click it to turn the warnings on and off. If you have turned them on, as shown in figure 9-28, you will find some very useful warnings underneath Rendering Intent. The warnings basically remind you that you need to leave printer color management turned on when the color management is left to the printer, and turned off when a profile is used to control it within the computer. You turn printer color management on or off in the printer driver — where and how depend on the printer and the operating system.

These are important warnings. Think of it this way: If you tell Lightroom to let the printer manage color, Lightroom simply sends a standard set of color information to the printer, then the printer interprets that information based on how its software (the printer driver) interprets color information to make the colors look their best with a specific paper choice. If you tell Lightroom to manage the colors, Lightroom then makes some adjustments to the colors so that they are optimized for a particular paper. At this point, the printer needs to just accept that adjustment and not add its own adjustments, which is why color management in the printer driver must be turned off.

Using the Template Browser

I am leery of many automated functions in programs for photographers. As a whole, photographers like more control over a photo than full automation allows. Luckily, Lightroom only uses its automated features, such as templates, as a way to get started, and you can tweak and modify any adjustments to the photo as needed. In addition, Lightroom enables you to remember consistent Print adjustments by creating your own, custom templates.

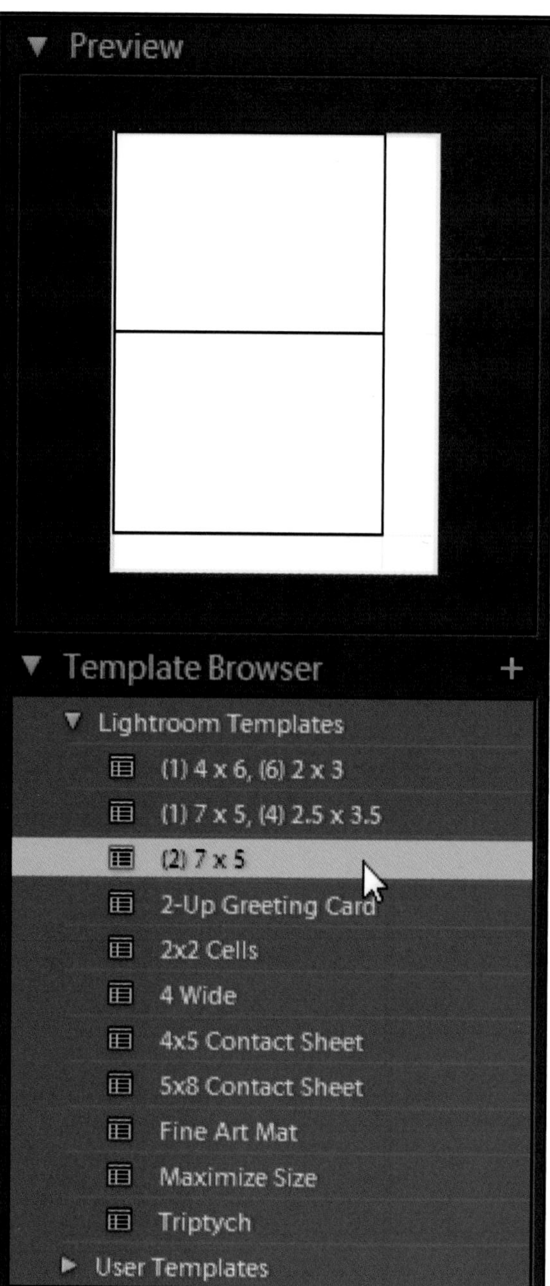

9-29

Print has a great set of templates for photographers, as shown in figure 9-29. As you move your cursor over them, a graphic of their layout appears in the Preview above Template Browser. A sample of them includes the following:

- **(1) 4 × 6, (6) 2× 3.** This is one of the Picture Package templates that gives you one 4 × 6-inch and six 2 × 3-inch images on one 8 ½ × 11-inch page.
- **2×2 Cells.** The 2×2 is not about inches but about a 2 × 2 grid of images printed on the page, as shown in figure 9-30. By default, it is a vertical, and vertical photos fill the cells. Horizontal images do not. Instead, they only use the width of the vertical cell for their width. Use Image Settings to fill out the cells, using Zoom to Fill to use the whole cell, Rotate to Fit for horizontals, and Repeat One Photo per Page to fill all cells with the same photo. Select multiple photos from the Filmstrip, and they appear automatically in the photo work area grid.
- **4 Wide.** This is a unique and dramatic layout for a page, as shown in figure 9-31, designed specifically for pro photographers' promotions. Each cell is a very wide, panoramic cropped format. In addition, photos come in sized to fill this width, meaning they are severely cropped (unless they are a panoramic photo to begin with). You can click and drag any photo up or down, or side to side to better fit the crop to the content. This template with its extreme crop doesn't work with every photograph or for every photographer. At the bottom, your Identity Plate is inserted — simply double-click on it and you will get a dialog box to change it as needed.

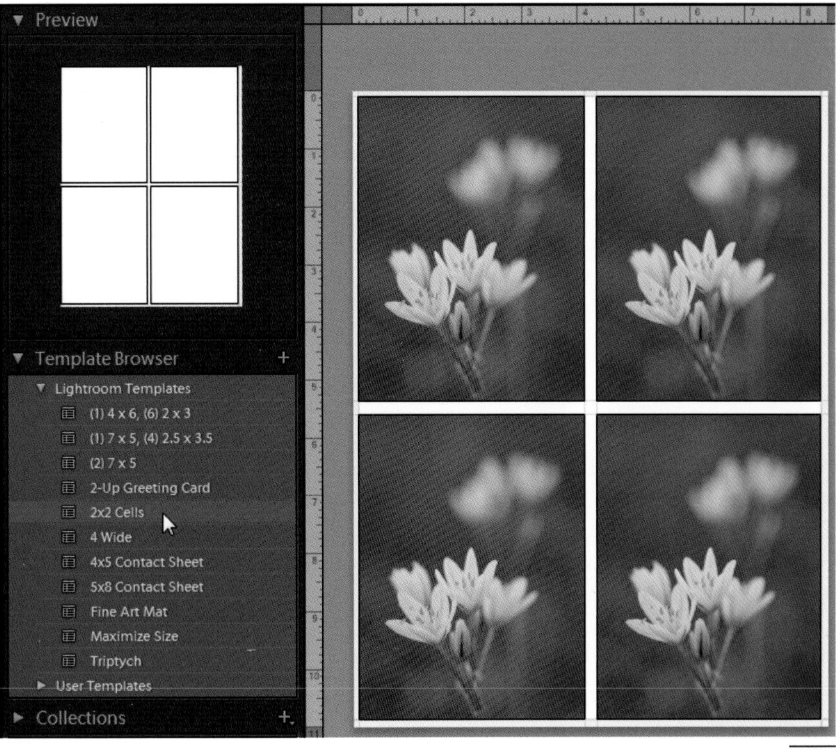
Preview
Template Browser
Lightroom Templates
(1) 4 x 6, (6) 2 x 3
(1) 7 x 5, (4) 2.5 x 3.5
(2) 7 x 5
2-Up Greeting Card
2x2 Cells
4 Wide
4x5 Contact Sheet
5x8 Contact Sheet
Fine Art Mat
Maximize Size
Triptych
User Templates
Collections

9-30

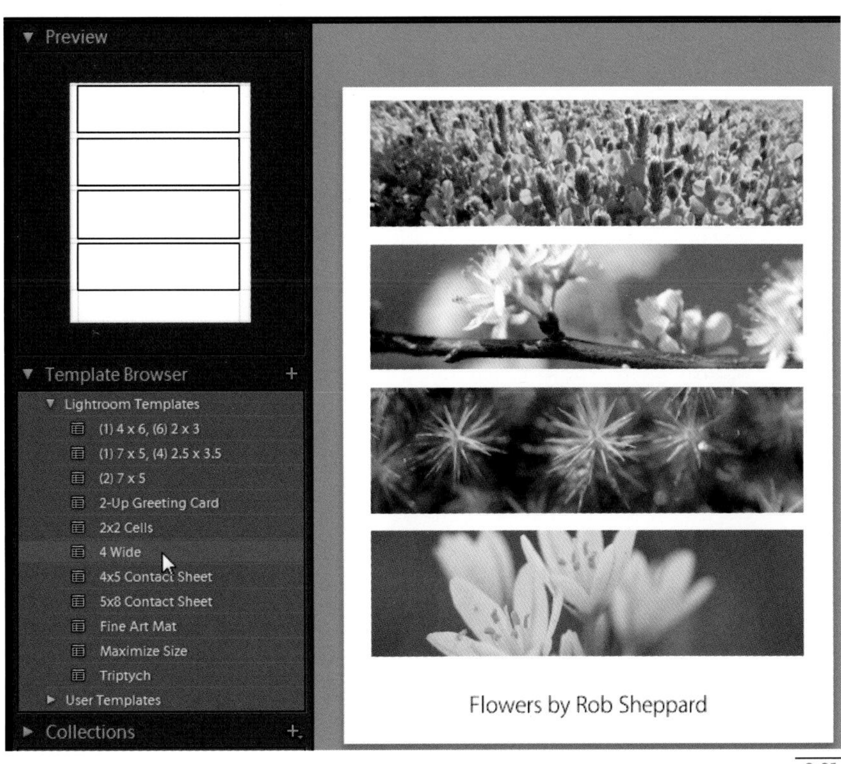
Preview
Template Browser
Lightroom Templates
(1) 4 x 6, (6) 2 x 3
(1) 7 x 5, (4) 2.5 x 3.5
(2) 7 x 5
2-Up Greeting Card
2x2 Cells
4 Wide
4x5 Contact Sheet
5x8 Contact Sheet
Fine Art Mat
Maximize Size
Triptych
User Templates
Collections
Flowers by Rob Sheppard

9-31

> **Contact Sheets.** The Template Browser offers two templates for a "contact sheet," a printout that includes many photos with key information beside them, including photo information from the metadata such as the file name, the date the photo was taken, its title, and the copyright (change metadata under Overlays). The 4 × 5 Contact Sheet gives four columns wide by five rows high for a total of up to 20 photos per page, as shown in figure 9-32. You do need to tell Lightroom to add photo information, such as Filename, with Photo Info in Overlays. The 5 × 8 provides five columns by eight rows for a total of 40 photos per page. Only images that are selected in the Filmstrip or Library Grid view appear on the printed page.

Use any of these, or other, templates with a simple click. You can add your own templates at any time by making printing choices specific to your needs based on everything discussed in this chapter, including Page Setup and Print Settings. When you have them set, click Add at the bottom of the left panel and type a name for a new template. That's it!

The two choices for contact sheets in Lightroom, 4 × 5 and 5 × 8, provide enough images per page to fit most needs for this type of printing. However, you can change these quickly enough by going to Page Layout tools and choosing different numbers for the Page Grid. As you do that, you may find that the images get too close or too far apart. Correct that by changing Cell Spacing or Cell Size.

PRO TIP

If you are a pro who is submitting photos to a publication, I highly recommend that you always print out a contact sheet with your submitted discs. This instantly puts you on the good side of the editor or art buyer. Many editors don't like disc submissions without photos because it means more time and effort out of their busy schedules to deal with a disc and their computer before they can even see what might be included. A contact sheet (or index print) lets them see what you have and which photos they want to look at quickly rather than forcing them to go through all of them.

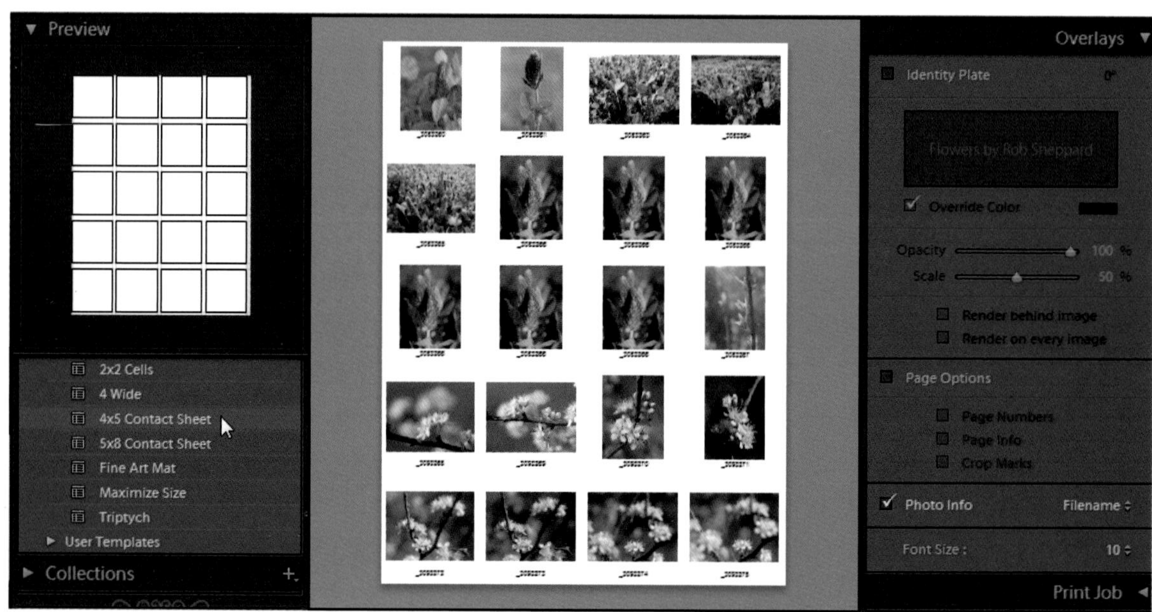

9-32

Print

After you make all of your adjustments, you are ready to print. You took care of Page Setup earlier. Now you need to set up your printer and print. This is one area where Mac and Windows operating systems differ completely. The Mac OS now incorporates the printer driver (the printer's software) into its own graphics and separates the options into one section, Print Setting, of a single Print dialog box, as shown in figure 9-33. (Older Mac operating systems had this information in more than one place.) The Windows OS accesses a unique printer driver dialog box through the Properties button in the Windows Print dialog box, as shown in figures 9-34 and 9-35 (these will look different depending on the printer you own). Regardless, the choices you make for a print are essentially the same in both systems.

The important parts of the print sequence can also be accessed in Page Setup and Print Settings, but frankly, you can go right to Print in Windows (on a Mac you cannot set paper size through Print Settings; you need to use Page Setup). Some photographers prefer to set up printing separately from making the print, hence the choice; plus if you want to quickly print using Print One, you have to have these set up previously. Here are the options you must confirm:

> **Number of copies to print.** This is pretty standard for all computer printing programs.

> **Paper or media type.** You must tell the printer what kind of paper you are using so it lays down ink properly for it.

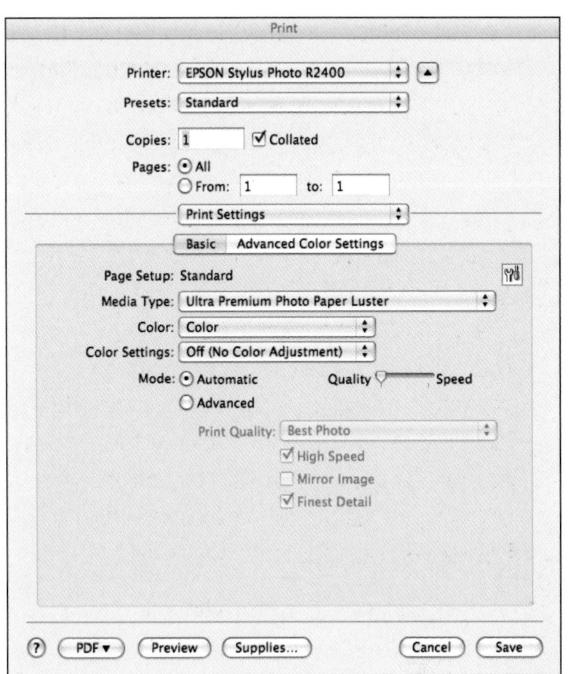

9-33

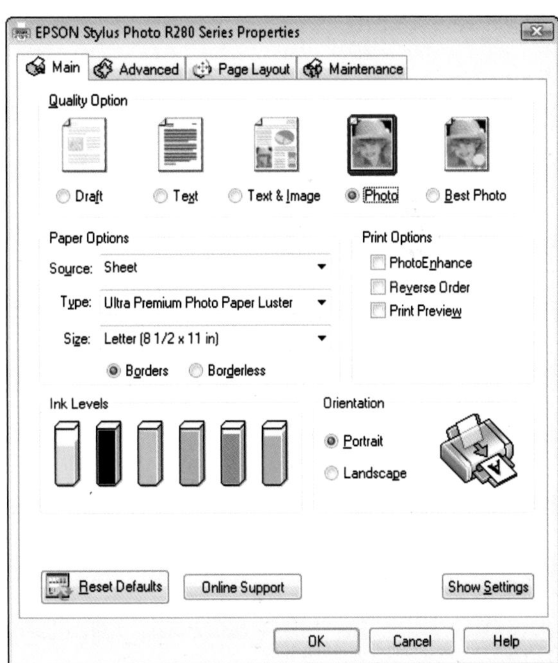

9-34

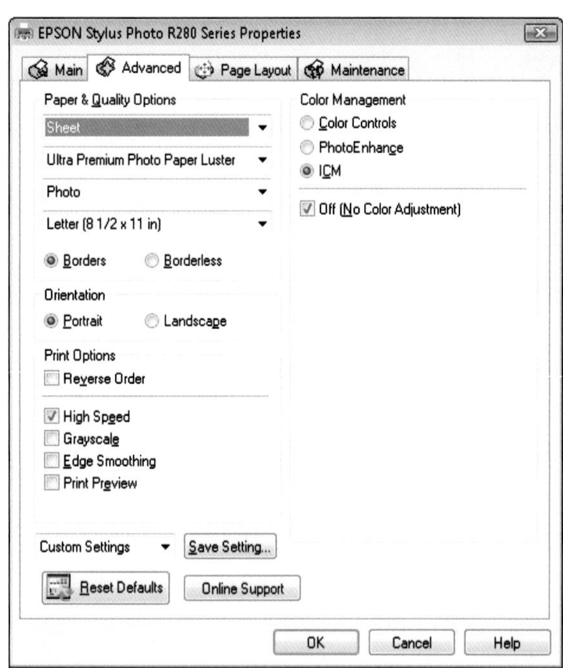

9-35

> **Color Management.** This goes right back to Color Management in Lightroom. If you selected Managed by Printer, you need to be sure the printer is managing the process, as shown in figure 9-36 for Mac (Color Settings) and 9-37 for Windows (usually Color Management). Unfortunately, the exact words used will vary from printer manufacturer to printer manufacturer, and this setting will be in different locations for Windows, too, so you may have to do some looking.

If you selected a paper profile, choose Off (No Color Adjustment), as shown in figure 9-33 for Mac and 9-35 for Windows. To reemphasize an important point: You will see different layouts and arrangements of options in these dialog boxes with different printers, but the key choices are still there. Setting color management properly in the printer driver is critical, because you do not want the printer trying to readjust colors already adjusted for a paper profile by Lightroom.

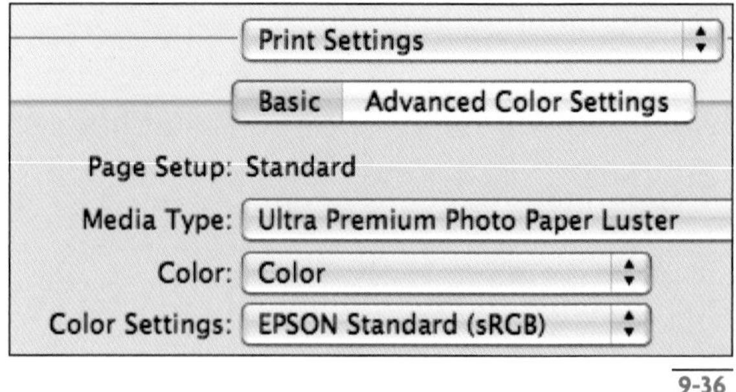

9-36

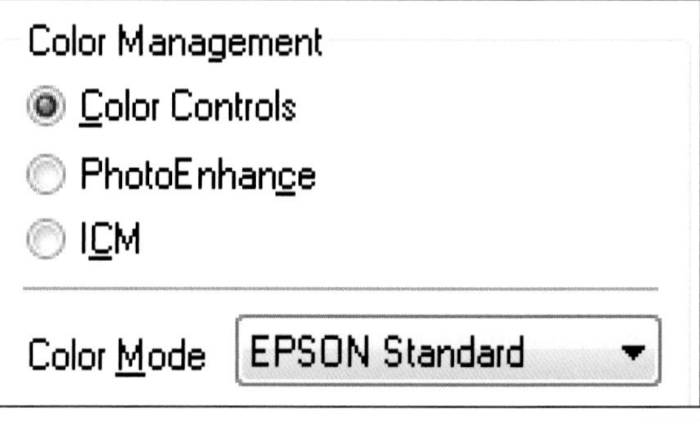

9-37

After you make your choices, click Print and sit back while Lightroom and your printer make the print for you. In Chapter 10, you learn how to use Lightroom to go from a good print to a great print.

Q & A

I have heard that you should use an image resolution that is a fraction of the printer resolution. They say, for example, that you should use 360 ppi with an Epson printer because Epson prints at 720, 1440, 2880, and so on, so 360 is a simple fraction. Does that work?

Logically, that might seem to make sense. After all, shouldn't the pixels in a photo somehow line up with the dots of an inkjet printer?

However, there are several problems with that theory. Modern printers print at variable resolution up to the maximum set. In other words, they might print a light area at a different resolution than a dark area, plus they may lay down different colors at different resolutions. So, if you want to work with an image resolution that is a fraction of the printing resolution, what fraction you will get is something that changes constantly depending on what color or tone is being printed.

Related to this, inkjet printers lay down ink with highly evolved patterns for color and tonality. These are so secret and are such prized possessions of printer companies that very few people actually have access to the algorithms that control this. From what I understand, these very sophisticated algorithms pay more attention to tonalities and color changes than they do to the actual pixels in an image. Plus, these patterns overlap ink dots in unique ways that don't always match pixels, either.

You talk about Lightroom's Color Management option as it relates to the printer and print. But what about the monitor? Doesn't this make the print match the monitor?

A lot of photographers are disappointed when the print doesn't match the monitor. Having a consistent color for your monitor that can be interpreted by the print is important, but the expectation of actually matching a print to the monitor can be both misleading and very frustrating. If nothing else, the mediums (screen and paper) are totally different anyway.

Color management, at any level, is about consistency first of all. You need to know that colors will be managed by the computer so that they will be interpreted correctly and consistently by every device used in digital photography, from the camera to the printer. While it is possible to even create profiles for a camera in order to better define its response to colors, it is rarely productive for most photographers. So, you set a color space in the camera such as sRGB or Adobe RGB, and then the computer with its programs recognizes it and interprets the colors appropriately.

On a very basic level, obviously, you want the computer to interpret a red from the camera as a red and not a purple at worst or a red-orange at best. Then you need the computer to translate that red into a red that the printer understands and can duplicate. That may or may not be exactly the same red that appears on the computer screen, but it better be consistent and done as accurately as possible. That is what color management is about.

Chapter 10

FROM GOOD TO GREAT PRINTING WITH PRINT

In the previous chapter, I covered everything you really need to know in order to use Adobe Photoshop Lightroom to create a good print from a digital image file. To refine your printing and get a better print, you have to make a lot of prints. I know of no other way to do this. Image printing is truly a craft, not just a set of "right choices" in a digital imaging program. It is about practicing with the program, learning the tools, and making the program conform to your expectations.

In this chapter, I help you make better prints by encouraging you to better learn the craft of printing through Lightroom. I am taking that further, though, and promising great prints. Of course, having a great subject or interpretation of that subject is up to you and can't be controlled by Lightroom. A great print, though, is one that truly expresses what your image and subject mean to you and that affects the viewer as well. I believe great prints are possible for anyone, but I repeat that this takes some time and effort to master.

Monitor versus Print

There is a pervasive, and I believe very misleading, idea that the best prints match the monitor. This idea can lead you in wrong directions as you strive for a great print. It is true that you should be able to get a good print that accurately interprets the colors and tonalities on your monitor, as shown in figure 10-1. Monitor calibration and attention to color management, as I describe in Chapter 9, helps you achieve that.

However, the monitor and the print are not the same. Here are some things to keep in mind:

> **The monitor displays colors from glowing RGB colors while the print represents its colors with reflected light on CMYK colors.** These two color spaces are very different. RGB is the standard computer space using red, green, and blue. CMYK is an ink color space using cyan, magenta, yellow, and black, and is a smaller color space than RGB. No matter how well each works, they present colors in their own way, plus we react differently to glowing versus flat ink colors.

> **A print is seen in a different place than a monitor.** Surroundings always affect how we see the print, and print locations are never the same as a monitor's position.

> **The size of an image changes it.** If you make a small 4-×-6-inch print, then a large 13-×-19-inch print, you will find all sorts of differences. Even compare the two images of the Costa Rican waterfall, La Paz, shown as a print and on a monitor in figure 10-1. You see color, contrast, details, and more quite differently when looking at different sizes. Yet a monitor is a single size and can never show the full range of sizes possible for a print.

> **A print is a different object altogether from a computer monitor.** You don't hold a monitor the way you do a print. You don't frame and move a monitor the way you do a print. These affect more than the physics of image handling — they affect your perception and your viewers' perception of the image.

> **No one ever asks a photographer to compare a print with what was displayed in Lightroom.** I have never seen computers set up at a gallery of photography so viewers could check to see if the print and monitor match.

> **Viewers of a print need to respond to that print and make a connection through it to you and your subject.** It is possible that an evocative print might have no relation to the monitor image, which might be used for a different purpose than the print one.

This is not bad news! Getting a good print used to be so hard when you were working with labs that the promise of a perfect print made by computer seemed awfully seductive. Get the right program, use color management right, and you get a perfect print, right?

10-1

That path leads you into making a technically "correct" print, but not necessarily one that truly connects with your viewer.

Why You Need a Work Print

Ansel Adams is considered one of the great print makers in photography. He died a little over 20 years ago, yet his influence on photography is still very strong. His prints are part of museum collections around the world, plus they sell at huge prices when any original print becomes available. How he worked and created those great prints offers some insight for getting your own great print from Lightroom. The name Lightroom is especially appropriate as it mirrors a darkroom, the place where Adams spent so much time making his images come to life on paper. Lightroom is the modern photographer's place for making digital images come to life on paper, too.

Adams was a master printer who had years of experience in the darkroom. He could "read" a negative and know what exposure to use with his enlarger when making a print from that negative. A lot of people would have been happy with such a print, and, indeed, they might have considered it a good one.

But Adams wanted more. He wanted a print that truly expressed his experience and feelings for the subject in the print as well as how he felt about the actual visual qualities of the print itself.

So, his first prints were always work prints. A work print was a common part of the film photographer's workflow in the darkroom. This was not meant to be anything final. It was a simple print that clearly showed what was in the negative (the original image capture) and offered insights to the potential of the image. In figure 10-2, you see a series of images that illustrate how an image might evolve from a work print (left) to a final interpretation (right).

From that work print, Adams would begin to formulate a plan of work. What needed to be darker? What needed to be lighter? What areas of the photo were unbalanced? Where was it too light? Too dark? And so on. Based on this, Adams would make a new print,

10-2

still considering that a work print, making revisions as to how the image needed to be adjusted to refine his vision of the scene. He would continue this for quite a while until he felt he had a master print that finally expressed his way of seeing.

It is true that in some ways, your monitor acts like a first work print. You should be evaluating what the image looks like — not simply what it looks like in Lightroom, but what it would look like if it were a photo hanging on the wall. That might seem obvious, yet I find many photographers don't do that. They adjust the photo until it looks good as a screen image on their computer. With experience making work prints, you can look at what is on the monitor and interpret it as a print. But to do that requires a different mental attitude. Once you start thinking that way, though, I guarantee you will start to see your photo differently before printing.

But sooner or later, you need to actually create a physical print that you use as a work print to evaluate what else is needed in Lightroom (or even if you need to do some work in Photoshop) to make this a better print, and, in the end, a great print.

One problem is that photographers sometimes see prints as simply a cost and don't want to "waste" paper and ink. An inkjet print costs far less than any traditional printing media from the old darkroom, especially when that print is in color. Consider the work print as an investment, a step toward truly wonderful photos, and not as only a "cost."

Evaluating a Work Print

How do you evaluate any photo? How, exactly, can you define a good print? A great print? There is no question that these are very subjective. What is a good or great print to one person may be something else to another, but then that is true for any creative medium. What is important is not finding some absolute or perfect great print, but creating a print that truly reflects your needs, interests, and feelings about your subject. It might be difficult to define an absolute, great print, but you will know it when you get it.

Getting to that print means making work prints, evaluating them, making adjustments to the image, printing a new photo, evaluating it again, and so on until you get the print you want. There are some things you can do to evaluate your print to get you more quickly through the work print process, as shown in figure 10-3. Here are some things to look for:

> **Are your blacks printing properly?** Look at the darkest parts of the photo. Are there blacks where they need to be? Are the black areas too small? Too large?

> **Are your whites and highlights printing with the right detail?** If something should be pure white, then it should be that white in the print. If a highlight area should be registering detail, look to see if that detail is too light or too dark.

> **Check your midtones.** They can have a major effect on the look of a print. If they are too dark, the image can look muddy. If they are too light, the colors can be weak and pasty. I have often seen prints that had the right blacks, but in setting them, the photographer did not reset midtones and made the print look heavy and dark. Another problem is midtones that are too bright because the photographer tried too hard to show everything in the image.

> **Check your dark tones.** These are the dark areas of an image that have strong detail. When they are too dark, the image looks heavy. When they are too light, you often lose the feeling of darkness in areas that should look dark, which plays havoc with the mood of a print.

> **Check your light tones.** These are the parts of a photo that have detail and are brighter than middle gray. If they are too dark, you will have a muddy, heavy-looking image. If they are too light, you can lose any feeling of substance in those areas.

> **Are your colorcasts correct?** Inappropriate colorcasts can make a photo look like a poorly adjusted television set. Skin tones can be sickly, neutral tones stained, and colors as a whole look like you are viewing them through some odd filter.

Check how blacks print
Note white detail
How do midtones look?
Check color in highlights and shadows

10-3

Subtle colorcasts can be hard to see precisely, yet they can create major problems for a photographer, especially advertising photographers working with products having defined colors or wedding photographers who better have the right white for the bride's dress.

> **Is the color in the shadows and highlights different?** This is often the case, so make sure that both areas display appropriate colors. Does one look right but the other look wrong?

> **Check your sharpness.** Make sure sharpness is appropriate to the subject. Is detail sharp where it should be sharp? Is the image oversharpened, leading to a harsh look for the subject?

Refining the Work Print

Lightroom's modular structure is the key to making a good print better. As soon as you notice an image doesn't quite work the way it should in the print, you can immediately go back to the Develop module, as shown in figure 10-4, and make some adjustments. You are not limited by a darkroom's processing times like the traditional film photographer is who works with an enlarger and processing chemicals. He or she could spend a day on a single print, but not because all that time is spent evaluating and changing prints. The time from when the enlarger comes on until the print is ready to be evaluated can take 20 minutes or longer per image.

Now, you can quickly make changes to an image, be ready to print again in minutes, and have a print in hand in less than five minutes. That helps many photographers feel freer to experiment as they fine-tune a print.

In addition, you can create one or more Virtual Copies (remember to right-click on the image to get the menu with this option) that offer variations for prints based on final print size, ultimate display location for the print, type of use of print, and anything else you might need. This lets you keep a "master" image with the original adjustments and as many Virtual Copies as you need.

After reading what I discuss about image evaluation just before this section, you might have already started thinking about how you can correct those things. Here are some ideas for doing just that, using the Develop module to refine your prints:

> **Weak blacks.** This is one area that I consistently see as a problem in prints. Check your blacks under Blacks in the Basic group of controls. Use the Alt/Option key to see where your blacks are.

> **Blacks cover too much or too little of photo.** Again, check Blacks in Basic. Use the Alt/Option key to see how much of the dark areas are truly black. You may be limited by your subject and exposure as to how far you can go. Try Basic ➪ Fill Light to lift and open dark areas. You can also try the Tone Curve — use the click-and-drag direct control (fully explained in Chapter 5) so you can click directly on the dark areas and move the cursor up to lighten them.

> **Whites have no detail.** Don't try to get detail in places you need no detail, such as a bright sky behind a person or in specular highlights (bright reflections of light in the scene). If you feel you do need detail, check Exposure and Recovery in Basic. Your exposure might also give you no detail to bring out, and you will see this as you try to change Exposure. You can also work the Tone Curve — use the click-and-drag direct control again, this time to click directly on the light areas and move the cursor down to darken them.

> **Highlights don't have the right detail.** While you can use Exposure to affect this, you are usually better off going right to Highlights under the Tone Curve.

> **Midtones are off.** For slight midtone adjustments to a print, you may find that Brightness and Contrast in Basic work very well and you don't have to muck around in the Tone Curve. If you find, though, that the midtones just look muddy or heavy, especially if they seem to have some contrast problems, then you will probably need to make some Tone Curve adjustments.

10-4

PRO TIP

Consider blacks (and to a degree, whites) in your print to be like the framework of a house. Without that framework, no matter what else is done to a house, it will never be whole without the proper framework. Now, a building that is only framework won't work too well, either. You need the rest of the structure to make a real house. That's what midtones provide to a print. They make a photo complete and make it work as an image for a viewer.

> **Dark tones are out of balance.** Start with the Tone Curve and Shadows. This isn't the only place you can go, however. You may find that the dark tones have a color problem that affects their tonal appearance — try adjusting the Shadows part of Split Toning. Also, check out the Hue, Saturation, and Luminance (HSL) controls. Sometimes it isn't the overall tonality of the dark areas that causes the problem, but rather a specific color that makes up a large portion of the dark areas is too dark or light in tone. Then you can try changing its Luminance in HSL.

> **Light tones are out of balance.** Start with the Tone Curve by changing Lights first, then Highlights. Split Toning doesn't have as big an effect on light tones (the colors don't react as much), though changing Luminance for specific colors in HSL can be worth a try.

> **Correcting colorcasts.** You can try making slight changes in Temperature and/or Tint in Basic first. Next, try the White Balance tool and click in a number of areas in the image. Another possibility is the HSL controls, which enable you to tweak specific colors, such as those represented in the colorcast, by hue (to change their actual color) and saturation. You may have to work more than one color slider to get the best results. Split Toning can affect the color in highlights (those areas often show colorcast problems the worst), and then shadows when the colorcast is not consistent across the range of tones in an image.

PRO TIP

It is rare that you would need to do major adjustments in color at this point. If you find it is necessary, check how you are setting up paper profiles and the printer driver. If that is correct, then you should reexamine your earlier color work, or at least, recalibrate your monitor. You might also do a test print with your printer to be sure it is working correctly and all colors are printing without nozzle clogs.

> **Correcting color in shadows and highlights.** Shadow and highlight colors are nicely affected by changes in Split Toning.

> **Getting optimum sharpness.** You have to make many prints at different sizes to start to get an intuitive feel for sharpness in the print. Be critical of how sharpness affects your subject and the mood of the photo, and then increase or decrease Sharpness to fix any problems. You may also need to check that Luminance and Color noise-reduction controls are not set too high (or they will affect small details in a photo). You can also try setting Luminance high if your photo looks sharp, but details, such as skin tone on a face, are too sharp.

NOTE

How many work prints do you need? Having read everything about them here, you might get the impression that you have to do a lot of them. That's not true. If you get all the information you need from one work print, it is enough. You don't need to keep printing work prints if you don't need them. You are only trying to refine your print so you get a truly expressive image that meets your needs. If that takes one print or ten, that's how many you need. There is no arbitrary amount to use. One idea you can try is to make several versions of your photo as Virtual Copies then print all of them on one sheet. Then you can compare the effects of your adjustments on one page.

The Principle of Visual Balance

Photography and the real world are very different. If one simply seeks to copy the real world, he or she will constantly seek the best in lenses, cameras, and so forth, but ultimately that search will be ever disappointing. The real world is not the same as a photograph and especially a print.

This idea has been a part of photography and other arts for a very long time, way before digital photography and the computer. The French painter Magritte once created a painting of a pipe, and underneath that used the words, "This is not a pipe." *LIFE* photographer Andreas Feininger talked a lot about this in his very popular books about photography written during the 1960s and 1970s, as I discuss in Chapter 6.

This concept is important to understand when looking at making a better print. Prints can quickly get visually out of balance, and that balance can vary based on the size of the print, as well as where it is displayed.

I believe it is very important to look at your print in terms of visual balance. This is where the local adjustment controls of Lightroom are such a tremendous asset. If you look at Ansel Adams' books, you will see him in his darkroom holding up prints and looking at them very carefully. One of the key things he looked for was this balance.

I think this is so important that I am going to reemphasize some of the points that I made in Chapter 6 about using local controls. Always keep in mind that the photograph is not captured by the camera in a balanced way based on how we see the world. This can be really noticeable in a print and can make the difference between a visually flat print and a print with some depth and dimension, as shown in figures 10-5 and 10-6, respectively.

10-5

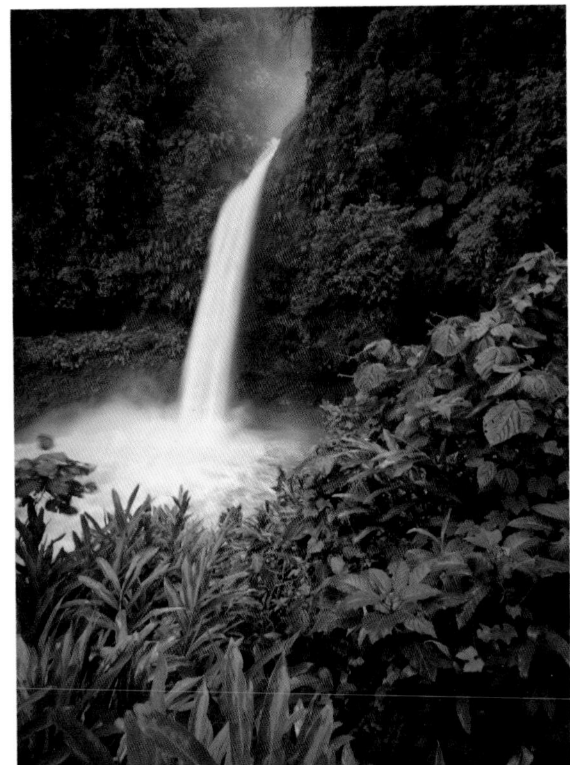

10-6

The adjustment brush and the graduated filter are great tools to refine your print in terms of its balance. Here are things to consider:

> Look for tones that are out of balance, where one part of the picture is too bright proportionally compared to another.

> Watch for colors that have too much or too little saturation compared to others. This can occur because of the way the camera captured them, because of the way the light affects them, or simply from contrasts within the image.

> Watch for colors that have the wrong hue compared to others, for the same reasons.

> Be aware that individual pictorial elements can be out of balance. This can happen if something is lit unevenly, for example.

> Look for ways to create emphasis in your image so that a composition is defined better or your subject stands out better.

And I really want to recommend again that if you want some inspiration on working a print, check out Ansel Adams' books, especially *The Print*.

Creating a Promo Sheet I

As you saw in Chapter 9, Lightroom has some flexible capabilities for making a contact sheet. Yet, a contact sheet is only one thing you can do with multiple images on a page. With a little thought and creativity, you can quickly do some attractive promotional pieces that you can print as needed. The easiest way to show you what is possible is to show you how to create a flyer or promo sheet that holds a group of photos.

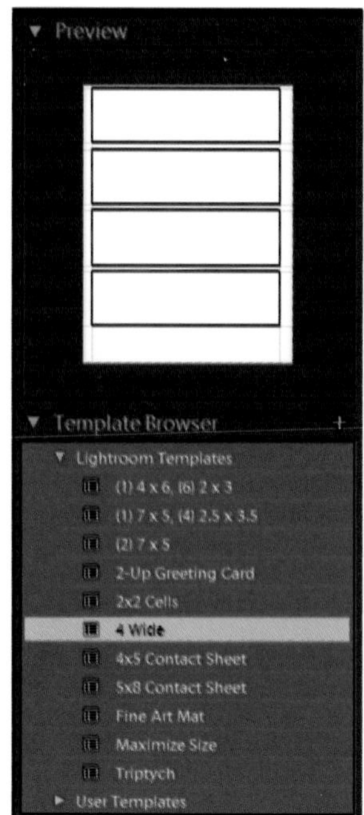

10-7

A good place to start is with the 4 Wide template in the Template Browser, shown in figure 10-7. This is a really cool combination of images cropped to a panoramic format, with your Identity Plate (including custom text) at the bottom. You can't use this for all photos, obviously, because the crop is pretty severe. However, with the right images, this creates a classy, dramatic look for a promotional piece. Here's how you can use it:

1. **Pick four interesting images.** You can go to your Filmstrip and work with a single collection or shoot. I recommend you go back to the Library module, add some photos for possible use to the Quick Collection, as shown in figure 10-8, and then use the Quick Collection for your image resource to do the flyer. In looking at photos for this grouping, remember that each one will be cropped severely to a short horizontal and that the four cropped images need to have some visual or contextual theme so that they look like they belong together.

10-8

2. **Bring them into the template.** In the Print module, choose 4 Wide in the Template Browser. Then multiple-select the four images you want from the Filmstrip. If you put just four into a Quick Collection, you can select them all by pressing Ctrl/⌘+A. They now all appear in the grid, as shown in figure 10-9.

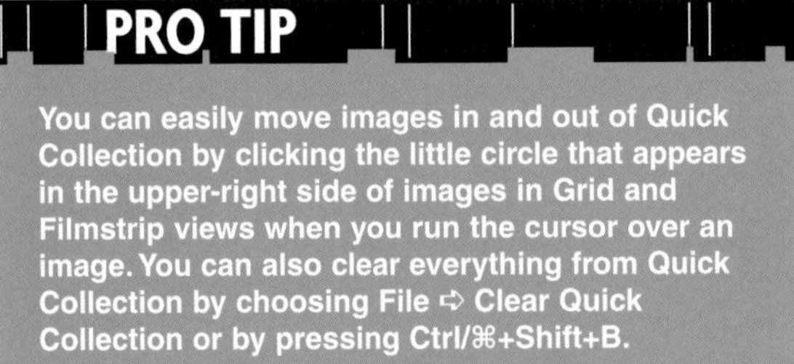

PRO TIP

You can easily move images in and out of Quick Collection by clicking the little circle that appears in the upper-right side of images in Grid and Filmstrip views when you run the cursor over an image. You can also clear everything from Quick Collection by choosing File ➪ Clear Quick Collection or by pressing Ctrl/⌘+Shift+B.

3. **Move photos within the frame.** Click and drag to move the images up and down within the crop area to find a part of each that works best with the shot, as shown in figure 10-10. You can't move them side to side because Zoom to Fill Frame is automatically selected in Image Settings, so the photos are zoomed to the full width of the crop.

4. **Arrange the photos.** Here it gets a little tricky. You can't simply click and drag photos around on the page. The order in which you shoot the photos is the order they appear on the page. You get around this by going to the Filmstrip. After first deselecting all the photos (click in a space where photos don't appear or use Ctrl/⌘+D), you can rearrange them in the Filmstrip by clicking and dragging the

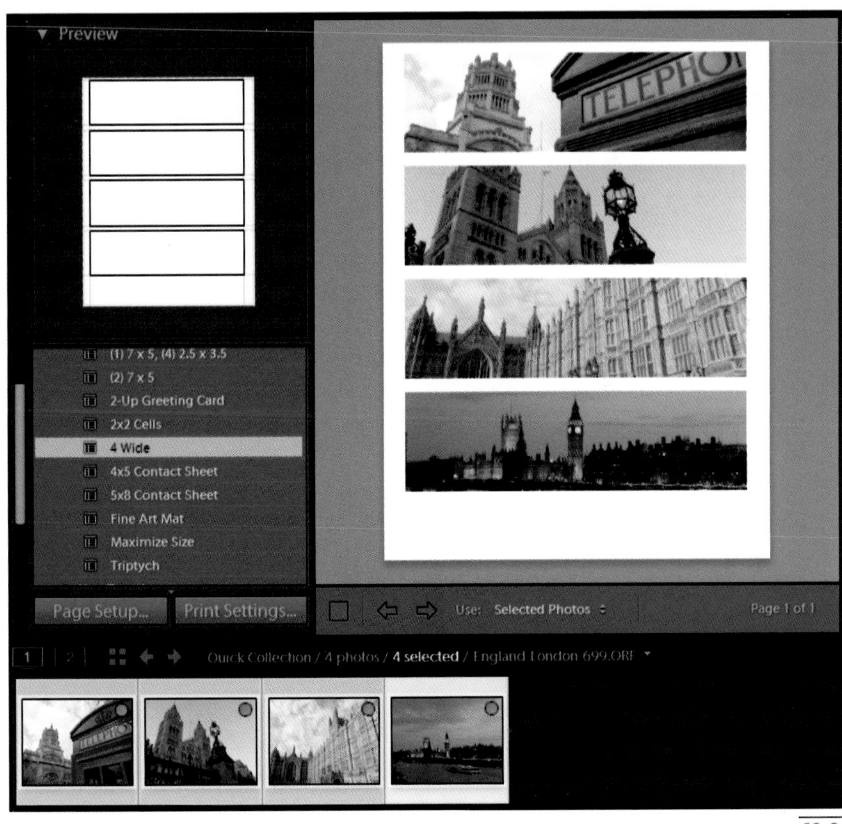

10-9

10-10

10-11

photos (watch for the vertical bar that appears to show you where you are moving an image to), and that order will show up in the central image area when you select them again, as shown in figure 10-11. This is a good reason for using Quick Collection because you will only have a few images to deal with as you rearrange them.

5. **Edit the Identity Plate.** The Identity Plate really finishes this printed piece nicely, as shown in figure 10-12. It appears at the bottom of the page. You can change it as you change any Identity Plate in Print as I describe in more detail in Chapter 2 (double-click the Identity Plate that appears to edit it or use Overlays). If you want to use an existing Identity Plate, but with a different color, you can use the Override Color check box in Overlays.

PRO TIP

The text editor for Identity Plate is pretty basic and somewhat awkward to use if you want something more than described here, such as a second line with a Web site address, but you can do it. Create a graphic that has everything you want in Photoshop using its text function, save it, and then import it as a graphic into the Identity Plate.

6. **Position the text.** Click and drag the Identity Plate to the position you want it. Sometimes you will find it looks best perfectly centered, but other times it looks best at the right or left side, lined up with the grid line that marks the edge of the photos.

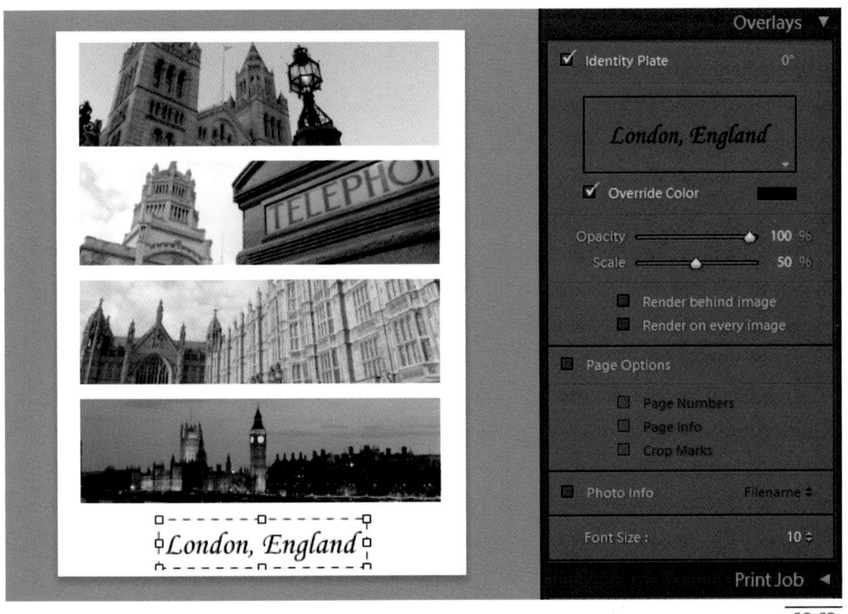

10-12

Creating a Promo Sheet II

Another way of creating a promo sheet, one with more photos that are not arbitrarily cropped, is to use another Contact Sheet template such as 4× 5 Contact Sheet or 5 × 8 Contact Sheet, and then include an Identity Plate. As a photographer who also has worked a long time as a magazine editor, I can't really recommend those numbers. It puts too many photos on a page for a promo sheet. They are fine for a contact sheet as a reference, but they make the images too small for any editor or photo buyer to really see them adequately. Here's what I recommend:

1. **Decide the number of images to go on a promo sheet.** I recommend nine images by using a four-row, three-column grid set up in Layout, as shown in figure 10-13. That gives a total of 12 spaces, but the bottom three give a space for the Identity Plate. This puts a good number of images onto the page, keeps them large enough to view easily, offers decent spacing for the photos, and presents a nice-looking page.
2. **Choose a group of photos for that promotion, as shown in figure 10-14.** At this point, you can see these are a mix of horizontal and vertical, but this will change. Again, I find a good way to do this is to use the Library module and put your photos into the Quick Collection. Or you can simply Ctrl/⌘+click the nine images needed from a larger collection from within the Print module, then choose Use: Selected Photos in the toolbar below the work area. Pick a group of photos that look good together and that show off your work. You can use the Quick Collection while still in Library to compare, contrast, and arrange images to be sure they work together.

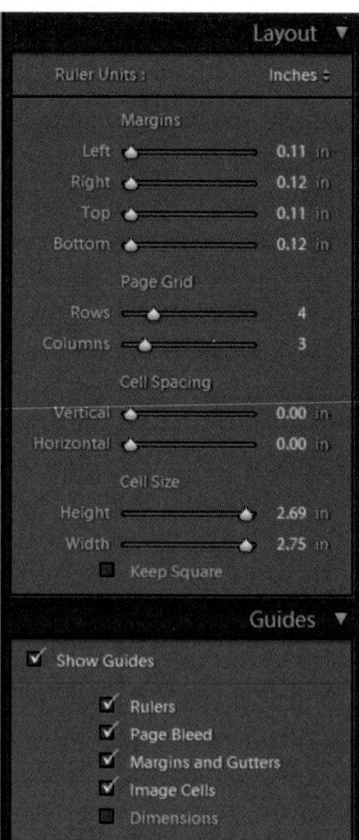

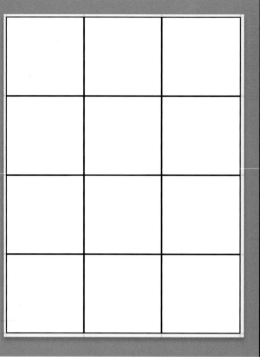

Layout
Ruler Units : Inches
Margins
Left 0.11 in
Right 0.12 in
Top 0.11 in
Bottom 0.12 in
Page Grid
Rows 4
Columns 3
Cell Spacing
Vertical 0.00 in
Horizontal 0.00 in
Cell Size
Height 2.69 in
Width 2.75 in
Keep Square
Guides
Show Guides
Rulers
Page Bleed
Margins and Gutters
Image Cells
Dimensions

10-13

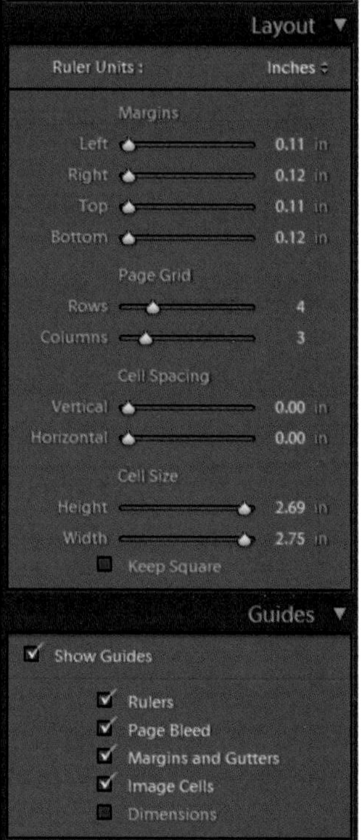

Layout
Ruler Units : Inches
Margins
Left 0.11 in
Right 0.12 in
Top 0.11 in
Bottom 0.12 in
Page Grid
Rows 4
Columns 3
Cell Spacing
Vertical 0.00 in
Horizontal 0.00 in
Cell Size
Height 2.69 in
Width 2.75 in
Keep Square
Guides
Show Guides
Rulers
Page Bleed
Margins and Gutters
Image Cells
Dimensions

10-14

3. **Vertical or horizontal?** I suggest keeping your photos for a given page all horizontal or vertical unless you are doing a square format like I am doing here. It is possible to mix them, but because you can't change the design of the page, the mix never quite looks right if the images are all oriented the same direction; that is, both horizontals and verticals read correctly. If you mix horizontal and vertical photos that are sized equally, they will not be oriented the same, so you will have to rotate your page in order to view individual images. That's not a good look to send to an editor.

4. **Set up the use of the photos.** Go back to Print, and select all of your photos so they now appear in the grid. In this example, I selected Zoom to Fill and deselected Rotate to Fit, as shown in figure 10-15. This keeps the cells filled and makes the overall "design" of the promo sheet look good as a pattern of squares. At this point, though, the images are all cropped to a square, which may or may not work for your photos. Images can be moved within that space, but not all photos look good as squares. The lines in the design shown here are guides and will not print.

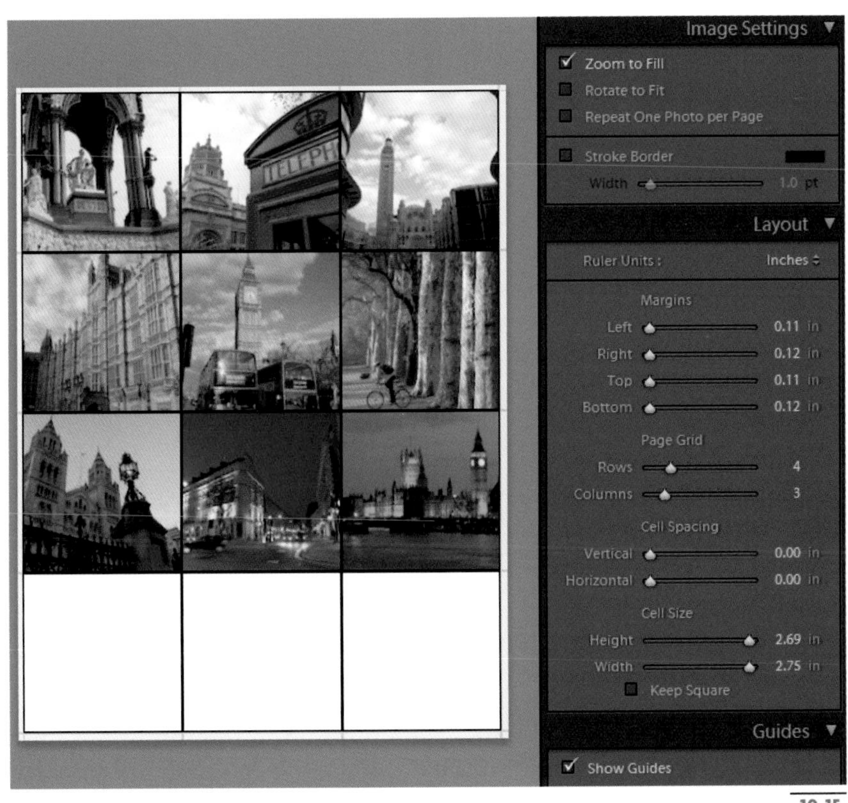

10-15

5. **Refine the photos, both how they display within the squares and their arrangement.** Click and drag on a single photo to move it within the square, as shown in figure 10-16. Go down to the Filmstrip to click and drag photos into new places that work better together, as needed. This is where it helps to have the photos in a small group, Quick Collection, or other collection. A hint: If you can't click and drag, it means your photos are all selected. You need to deselect them by clicking off the photos in the Filmstrip or pressing Ctrl/⌘+D.

10-16

6. Adjust the cell size by changing Cell Size in Layout. Move the Height slider until you like the look of your photos; for example, if you want more horizontal photos. You might also want more space between the photos — you can do that in Cell Spacing, as shown in figure 10-17. (Show Guides is off to show the spaces better.)

PRO TIP

Experiment with cell spacing. You can get a very interesting look with groups of photos butting up against each other (0-inch horizontal spacing for vertical photos; 0-inch vertical spacing for horizontal photos) that create rows of linked photos. You can also try the "block" look with 0-inch spacing all around.

7. **Add and edit the Identity Plate.** In Overlays, select Identity Plate. It is placed at the bottom of the page in the empty cells — drag it to where you like it best, as shown in figure 10-18. Edit it as needed (double-click on the frame). As I note in a Pro Tip, a very classy way to use an Identity Plate is to create a Photoshop graphic for it with your name and Web site or phone number.

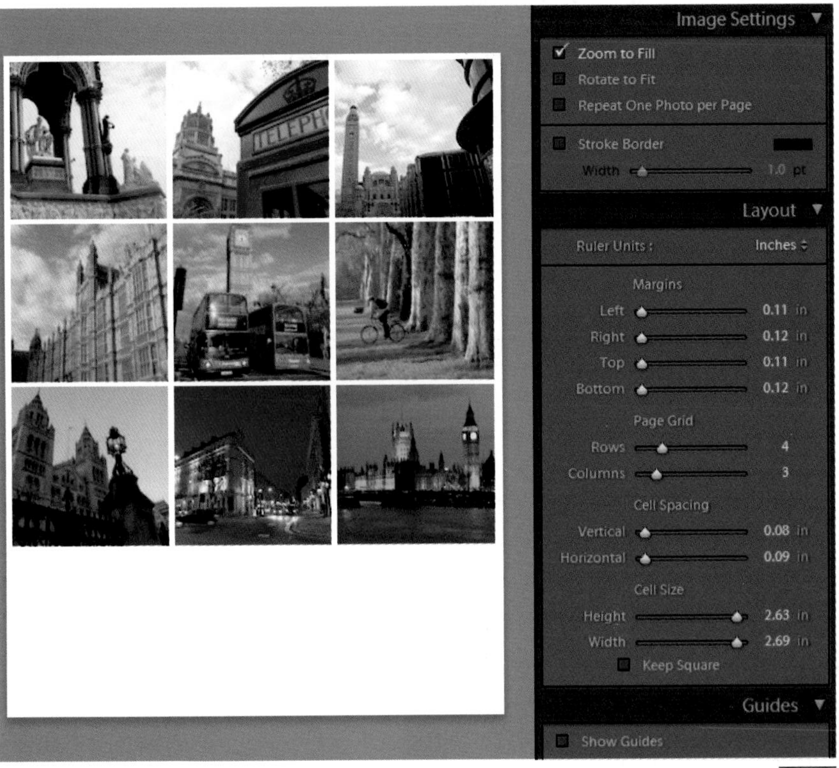
Image Settings
Zoom to Fill
Rotate to Fit
Repeat One Photo per Page
Stroke Border
Width
1.0 pt
Layout
Ruler Units :
Inches
Margins
Left
0.11 in
Right
0.12 in
Top
0.11 in
Bottom
0.12 in
Page Grid
Rows
4
Columns
3
Cell Spacing
Vertical
0.08 in
Horizontal
0.09 in
Cell Size
Height
2.63 in
Width
2.69 in
Keep Square
Guides
Show Guides

10-17

Rob Sheppard Photos
Image Settings
Layout
Guides
Overlays
Identity Plate
0°
Rob Sheppard Photos
Override Color
Opacity
100 %
Scale
69 %
Render behind image
Render on every image
Page Options
Page Numbers
Page Info
Crop Marks
Photo Info
Filename
Font Size :
10
Print Job

10-18

Q & A

Making a lot of prints, especially work prints, seems costly and wasteful. I realize that I can't just use a cheaper paper so I don't waste the good paper on them. But what can I do to make this more efficient?

Early on in the transition to digital printing, the idea of using cheaper paper came up a lot, as prints could be expensive. Now that paper and inks cost much less, your idea that this is not a good idea is right. In general, you want to only use the paper you want the final print on as that is the only way to truly evaluate what an image will look like. Papers do change the look of colors, contrast, and tonalities.

So what can you do? Here are a few ideas:

- **Stop bad prints as soon as you see they are off.** Most printers have a stop button. If you see the print is too dark, too light, off-color, and so on, stop the print from continuing. This can happen because you set the printer driver wrong (and we all do that at times — you go through the process too quickly and forget a key step, such as turning off color management in the printer driver). By stopping the print, you obviously use less ink. In addition, you often get a large bit of blank paper that you can use again for a work print or, at least, a small print.
- **Print small images at the start.** You will need a full-size work print at some point because you need to see how the image looks at its final size. However, creating a small print for initial evaluation gives you a quicker print using less ink and, even, smaller paper (or at least you can print more than once on the same larger sheet by putting it in the printer again in a different orientation).
- **Crop images for test prints.** Often there is a critical part of a photo that you can print to get most of the information you need for the final image. Go to Develop, crop the photo to a strip through that area, and then just print it. You can shift the strip to the right or left on the page using the Page Layout tools and run the paper through the printer more than once. Because all work in Lightroom is non-destructive, this cropping doesn't hurt anything, so you can "uncrop" the photo for full-size work prints and the final print without hurting anything in the image. You can also use a Virtual Copy for the cropped version.

The promo sheets sound like a neat way of creating a group of photos. Could you put the Identity Plate over a photo or a group of photos for a different design? And what about other uses than strictly marketing?

The first part of this question brings up a great idea: using a photo as a background for the Identity Plate. This can be a standard, iconic photo for your business, for example, that you can use on all promo sheets. You simply need to import it into a folder in Lightroom in order to use it. You could also build the text and photo together in Photoshop so it would be imported as a graphic.

The biggest thing to consider about using a photo behind the Identity Plate is that the photo has to be subordinate to the text or logo in that plate. You don't want a strong photo that competes with the plate or other images on the page, or why bother doing this? You can make an adjustment to a photo to make it lighter, darker, or less saturated (even black and white) so that the text or graphic shows up better against it. If you decide to use such a photo a lot with that adjustment, you might consider exporting it as its own file, then reimporting that adjusted photo back into Lightroom just for this use behind the Identity Plate.

The second part of the question brings up many possibilities for how you can use these promo sheets. They are simply a quick way of neatly grouping photos together, and then, with the Identity Plate, adding some text. Maybe these ideas will stimulate more based on your specific situation:

> **Article query.** Put together images that support an article idea, and then put something about the idea along with your name and contact information in the Identity Plate and use this to support a query letter to a publication.

> **Organization flyer.** If you photograph for a community organization, whether it's your church, soccer league, or kids' school, consider gathering some of those images into a group that you can use together to support the organization, using the Identity Plate to identify the organization.

> **Graduation announcement.** What if the group of photos shows off your senior's past year's activities? I shoot all digital and photograph images both as a writer/photographer and as a dad, so it would be pretty easy to gather a series of photos for that announcement, using the Identity Plate for information about the senior.

> **Family story.** You take a great vacation with your family, but then the photos rarely get seen. Make a selection and put them onto a promo sheet form using the Identity Plate to identify the location of the trip.

Chapter 11

THE WEB MODULE

Photoshop and other imaging programs often have a Web component to them, but few have such a strong and easy-to-use section like Photoshop Lightroom's Web module. The Web has become an extremely important place for photographers and their images. For pros, it has become pretty much a necessity, as shown in figure 11-1 (which was made in Lightroom). Even amateurs are using it extensively as a way of displaying images for friends and relatives across short and long distances.

Let's be straight about this, though. This is not the program for anyone doing extensive Web work. The Web module follows the concept of the rest of the program — making digital photography easier and simpler for the photographer. And it does exactly that for Web galleries, a standard need for photographers, but it won't give you the tools to create a complete Web site. Still, a lot of photographers have their Web site designed professionally, and then upload new photos regularly. The Web module is designed to make that task easier and more efficient for a non-Web designer — the photographer.

This is not to say that there is nothing here for the photographer who is more sophisticated in his or her Web use. The Web module does offer anyone a quick and easy way of creating picture galleries for Web use.

Web Module Layout

Like all other Lightroom modules, the Web module has its main adjustments on the right, its presets on the left, and a work area in the center, as shown in figure 11-2. Here's what you find in this module's interface:

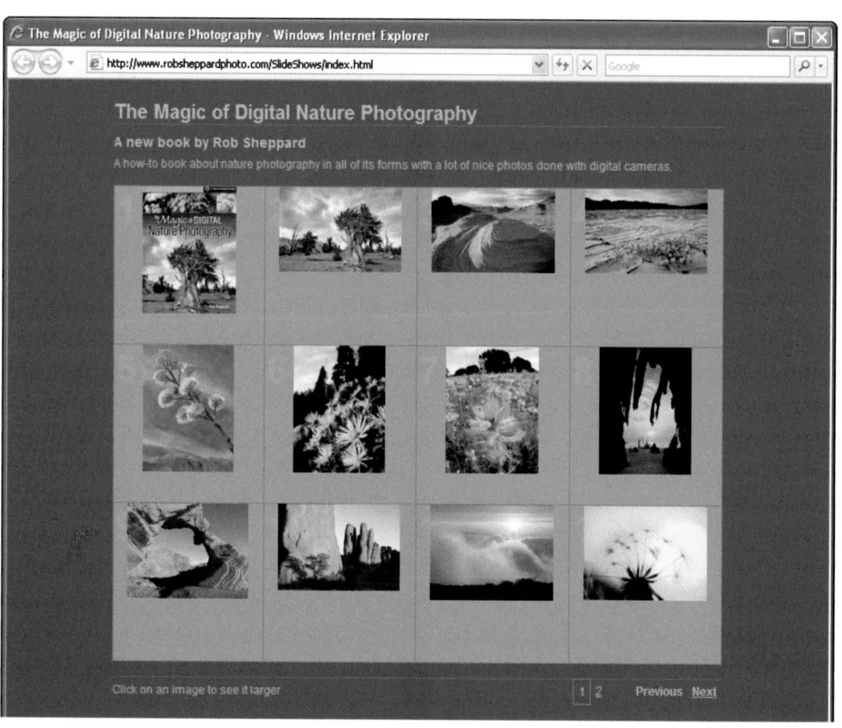

11-1

> **Center work area.** As usual, this shows you what you are doing in a Web gallery with photos (although for the monitor resolution needed for this book's screenshots, the whole gallery does not show up when all panels are visible). In this module, you see only the complete Web page as it is being constructed. You immediately see how your photos will show up in the Web gallery based on what is in the Filmstrip, including links to different Web views of the photos. If you remember, Print calls the active image area a "cell," which the Web module continues. The bottom has a very simplified toolbar. Images in the central area are active like on a Web page — if you click on a small photo, the interface changes (how it changes depends on the type of gallery). Or, if you see Previous or Next buttons (links), you can click them and the photos change.

> **Right panel.** The standard of Lightroom, the right side panel holds the controls. Here is where you change how your photos appear on a Web page: the type of gallery, the information that is included with the page as well as with individual photos, the size of the images, and so forth. At the bottom are Export and Upload buttons to move your Web gallery out of Lightroom.

> **Bottom Filmstrip.** This is the standard photo display area that allows you to arrange the photos in the gallery.

11-2

- > **Left panel.** Once again, here is a Template Browser, plus a preview area that shows what the galleries look like as you move your cursor over the presets. At the bottom is a Preview in Browser button to show your work in a real Web browser.

PRO TIP

For a lot of Web gallery work, you don't need the filmstrip at the bottom or the presets at the left. Close those panels to give more space for your work area, the actual Web page, as it develops.

Choosing Your Web Gallery Type

The first step you will always do is to choose the Web gallery style. You have several choices: the standard HTML, as shown in figures 11-3 and 11-4; Flash, as shown in figure 11-5; and Airtight Flash viewer, as shown in figure 11-6. Notice that in the Flash and Airtight examples, you can see small images and a larger image at the same time. In HTML, you see an index view first (figure 11-3), then click on an image to get a large image (figure 11-4). In the HTML gallery, you move from image to image using the Previous and Next buttons. (Index takes you back to the index view.) In Flash, you always have a larger image that is a slide show. In that area you have play-back-style buttons to play a slide show or move from image to image.

HTML and Flash (including Airtight Viewers) are different ways of creating Web sites and the browser. HTML is the traditional authoring language for Web sites. All Web sites use it. It defines and structures how a Web site looks, acts, and interacts with the visitor. It allows for many designs, but not for a lot of activity in that design.

Flash, on the other hand, lends itself to some lively uses of images on the Internet. With this technology, slide shows and fun actions with photos become very easy to do. Flash technology is one of the primary tools for adding animation and interactivity to Web pages. You won't be doing that in Lightroom. In this program, Flash is primarily used to animate the Web gallery.

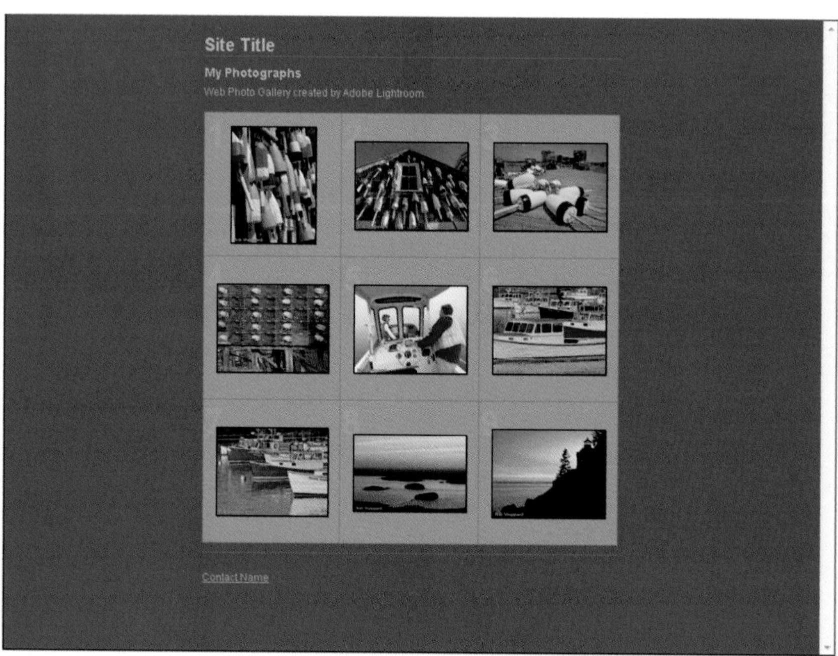

11-3

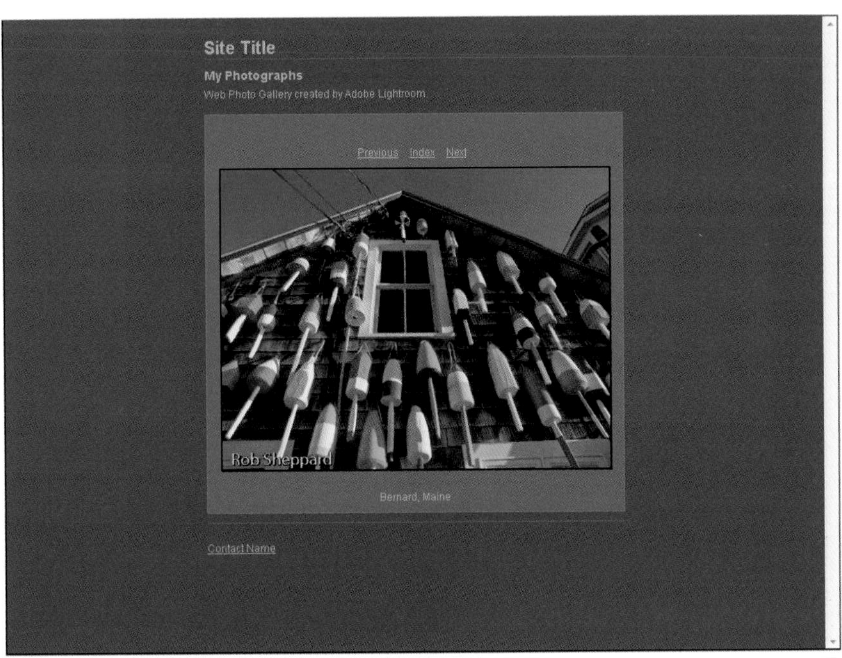
Site Title
My Photographs
Web Photo Gallery created by Adobe Lightroom.
Previous Index Next
Rob Sheppard
Bernard, Maine
Contact Name

11-4

Site Title
My Photographs
Contact Name
Rob Sheppard
Bernard, Maine
4/9

11-5

11-6

The type of gallery you select influences everything else and changes the options on the right panel, so you need to know right away which one you want to work with. You make this choice at the top of the right panel in Engine, as shown in figure 11-7. Some readers might wonder why I would say that you need to choose right away given the Web module, like the rest of Lightroom, is non-destructive, simply providing instructions for adjustments, not the actual adjustments. You can change anything at any time, including the Web gallery style; however, I don't recommend going arbitrarily back and forth among Web gallery styles. The reason is that you are dealing with a graphic treatment of Web pages and radically different visuals for HTML, Flash, and Airtight designs (actually, Airtight viewers are special Flash designs). These visuals are affected by everything included in their layout, from the colors to the text used.

Your best-looking page comes from making an early decision about which style best fits you, your personality, and your needs, and then choosing all modifications to it based on that specific style. You may want to play a bit with the gallery types and your photos, plus try out the templates from the Template Browser on the left panel before you make a final decision.

11-7

As you look at the options for galleries in the Web module, you will discover that there are advantages and disadvantages to Flash and HTML. Think about these things:

> **Flash is lively and modern.** It can make your Web site seem more up-to-date and "hip." You can display the photos in different arrangements, all based on a Flash slide show (the Airtight

Viewers are good examples of this). The gallery even allows viewers to get a full-screen slide show. It is quite appropriate for a sequenced presentation where the images have some sort of order or story.

> **The HTML gallery is tried and true.** It lets you show off a larger number of photos immediately, then access individual shots as larger views by clicking on any photo. The HTML design works quite well for dealing with something more like a light table presentation, where you see images individually. It has a conservative look to it, too, which can be important for certain businesses. But probably the most important thing is that it can be read by all Internet browsers. With Flash-made Web sites, you need a plug-in inside your Internet browser to read it, and some people simply don't have it.

So for the simplest gallery that everyone can see, go with HTML. On the other hand, if you want something a little more hip and modern, go with Flash.

I know there are photographers who want a recommendation as to which is best. Which style should they really use? That's not a recommendation I can give. A gallery style is not simply about computer technology and software code. It is also a distinctly visual graphic that affects the personality of your Web gallery. That makes it a very personal decision. The nice thing about Lightroom is that you can quickly compare each style with your photos inserted, making it easier to see the differences.

Setting Up the Gallery Page

Once you have chosen a gallery, you typically modify the gallery page look next. The controls are in Custom Settings in the right panel. However, if you are like me, Web page galleries are not something you do every day, so you might like some inspiration here. That's why in this module, I highly recommend you go to the Template Browser first. You can find a lot of ideas there — ideas that you can use as is or customize for your specific needs.

If you included a copyright in the adjusted metadata when you imported your photos, you see a copyright notice on the images when working in the Web module.

Choices in the Template Browser

You get a lot of choices to start in the Web module's preset Template Browser, as shown in figure 11-8. Most photographers can also use the Template Browser to create new presets for Web galleries that are unique. Each template shows up in the preview as you move your cursor over it. Also, you will see a lowercase *f* for Flash and *HTML* for HTML in the lower left of the preview.

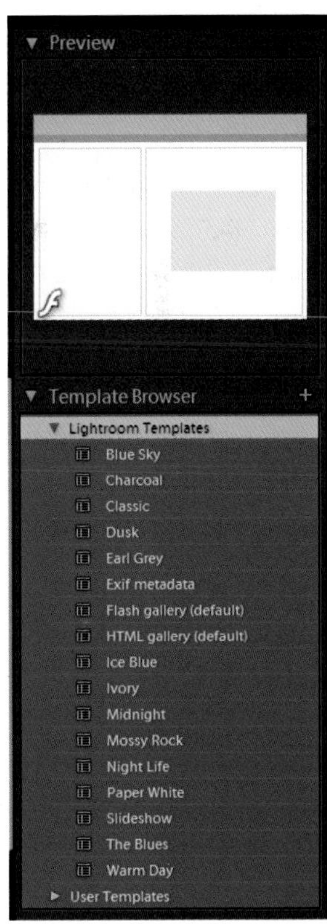

11-8

11-9

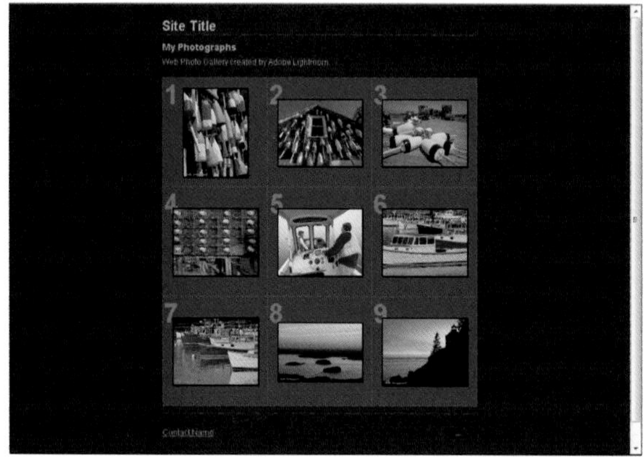

11-10

Each template uses a specific set of colors with either a Flash or HTML gallery. Here are your choices (the text shown is simply the default text — I discuss changing text later in the chapter):

> **Blue Sky.** This Flash option uses a nice blue set of tones with a white background, as shown in figure 11-9, for a Flash gallery showing images on the left with the slide show in the center.

> **Charcoal.** This is very close to the default HTML option and uses neutral tones around the images, as shown in figure 11-10, set up first as a grid of 3 × 3.

> **Classic.** This Flash option is basically a white design with neutral grays for the colors used and a left filmstrip to go with the slide show in the middle, as shown in figure 11-11.

> **Dusk.** This HTML option has a dark tone to it, using mostly blues, as shown in figure 11-12. The Identity Plate is included automatically and there is a grid of 4 × 3 images. This is a pretty heavy-handed use of color for most photography sites, though.

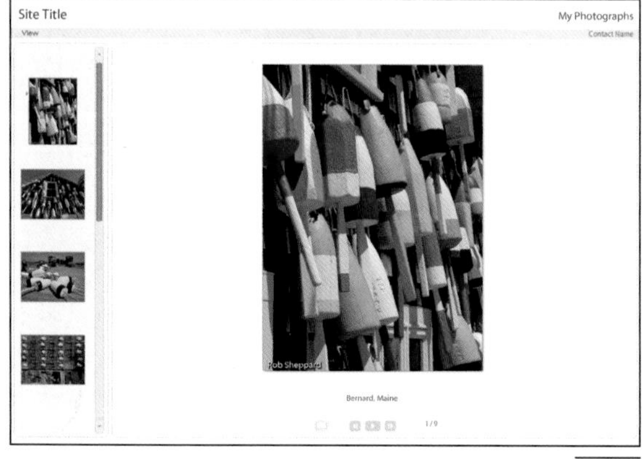

11-11

11-12

- **Earl Grey.** This Flash option is a simple, black and gray design that keeps the photos as the stars, as shown in figure 11-13. The slide show is at the right, a filmstrip at the left.
- **Exif metadata.** This is a simple, gray, HTML design that automatically includes selected metadata in the larger view, as shown in figure 11-14.
- **Flash gallery (default).** This Flash option uses a very dark setting, as shown in figure 11-15, that makes the right-side slide show look like a show in a darkened room. The filmstrip is on the left. This is the default HTML design that first appears when you first open the Web module.
- **HTML gallery (default).** This is a very basic HTML gallery that uses middle and dark gray tones to set off a grid of 3 × 3 images, as shown in figure 11-16.

11-13

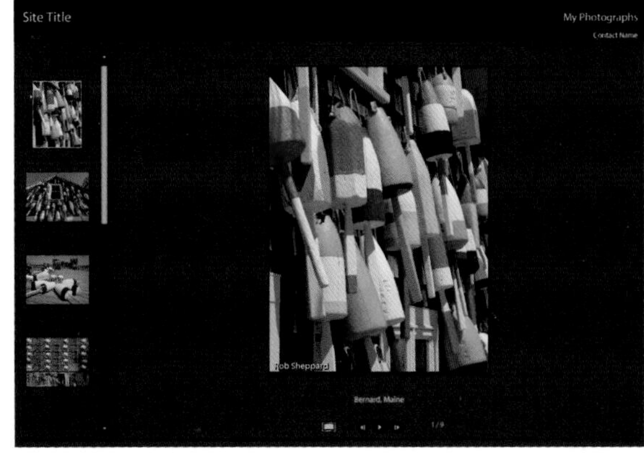

11-15

11-14

11-16

11-17

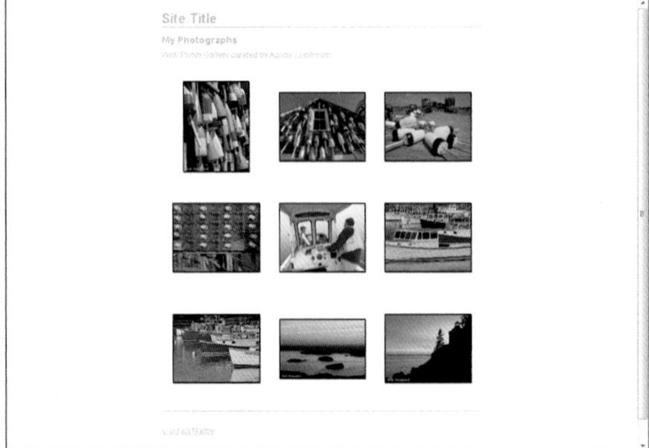

11-18

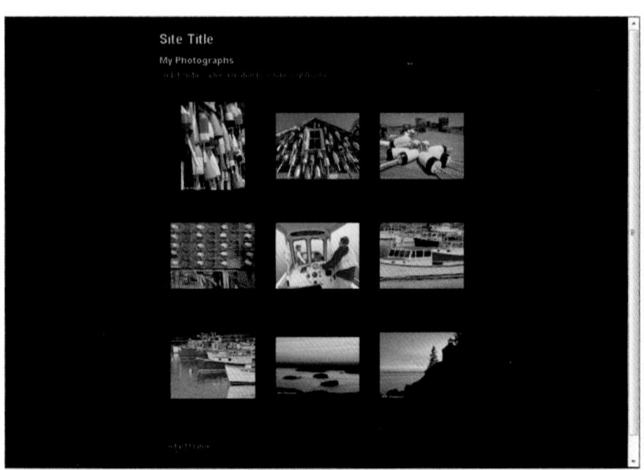

11-19

- **Ice Blue.** This is a mostly white, HTML design, with low-saturation blue accents, that uses a long 5 × 3 grid, as shown in figure 11-17.
- **Ivory.** This is another very simple, white, HTML design where the photos seem to float on the background, as shown in figure 11-18.
- **Midnight.** This option is the reverse of Ivory, presenting images in a very simple, pure black, HTML design where the photos seem to glow through cutouts in the page, as shown in figure 11-19.
- **Mossy Rock.** This Flash option is colored as you would expect from a mossy rock, green, as shown in figure 11-20. The color is so strong that it limits what you can use with it; frankly, it is so strong that I am not sure what photographer would want to use it because it overpowers the photos.
- **Night Life.** This option is really the HTML Midnight option done in Flash — a very simple, black design that makes images look like they are glowing, as shown in figure 11-21.

11-20

- **Paper White.** This is the HTML Ivory option done in Flash — a very simple, white design where photos seem to float in the space, as shown in figure 11-22.
- **Slideshow.** This Flash option is pure slide show with no Filmstrip and the image is displayed large against a black background, as shown in figure 11-23.
- **The Blues.** This Flash option is strongly colored like Mossy Rock, this time in blue, as shown in figure 11-24. The color is, again, so strong that it limits what you can use with it and is probably not going to be all that popular with photographers who care about their images.
- **Warm Day.** This Flash option uses some strong colors as accents; though the background itself is warm neutral, as shown in figure 11-25, it is not overpowering. Still, the colors used in the accents are so strong that they may limit what you can use with it. The Filmstrip is on the bottom.

These presets may give you exactly what you need right from the start for your Web gallery. Seeing the options here as an overview should help you better compare them, too. If they don't exactly meet your needs, they should at least give you ideas of things that you might like to try.

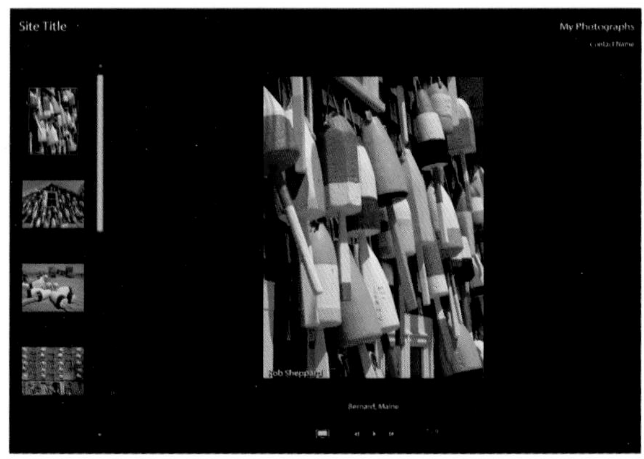

11-21

11-23

11-22

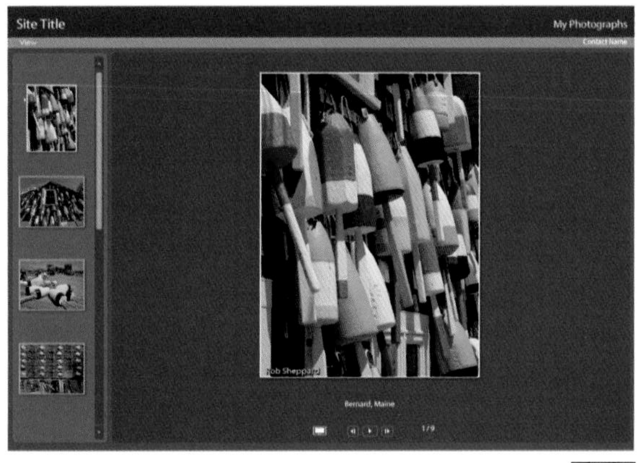

11-24

11-25

If you do modify the look of any of these templates, or you create a Web page look that you really like, you can save it as a preset for the Template Browser. You do this quite simply — once you have completed your work gallery, click the + button at the right of Template Browser. This opens a New Template dialog box, as shown in figure 11-26, where you can give a name to your template and put it into User Templates or create a new folder for it. Just click Create and this information is now retained within Lightroom. You can go back to this same gallery setup at any time with new photos.

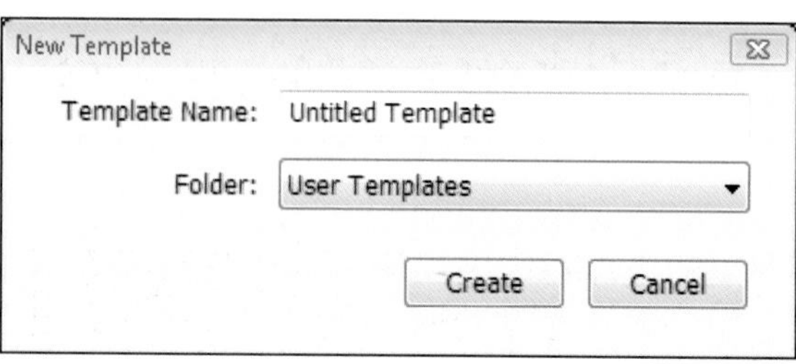

11-26

PRO TIP

To better see your whole gallery as you work, hide the left and Filmstrip panels. You really don't need constant access to them as you develop your gallery. By hiding these panels, you allow more room for the work area so that your Web gallery displays full-size (or close to it) and you can look it over as a complete visual whole.

Organize Your Images

Once you have a basic look for your gallery, you need to organize your photos. You can change the color of the background, title bar, text, and so forth, but because your images are really the stars here, I believe you should consider their order now. It is especially important to choose a first photo with impact as that is the one that every viewer of the gallery sees first, either as the top-left photo in an HTML gallery or the first image in the slide show.

Click and drag photos in the Filmstrip to move them from place to place. Once you have a first image, look at how the rest of the images fit together. This is especially important in the Flash gallery as there is a slide show there that shows images one after another. You can use some of the ideas discussed about slide shows in Chapter 8 to help organize images for a Web gallery.

Making Titles for Your Gallery

For a Web module gallery, you get a number of different places to add information to the page in the Site Info section of the right panel, as shown in figure 11-27. Before you start typing in information, think a bit about what you want to say on your Web page. You are best served if you choose what you want to put into the text areas before you start typing. I say that because there are distinct places in Site Info for information, including Site Title, Collection Title, Collection Description, Contact Info (which should always go on a pro's site), Web or Mail Link, and,

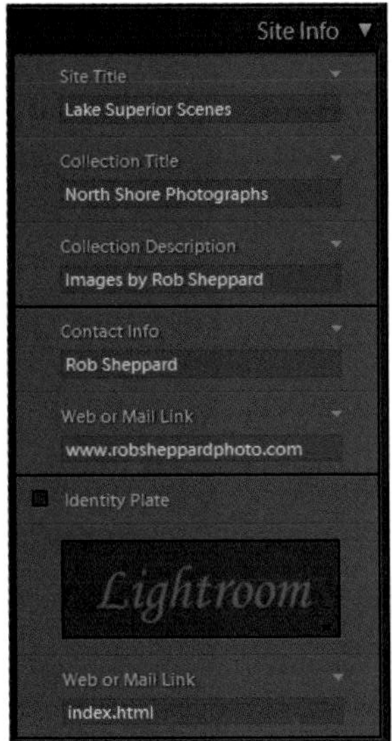

11-27

when you are in an HTML design, the use of an Identity Plate. The specific options available to you will change depending on whether you are working on an HTML or Flash design.

Organize these text areas to get the best impact from your gallery. How do you want to use this information? What do you want to put where? The Site Title could relate to your overall Web site or it could be something specific for the gallery. The Collection Title might refer to a specific grouping of images, a description of the subject (Mountains of California), or even a specific client job. The Collection Description gives you the option to include a bit more about your collection — but exactly what? And can you say it in a brief set of words?

Here's how to use Site Info once you have decided what information you want to give to your viewers (whether you can do each of these will be dependent on the Engine setting):

> **Site Title.** This first entry enables you to add a dominant title to your gallery. You can use a name appropriate to your work, your Web site, or maybe your business. You want to have visitors to this gallery always remember who you are and associate your photos with you. Click the text either under Site Title or click the text itself on the Web page being built in the central work area, as shown in figure 11-28. Keep the title simple, with only a few words. Press Enter/Return to accept the words.

> **Collection Title.** In this section, you can give more information to the viewer about the collection of images seen in the gallery, as shown in figure 11-29. Insert whatever makes sense. I recommend something that quickly explains what the viewer is seeing, such as "Portfolio," a shoot name such as "London," or even "Recent Photojournalism Assignments." Keep it simple, however, because you don't want viewers to struggle with reading text in this position.

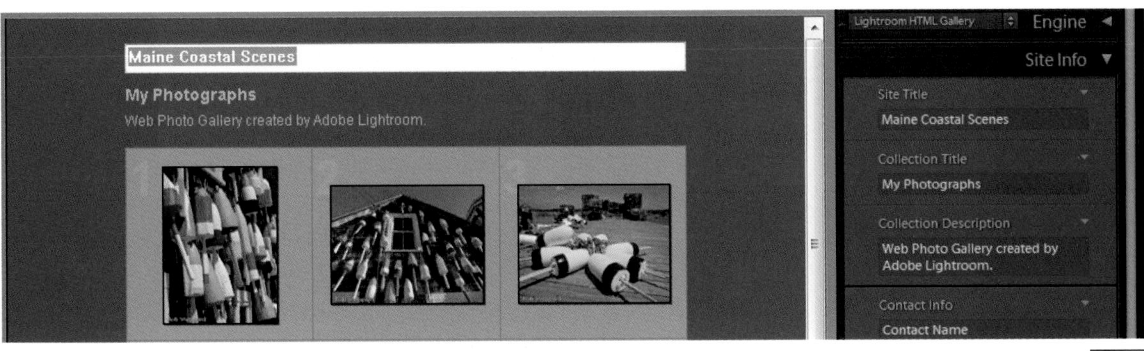

11-28

- **Collection Description.** Now you can get a bit wordier to explain what appears on this page. You could describe the work in terms of a specific job or give more information about a location than you included in the Collection Title, as shown in figure 11-30.
- **Contact Info and Web or Mail Link.** Having worked at several magazines as an editor receiving photos from photographers all the time in many forms, I have to tell you that Contact Info is extremely important. Too often photographers forget this on printed promotional materials, and then continue to forget it on their Web sites. Pros should find these choices, as shown in figure 11-31, valuable reminders to add contact info to their Web sites at all times. Web or Mail Link info does not show up on your Web gallery, but is linked from the Contact Info if a visitor clicks on it.
- **Identity Plate.** The Identity Plate works here the same as in so many other parts of Lightroom. You can learn more about it in Chapter 2. It appears at the top of the gallery and can be a nice graphic treatment to tie the gallery to the rest of your Web site. You can link it to your home page, for example, with the Web or Mail Link.

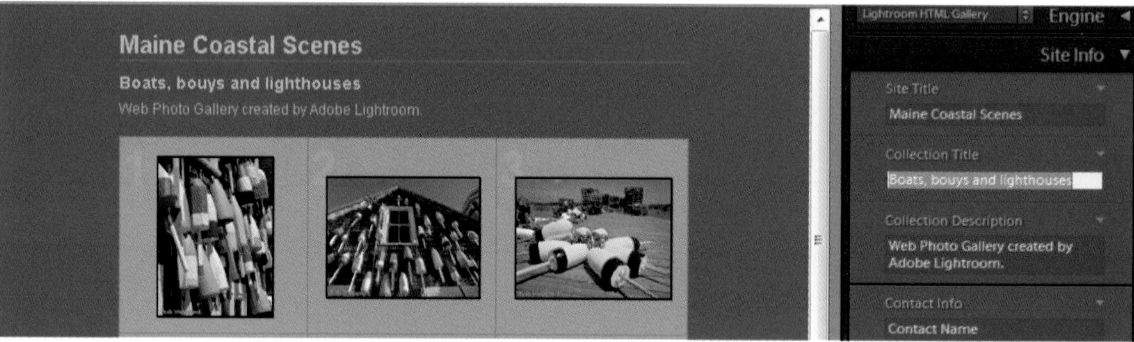

11-29

11-30

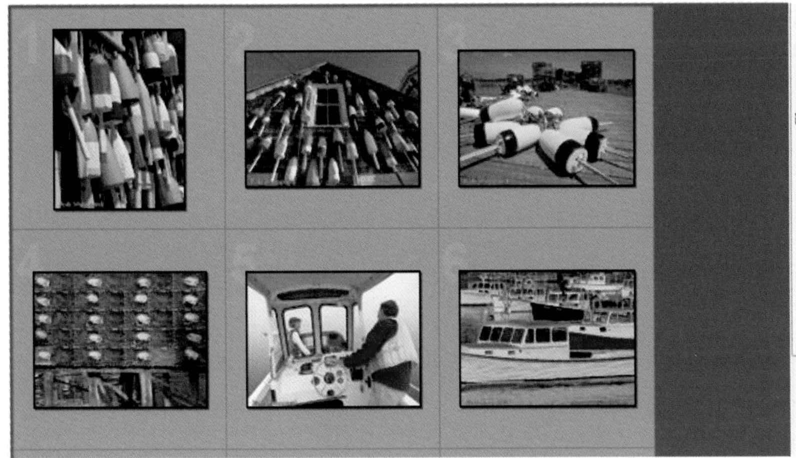

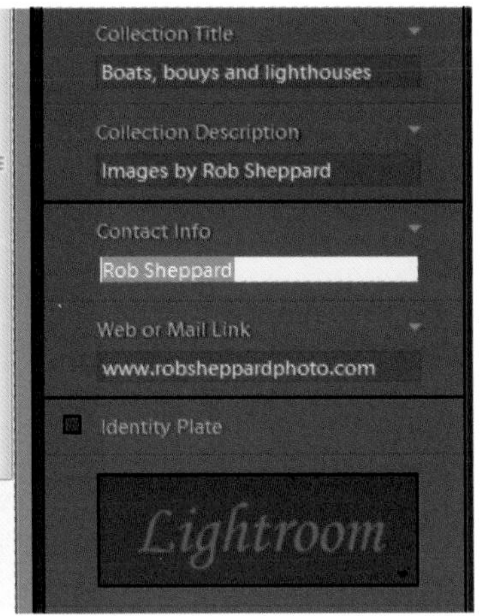

11-31

As you do work on a Web gallery in this module, Lightroom remembers your choices. If you click the arrow to the right of each title, you get a drop-down menu of what you have used for it. This can be helpful as you work to make changes to the gallery.

Changing Colors

The next section of the Web module, Color Palette, deals with the colors of elements on the Web gallery (though, once again, the choices in Engine will give you more or fewer options in this area). This is a very straightforward section, as shown in figure 11-32. To stay consistent with the gallery, I am going to illustrate these with the HTML design. Flash galleries use the colors in the same ways. Here's how to work the choices:

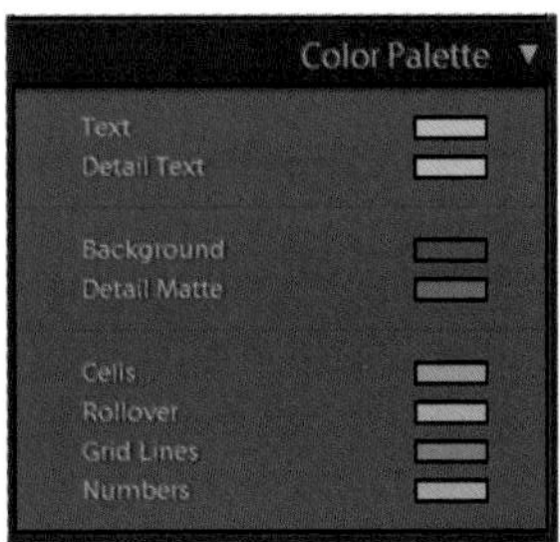

11-32

- **Text.** Click the little rectangle to the right of Text to choose a new color for the main text of the gallery. A Color Picker dialog box appears that allows you to pick almost any color or tone. You need color that makes the text readable, yet you don't want something too obtrusive. This is one place you can sometimes add some color to the page without causing competition among a variety of colors. One idea is to use a color here that is complementary to your logo when it is used as an Identity Plate. Whatever the color you use is, however, it needs to work with the background color (which is explained later), so you may want to choose a background color first.

> **Detail Text.** This is a minor use of text, which is used on the Detail page of an HTML design, but it can still be distracting if too strong.

> **Background.** This color, shown in figure 11-33 (the color is only for illustration), is set in the same way as the Text color — click the little rectangle to the right of Background to open a Color Picker dialog box. Background and cell color are two interrelated and very important choices for your Web gallery. This is what sets off the entire gallery page, and, in many ways, is what your viewer sees first. It is possible to use a more vibrant background color and a neutral cell color, because the cell color is what actually surrounds the photos. However, I recommend you choose saturated colors very cautiously. They don't always display properly on a Web site and can really distract from the real reason for your gallery page — the photos. I suggest you try neutral tones or light colors with low saturation. I think it is a nice effect to have a background different from the cell color so that it acts like a frame to the images.

> **Detail Matte.** This is another more specialized use of color. It shows up with detail views such as that shown in figure 11-34 (again, color is only for illustration). Color is set the same way as other options.

> **Cells.** As mentioned in Background, this is one of the key areas of color. Though you see it brightly colored in figure 11-35 for illustration, I recommend you use neutral colors so as not to compete with the photo colors (Ctrl/⌘+Z will undo any change that you don't like). This is a very important part of Color Palette because it changes the color directly around your photos.

11-33

11-34

11-35

> **Rollover.** The Rollover color (the color that highlights the cell when you roll over an image with your mouse to select it) can be many colors because this is only temporary. In fact, it can work well to use a brighter color for this, as shown in figure 11-36, so it is obvious which photo is being selected (however, don't overdo the brighter color idea).

> **Grid Lines.** Having a bit of color for the Grid Lines can add a nice touch — the lines aren't big enough to really compete with your photos.

> **Numbers.** I advise you to be cautious about making the numbers anything other than the default color. They are right by the photos and big enough to be a serious distraction if too bold in color or tone.

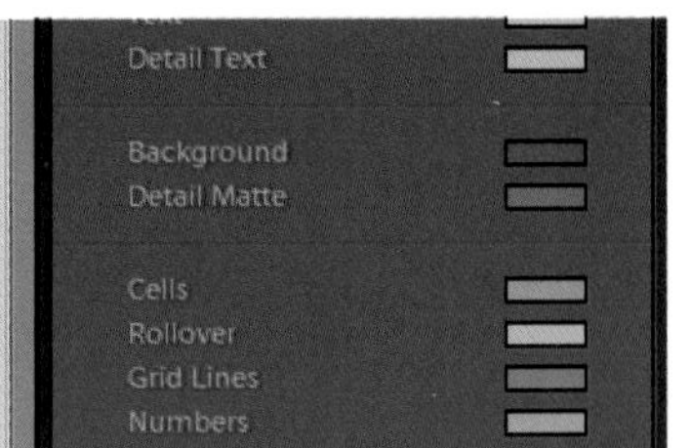

11-36

Changing Appearance

Appearance enables you to change several things on the gallery including the rows and columns in an HTML gallery, as shown in figure 11-37; the layout of Filmstrip and slide shows, as well as the use of an Identity Plate in a Flash gallery, as shown in Figure 11-38; and specific options for Airtight viewers, as shown in figure 11-39. These are very helpful tools in refining the look of your work. You will find additional options with specific gallery choices; the examples here will get you started.

Here's how to use some of these tools:

- **Number of Columns and Number of Rows.** This section allows you to change how many of your images show up on the page when in an HTML layout — just run your cursor over the grid to see new cells highlighted and click when you see something you like. The default numbers of three columns and three rows are good for a Web gallery. You can increase both columns and rows, but this doesn't fit more images in the viewing area. It adds images to the page, which results in many viewers having to scroll the page to see them all.

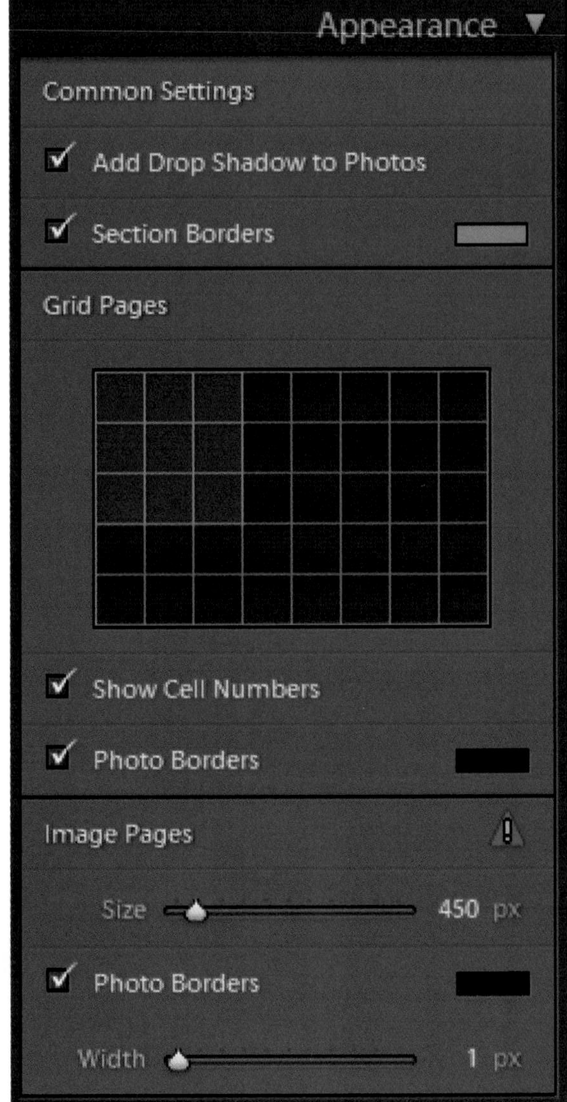

11-37

11-38

11-40

11-39

- **Layout.** When you select a Flash gallery, you can choose from four different layouts, as shown in figure 11-40, when you click the drop-down menu at the right of Layout. These include Scrolling, Paginated, Left, and Slideshow Only. Scrolling is a very popular way of dealing with images in Flash. In this form, you have a large photo on display in the top half of the page, while all other photos in the gallery appear as thumbnails in a scrollable Filmstrip at the bottom. The viewer selects the top photo by clicking any image in the Filmstrip. In all Flash layouts, the large photo can also become a slide show of all of the gallery images when the viewer clicks a play button, or the user can click the other "step" buttons to step through the gallery images one at a time.

  The Paginated option changes the look so that now the large image is on the right half of the page, and the gallery photo thumbnails are on the left. The gallery thumbnails are now grouped in pages. Left is very similar, but uses a scrollable Filmstrip on the left. The last view is Slideshow Only and no thumbnails are available.

- **Identity Plate.** This option is for Flash galleries and is the same as the one in Site Info for HTML. It puts the Identity Plate either on or off your Web gallery page. It is placed at the upper left, over the site title text. I describe Identity Plates in detail in Chapter 2.
- **Large Images and Thumbnail Images.** These two options change the size of the photos displayed in a Flash Web gallery. Large Images refers to the size of the large photo, while Thumbnail Images affects the size of the small photos in the Filmstrip. The default sizes work pretty well as a balance between size and upload time.

PRO TIP

Be careful of adding too many images that are hard to really see by your Web site visitor. I can tell you from experience as a magazine editor that images start to get lost in the viewer's mind as the numbers go up. They just compete with each other. I suggest choosing a number of cells from 9 to 12 for most purposes.

The Importance of Color for the Web Gallery

The effect of your Web gallery on a viewer is strongly affected by color, which I touched on earlier. Having seen a lot of photographers struggle with selecting colors that appear around or near a photo, I thought it might be helpful to emphasize a few ideas in a separate section to summarize and complement what I said earlier in the chapter.

- **Choose colors carefully for areas that are physically close to the actual photos.** As I mentioned, neutral colors are good because they do not compete with your photos. Black and white are extreme and can make a gallery look harsh, though. Try shades of gray. Then try unobtrusive colors that are low in saturation. Avoid really bright colors — they are extremely difficult to use without the bright colors competing too strongly with your photos.
- **Choose text colors for readability.** I've seen people try to get cute with odd colors for text. Text needs to be legible or what is its point? Select colors for text that contrast with the colors or tones that the text is read against. Avoid highly saturated colors as they can be hard to read. Be cautious in the use of blues as they can make text look out of focus for many people.
- **Use grid and line colors for accents.** As the lines around the active areas of the gallery or grid lines are not large, you can use all sorts of colors for them without too much of a problem. Try colors that contrast with the neutral colors of the rest of the gallery page to enliven it. However, watch for unintended effects when certain line/background color combinations are used — lines can look too vibrant, almost like they are vibrating.

Using Image Info Settings

Image Info is a section that sets up text that appears with the larger photo display in your Web gallery. The text does not appear with thumbnails; it only appears with the large slide show image of a Flash gallery or with the large images that appear when a viewer selects a thumbnail in the HTML gallery. The text you choose here appears the same with all photos as they are enlarged — you do not have the ability to change text per photo in the Web module.

You have two choices for text: Title and Caption. These are very similar in their options, but affect where text is placed — a title shows up above the photo, a caption shows up below.

- **Title.** At the right of Title is a drop-down arrow that gives the choices shown in figure 11-41: Caption, Custom Text, Date, Equipment, Exposure, Filename, Sequence, Title, and Edit.

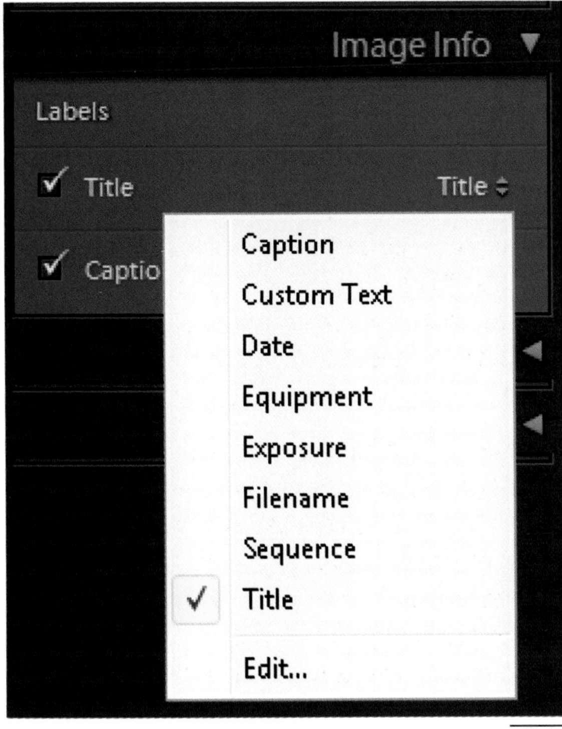

11-41

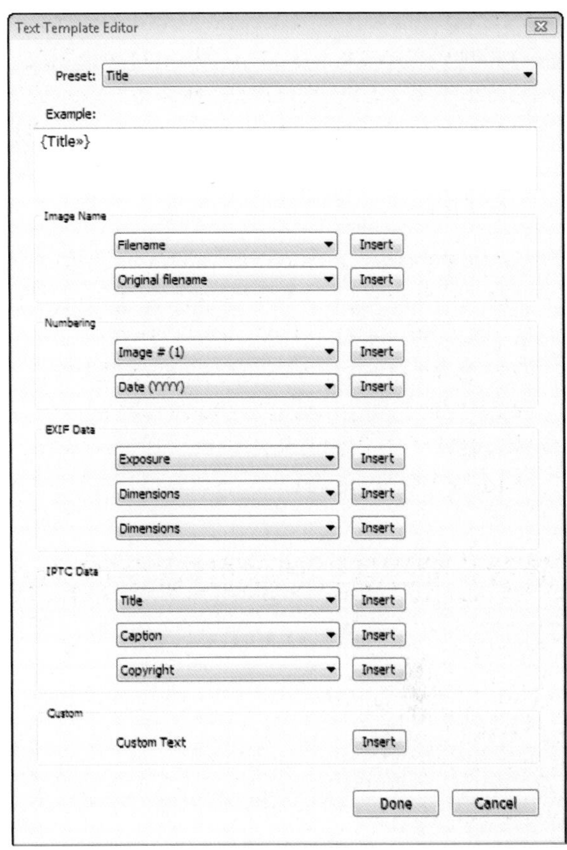

11-42

These are all pretty much exactly as the names suggest, come largely from the metadata, and will be the same on all photos (even Custom Text). Choose Edit, and the Text Template Editor dialog box appears. It contains a lot of choices for what appears in the title, as shown in the dialog box in figure 11-42. Many of these options, to be honest, are very specialized and unlikely to be used by the average photographer.

> **Caption.** Caption does not give unique captions for your photos. It is, in reality, a variation of Title. If you want unique captions for your photos, you can use IPTC (International Press Telecommunications Council) caption information in your metadata. Image Settings do allow you to select that in IPTC data. This can be caption info that you added to the metadata of your image back in the Library module, or you can go back to that module and add the caption info now. Select the Caption check box and the metadata attached to your photos now appears with your photo, as shown in figure 11-43. (You can also see a Title above the photo.) You can change what appears here by clicking on the drop-down menu, as shown in figure 11-44. Caption itself is, in a sense, a way of adding more information under the photograph, while Title adds info above the photo. You might consider them Caption 1 and Caption 2.

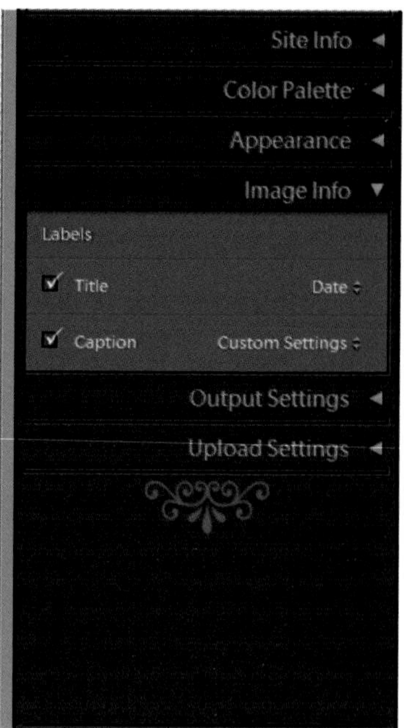

11-43

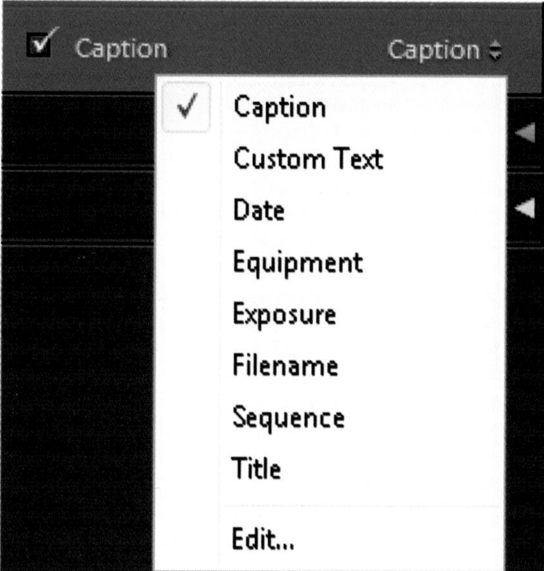

11-44

Choosing Output Settings

The Output section of the Web module, shown in figure 11-45, is a really simple little section that affects what your photos look like in the gallery. Large Images affects the JPEG compression of the JPEG files used for the gallery; a lower quality setting gives smaller image files that download faster. The options available to you will be dependent on the Engine you have chosen.

Add Copyright Watermark adds your name to the photo, as shown in most of the figures in this chapter. It finds your name from the metadata you added to the photos (probably when they were imported into Photoshop Lightroom if you follow some of the ideas in the Library chapters). If you want the word *Copyright* or the copyright symbol with your name, you need to add it in the metadata in Library. Sharpening is output sharpening and optimizes the image for use on the Web.

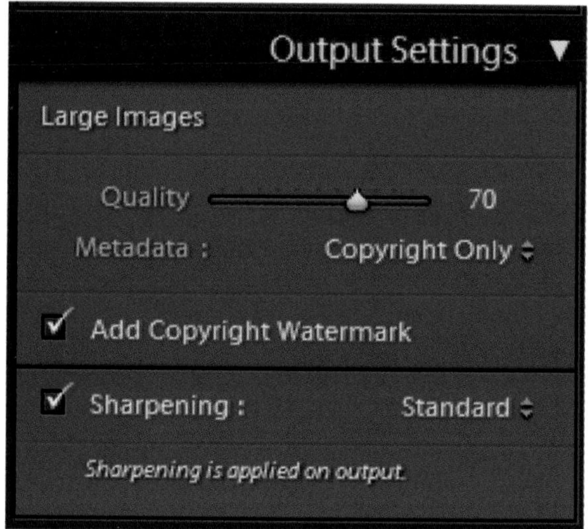

11-45

Working with Upload Settings

The Upload Settings section of controls is fairly straightforward, as shown in figure 11-46. It is where you tell Lightroom how to deal with the Web gallery you are working with, including the settings for uploading it to your Web site.

FTP Server tells Lightroom where to upload your gallery. You have to click Custom Settings to get a drop-down menu arrow, then select Edit to set this up. The Configure FTP File Transfer dialog box is shown in figure 11-47. Here you name your preset and put in your server address, name, password, and so forth to allow an upload to your Web site. When you have set this up once, a preset name automatically appears that you can choose in the future.

11-46

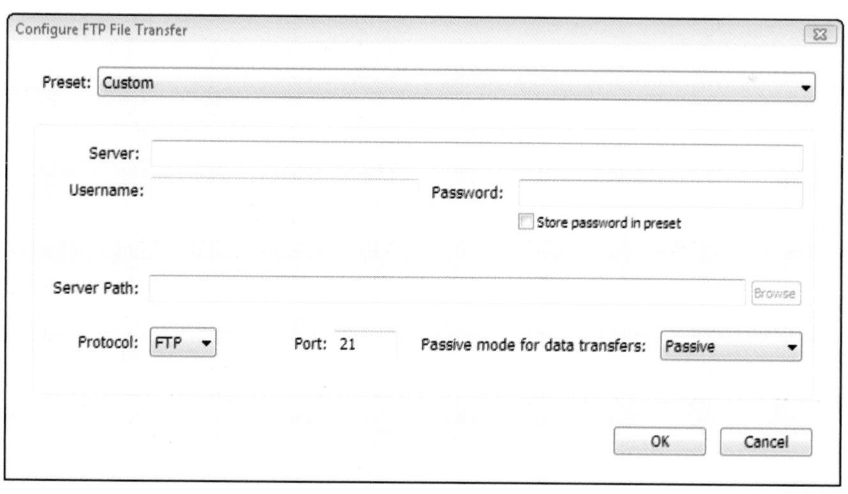

11-47

Using the Export and Upload Buttons

Export and Upload buttons are at the bottom of the control panel side of the Web module, as shown in figure 11-48. Export enables you to save your Web gallery on your hard drive. It saves a set of files appropriate to either a Flash or an HTML Web site, depending on the form you choose.

Upload uses your FTP presets and server output path you put into Output. This enables you to send your page directly to your Web server and get it onto your Web site. Even if you do go directly to your server from Lightroom, I recommend you always save (Export) your Web gallery first. This just protects you so that the work you put into the gallery is saved; you can at least use it directly from that file if you go on to other things in Lightroom and go out of your Web gallery, yet later you discover the FTP transfer didn't do what you expected and the gallery did not go to your site properly. If you really like your gallery design, I also recommend you save it as a preset in your Template Browser.

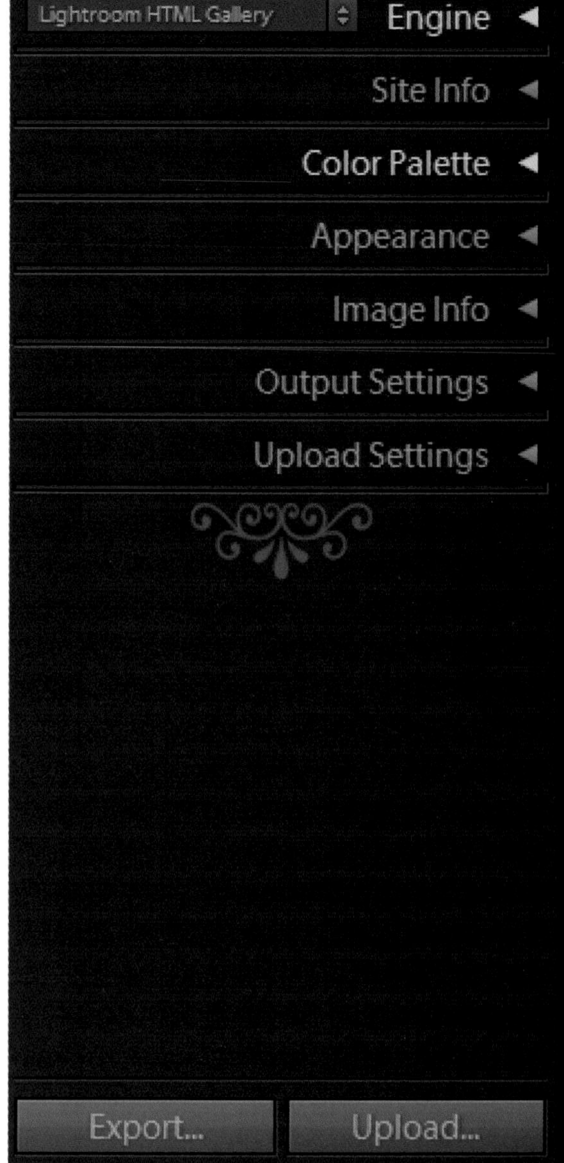

11-48

Q & A

I am not much of a Web expert. I have someone who knows the Web who is doing my Web site. I don't fully understand all the FTP business with Output. What do you suggest I do?

This is very common. A lot of photographers do not do their own Web sites and are not familiar with the information in Output. They are busy taking pictures and not spending time doing Web sites! I am no Web site expert, either. I have a Webmaster who handles those details for me. Still, I like the gallery options in Lightroom — they make it very easy for a photographer to quickly create his or her own gallery without waiting for help.

Once a gallery is done, I would do one of two things:

> Talk to your Webmaster and get the appropriate information from him or her. Just tell this person what Lightroom asks for in the Output section, FTP Preset, and ask how you can best use that to work with your Web site.

> Save your gallery and send that "file" (actually a folder of files) to your Webmaster to upload.

What if I don't like the fonts for the Web gallery? How can I change them?

Unfortunately, at this point in the development of Lightroom, you can't. This isn't all bad. The fonts used are a simple, easy-to-read typeface that displays well on a Web page. Most photographers aren't Web designers, so offering a lot of choices in the Web module is probably counterproductive and Adobe was smart to avoid that. If you really do know how to design a Web page and select fonts properly, then Lightroom's Web module is probably not the software you should be using.

I am still undecided. Should I use the HTML, Flash, or even the Airtight Viewer gallery? They all seem to have advantages and disadvantages, but I am thinking mostly from a visual perspective. They show images quite differently. Which do you think affects viewers more?

That's really a hard question to answer. It is based on such personal, subjective ideas. You really have to look at several things in making this decision:

> **Your existing Web site.** Which type of gallery seems better suited to the tone and personality of your Web site? Try opening your Web site in your browser, and then go back and forth between the Web gallery in Lightroom and your Web site to see how they look together. You can use Alt or ⌘+Tab as a keyboard command to go back and forth between these programs without using your mouse and a toolbar.

> **Your audience — who is most likely going to view your gallery?** If you expect a lot of hip designers to visit, maybe the Flash gallery is better. On the other hand, if you know that photo researchers from book publishers are visiting, they may prefer the HTML gallery because of the way it presents more images to them.

> **Your photos and the subject matter.** You may find that some photos really go together nicely in a slide show format, making the Flash gallery ideal. On the other hand, another group of photos might be such stand-alone images that they never quite work when blended into a slide show, so the HTML gallery will be better.

> **Your personality.** You may just like the way a slide show looks on your Web site. If this is the case, obviously the Flash gallery is the better choice. On the other hand, you may be the type of person that prefers images to stand alone as single pieces of art, so the HTML gallery is the way to go.

Part III

THE PHOTOSHOP PARTNERSHIP

Chapter 12

GOING BETWEEN LIGHTROOM AND PHOTOSHOP

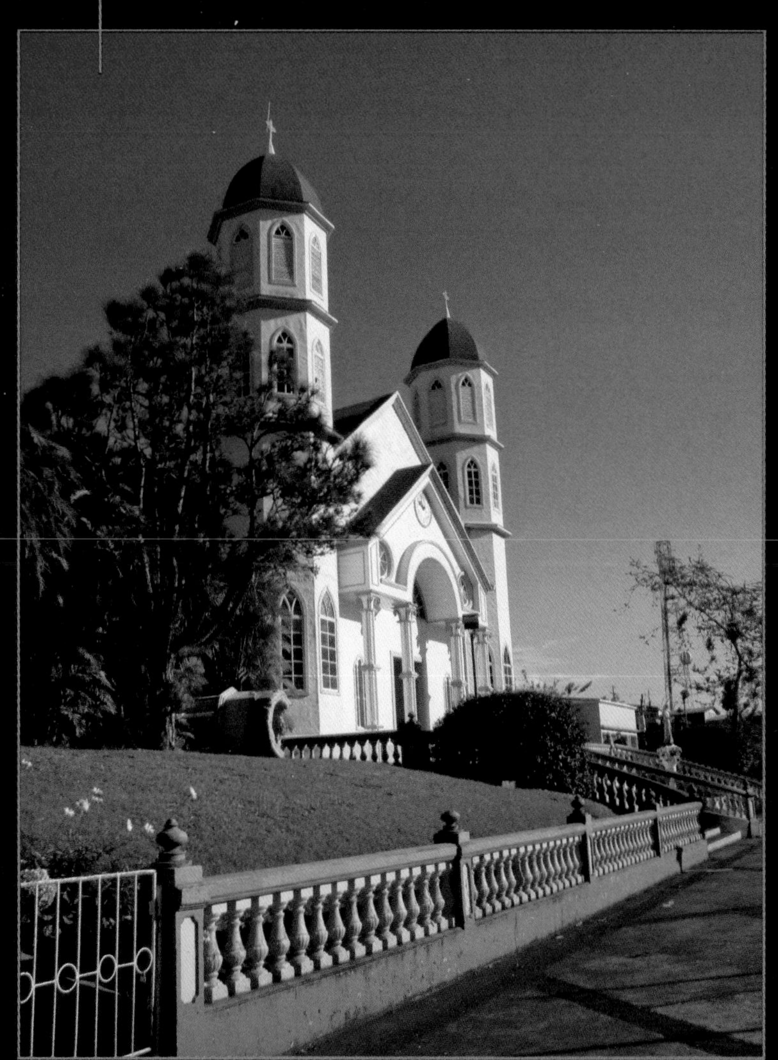

As I worked on the first edition of this book and learned to master Adobe Photoshop Lightroom 1, I got a lot of questions about Photoshop itself from photographers who knew I was doing this. The big question was, "If I have Lightroom, do I still need Photoshop?"

That was not a simple question or an easy one to answer. "It depends" is rarely a satisfying answer, yet then, it really was true. With Lightroom 2, that question is easier to answer. The addition of local controls makes Lightroom a fully capable program for most photographers. There are reasons to use Photoshop, but frankly, many photographers will be perfectly happy never going to Photoshop. Any photographer who needs to do a lot of compositing, however, must go to Photoshop as Lightroom has no compositing capabilities. I think many photographers will even find that Lightroom now does so much for them that they only need Photoshop Elements, not even Photoshop, for occasional work in layers.

Adobe makes it easy for these programs to work together — in fact, that is part of the reason that Photoshop is included in the official name, Photoshop Lightroom. But remember that Lightroom and Photoshop are designed for very different purposes. Lightroom is a program for dealing quickly and easily with a lot of photos, and then working on them fluidly from one to another. It is not a program for doing detailed work on individual photos, whereas Photoshop is. Photoshop was designed from the start to deal with single images and for very concentrated, meticulous work on them. Adobe Bridge was later developed to try to deal with multiple photos, but it really was an add-on patch rather than something integrated into the program from the start.

For now Photoshop is the detailed image processor that includes layers and layer mask controls; Lightroom is the multiple photo organizer and overall image processor. In this chapter, I discuss some of the possibilities of having Lightroom work together with Photoshop. For the Photoshop power user, this chapter is pretty basic.

However, I know that many Lightroom users are not sophisticated Photoshop users and want some guidance in going to and from Photoshop. That's what this chapter is designed to do. This is not a book about Photoshop, so I am not covering every specific command or the location of controls. If you are not sure of some of them, there are many excellent Photoshop books on the market that can help.

Moving Between Lightroom and Photoshop

Lightroom is set up to move a photo to Photoshop (or to any other program, such as Photoshop Elements) pretty easily. Usually, you will be exporting from the Develop or Library module, but you can be in any module with a photo selected (in Library, Develop, Slideshow, and Print, that includes the central work area and Filmstrip; in Web, it includes just Filmstrip). Simply right-click a photo (yet another reason to get that right-click mouse for Mac users if you don't already have one!) to get a menu, as shown in figure 12-1. Among the choices are Edit In, which takes you directly to Photoshop, and Export, which gives you more options as to how to export an image out of Lightroom. These options are described in detail in Chapter 6 in the Export section.

With any of the Edit In options, Photoshop is launched (if it isn't open) and the image is opened into it as a 16-bit file, as shown in figure 12-2. If you save that image immediately (using Save, not Save As), it will be saved in the same folder as the original as a TIFF file using the same name as the original with the addition of Edit at the end. You can have it added semi-automatically to the Lightroom Folder where the original is cataloged, so if you access that folder, you find both the original and the new PSD file. You do this by right-clicking the folder in Library and choosing Synchronize Folder. This gives you the dialog box shown in figure 12-3. Lightroom finds the differences between what is in your folder and what is seen in the program. Click Synchronize when the button becomes active (that may take a moment if you have made other changes to the folder). If you use Save As in Photoshop to save the image with a different name into the same folder, you can do the same thing.

With the Export options, you get a whole set of choices for exporting your photos. This is my preference as it allows me to very precisely control where my image is stored once it is processed, plus I can decide if I want 8-bit or 16-bit, a name change, and so forth, including editing in Photoshop, as shown in figure 12-4 (this is explained in more detail in Chapter 6).

NOTE

If you are working with JPEG files, you will find a different dialog box altogether when you click Edit In then Edit Photo with Adobe Photoshop. Most photographers will not use this. You will find three options there, and all are explained in the dialog box itself. If you do use this, I would suggest using the Edit a Copy with Lightroom Adjustments choice unless you have some very specific requirements.

12-1

12-2

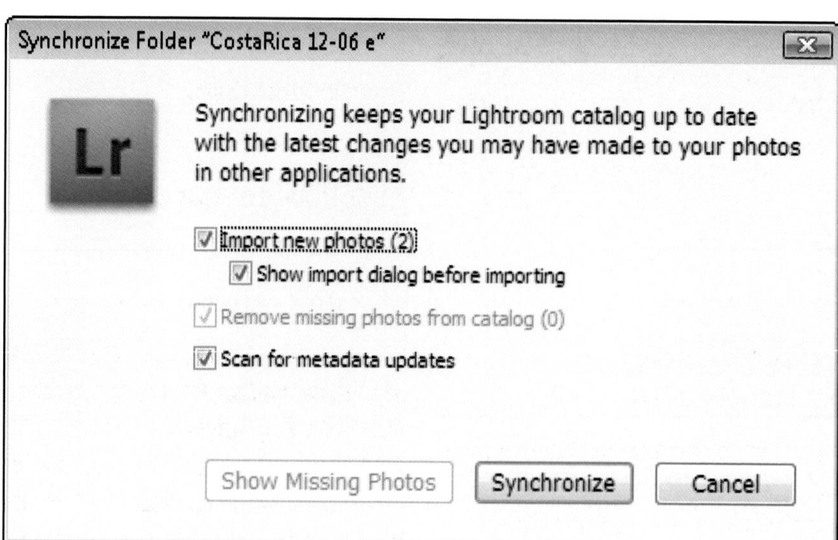
Synchronize Folder "CostaRica 12-06 e"
Lr
Synchronizing keeps your Lightroom catalog up to date with the latest changes you may have made to your photos in other applications.
Import new photos (2)
Show import dialog before importing
Remove missing photos from catalog (0)
Scan for metadata updates
Show Missing Photos
Synchronize
Cancel

12-3

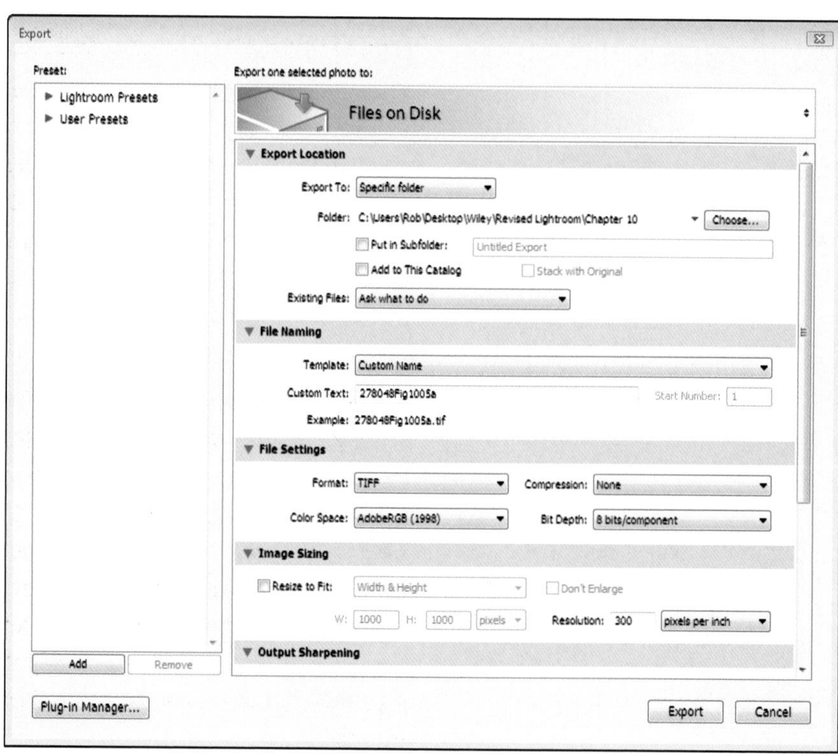
Export
Preset:
Lightroom Presets
User Presets
Add
Remove
Plug-in Manager...
Export one selected photo to:
Files on Disk
Export Location
Export To: Specific folder
Folder: C:\Users\Rob\Desktop\Wiley\Revised Lightroom\Chapter 10
Choose...
Put in Subfolder: Untitled Export
Add to This Catalog
Stack with Original
Existing Files: Ask what to do
File Naming
Template: Custom Name
Custom Text: 278048Fig1005a
Start Number: 1
Example: 278048Fig1005a.tif
File Settings
Format: TIFF
Compression: None
Color Space: AdobeRGB (1998)
Bit Depth: 8 bits/component
Image Sizing
Resize to Fit: Width & Height
Don't Enlarge
W: 1000 H: 1000 pixels
Resolution: 300 pixels per inch
Output Sharpening
Export
Cancel

12-4

PRO TIP

I know I constantly nag Mac users to get a right-click mouse. Sure, you can Control+click to substitute for the right-click, but why do this when the right-click is so easy and convenient? Right-clicking gives you context-sensitive menus in so many programs.

When Photoshop Might Complement Lightroom

You can obviously do anything to an image brought into Photoshop that Photoshop Lightroom is also capable of. Lightroom has streamlined many functions nicely, so it seems pointless to do in Photoshop what could be done in Lightroom. Keep adjustments in Photoshop focused on what Photoshop does best.

Generally, you will go to Photoshop for very definite controls. I suggest thinking specifically about what is missing in a photo so that you enter Photoshop focused on a distinct task for your image. The following Photoshop image adjustments complement Lightroom for the photographer and make the use of both programs stronger. While it is by no means complete, I offer the list as a checklist of sorts that you might use to identify your needs in Lightroom and focus your work in Photoshop.

- Layers
- Layer masks
- Double processing RAW images for one final photo
- Merging two exposures into one final image
- Any compositing effects
- Sophisticated selection effects
- Advanced cloning
- Complete set of healing tools
- Correcting perspective
- Correcting distortions
- Filters for special effects

I could write a book on these techniques (and I actually did in *Outdoor Photographer Landscape and Nature Photography with Photoshop CS2*, Wiley, 2006). In this chapter, I want to offer a perspective on working between Lightroom and Photoshop by summarizing some of these adjustment tools in the context of these two different programs.

Layer Benefits and Using Layers

Layers are not possible with Lightroom. In a sense, you are adding layers of information on how to process an image file when you use the Develop module (including the use of local adjustments), but you can't access these layers, nor can you see them. The isolation of controls that layers give you is a strong benefit of Photoshop and a major reason why you might finish processing an image there.

In doing workshops around the country, I hear from a lot of photographers that layers give them problems. While layers are an extremely important part of Photoshop and Photoshop Elements, and many people consider them to be the ultimate advantage of the program, they are certainly not very photographic. Or at least they don't seem to be. If you know and are comfortable with layers, you can skip this section. But if you aren't, this section is an overview of what layers can do for you.

You see a photo of an Alaskan flower, a nagoonberry, in figure 12-5, with seven layers. It illustrates very well why you might go to Photoshop or Photoshop Elements after Lightroom. If you are not comfortable with layers or you need a review, you might find this figure anything from obscure to intimidating.

I like to tell photographers that they already know a little about layers, information that you can translate directly to figure 12-6. Think about if you put a stack of mail on your dining room table — some bills in standard-sized envelopes, a larger envelope promoting some credit card offer, a magazine or two, and some miscellaneous, mostly worthless, flyers. You know what I'm talking about.

That mail stack is a pile of layers. You can affect any part of the stack without changing any other part (except its position, probably). You can write on a part of an envelope sticking out from the pile and have that writing appear nowhere else but on that envelope. You can remove a magazine without removing other parts of the stack. You might not be able to read the blurbs on the cover of a magazine at the bottom because it is covered by other "layers" above it.

If you deconstruct that pile and write down each envelope, bill, flyer, magazine, and so on, in order, top to bottom, on a piece of paper, you have the equivalent

12-5

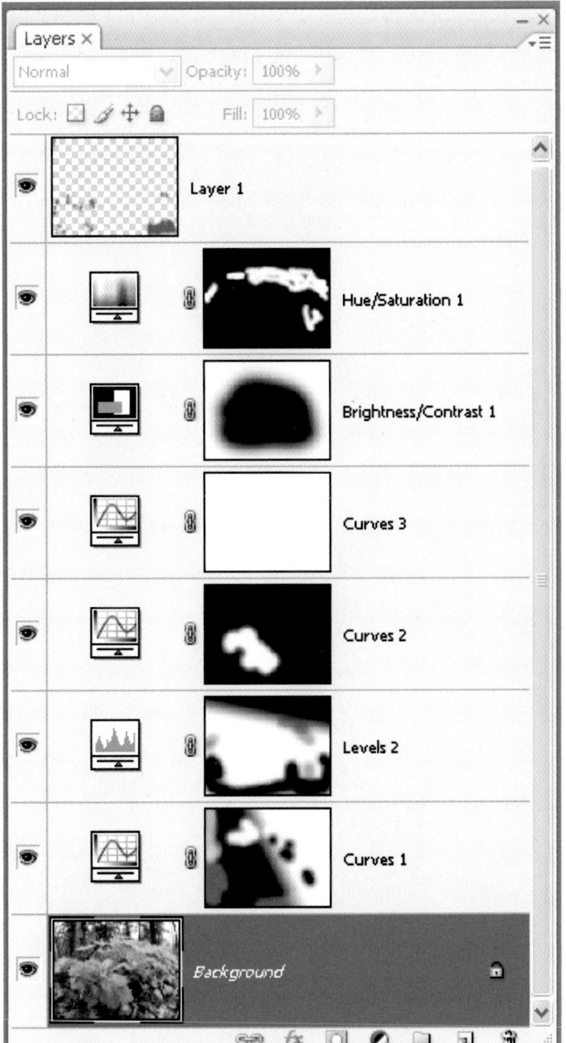

12-6

of the Photoshop Layers palette (illustrated in figure 12-7). That palette works just like the stack of mail. You read it from the top down; opaque things on top block your view of things underneath. The same thing happens with the Photoshop Layers palette.

I will deconstruct the photo and its layers so you can see how the layers apply unique and specific controls to the image. Layers are generally added to a layer stack from the bottom up, just as you usually put letters in a pile, so I start from the bottom. Figure 12-8 shows the photo fresh from Lightroom with its blacks and whites set properly as well as its midtones. However, the light causes a visual imbalance, changing the scene to something rather arbitrary in tonalities, rather than the way the eye sees it. The flower is too dark, while the background is too light. In part, this happens because I photographed the flower with an extreme wide-angle lens up close, which means I shaded it slightly. Some of this imbalance could now be corrected in Lightroom with the local adjustments, but this particular image has some involved local adjustment needs that are done more simply and effectively in Photoshop.

In figure 12-9, I add an adjustment layer. I use Curves to darken the background, then use the layer mask to limit the darkening to the background and some localized areas. This is shown with its layer mask detail in figure 12-10 — blacks block the effect of the layer, white allows it, and grays are in between (I explain layer masks more fully later in the chapter). This photo is becoming better balanced. This type of control with the layer mask restrictions can be mimicked in Lightroom, but it can get a bit confusing with a lot of individual brush stroke additions.

MailStack.jpg @ 23% (RGB/8)
Layers
Darken
Opacity: 19%
Lock:
Fill: 100%
Layer 1
Hue/Saturation 1
Brightness/Contrast 1
Curves 3
Curves 2
Levels 2
Curves 1
Background
23%
Doc: 14.4M/14.4M

12-7

12-8

12-9

12-10

The next layer brightens the flower and the leaves near it with a Curves adjustment layer. You can clearly see the change in figure 12-13. The layer mask in this case is really limiting, as shown in figure 12-14 — you can see that only a small area of white is in a large field of black. This means that only the area over the flower and nearby leaves can be affected by the change in Curves.

I add another adjustment layer because the greens of the leaves are now too dark over the whole image, yet I don't want the bottom or top of the photo to get brighter, too. I use a Levels adjustment layer to create the new tonalities shown in figure 12-11 and use its mask to limit the changes to mainly the leaves, as reflected in figure 12-12.

12-11

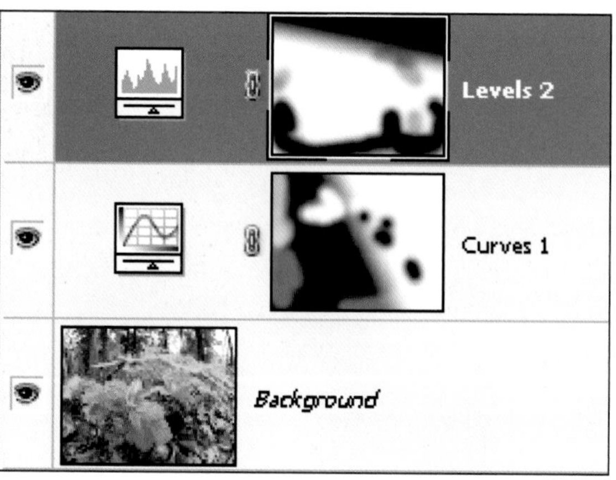

12-12

The fourth layer is a bit subtle for the printed page so I do not show a full image here. This is a Curves layer that just darkens some of the darker midtones slightly and shows up in a print. No layer mask is used, as shown in figure 12-15.

I add another adjustment layer — this time Brightness/Contrast, as shown in figure 12-16. Brightness/Contrast is a blunt and coarse adjustment tool; it is not something for general use, but is perfect for this purpose, which is to darken the outside edges

12-13

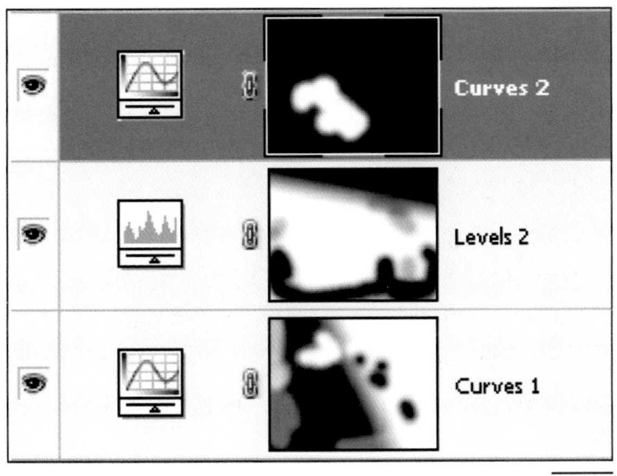

12-14

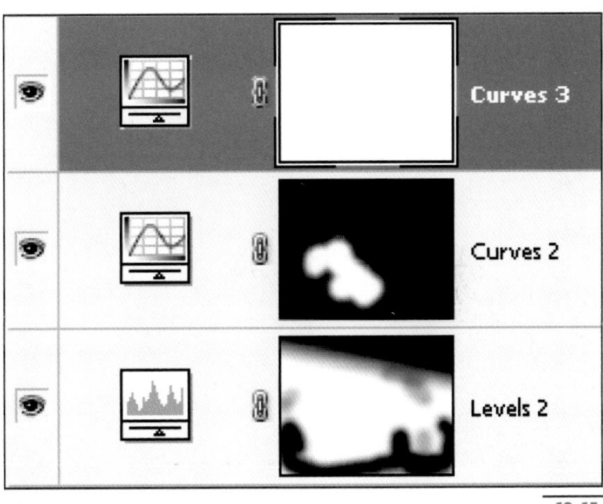

12-15

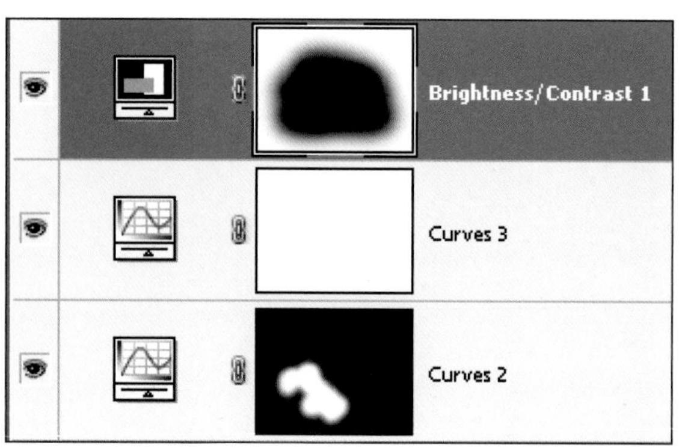

12-16

of the image, as shown in figure 12-17. This is a traditional technique used by classic darkroom workers such as Ansel Adams and W. Eugene Smith. They darkened the corners and edges of a photo to give it more dimension and keep the viewer's eye from wandering off the image.

You don't want or need the control of Levels or Curves to do this in Photoshop — in fact, they don't create the same traditional darkening effect, and Brightness/Contrast does. I simply use the Brightness slider to darken the image and then a layer mask to limit that adjustment to the outside edges and corners. You can do this with the Vignettes sliders in Lightroom, but you do not have the same control that you can get using this layer technique.

In the sixth layer, I use a Hue/Saturation adjustment layer to change the color of the background leaves. The saturation and hue of the green leaves behind the main subject are competing with it and need to be toned down, as shown in figure 12-18. This is not a big change (I am not trying to make the leaves something other than what they are) and you won't see much on the printed page in a book, but in a print it really makes a difference. You can see from the layer mask, as shown in the Layers palette in figure 12-19, that the area controlled by the layer (the white) is very restricted.

12-17

12-18

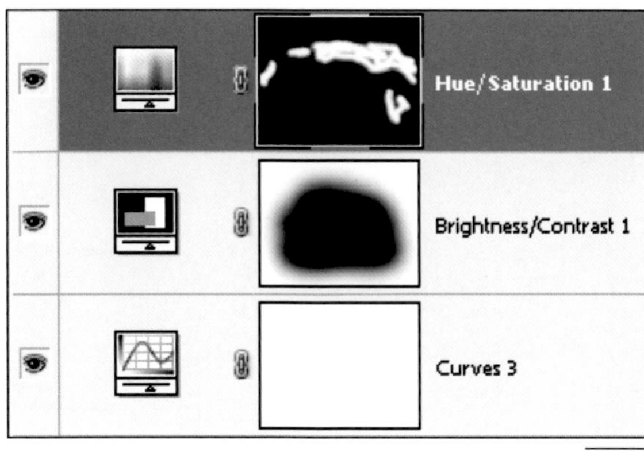

12-19

The last and top layer is a pixel layer. There are a few places in the old leaves that are too light. They did not darken properly with the right color when using any adjustment layers. I picked a color from a dark leaf with the eyedropper, which puts it in the foreground color. I then used a paintbrush and painted over those areas on a new layer, as shown in figure 12-20.

I changed the layer blending mode to Darken and reduced its Opacity until it looked right. The result appears in the final image, shown in figure 12-21 (which has also been sharpened).

Using layers is a matter of applying them step by step, as shown by this example, each time affecting one thing on the image. I do not try to make a layer do multiple things — that makes it harder to control the effects in that layer. You can see from this example how much control you can get from layers. You may have noted that I said early in this chapter that a lot of photographers could easily work with just Lightroom and Photoshop Elements. Everything I am showing with this example can be done in Photoshop Elements.

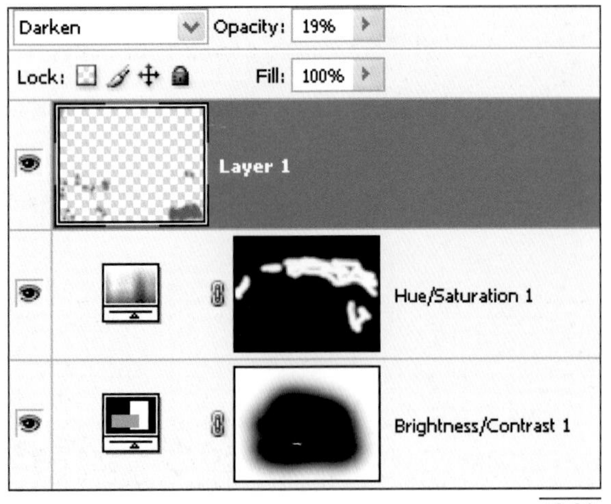

12-20

Working with Layer Masks

A very important part of this image, as you saw in figures 12-10 through 12-21, is the layer mask. This is a hugely valuable part of using layers because it offers you a level of control in Photoshop that you cannot achieve in Lightroom. To be honest, not all photographers will really need it now that Lightroom has local adjustments. However, when you do need this control, it is invaluable.

Yet the layer mask is also one of the most consistently confusing parts of Photoshop for many photographers. It is extremely helpful to understand layer masks, however, and I strongly recommend spending some time learning them. In this section, I give you

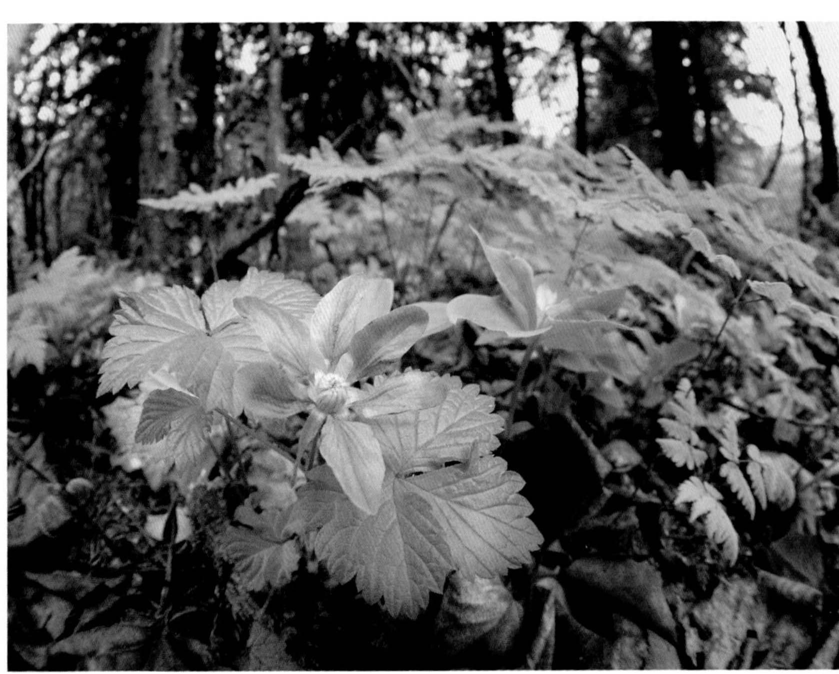

12-21

enough information to get you started with layer masks (and to see how valuable they can be) so you can practice on your own.

A *layer mask* is an invisible layer control that allows some, all, or none of a layer and its effects to work. Masks have been long used by advanced darkroom workers, publication printers, and Hollywood to block part of an image so something unique can be done in the blocked area with a different visual. You may know that many movies of imaginary locations use a computer-generated scene, for example, to represent that location in the distance while the hero and heroine appear in the lower part of the image. The actors are often in common California hills, but a mask blocks the hills in the background so the computer-generated scene can replace it, resulting in a fantastic image that has no real-world connection.

You can do exactly that in Photoshop with layer masks, and, in this section, I explain how to use them to control how changes to an image are applied through layers.

The layer mask is represented in the Layers palette by the white box (layer mask thumbnail) to the right of the layer thumbnail, as shown in figure 12-22. It is actually an invisible mask on the image itself (though you can make it visible). When the mask is being used, the layer mask thumbnails have black and white patterns in them, as shown in figure 12-23. These patterns show the actual mask being applied to the layer.

In a layer mask, black creates the masking effect, while white acts like it is the transparent area around a traditional mask. As a photographer, you may find it helpful to keep several things in mind about the effects of black and white in a layer mask:

- **Black blocks anything that a layer might do.** This could be an adjustment layer making the photo lighter, darker, more saturated, less saturated, and so on. No matter what the control, black blocks it from changing the photo.
- **White allows anything that a layer might do.**
- **Black and white do not affect the photo, only the layer effects.** That is important to keep in mind. Using black to block one effect in a particular layer might make the photo lighter, while in a different layer and with a different effect, it might make the photo darker. This is because that black cannot change the actual effect, only whether the effect works or not.
- **Gray partially allows a layer to act (or partially blocks the effect).**
- **Some photographers like to remember this: Black conceals, white reveals.**

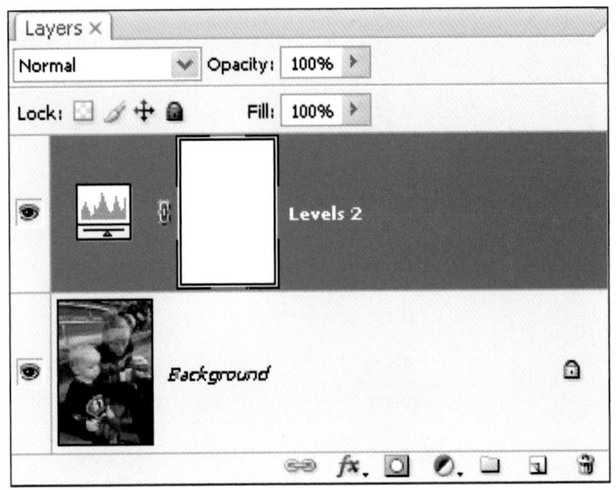

12-22

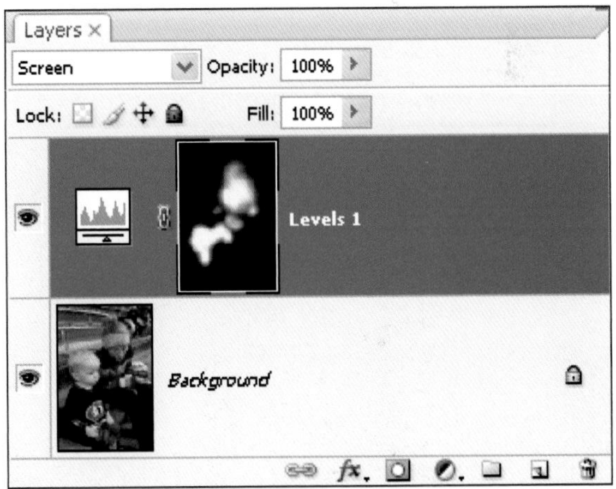

12-23

In the photo of the two kids at a hockey game that appears in this section, you can quickly see the effects of a layer mask. Figure 12-24 shows the image with its overall Lightroom processing. Figure 12-25 shows the effect of adding a layer to lighten the dark face of the girl and the shirt of the boy and using a layer mask to control where that lightening appears. Without anything in the layer mask, the whole image would be lighter, but it should not be.

PRO TIP

Use the Paintbrush tool plus the foreground color in the Toolbox to paint black or white in a layer mask. Choose a brush that is as big as the area you want to work with; that is, don't make it too small. A small brush does not blend as well and you should only use it to fix certain details. You should also use the brush at maximum softness (0 Hardness in the brush options) so it blends better.

12-24

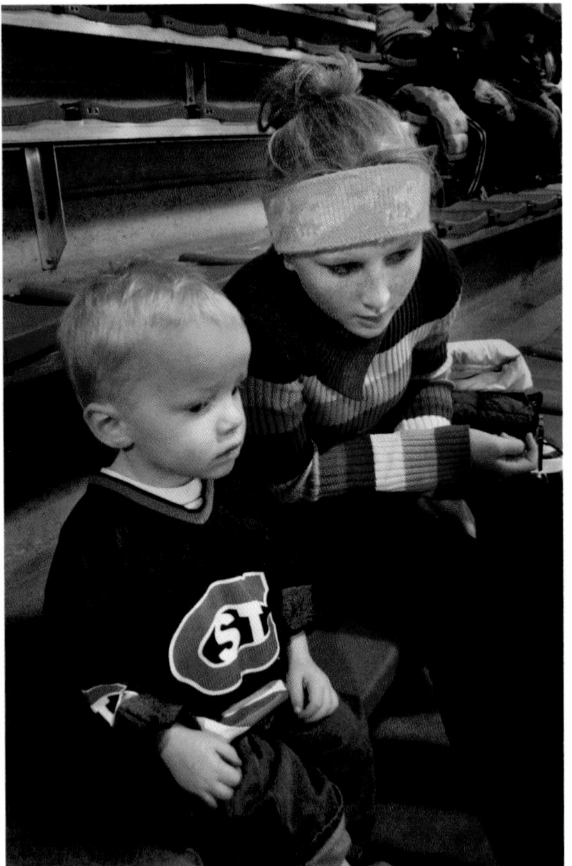

12-25

In figure 12-26, the layer mask used is shown (Alt/Option+clicking on the layer mask icon reveals the mask). By default, the layer mask is white, which allows the layer to work normally. Black is filled into the layer mask to block its overall effect (choose Edit ➪ Fill ➪ Black), and then white is painted over the girl's face and nearby dark areas. This reveals the adjustment layer's effects, but only in the areas of the mask that are white.

A great advantage of a layer mask at this point is that it is infinitely changeable with no adverse effects on your photo. You can fill it with black at any time to block the effect overall. You can fill it with white at any time to reveal the overall effect if your mask work is going in the wrong direction. You can also go back and forth between black and white while painting to refine where an effect is concealed or revealed as much as you want.

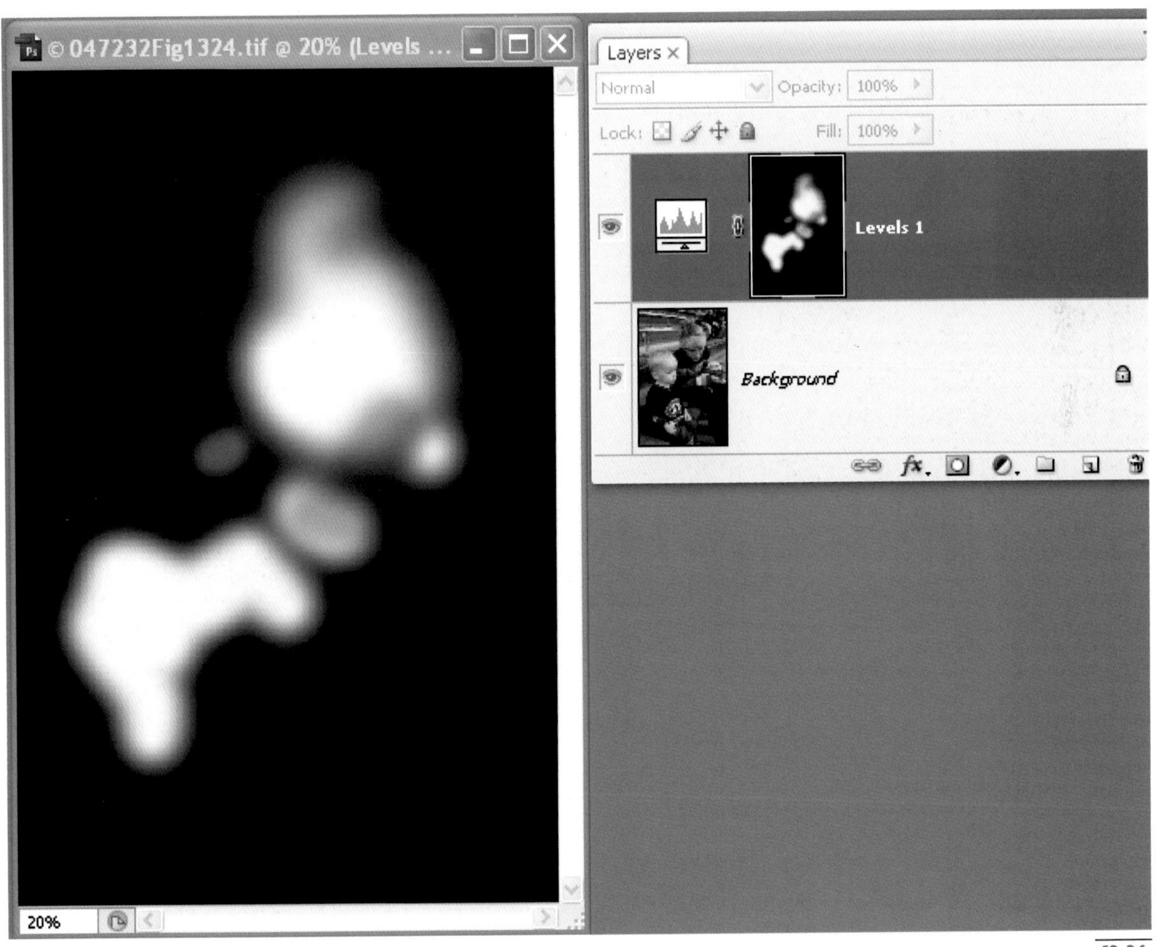

12-26

Layer Masks with Pixel Layers

In figure 12-27, a layer mask is used to limit the effect of sharpening a pixel layer on the photo of the nagoonberry from Alaska. There is no point in sharpening the whole scene because only the flower and leaves in the foreground are actually sharp. When you sharpen out-of-focus areas, you often introduce unwanted artifacts from the sharpening. By sharpening a layer, you can use a layer mask to limit where the sharpening occurs, something that cannot be done in Lightroom. You can use the adjustment brush set to sharpen in Lightroom to get a similar effect, but you will not gain the same control you can get here.

An important note: You have to have pixels to sharpen. You can flatten your photograph before sharpening to get those pixels. Or you can create a pixel layer with all of your adjustments on top of the layer stack. You can do the latter by selecting the top layer, then pressing "all the modifiers" plus E (if you have an older version of Photoshop, press N before E) — those modifiers are Shift+Alt+Ctrl+E for Windows and Shift+Option+⌘+E for Mac.

You can add layer masks in Photoshop (though not in Photoshop Elements) to a pixel layer either through the menu (choose Layer ➪ Layer Mask ➪ Reveal All or Hide All — reveal is white; hide is black) or through the layer mask icon at the bottom of the Layers palette (the little gray rectangle with a white circle in the center). In this case, I want to remove any evidence of this sharpened layer, and then paint its effects back in only on the flower and nearby leaves. If you press Alt/Option while clicking the layer mask icon, you get a black mask. (In Photoshop Elements, you have to erase the parts of the top layer that you don't want.)

Then I simply use a white paintbrush to bring the sharpening back to the flower. This selective sharpening technique can be very useful in many situations, and it can be especially helpful in low- or available-light photography where noise can be high. This enables you to avoid sharpening the noise where it does not need to be sharpened. If you have trouble seeing where to use the layer mask to bring the sharpness in or leave it out, turn off the bottom background

12-27

"layer" (it is not technically called a layer, but it still is your bottom layer) by clicking the eye icon at its left. This allows you to see exactly what becomes visible from your layer mask work. Then click it back on when you are done.

You can paint in and out the effects or appearance of any layer, from pixels to adjustments, simply by using a layer mask. For example, you could put two photos together on a page, using separate layers for each, overlap them, and then blend them together with layer masks. That's exactly how you do a panoramic image.

NOTE

You cannot add a layer mask to a pixel layer in Photoshop Elements. There are work-arounds to this that you can find from a search on the Internet, but you can also just erase parts of the top layer that you don't want sharpened.

Local Adjustments and Photoshop

Using adjustment layers and layer masks gives you a lot of control over small areas of a photo. This local control or adjustment is also what the local adjustments allow you to do in Lightroom now. Ansel Adams used to talk about using dodging and burning for adjusting the exposure and contrast of local areas in a print that would not affect the overall exposure or contrast of the image. This was an important part of the work of many famous darkroom workers from nature photographers like Adams and Edward Weston to photojournalists like W. Eugene Smith.

Photoshop has Dodge and Burn tools that even look like the tools used in the traditional darkroom. However, they really don't work as well as true dodging and burning in the darkroom for large areas of an image. By large areas, I mean something more than a spot or tiny fraction of a photo. Local adjustments are needed whenever you must affect part of a photo without changing the whole image, so this can mean a large fraction of a picture, as well as very small parts of it. This is what I did in the previous examples showing layers and layer masks.

The Photoshop Dodge and Burn tools provide you with far less control than you can get with an adjustment layer and the layer mask. You can adjust and readjust an adjustment layer, plus alter the layer mask as much as you want to give you exactly what you want, where you want it. This is simply not possible with the Dodge and Burn tools. Perhaps you have heard of using a dodge and burn layer, a gray-filled layer set to the Overlay mode — the gray is neutral in Overlay. In it, you can darken (burn) or lighten (dodge) that gray to make areas of the photo lighter or darker. This still has less control than an adjustment layer with a layer mask and is far less flexible. In addition, using the Burn tool can cause splotchy patterns over large areas no matter how you use it.

Local control extends to more than image brightness and contrast. That's a great thing about using adjustment layers and layer masks. You can use exposure, contrast, and color controls. You can color correct a part of a photo, for example, without changing any other part of the image. This can come in very handy if you shoot a scene with the available light there and the lighting sources are mixed. The human eye-brain connection compensates for this, and you don't see the strong color difference that the camera, unfortunately, captures. You cannot correct this in any overall adjustment. Sometimes you can make small area color adjustments in Lightroom using the color tools in local adjustments, but they are much more limited than what is available in Photoshop. In Photoshop, you can easily add a special adjustment layer to correct the problem color. You then use the layer mask to control that correction to only the problem areas.

Using the Cloning Tool Missing from Lightroom

Lightroom has a simple cloning and healing tool that helps remove things like specks from sensor dust in the photo. It does not have a cloning tool like that in Photoshop, which, along with layers, offers much more control over dealing with problems that need to be removed in an image. There are many things that can use the help of this tool (and its cousins, the healing brushes): flare artifacts, unseen distractions along the edge of the photo, and so on.

You can use cloning to radically change a photo, but I am not a big advocate of that. I like photo fantasies that are meant to be just that — fairies in flowers can be great fun. However, there are better techniques for doing this than cloning. When simple image-processing programs exploded a few years ago (and since then have largely disappeared), marketing people used to promote the cloning tool by adding a third eye to a portrait's head — possible to do, but hardly something worth doing except as a party game.

You do cloning using the Clone Stamp tool in Photoshop. It is important for cleaning up good images. Many photographers use this tool, but have problems with cloning artifacts. Cloning artifacts are details that begin to show up from cloning that did not originally exist in the photo. They appear purely from the cloning. The most obvious examples are repeating patterns or duplicate details. These are a sure sign of poorly done cloning, and people do notice.

Figure 12-28 is a summer beach scene near San Diego, California. The sun is important to the composition and gives a strong feeling of being at the beach on a sunny day. However, a nasty, bright bit of flare shows up at the bottom, as shown in figure 12-29. That area is really treacherous for using a cloning tool because of the pattern there (which also makes the healing tools difficult). Here's how to use the Clone Stamp tool:

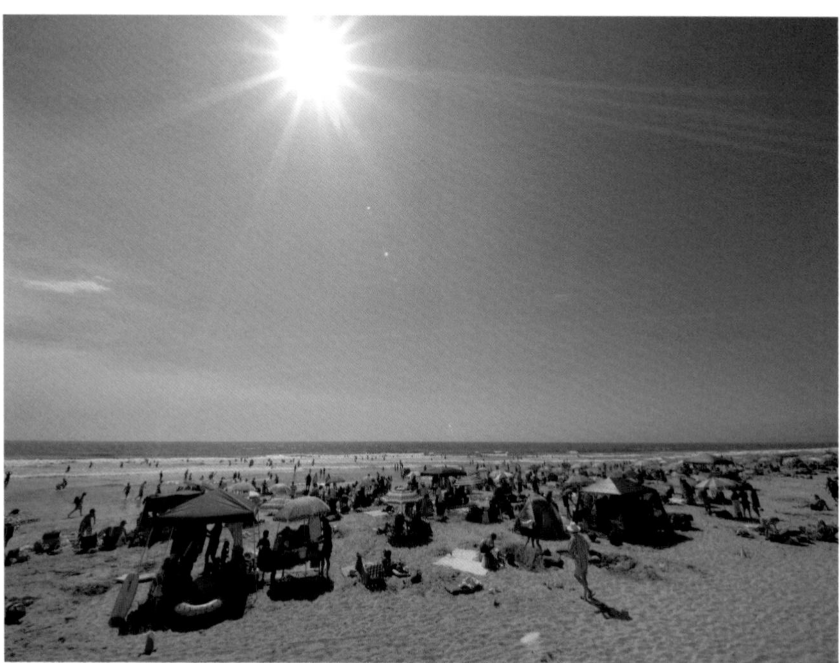

12-28

1. **Enlarge the area to the location that has the problem, as shown in figure 12-30, and select the Clone Stamp tool in the Toolbox.**
2. **Choose a brush size appropriate to the area in which you are working.** The Photoshop Clone Stamp tool is a brush tool and you can size it in the Options bar (below the menus) so that it is close in size to the area that needs to be cloned out, also shown in figure 12-30. Choose a soft-edged brush.
3. **Start with the brush at 100 percent opacity and lower the opacity to help blend in a cloned area when needed.**
4. **Clone to an empty layer, as shown in figure 12-31.** Add a layer before beginning cloning by clicking the Add Layer icon at the bottom of the Layers palette (the second icon from the right). Cloning to a layer gives you a lot of flexibility to clone because you cover the original problem, you do not change its pixels; plus you can use layer masks for refinement of the cloning work.

12-29

12-30

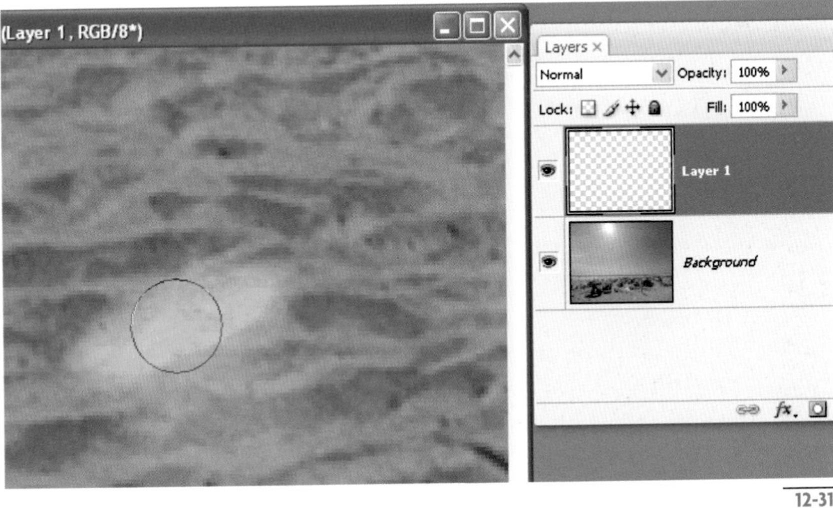

12-31

5. **Start with the brush at Aligned and Sample All Layers.** In the Options bar below the menu headings, you see these two options that you can check on or off (in general, leave everything else at the defaults). Aligned makes your cloning point follow your cursor at the same distance and angle from the start of your cloning, even if you release the mouse button (or move the graphic tablet pen from the tablet). Sample All Layers lets you clone to your new layer. You only turn this off when you need to keep your cloning limited to one layer (both the clone-from and clone-to points).

6. **Set your clone-from point (the place where there is detail you want to copy over the problem) by pressing Alt/Option and clicking with the cursor at that point.**

7. **Move your cursor over the problem and start cloning by clicking your mouse (or using your graphic tablet pen).**

The flare problem is hidden in figure 12-32, but there are some new problems due to the cloning. Notice the three ridges in the center that are identical — this is a cloning pattern artifact that will always draw attention to your cloning work.

Here are some tips on getting the most from the Clone Stamp tool and avoiding such problems:

> **Be quick to use the Undo command (choose Ctrl/⌘+Z).** If you find you picked the wrong clone-from point and your cloning starts out looking off, stop immediately, undo what you've done, and try a new clone-from point. Do not try to make the cloning work by continuing to clone when it looks off from the start.

12-32

- **Avoid cloning with a single click and drag of the mouse (or pen).** Unless you have a very small spot (like a dust speck), you will not blend and merge the cloned area with its surroundings if you just click and drag. Do it in multiple clicks.
- **Change your brush size as you go.** Keeping the same brush size as you clone tends to aggravate cloning artifacts.
- **Change your clone-from point as you go.** This is especially important for larger clone areas, such as flare removal. Keep finding new spots to clone from (Alt/Option+click) around your cloned area. This is another technique that really helps you avoid cloning artifacts.
- **Clone into cloning artifacts.** Break up a cloning artifact by setting a new clone-from point and using a smaller brush size, and clone directly into the artifact. This is how the problem seen in figure 12-32 is corrected, as shown in figure 12-33. (In this small of an area, the cloning work looks fine — some photographers will want to go further with cloning in areas that are more prominent in a photo.)

You can do all of the cloning work shown here in Photoshop Elements the same way you can do it in Photoshop.

12-33

Q & A

Suppose I work on a photo in Lightroom, then export it to Photoshop and work on it there with those tools specific to Photoshop. What if I decide I need additional adjustments that I can do in either program? Which one would be best to use?

This is not a simple question to answer. There really is no quality difference if you use adjustment layers in Photoshop. The answer depends largely on workflow. If you are working on an image that is going to go straight to a client or other single use, it might be best to finish the image in Photoshop. This takes less time and you are done.

However, if you need to keep that image consistent with a group of photos (from a given Folder or Collection, for example), it is probably best to go back to Lightroom. That is certainly easy if the photo was saved into the Folder it originally came from when it was saved from Photoshop. Once there, you can adjust the image to match the others, or even use those adjustments and copy or synchronize them to other photos. You can do this in Photoshop, but it is much harder to do because Photoshop is not designed to handle multiple photos.

When I discovered Lightroom, I thought I had found exactly what I needed. I really didn't like spending so much time in Photoshop. Now you are telling me that I need to use Photoshop to complete my photos. What happened to the simplicity of Lightroom?

This chapter is not meant to imply that everyone needs to go to Photoshop. Lightroom 2 makes it easy for many photographers to skip Photoshop altogether. The great thing about photography, I think, is that it fits so many different needs and personalities. Photoshop is not for everyone, nor is Lightroom. Both programs are simply tools that can help photographers achieve whatever their photographic goals are. If one tool gives you what you need without you having to use the other, that's no problem.

I do know that many photographers start feeling guilty because they are not using a certain technique, workflow, file format, and so on, that they heard they "should" use. I believe that photography should be fun. As soon as the "shoulds" start taking over, you quit having fun. That's not good.

Don't be intimidated by any expert into thinking you have to do something that expert's way. I know the feeling. As I started learning Photoshop years ago, I would hear about things that I "had to do" to "do Photoshop" right. Sometimes they worked just fine, sometimes not. Yet, even if I found a certain way of working that really fit my needs, I sometimes felt uneasy because that was not what the experts of the time said I should be doing.

I admit that this helped me learn a whole range of techniques. But the "guilt" was totally unnecessary. To this day, I get into disagreements with experts who want every photographer to do something their way. I just can't support that idea. Photographers are different and unique, and all have needs and attitudes that are not satisfied by one-stop shopping. I really believe you have to find the way that works best for you.

Your photography is yours, and your workflow should be yours, too. Have fun and stick with what seems to best fit your needs.

PRO GLOSSARY

Adjustment Brush A local adjustment tool in Develop that allows you to brush on a specific effect in a limited area.

Adobe RGB A working color space based on the standard computer RGB colors created by Adobe Systems. It includes a wide gamut of colors that makes it a very flexible color space for use in Photoshop.

Algorithm Computations, formulas, and procedures — the software-based steps or instructions used in digital devices and programs to process data.

Anti-aliasing Using software to soften and blend rough edges (called aliased).

Archival storage Using external nonmagnetic media such as DVDs and CDs to store information long term.

Artifact A defect in an image or other recorded data created by the tool used to record or output; something in an image that did not exist in the original scene but was inadvertently added to the photo by the technology.

Aspect ratio The proportion of an image comparing the height and width.

Background color The color chosen in Slideshow for the background behind the image.

Batch processing A way of making one or more changes, such as brightness or color adjustments, to a group or batch of image files all at once.

Bit The smallest unit of data in a computer.

Bit depth The number of bits required to represent the color in a pixel. With more bit depth, more colors are available. This increases exponentially (in base 2). True photo color starts at 8-bit but has limited adjustment range; 16-bit color offers a much larger amount of data that can be adjusted.

Browser 1) A program that's used for examining sites on the World Wide Web; 2) A software program designed to show small, thumbnail images of digital

Cast shadow A virtual shadow that appears like it is under a photo, making the photo look like it is floating over the background; often called a drop shadow.

CCD (charge-coupled device) A common type of image sensor used in digital cameras. The CCD actually only sees black-and-white images and must have red, green, and blue filters built into it in order to capture color.

CD-ROM (Compact Disc Read-Only Memory) A compact disc (an optical medium) that contains information that can only be read. It cannot be updated or recorded over.

Cells The units on a page that hold images for prints and Web galleries in Lightroom.

Chip A common term for a computer-integrated circuit; the place where the data in a computer is processed.

Chroma The color component of an image; it includes the hue and saturation information of color.

Clone Stamp tool Photoshop's cloning tool; this brush-based tool lets you copy small areas from one spot and clone them (paste them) over other places in the image; often used to cover up or fix problems or defects in the photo.

CMOS (complementary metal-oxide semiconductor) A common type of image sensor used in digital cameras. Like the CCD, a CMOS sensor typically sees only black-and-white images and must have red, green, and blue filters built into it in order to capture color. CMOS sensors use less energy than CCD chips.

CMYK (cyan, magenta, yellow, black) These are the subtractive primary colors and the basis for the CMYK color space. They're used in so-called four-color printing processes used in books and magazines because they produce the most photolike look for publications.

Collections A basic form of image organization in the Library module that allows you to create unique groupings of photos.

Color noise Noise in a digital image that has a strong color component to it; commonly found in dark areas in long exposures. Also known as chromatic noise.

Color Picker A color palette dialog box that allows you to pick colors based on hue (the actual color), saturation (the intensity), and tonal value (from black to white); it appears when you click in color option boxes in Slideshow, Print, and Web modules.

Color space Models of color that are based on a range of colors that can be interpreted by a particular digital device from camera to printer. This is its color space. There are many color spaces, though the two main ones used for photography are RGB and CMYK. Within those spaces are subsets of spaces such as Adobe RGB 1998 (larger) and sRGB (smaller).

Color wash A graduated color background used behind images in Slideshow; it blends two colors equally from top to bottom, side to side, or any other angle.

Compression The use of algorithms to reduce the amount of data needed to save a file in a smaller form.

Continuous tone The appearance of smooth color or black and white gradations, as in a photograph.

Copy This Lightroom command copies adjustments from one photo that can then be applied to another.

Copyright A legal term that denotes rights of ownership and, thus, control over usage of written or other creative material. All images, unless otherwise noted, are assumed copyrighted and can't be used by anyone without permission of the photographer.

Dpi (dots per inch) The resolution of a computer peripheral as a measurement of the number of horizontal or vertical dots it's able to resolve in input or output. This is confusing because dpi for a scanner is the same as ppi (pixels per inch) of an image, yet both are different from the dpi of a printer. Dpi for a printer refers to the way ink droplets are laid down on paper.

Drop shadow A virtual shadow that appears to be under a photo, making the photo look like it is floating over the background; in Lightroom, it is called a cast shadow.

Dynamic range The difference between the highest and the lowest values, as in the brightest highlights and the darkest shadows, in an image.

EVF Stands for electronic viewfinder.

EXIF data Special metadata added to a photo file by the camera that includes such things as shutter speed, aperture, ISO setting, and so forth. EXIF stands for Exchangeable Image File.

Export Sending photos out of Lightroom; this means the image is fully processed as a finished file based on Lightroom's adjustments.

Exposure 1) The combination of shutter speed and f-stop used in a camera to control the light hitting the sensor or film; 2) A specific control in Lightroom that affects brightness and highlights.

File format How the data that makes up an image is defined and organized for storage on a disk or other media. Standard image formats include JPEG, RAW, PSD, and TIFF.

Filmstrip 1) A linear sequence of images; 2) The bottom panel of Lightroom.

Filter 1) In traditional photography, this refers to colored optical glass or a plastic sheet that goes in front of the lens and affects how the image is captured; 2) In Photoshop, this refers to special effects applied to a photograph through the Filter menu.

FireWire A very fast connection (meaning lots of data is transmitted quickly) for linking peripherals to the computer; also known as IEEE 1394.

Flash A multimedia system designed to create programs of slide shows and more for computers; programs that showed much interaction among the visual elements, yet could be stored and played back from a small file size; originally developed by a company called Macromedia, which was later bought by Adobe.

Folders The groupings of images as imported into Lightroom.

FTP server (File Transfer Protocol server) A standard for transfer of images from one computer to another, typically used to transfer large files (such as photos) or multiple files to a server; hence, FTP server.

Graduated Filter 1) A local adjustment tool in Develop that allows you to add a specific effect in a limited area by creating a gradient from maximum to minimum by clicking and dragging across that area; 2) A filter used on a camera that is part dark and part clear, and has a gradient across the middle to blend those areas together.

Graphics tablet and pen A way of controlling your cursor's movement and actions by using an electronic tablet that senses where its graphic pen is moving; an alternative to the mouse.

Gray scale (or grayscale) A black-and-white image composed of a range of gray levels from black to white.

Guides Lines that appear in a work area to guide or structure the placement of an object, its sizing, and other changes to a photo but are not part of the image; they can be turned on or off.

Histogram An important tool for reading the exposure of a photo that is a graph of pixels at different brightness levels in the photo, with dark tones represented toward the left, bright tones to the right, and midtones in the middle.

History An interactive chart of the actions taken on your photo in the Develop module; it gives the photo's history, so that you can see what you've done and back up to earlier actions.

HTML (Hypertext Markup Language) HTML is the standard language used for instructions that structure text and images to create Web pages.

Hue The actual color of a color.

Identity Plate A unique and customizable text or graphic element that can be added to Lightroom in place of the program logo and can be used with prints, slide shows, and Web pages.

Import Bringing photos into Lightroom; the identification and recognition of image files so that they can be brought under Lightroom control.

Inkjet A digital printing technology where tiny droplets of ink are placed on the paper to form characters or images.

Interpolation A way of increasing or decreasing the apparent resolution of an image by using algorithms to create additional pixels in an image by smartly filling in the gaps between the original pixels or by smartly replacing them in order to get to a smaller file size.

IPTC data A set of writable metadata that is based on a standard that can be readily used by pros and publications; IPTC stands for International Press Telecommunications Council.

JPEG (Joint Photographic Experts Group) A file format that smartly compresses image information to create smaller files; the files are reconstructed later. JPEG files lose quality as compression increases. Technically, JPEG is a compression standard rather than a file format (the term JPEG really refers to the standards committee), but through common use it has come to mean a file format.

JPEG artifacts Image defects due to file size compression that look like tiny rectangles or squarish grain. They appear from high compression levels or multiple compression of a single file.

Keywords (keyword tags) Unique words that can be attached to images in their metadata so that specific images can later be easily found from a search for keywords.

Layer mask A special part of a Photoshop adjustment layer that allows you to turn the layer effects on and off by painting in white or black, respectively.

Layers Separated elements of a Photoshop digital image in which each part has its own isolated plane or level.

LCD (liquid crystal display) A display technology used for computer monitors as well as small monitors that act as viewfinders and playback displays for digital cameras.

Lens aberration A defect in the optical path of a lens that creates optical artifacts, such as color fringing, that can affect color definition and sharpness of a lens.

Levels A key tonal adjustment tool in Photoshop; this uses a histogram and three sliders under it to affect the image: the left is for dark areas, the middle for middle tones, and the right for bright areas.

Lights Out A Lightroom mode that darkens the whole screen except for the selected photo being worked on (accessed by pressing L).

Lossless compression Any form of file size reduction where no loss of important data occurs. (Redundant data is lost.)

Lossy compression Any form of file size reduction technique where some loss of important data occurs.

Loupe A single-image view in Lightroom that can be magnified with a single click on the image; loupe is a name for an optical magnifier.

Luminance noise A special type of noise in a digital image that looks like sand across the image — a dark/light pattern without colors in it (other than the original subject colors).

Metadata This means information about information; for photos, it refers to data stored with an image that describes exposure, camera type, copyright, and so on. Lightroom allows much additional information to be written to the file in the metadata.

Navigator A small preview image in Lightroom that lets you see the whole photo when the central work photo is magnified, then move around in it; it is also used as a preview of certain adjustments.

Noise An artifact of digital technologies, largely the sensor, that shows up in the photograph as a fine pattern that looks like grain or sand texture.

Overlays Details about a photo, including text and rating stars, that Lightroom adds to the exported image in a slide show or a print.

Paste In Lightroom this applies copied adjustment information to new files.

Photosite The individual, actual photosensitive area on a sensor that captures the brightness for a single pixel in the image. There is one photosite for every pixel in the original image.

Pixel Short for picture element (pix/picture, el/element). The smallest element of a picture that can be controlled by the computer.

Ppi (pixels per inch) A way of measuring linear resolution of an image and refers to how the pixels are spaced, meaning the number of pixels per inch in an image; often used interchangeably with dpi (dots per inch).

ProPhoto RGB A working color space based on the standard computer RGB colors created by Kodak. It offers an especially large gamut of colors that covers more colors than most cameras and printers can handle. It is a very flexible color space but must be used in 16-bit or there can be color issues such as posterization. (Posterization is a visual effect that occurs when there are not enough tones to display a gradient, so the tones start losing subtlety and become blocks of tone and color that look like something from a poster.)

PSD file The native file format for Photoshop and Photoshop Elements. It allows the saving of layers, layer masks, and more.

Quick Collection Lightroom's semiautomated way of grouping images together quickly though temporarily.

RAM (Random Access Memory) The computer's memory that's actually active for use in programs. Anything in it is temporary and disappears when a program is closed or the computer is shut down.

RAW file An image file that is minimally processed after it comes from the sensor in a camera. Data comes from the sensor and is translated to digital in the A/D converter; that data is then packaged for the RAW file. A RAW file is not generic for all cameras; there are actually proprietary files made by each camera manufacturer.

Resolution The density of pixels in an image; the number of pixels or dots per inch in an image; or the number of pixels that a device, such as a scanner, can capture.

RGB The primary color system of a computer based on red, green, and blue, the additive primary colors. Computer monitors (CRT and LCD) display RGB-based screen images.

Saturation The amount of brilliance or intensity of a color; how colorful or dull a color is.

Sensor The light-capturing part of a digital camera, usually a CCD or CMOS chip.

Smart Collections A unique collection in Library that automatically adds photos to its group based on preset criteria so that whenever a new photo appears in Lightroom with that criteria, it is also added to the collection.

Snapshot A stage in image adjustments in the Develop module remembered by Lightroom; it is a snapshot of what the image looked like at that point in processing.

Split Toning Coloring of an image so that the shadows and highlights are colored differently.

sRGB A common color space in the RGB color system that is more restricted than others.

Stacking The grouping or arrangement of images in the Filmstrip or Library so that different images sit on top of each other in a virtual stack.

Stroke A fine line around a photo that acts as a thin border.

Sync metadata and sync settings Sync in Lightroom is used to synchronize settings among a series of individual photo files; sync metadata matches metadata among those files, while sync settings duplicates adjustment parameters.

Thumbnail A small, low-resolution version of an image that is used for browsing many images at a time.

TIFF (Tagged Image File Format) An important, high-quality image format common to most image-processing programs.

Tonal range The difference in brightness from the brightest to the darkest tones in an image.

Tone Curve An adjustment for tonal values in an image that offers a great deal of flexibility. It appears first as a 45-degree angle line running up to the right in a graph. When that line is clicked on and moved, it changes tones in the image. The upper part of the curve is light, the bottom dark. Moving the curve up lightens tones; moving it down darkens tones. It is possible to move parts of the curve in different directions.

Unsharp Mask (USM) The name is misleading because it is based on an old commercial printing term; it is a highly controllable Photoshop adjustment used for sharpening an image and includes three settings: amount, radius, and threshold.

USB A standard computer connection for linking peripherals to the computer; Hi-Speed USB 2.0 is very fast, comparable to FireWire.

Vibrance Similar to the Saturation control, vibrance also affects the intensity of colors, but uses a different algorithm.

Vignetting The darkening or lightening of the outer part of an image due to the way the photograph was shot (either the lens used or special vignetting techniques employed).

Watermark In Lightroom, this is a copyright text with the photographer's name that is added to images in Web galleries.

White Balance A special digital control that tells digital cameras how to correctly represent color based on the color temperatures of different light sources. All digital cameras have automatic white balance; most also let photographers adjust it manually.

index

D

E

F

G

H

M

N

O

P

Q

R

S

Z